LOOKING CLOSER 2
CRITICAL WRITINGS
ON GRAPHIC DESIGN

EDITED BY
Michael Bierut, William Drenttel,
Steven Heller, and DK Holland

INTRODUCTION BY
Steven Heller

ALLWORTH PRESS
NEW YORK

Copublished with the American Institute of Graphic Arts

Published by Allworth Press, an imprint of Allworth Communications, Inc.
10 East 23rd Street, New York, NY 10010

05 04 03 02 01   8 7 6 5 4 3

ISBN: 1-880559-56-0

Library of Congress Catalog Card Number: 93-83003

Cover and book design by Michael Bierut, Pentagram, New York
Page composition by Sharp Des!gns, Lansing, Michigan

Printed in Canada

FOR PAUL RAND (1914–1996)

He was graphic design.

CONTENTS

ACKNOWLEDGEMENTS

The editors would like to thank Ted Gachot for dogged supervision of *Looking Closer 2*. Gratitude also to Tad Crawford, our publisher, for his continued support. Thanks as well to Charlie Sharp for design help, Suzanne Caltrider and Melissa Madsen for editorial assistance, and Rudy VanderLans for providing helpful information.

INTRODUCTION
A CLOSER LOOK AT LOOKING CLOSER
Steven Heller

More than a decade ago Massimo Vignelli argued for graphic design criticism as a means to elevate the field from service to profession. Using architecture as the model, he asserted that serious introspection in graphic design magazines and trade journals would have remedial effect on our professional self-esteem, as well as inspire mainstream journalists and scholars to be more respectful of our achievements. Vignelli got more than he bargained for. Since the late 1980s, and certainly since 1994 when *Looking Closer* was first published, graphic designers have become gluttons for criticism. Writing about graphic design has so greatly increased in publications and on the Internet that criticism has become a virtual trend. What Vignelli believed would proffer common standards and mutual respect has developed into a body of literature that challenges the canon and the canonizers, including Vignelli himself.

As an anthology of published articles and essays, *Looking Closer* cannot claim credit for launching the graphic design criticism movement, but it was certainly the first book to proclaim it. Now the movement has grown considerably with writers kicking up dust on a wide variety of contemporary issues. And the editors of *Looking Closer* have noticed a significant demographic change in just two years from when the first volume was published. Today there is a proven readership of students and professionals hungry for intelligent critical writing about design.

Looking Closer 2 addresses the issues that have sparked discourse and discord over the past two years. And like the first, the second volume serves as an ad hoc textbook of graphic design criticism. In the absence of a critical graphic design vocabulary, various models (based on -isms, -ologies, and -otics) have been adapted from academia and journalism, running the gamut from scholarly exegesis to investigative profile. This includes commentaries, manifestos, reviews, editorials, and reportage. Many are highly opinionated, though not all are entirely subjective. Most speak of passions, though some are curiously dispassionate. Some attack, others defend. A few are wise.

Readers will find that graphic design criticism is a diverse and disparate discipline. The methodologies, indeed the writing styles, comprising the critical essays in this book—from Robin Kinross's incisive critique of contemporary typographic excess in "Fellow Readers: Notes on Multiplied Language" to Susan Sellers's precisionist history of the evolution of an archetype in "How Long Has This Been Going On? *Harper's Bazaar, Funny Face,* and the Construction of the Modernist Woman"—vary considerably in tone and approach, perhaps because the definition of what is graphic design criticism has yet to reach a mature stage.

Criticism, it is argued, expands knowledge by revealing otherwise hidden meanings. The so-called "positive" method examines a maker's intent and rationale; a work's structure is scrutinized and the factors that inform it are contextualized providing the basis for balanced analysis and historical categorization. Conversely, the so-called "negative" method is a kind of faultfinding exposé of flaws in a process or result. The purpose is ostensibly to reinforce a set of standards used to judge success or failure. Both methods are useful in addressing the form and function of design. But for designers who have been accustomed to peer critique through omission—i.e., not getting work accepted into competitions and annuals—overt criticism is threatening. Designers tolerate the conventional classroom or client "crit," but critical public notice, even if it's not always a harsh rebuke, is difficult to swallow unless, of course, it's happening to somebody else.

Until recently, graphic design, whether a total identity system or an individual poster, has been immune from the kind of public scrutiny given books, films, plays, painting, and sculpture, even advertising. Graphic design has been seen but not heard about. Only those media that are directly marketed to the public and play a more integral cultural role are deemed worthy of a place in the critical limelight. In the past, graphic design was not criticizable because authorship was comparatively invisible, and, moreover, design routinely served a supporting role. There was also a gentleman's agreement within the graphic design community that a demonstrative critical voice was simply unnecessary. Although certain trade magazines from the 1920s and 1930s published angry critiques of European typefaces, the Bauhaus, and the New Typography (notably Thomas M. Cleland's 1939 diatribe against American moderns in the essay "Harsh Words," and the occasional privately published manifestos on the nature of good design by W. A. Dwiggins), the majority of articles found in magazines were celebrations of a particular genre or designer. Distinctions within the field between good and bad design—i.e., crass commercial art was bad, sophisticated modern design was good—were pronounced through the results of art directors' competitions where the reasons for inclusion or exclusion were rarely articulated. Other than the positive reinforcement of winning a medal, designers were not held individually accountable. Seldom, therefore, was an individual graphic designer's body of work critical grist.

Vignelli was the first of the moderns to call for public graphic design criticism of the kind that twentieth-century cultural critic Walter Benjamin referred to as "romantic"; the ennobling of contemporary work through intense scrutiny. Applied to graphic design, ignoring the negative would preserve the gentlemanly façade of professional discourse while serious critique of the positive would intellectually validate the work. In the late 1980s, what happened instead was that criticism took a more strident turn, and what emerged was an argumentative form that challenged the credibility of work while proposing both aesthetic and ideological alternatives. This form of writing was actually practiced in arcane publications during the late 1930s and 1940s when modernism challenged conventional commercial art. But by the 1950s, with the battle won and the modern method accepted, feisty critical discourse was reserved for the privacy of classrooms and after-dinner conversations at art directors clubs. Disagreements among designers over specific methods or practices were rarely, if ever, made public, or written about.

When critical discourse did occur during the 1950s and 1960s, it was usually in the academic arena. Books like László Moholy-Nagy's *Vision in Motion* (1947) and Gyorgy

Kepes's *Language of Vision* (1945) were models of theoretical writing that served as the only critical design textbooks. *Visual Language,* founded in 1966 by editor Merald E. Wrolstad, a unique journal of visual communications theory, history, and psychology published through the Cleveland Museum of Art, set a similar standard for scholarly writing and covered a range of communication disciplines. Meanwhile, the graduate design faculty at Yale University, and most notably Paul Rand, invoked leading cultural critics in texts and lectures to apply the realms of aesthetics and cognition to the study of design. Students were routinely given class crits informed by the language of critical modern theory. Further reading and interpreting such texts were required for the completion of thesis projects. Similar graduate-level design programs at other institutions encouraged intensified critical thinking and set the stage for the next logical step, the development of a body of professional critical writing. Owing to timidity among the editors of trade magazines, however, such critical writing would take a relatively long time to surface in the mainstream design press.

In the late 1970s, alternatives to orthodox modern practice marked the advent of the so-called postmodern era of graphic design. The modern canon was under fire from designers who questioned the old and sought to establish new standards—to break free from the strictures of the grid. The re-evaluation of modern type and design conventions notably taught in Wolfgang Weingart's classes in Basel, Switzerland, was imported to America by his students and acolytes, including Dan Friedman and April Greiman, who designed in ways that were indeed foreign to modernist America. They in turn became teachers, and the approaches they taught began to surface in design competitions. Similar approaches rooted in semiology and deconstruction also began to emerge from other design academies, notably Cranbrook, University of Cincinnati, and Rhode Island School of Design. At the same time that these new antigrid typographic and compositional methods were advanced, more sophisticated ways of discussing design became necessary. By the mid 1980s the typical showcase articles on veterans and promising newcomers were no longer rigorous enough to address changes in design method and thought.

Most mainstream trade journals tried desperately to ignore these changes. The typical designer profile was more or less objective reportage comprising a collection of celebratory quotes by clients and colleagues interwoven with biographical facts that were peppered with the subject's own philosophy and descriptions of their working conditions. In contrast, the new design writing that was slowly emerging took a critical slant, and sometimes bite, that went below the epidermal levels of ego and artifice. At first, such design commentaries were found in isolated critical columns of the professional magazines so as not to shock the readership (or the advertisers). But eventually, critical perspectives surfaced in the feature wells of magazines like *Print, Communication Arts, I.D.,* and *Metropolis.* Commentaries in the form of op-ed articles and investigative reportage soon became the meat of institutional publications, as well, including *The AIGA Journal of Graphic Design, STA Journal,* and *ACD Statements.* In addition to *Visual Language,* the scholarly journal *Design Issues* further situated graphic design in a larger academic arena along with industrial, environmental, and product design. In 1985, *Emigre* premiered as a "culture tab," or large format chronicle of contemporary art and society, but within two years it was transformed into the clarion of a new design aesthetic. Amidst the unedited fanzine-styled interviews with a growing number of influential anticanonical typographers and designers, it became the forum for a fair number of critical essays and debates on experimentation in theory and practice (and in 1995, it was reformatted to become a journal of criticism). In 1990,

Eye, a London-based graphic design magazine, premiered as an alternative to the dominant trade journals in England with a unique mix of commentary, reviews, and critical academic and journalistic writing. By analyzing the warts and all of individuals and phenomena, *Eye* became the foremost "design culture" magazine.

There have been other benchmarks of graphic design criticism. "Dangerous Ideas," the theme of the 1986 design conference of the American Institute of Graphic Arts in Austin, Texas, announced a new epoch in which environmental, political, ethical, and aesthetic concerns were publicly addressed for the first time, and papers from the event fueled critical columns for some time after it was over. This was also the first time that personal methodologies were scrutinized when conference co-organizer Tibor Kalman, then principal of the New York design firm M&Co, engaged Joe Duffy, principal of the Minneapolis firm The Duffy Group, in a heated debate about the efficacy of how each catered to his corporate and business clients at the expense of a larger ethical scheme. This was the end of the gentleman's agreement, and the beginning of what would turn into a period of harshly critical professional self-reflection.

This early stage of the new design criticism was, however, surprisingly focused, and the first volume of *Looking Closer* can be summed up as expressing a single theme: the shifting modern paradigm. Most of the essays were ostensibly attacks on, responses to, and explanations of this shift; as such they heralded the most significant reappraisal of design practice and education since the 1940s. This writing directly or indirectly addressed the changing paradigms that *Looking Closer* could not help but mirror. *Looking Closer 2* does not contain such an overriding focus, but it is representative of the aftermath of these shifts and the ensuing concerns about where design fits into culture. The editors have, therefore, made selections that reveal two intersecting stories: the first is about the development of graphic design criticism itself; the second is about the state of the art and craft of design.

Looking Closer 2 is organized into six sections:

- "Design as Language" encompasses the belief that design form, and especially type and typography, is a manner of address as structured (and chaotic) as any linguistic form. Designers may swing around the maypole of legibility, but even more important is how we communicate through codes and styles. The essays here range from a critical survey of our typographical slang, in Véronique Vienne's "Soup of the Day," to how the digital environment is forcing us to reckon with the new standards in Jessica Helfand's "Electronic Typography: The New Visual Language."

- "On Teaching and Learning" addresses how our languages will be translated and ultimately taught. The fundamental ideas have challenged educators for decades, since commercial art instruction became design education. The essays included are concerned with establishing links between opposing views and methodologies (Rick Poynor's "Building Bridges Between Theory and Practice") and reconciling academic and work environments (Gunnar Swanson's "Graphic Design Education as a Liberal Art").

- "Changing Paradigms" leaves the academy for the real world. Here a variety of commentaries on the practice of design and design history examine how designers and scholars will (and should) perform: how changes in technology affect the creative process in Paul Saffo's "The Place of Originality in the

Information Age" to how designers should understand the images they use in Fath Davis Ruffins's "The Politics of Cultural Ownership."

- "Design as Strategy" moves abruptly from paradigms to professionalism. Missing from the first *Looking Closer* are critical perspectives on the nature of business, which the editors believe are as important to the enlightenment of the field as are the cultural manifestations. In the past, so-called professional practice articles have been dry and pedantic; here, arguments about standardized requirements for designers found in Ellen Shapiro's "Certification for Graphic Designers? A Hypothetical Proposal" and Gunnar Swanson's "The Case Against Certification" serve to measure the standing of the profession against how rigorous our standards of accomplishment are. In a passionate attack on the ills of designer-client relations in an age of downsizing, Milton Glaser's "The War Is Over" tells a woeful story of the devaluation of design.

- "Public Works" proceeds from the business of making profit to the profit earned from working for community. Pro bono work has become the catchall that absolves designers of myriad sins, but truly engaging in the public sphere is more complicated. The essays here explore such themes as the nature of the ethical society, the design of hate, and the marriage of design and politics.

- "Critical Profiles" presents possible models for researching and writing investigative analyses of significant practitioners. The examples here represent this comparatively uncharted, and not yet perfected, practice of wedding commentary and biography. These are not the salutary peer reviews in the showcase tradition, but rather stories that pierce the façade of the subject in order to report on and explain the designer's motivations and goals.

Schisms between old and young generations, modern and postmodern ideologies, and theory and practice appear to dominate current critical debates. Such disagreements have absorbed a fair amount of ink. But the current state of design criticism should not be seen as venting. Even within the past two years, published criticism has noticeably shifted from offensive and defensive to reasoned and enlightened. While *Looking Closer 2* includes some rather contentious arguments about style and content, most of these essays attempt to unravel levels of complexity that previously have been ignored by or unknown to designers. While still restricted to design magazines and journals, the writing is more rigorous and more informed by the vocabulary and methods of other creative fields. The next challenge for design writing (and writers on design) is to be considered as viable as other cultural studies, and as visible to the public.

DESIGN
AS
LANGUAGE

SOUP OF THE DAY
Véronique Vienne

The most devastating experience for me as a magazine writer is seeing my work in print. I can't figure out why anyone would want to read what I wrote. The text is only texture, a decorative element. The type is too small, the lines too long, the title too obscure, and the layout too complicated. I get nauseous just staring at it—loss of creative control feels a lot like a hangover.

Authors are no longer authority figures. Art directors and type designers, kept for many years in a subordinate position, have taken over and claimed authorship of the page. The electronic revolution has given them the advantage. Their victory leaves the rest of us to sift through the visual wreckage—tangled headlines, blurred letters, floating pull-quotes, and distressed imagery—unable to figure out what an article is all about. Somewhere in the swelling sea of digitized information, the author's original intention has capsized. This illegible medium is the new message—adrift in a bottle.

In a recent issue of *Interact*, a journal published by the Chicago-based American Center for Design (ACD), two writers were allowed to express their objections to the layout of their article, which had been set in a series of copy blocks shaped like footprints. "We were not offered the opportunity to work collaboratively with the designers," wrote Lauralee Alben and Jim Faris. "This is ironic, given the subject of our article [inter-disciplinary dance], which discusses various models of collaboration and the degree to which they foster or hinder effective design." The editor's note, written in response, had an unpleasant tone: "ACD considers design a form of authorship, and does not generally ask its designers to rework their proposed solutions based on subjective criteria, just as it does not ask authors to rewrite their contributions to reflect a different point of view should someone disagree." Conflicts between icon makers and wordsmiths are as acerbic as those between estranged husbands and wives.

I used to be an art director and can attest that I was often asked to rework my design solutions based on the subjective criteria of editors, publishers, circulation experts, commu-nication consultants, marketing executives, advertisers, and even, sometimes, writers. But those were the old days when the pen was mightier than the mouse.

Just when I thought computers would further erode my ability to function as a designer, I became a writer. I should have known better—whenever I switch lanes at the checkout counter, I always pick the wrong one and get stuck behind someone who is returning a defective product and filling out triplicate forms for a full refund. Although I, too, feel like asking for a refund when I see my articles in print, I also find myself cheering for my old team. Let designers have the ball for a while. Reading is, after all, a spectator sport.

Printed words have lost their authority because they are no longer printed, but rather "published." Not long ago, their weighty presence was a by-product of the heavy printing equipment necessary to produce them. The massive engraving plates, sturdy oak drawers packed with steel punches, and vats full of melting lead were indeed *impressive*. In contrast, digitized documents stored on wafer-thin disks don't seem real. Flickering on screens—bit-mapped at 72 dots per inch—and translated into software language for various output devices, these words are now elusive entities. Without their metal shells, they are vulnerable, unprotected. Fontographer, a software program by Altsys, creators of the popular illustration software Aldus FreeHand, allows designers to modify traditional iron-age typefaces, pushing letters to the limit of their readability. Easily layered, meshed, and woven together into a seamless electronic fabric, these rasterized words are eventually transcribed onto paper—almost as an afterthought.

The page is now a living surface. Fluidity is the order of the day. Your typical type foundry is a converted space—an office, loft, or bedroom—with a couple of Macs in the corner. Fontographer users are a volatile group, more artists than technicians. Twenty-six years old on the average, they are usually middle-class college graduates—from Eastern Michigan, Cranbrook, Art Center, CalArts, Yale—who've read Claude Lévi-Strauss, Roland Barthes, and Jacques Derrida. Few live in Manhattan; they prefer the off-campus, informal atmosphere of a smaller town. The new typographical movement is a regional phenomenon with its local heroes: Dutch graphic designer Rudy VanderLans, founder of *Emigre* magazine, lives in Sacramento; Rick Valicenti, principal of Thirst, and Carlos Segura, who master-minded the prolific foundry T-26, are both in Chicago; Scott Makela has moved his Words+Pictures design office to Minneapolis; David Carson used to art direct *Ray Gun* from Santa Monica.

The traditionally macho field of typography is accommodating women who are gaining access to the keyboard. One of the first type designers to publish her own fonts under the *Emigre* label was Zuzana Licko, VanderLans' wife and partner. Her bold, vigorous, and popular font designs (Modula, Matrix, Journal, Citizen) changed forever the face— and the gender—of graphic expression.

Sexually depolarized, identified by area codes rather than style, physically isolated in front of their screens, font artists are marginalized. They see no reason to join the system. With the click of a mouse, they can distort, smudge, blur, or shrivel any letterform and challenge the sanctity of the written word.

The first generation of graphic design students who trained on Fontographer is now entering the work force. These young professionals think that text is something that's meant to be infused with irreverence—not necessarily read. To a large extent, they are right: the projects they design are album covers, posters, catalogues, brochures, greeting cards, and, occasionally, annual reports—graphic showpieces no one ever reads. Most of the time, junior designers don't deal with real readers. The only victims of their personal style are people who receive invitations to gallery openings and can't make out the day, the time, or the location.

"The new, popular medieval typefaces, Coptic-looking glyphs, and Victorian scripts, are symptomatic of a return to individuality," says Jonathan Hoefler, who created elegant faces for such publications as *Esquire, Rolling Stone,* and *Harper's Bazaar.* "This revivalist trend is not retro—it's politically subversive. What you are witnessing here is the crumbling of the paternal authority of the word. Some typesetters, Erik van Blokland and Just van

Rossum in particular, have programmed a progressive and randomized decaying of their typeface right into the system." Today, printed matter is viewed as trash, even before it gets to the dump.

Illegibility is a deliberate act of avoidance. Jonathan Barnbrook, an influential British type designer, confessed in an article in *Emigre* that he "finds it difficult" to use his own typefaces (appropriately named Bastard, Exocet, Manson, Prozac, Nixon). "I see them as individual elements rather than part of the larger discourse," he writes. That "larger discourse" is one writers and editors know all too well. The economic reality of magazine publishing can turn the most substantial editorial content into mere stuffing—into processed food for thought sandwiched between white bread ads. "The tension between authority and its destruction is a constant theme in my work," says Barnbrook in a recent *Eye* magazine interview.

But is this communication? Rudy VanderLans, the art director/editor/publisher of *Emigre,* the now legendary West Coast graphic design publication, takes a philosophical approach: If you can't read something—never mind, it probably wasn't written for you. "People who complain about not being able to read the type are usually not the audience the piece was destined to reach," he says.

But what's most striking about this ambiguous type trend is the fact that it has become a coded language for an entire generation. Illegible typefaces are the graffiti of cyberspace. And in the computer age, things have a way of springing into the mainstream in the blink of an eye. Today, type designers like David Carson, former art director of the music and youth culture magazine *Ray Gun* (probably the most illegible magazine to date), are worshiped by those whose job it is to capture the attention of a visually overloaded public. In the last year, Carson has acquired some pretty big corporate clients, including Nike, Levi Strauss & Co., and Hardee's. "I figured that if I didn't work with them, someone else would—using a bastardized version of my style. I have done the illegible stuff for ten years."

The message-driven Nike T-shirt department is one of the company's fastest-growing divisions. Valerie Challis, a Nike senior art director, explains that illegibility is "appropriate to the function" of the product, which is to express irreverence. "Different ideas or messages call for different typefaces," she says matter-of-factly. Wieden Kennedy & Associates, Nike's advertising agency, has teams of copywriters working around the clock to come up with hip, jargon-of-the-moment slogans. Raised on a visual diet of cartoons, TV sitcoms, and videos, their twentysomething target audience has only recently discovered the power of words and they're hungry for more.

In an interesting about-face, Carson is now de-emphasizing the typographical exuberance that won him his fame for the benefit of tone, attitude, color, and shape. "I want to redesign the magazine—which is tricky since *Ray Gun* had no format to start with," he says. "I've had enough of weird scripts and fractured letters. One should be able to solve anything with one typeface. There is this new straightforward font I like, with a name I can't spell, something like 'DINEngschrist.' I don't even know where I got it."

Watch out, David. People may not like the new *Ray Gun*. I recently picked up this cryptic message posted on one of the handful of graphic chat lines on America Online: "Sorry, but *Ray Gun* isn't meant to be read. It is a forum for design disguised as a music mag forced upon the unbeknownst musicians who purchase it." (Signed TKween9.)

"Letters are legible," wrote Dutch designer Peter Mertens in 1990 in *Emigre 15,* a landmark issue devoted to typography. "If they are not legible, then they are not letters. Illegible letters do not exist. Illegibility does not exist." This statement has since become the *Emigre* credo. By making the controversy black and white—either you can read the type or you can't—Mertens was hoping to cut the Gordian knot. But five years later, font designers are still tangled in the same inextricable debate.

Jeffery Keedy, a type designer also known to his fans as "Mr. Keedy" (at age thirty-six he thinks of himself as "an old man"—the Mr. Rogers of the new typographical age), believes that legibility is an American obsession. "In Europe, people give themselves permission to interpret the text. Here, we hold on to the illusion that what we read is true—that there is no misinformation or lies in the press."

Zuzana Licko offers a conciliatory explanation: "Typefaces are not intrinsically legible," she argues. "Rather, it is the reader's familiarity with the faces that accounts for their legibility. Studies have shown that people read best what they read most. For example, the scientific assumption is that words typeset in lowercase are the most readable—but aren't they also the most ubiquitous? It seems curious that Gothic letters, which we generally find illegible today, were actually preferred during the Middle Ages," she notes. Totally Gothic, a "medieval" typeface she designed in 1990, was considered hard to read when first introduced to the market. Five years later, it is regularly used, in small sizes, by conservative art directors. The extra time people spend deciphering the words seems well worth the gratification they derive from the exercise.

What's read most these days—newspapers, magazines, catalogues, ads, promotional material—would probably be unreadable to an erudite twelfth-century monk. And vice versa: today, the Gothic letters he painstakingly fashioned might be deciphered as slowly as he wrote them. Modern readers are visually literate; most things aren't read, they're read *into.* People can glance at a corporate brochure and instantly deduce if the company had a good or a bad year. They scrutinize an ad to evaluate a product's worth. It's possible that we read different kinds of things with different expectations of comprehension. So how's a designer to know what to do? A monk only had to communicate the eternal glory of God.

Communication is not simply problem solving. The readability of a typeface is often directly proportional to its emotional context. To communicate via fax-modem with my parents in France, I ordered (from a company called Signature Software) a customized typeface that's a digitized version of my handwriting. Named Colette, after my mom, my personal font gets the job done. Although she knows I didn't scribble a note to her, my mother reads my electronic messages with something that resembles pleasure. "The Vs and the Rs are realistic," she says. "Too bad the lines are so regular."

Readability can be off-putting. Just last week I received a "Dear Véronique" letter, beautifully typeset on blue paper, and instantly assumed it was junk mail. I trashed it without even reading it. When I emptied the wastebasket I realized it was written by a close friend of mine.

The type market is flooded with experimental fonts that express the delicious idiosyncrasies of their makers. They quickly become addictive. Mara Kurtz, who teaches typography at New York's Parsons School of Design, collects typefaces the way Imelda Marcos collects shoes. "There is no way I can use them in my work," she says, "but I am hooked. Type today is not about excellence, it's about diversity."

My favorite new faces are those that take my eyes where I didn't know they wanted to go. A decorative engraver's face, Bronzo, designed by Rick Valicenti and Mouhli Mauer and distributed by Thirst, features overemphatic horizontal strokes that lend an irresistible zippiness to the stream of letterforms. You don't decipher words set in Bronzo because they are easy to read, but because they chase each other from line to line. Randomun, an engaging brushstroke font by Todd Munn distributed by T-26, reads like a series of footprints, leaving on the page a trail of fascinating tracks that lead the reader, step by step, to the end of the sentence. A hard-to-read typeface called Indelible Victorian, designed by Stephen Farrell for T-26, becomes legible when seen in the context of a phrase—its faded letters with their broken and frayed edges forming a fragile yet compelling message.

Sorting out the visual context to extract relevant information always was—and still is—a genuinely creative act, one that demands judgment, good sense, and aesthetic discernment. In the last analysis, it is the reader, not the writer or the designer, who is the ultimate arbiter of the implication of a text.

A love of words—and a need to exert more control over my work—made me switch careers. In the process I became fascinated with the way written language performs. Its power is in its sheer simplicity. An active voice, a vigorous choice of adjectives, and a healthy respect for grammar give sentences their potency. A good writer, I soon learned, is not timorous. *That's what it must feel like to be a guy,* I thought. Real men don't mix metaphors.

Annoyed by a culture that rewards assertive writers and celebrates must-read male authors, women designers are at the forefront of what Pamela Mead calls "hairiness." An interface communication specialist for InForm in Boston, Mead advocates a fuzzier interpretation of readability standards. "Hairy is a philosophy, not a set rule," she wrote in *Interact.* "It should add a degree of pleasure and surprise, taking advantage of the human tendency to take a chance and explore." She proposes, for example, friendly ATM machines that give users a chance to play with the visual representation of their cash transactions.

Rebeca Mendez, former design director of the Art Center College of Design in Pasadena, California, wants to use typography to re-script cultural assumptions about the best way to communicate. "If you are too overt about challenging authority, people dismiss you as crazy," she says. "It's more effective to subtly undermine the grid system from within, with imperceptible tricks, such as delicate curves in the baselines, slight corruption of the letterforms, and strategically placed *mistakes.*" Pleasing and legible, her irregular text treatment suggests an exquisitely flawed material—a skillfully woven fabric delicate enough for the emperor's new clothes.

Margo Johnson, a graduate from the California Institute of the Arts in Valencia, applied mathematical variables to existing typefaces and recorded each step of the process as the alphabet fell apart. The results were sixty expressive hybrid fonts that retrace, backward, the story of the evolution of typography, from elegant cursives to primitive ink-spots. "There is a trend in the multimedia field to turn type into pictures," says Johnson. "I used to think of myself as a type designer—now I tell people I am an illustrator." While male designers enjoy blurring words, women seem to prefer blurring the boundaries between words and pictures, typographers and illustrators, designers and artists. Rather than re-script narrative expression, women choose to de-script it.

To promote Concrete, her Chicago-based design office, Jilly Simons produced what she calls a "tautological piece," a handsome series of captionless photographs held together by a wide rubber band imprinted with the phrase: "How does it feel to think?" It's definitely a stretch. "Words make it too easy," she explains. "I want to challenge people to think for themselves. I want them to create their own story. I find text with pictures somewhat redundant." Not everyone got it. She adds wistfully that she received more inquiries about the printing on the rubber band than about her company. "The focus of my work is to use pictures to create a dialogue. I welcome different interpretations. For me, a truly interactive piece is poetry."

Few graphic designers can afford to develop truly sophisticated interactive presentations of their work, like CD-ROMs or multimedia films. "There is never enough money in interesting projects to hire the right people," says New York designer Barry Deck. "So when I want something, I simply design it. I collaborate with myself. It's the only way I can control my work. I script it and design it." While his fonts are used by Nickelodeon, *Details, Mademoiselle,* and QVC, and his bootlegged Template Gothic shows up everywhere from missing pet posters to Fortune 500 annual reports, Deck likes to keep techno-jargon to a minimum. "Yeah I get on America Online, but mostly to check the *New York Times* highlights. It saves paper—I don't like murdering trees."

Nevertheless, the page is the typographer's and the reader's preferred medium. Interface design—strictly for monitors—is still mostly in the hands of engineers who have minimum graphic design training. As a result, even the most popular CD-ROMs are awkward in their visual delivery. Images are lavish, but the text—or "hypertext"—is seldom an integral part of the overall concept. You still read blocks of copy stuffed in compartments and click icons to activate dialogue boxes. The little booklet that comes with the disc is usually the most graphically exciting part of the software package.

"Today, words are objects," says Fred Brady, Adobe's manager of new typographic developments, and a designer who's helped define the type company's aggressive strategy. "A word can be set in an illegible, ephemeral font and still be readable—yes, people can decipher a couple of words in a large size, no matter what they look like. But no one reads text unless it is set in a permanent typeface." With multiple master technology, which allows variations of sizes, weights, widths, and styles, the Adobe font user can now instantly create hundreds of fonts from one typeface. Composition families, as Adobe typefaces are now called, support creativity while preserving legibility.

Minion is a good example. A classic serif, it looks substantial and unambiguous in any size or permutation. You can slant it, squeeze it, stretch it, shrink it, or enlarge it—it never fades or falls to pieces. So how come David Carson doesn't play with it in *Ray Gun?* Maybe it's because Adobe's fonts aren't vulnerable enough: they take abuse and keep going, a sure sign of a corporate mind-set.

Another type resource, the International Type Corporation (ITC) in New York, recently completed a three-year project to replicate, in the digitized realm, the "warm, irregular, and human" feel of the original Italian Bodoni face. "To appeal to designers today, we knew we had to preserve the stylistic idiosyncrasies of the eighteenth-century face," says Ilene Strizver, ITC director of typeface development. "An interpolation between the small and the large sizes gave us what we were looking for—a consistent style and flavor—and the proof that the computer had captured Giambattista Bodoni's attention to details." Less pristine and luminous than Minion, ITC Bodoni is robust, friendly, and easier on the eye.

Clarity is not always synonymous with readability. On America Online, the *New York Times* is exceedingly legible—set in Geneva, a digitized version of Helvetica. But practically speaking, it is unreadable: you have no perspective on the news; the articles are reproduced on the screen in a uniform format—with no columns, photographs, or captions to support the flow of the narrative; you can't glance back and forth at other headlines; you can't savor the irony of journalistic juxtapositions. There is no hierarchy, urgency, or drama. And dare I say it? I miss the Lancôme ads.

To make matters even more confusing, good typography is not always synonymous with good design. With unquestionable graphic dexterity, the Oregon firm of Johnson & Wolverton designs *SAY,* Amnesty International's award-winning magazine for young people. Trendy with just a touch of funkiness, the magazine is technically readable but practically illegible: it's humanly impossible to concentrate on the subject matter—torture—in such a slick visual environment. "We are not commenting on politics," explains designer Hal Wolverton. "Our goal is to inform and motivate. We made an early decision to avoid gruesome imagery, to focus instead on emotions the reader feels capable of acting upon." Here, reading is not as important as joining. *SAY* is not a magazine but a highly successful pamphlet—the youth section is the most active division of Amnesty International.

To make sense, text must be more than simply copy. "All the world's a text," says Robert Scholes, author of *Protocols of Reading* (Yale University Press, 1989). J. Abbott Miller would agree. Ten years ago he founded Design Writing Research, a "formmaking and text-making" studio in New York, with his partner and wife, Ellen Lupton. He art directs *Dance Ink,* considered to be one of the most appealing magazines at the newsstand. What makes the quarterly publication so accessible is not its type or its layout—both low-key—but the genuine curiosity with which the designer seems to approach the content. A prolific writer on design criticism and history, Miller describes white space on a page as "absence of narrative." Here, the text—in the structuralist sense of the term—is legible. In *Dance Ink,* the narrative is a choreography between words and images. We don't read what's clear or orderly—we read what's spellbinding.

Case in point: a modest literary magazine, *Cellar Roots,* published once a year by Eastern Michigan University. Designed by graduate students Sharon Marson and Craig Steen, who created a slightly idiosyncratic format and two memorable typefaces, a recent issue was unanimously selected for the prestigious American Center for Design's seventeenth annual 100 Show. Three judges, representing a wide range of typographic styles, picked it without hesitation. "It's an oddity, a real curio," says Stephen Doyle, of New York's Drenttel Doyle Partners. "The classical type is surrounded by very peculiar ornamentation," explains graphic designer Laurie Haycock Makela. "It's the balance between familiarity and experimentation that holds my attention," adds Rudy VanderLans. If you look closely at *Cellar Roots,* there is nothing much to the design. Classical borders overprinted in yellow fracture the text without ever interrupting it. "We challenged ourselves to be smart while pleasing our conservative audience—artists and poets who were disappointed with how their work was presented in the past," says Steen.

Cellar Roots' writers knew instinctively that, without readers, their thoughts would forever remain illegible. Authorship is a shared experience between writer, type designer, and reader. As French semiologist Roland Barthes once wrote, "Reading is: rewriting the text of the work within the text of our lives."

Originally published in: Metropolis, *March 1995*

TOWARDS THE CAUSE OF GRUNGE
Tobias Frere-Jones

Why has grungy typography become so attractive to so many designers? Where legibility and clarity were highly prized, tension and noise are the new goal. Album covers, magazines, commercials and posters shiver and twitch with entropy and decay. Why did *Sassy* magazine commission Jonathan Hoefler to draw a rough, irregular rubber-stamp type for its headlines? Why is Barry Deck's Template Gothic appearing on NBC promo spots? Why does Remedy show up everywhere?

The current trend may never be properly explained until it has passed. But as dirty type becomes increasingly common, its causes become apparent. Here are two causes out of many, one from the graphic designer in the marketplace, the other from the type designer in the technological environment. While both are plausible on their own or in tandem, neither discounts any undiscovered causes.

THE PITCH

Desktop publishing has left much of the design community in disarray, wondering how to explain its services to potential clients. As Michael Rock explains, there are two ways that a designer can validate his or her authority. The first, more modernist approach, is to package oneself as a "visual engineer" or some other quasiscientist. Here, the designer studies the problem and returns with the most efficient and clear method of communicating. This is what many of us were taught in design schools and academies. The second is to emphasize the "artistic" nature of the design product. Here, the client comes to the designer in hopes of a product that embodies a specific Gestalt. The measure of legibility is allowed to slide in favor of creating an atmosphere. The audience's gut reaction is just as valuable as legibility, and far more memorable.

With thousands of computers in place around the world and software flowing like water from mail-order distributors, the modernist design agenda begins to feel not only redundant, but also very hard to sell. Why should anybody pay a designer thousands of dollars for an annual report when all the necessary equipment is already in the data entry department? The ingredients for design are now available to everybody, even if the less obvious skills are not. The great "democratization" of typography will threaten the livelihood of many designers unless they change their selling tactics. To justify the costs of design commissions, the benefits must become obvious: the designer must provide what the secretary cannot. Why be clear and legible when ANYBODY can do that now? The folks in data entry can now make a fairly good facsimile of the Bauhausbücher series (to the eyes of the accountants, at least) but they can't make *Ray Gun*. For designers who want a nonmodernist and individual portfolio, grunge becomes a seductive method of self-identity.

THE MACHINE

Of all the branches of graphic design, type design is always among the first to become involved with a new technology. Type is a tool and not an end product, so type designers must behave as engineers as well as designers. Drawing a font implies being able to reproduce it mechanically somewhere else, so a change in the technical environment has a profound impact on the type community. With the introduction of copperplate engraving, lithography, wood type, and phototype, designers were suddenly allowed to create forms and systems that were previously impossible. At each new stage in history, another set of constraints was lifted, and with varying degrees of seriousness, designers would investigate the potential of new media. In the nineteenth century, wood type manufacturers seized upon the new methods of die-cutting and routing to create the loudest, most garish designs conceivable. The wood studios released fonts with outlines, spurs and knobs, inverted contrast, double-tone shadows, and chromatic fills, all at sizes worthy of billboards. Phototype studios of the sixties and seventies took advantage of the flexibility of spacing allowed by film, and designs with interlocking characters and exuberant swashes filled the specimen books. All the popular faces of the day, from Bookman to Times to Univers, were adapted to the filmsetter's format, but not before swashes, finials, ligatures, and biform alternates were added. One film version of Univers 55 totaled nearly three hundred characters. The tyranny of lead was officially over, and the designers had a field day.

A new technology has arrived, and with it, a new age of experimentation. Now it's perfectly reasonable to produce an entire font (or three or four, while you're at it) in a day. The length of time needed to develop a full character set has imploded to the point of being almost negligible. In addition to the inherent functions of digital type, the ability to generate fonts instantly has let any idea find its way into a consumer product. Every source, from venerated history to random experiment, can now be exploited for material. Drawings for the early design of Futura, before Paul Renner honed it to the form we know, have been digitized and released. The Bauer Foundry, which published Futura in its refined form, would never have considered releasing the early version of the font, even as an alternate member of the family. The risk of time and money were too great to justify. Now, the designer only needs to risk a few hours and a blank disk. This change in the time required is the most profound change in font development. If the design of a font still had to last weeks and months (it still can, if anyone wants it to), then we would see many fewer grungy fonts for sale.

Each set of experiments has been followed by a condemnation of new designs as lurid, grotesque, and useless. From many quarters, this call is being raised again. Is anyone checking to see if these new products are useful? Did anyone need four-foot-high wood type? Did anyone need hundreds of swash alternates? When the customers saw it, they wanted it and felt they needed it. Supply does not always follow demand. Given the right atmosphere, any new design can create its own need; it was only when art directors saw fonts like Remedy and Trixie that they thought of actually using them. The sheer force of novelty was enough to install them on art directors' hard drives.

The livelihood of studios and foundries has always been based on following the technology closely and generating products that nobody else can. Each time a new medium arrives, a new crop of designs comes with it. At each point in history, designers and manufacturers have exploited what is specific to the new technology. While some of the fonts currently in production may be difficult to use or read, they are very easy to make; many of these new designs are being produced exactly because it's possible. For the first critical years in a new market, having a best-seller is far more important than having a slow, but steady, classic. From the financial view, grunge is the debris from the marketing wars of different foundries. Every font manufacturer from Adobe to FontFont is scrambling to add dirty, crunchy or decayed type to its library because everyone else can—and is—doing it.

Against a backdrop of defaults and prepackaged templates, grunge stands as a rebellion against the default of the computer. If left alone, a digital environment will produce forms of perfect alignment and straight edges. It's amusing that the tool that makes for such mechanical exactitude is what makes all the grunge possible. Behind all the grunge is a quiet joke that such a precise tool is being configured to spout dirt.

The new ability has become the new aesthetic. This attachment to new possibilities is far from reprehensible. Designers should search out every function of new tools before these tools become commonplace. But like any other trend, grunge has firmly dated itself and many are already tired of it. Like the arabesques of the 1880s and the swashes of the 1970s, the contortions of the 1990s will fall out of favor, but not before showing us what the new tools can do.

Originally published in Zed, *1994.*

FELLOW READERS: NOTES ON MULTIPLIED LANGUAGE
Robin Kinross

FREE-FOR-ALL MEANING

It is the world of words that creates the world of things."[1] Jacques Lacan's motto —extreme, absolute, unreal—sums up as clearly as can any single formulation the tendency of poststructuralist theorizing. Over the last twenty years the quite rarified ideas of a few thinkers in Paris have become common currency in intellectual discussion. And now, late in the day, and after they have been seriously questioned at their source, these ideas have turned up in the rude world of design. A full discussion would need to consider the ways in which this theory has been applied to typography and graphic design, with illustrations drawn both from design work and from theoretical writing. But, for the purposes of the present brief argument, this tight, self-enclosed circuit of ideas might be adequately described in a summary such as the following. We know the world only through the medium of language. Meaning is arbitrary: without "natural" foundation. Meaning is unstable and has to be made by the reader. Each reader will read differently. To impose a single text on readers is authoritarian and oppressive. Designers should make texts visually ambiguous and difficult to fathom, as a way to respect the rights of readers.

This mishmash of the obvious and the absurd goes under different names: poststructuralism, deconstruction, deconstructivism, and—more generally and much more vaguely— postmodernism. One could have a theological discussion of these terms; but not here. This essay is a loose and informal tour around some of the issues raised by deconstruction in typography and graphic design. I will wander off the path at times, believing that the academic discussion of typography, and of design in general, is too often hermetic and unreal: in unholy partnership with the proud anti-intellectualism of many practicing designers.

Let us go back to the main theoretical source at the root of these ideas about reading. This is the book known as *Cours de linguistique générale* by Ferdinand de Saussure: "Course in general linguistics." Saussure was a professor of linguistics at the University of Geneva. He died in 1913, and this book was first published in 1916. Its text is a reconstruction of lectures, based on notes taken by students and edited by some of his colleagues. This helps to explain why professional linguists—not to mention amateurs without any special competence in linguistics—have found it an enigmatic and difficult text, though commentaries and improved editions have cleared up some mysteries.[2]

Saussure dismisses the simple-minded notion that words correspond to real objects; that, for example the word "tree" corresponds to the real thing that we know as a tree. Instead he introduces a more complex notion of what he calls the sign (*la signe*). "A linguistic sign is not a link between a thing and a name, but between a concept and a sound pattern."[3] And Saussure goes on: "The sound pattern is not actually a sound; for a sound is something physical. A sound pattern is the hearer's psychological impression of a sound, as given to him by the evidence of his senses." Coming to the end of this discussion he proposes to substitute *concept* ("concept" in this translation) and *image acoustique* ("sound pattern") by the terms *signifié* and *signifiant*, which, in the English translation followed here, are "signification" and "signal." This pair in combination constitutes the sign.

Saussure then describes the two fundamental characteristics of a sign: that the link between signal and signification is arbitrary; and that the signal is linear in character (it occurs over time). The first of these characteristics is at the root of the debate over typography and the reader.

As one reads Saussure's remarks on arbitrariness, it is hard, I think, to disagree. He says that different languages have different words for the same concept: the animal which the French know as *un boeuf*, the Germans know as *ein Ochs*. And this is enough to prove the arbitrariness of the linguistic sign.

Two paragraphs after this, Saussure drops in a speculation about semiology, the science which, he predicts, will extend the principles of linguistics to the understanding of every aspect of human life. This is why Saussure has assumed so much importance outside his part in linguistics. A few cryptic remarks in this text became foundation stones for the semiology that was developed half a century later. Semiology became part of the larger project of structuralism, worked out most notably in the anthropology of Claude Lévi-Strauss. Then later—gradually—semiology and structuralism turned into poststructuralism. The development of Roland Barthes's writing—from the scientific pretensions of the early work to his frankly poetic later prose—exhibits this transition most clearly. Poststructuralism renounces the notion of the heart, center, or essence; but if it had such a thing (and perhaps its center lies in its wearying championing of the periphery?) then this concept of the arbitrariness of the sign lies there. Another two paragraphs further on, Saussure says the following:

> The word arbitrary also calls for comment. It must not be taken to imply that a signal depends on the free choice of the speaker. (We shall see later that the individual has no power to alter a sign in any respect once it has become established in a linguistic community.) The term implies simply that the signal is unmotivated: that is to say, arbitrary in relation to its signification, with which it has no natural connection in reality.[4]

It seems that the deconstructionists never read this. Or if they did read it, they never made their disagreement clear. Language, Saussure reminds us, is created by a community, and we use it within the constraints of this larger, communal understanding. In this fundamental sense, signs are not arbitrary, and we would do better to use the term "unmotivated" to describe the quality of fortuitousness in our pairing of signal to signification. So deconstruction contradicts Saussure, without acknowledging this contradiction. Certainly in its degraded forms, as in the recent typography debate, this theory very simple-mindedly asserts that there is no such thing as community, or society— as Margaret Thatcher notoriously formulated it, at around the same time.[5]

Saussure regards language as a collective, social endeavor. But typographers and other designers who share that view should nevertheless have a deep disagreement with Saussure. The language that he considered was almost exclusively spoken language. Saussure's idea of language is a very theoretical and intellectual one. It is less material even than human breath. He remarks that "a sound is something physical." Can one sense a tone of disdain here? Then he turns away from such crude materialism to concentrate on concepts and sound patterns. The diagram in the *Cours de linguistique générale* of how sounds are produced by the organs of speech is about as material as Saussure gets.[6]

In the *Cours de linguistique générale* there is not even much sense of human beings talking with or to one another. It is true that Saussure's famous distinction between *la langue* (the system of language) and *la parole* (individual acts of speech) makes provision for this, in this second term. But then his emphasis falls so largely on the speaker. And if you look for the form of language that most interests typographers—the language that uses letters, characters, images, of ink on paper, of scans across TV screens, of grids and bit-maps, of incisions in stone—there is a large gap. Early in the lectures, Saussure has some pages on writing, but only to put it in its place: "A language and its written form constitute two separate systems of signs. The sole reason for the existence of the latter is to represent the former. The object of study in linguistics is not a combination of the written word and the spoken word. The spoken word alone constitutes that object."[7] This may have been a revolutionary attitude to adopt then: linguistics had been shaped as a study of language in its written forms. But its legacy has not been helpful to any discussion of the material world of the making and exchange of artifacts: the world to which typography belongs. The wish of semiologists, to study and explain the social world, suffers from this crippling weakness: it has no material foundations. So, after his brief discussion of writing, Saussure confines himself to spoken language. Indeed he uses the word "language" (*la langue*) to mean just "spoken language."

Some attempts have been made to correct the blindness of linguistics to writing. From within linguistics itself, one could cite the work of Josef Vachek, and maybe others.[8] From a vantage point outside linguistics, the English anthropologist Jack Goody has produced a stream of books and essays on writing, understood in its full historical and material sense.[9] *The Domestication of The Savage Mind* may be his most accessible and directly relevant book for typography. Goody here points forcefully to the distinctive properties of written language as a system apart from and in mutual reciprocity with spoken language. His work also has the distinction of examining ways in which writing may be configured other than as continuous text: in tables, lists, formulae, and other related forms for which we hardly have an agreed descriptive terminology. These systems of configuration may be used almost unthinkingly, every working day, by typographers, editors, typesetters, and typists. And yet discussions about reading, legibility, print, and the future of the book seem to know only continuous text (a page of a novel, most typically) as their object of reference. The real world of typography is far more diverse and awkward. If reflection on what is there before us is not enough to persuade semiologists about the reality and difference of written language, then a reading of Jack Goody should be persuasive. Afterwards it will be impossible to parrot Saussure on "language."

SHARED COPY

The recognition and analysis of written language is an essential correction to the Saussurian theory, but it needs to be developed further. There is writing and there is printing: two different phenomena. Writing exists in one copy; printing makes multiple copies of the same thing. Yes, you can duplicate writing: you can photocopy it or photograph and make a printing plate from it. The more exact difference is between writing and typographic composition of text. But some such differentiation must be made: between the written and the typographic/printed; or, more widely (to include film, TV, video, tape- and disc-stored information) between the single and the multiple.

Semiology, based on an abstract notion of language that does not recognize the independent life of writing, is no help here. Theorists who do discuss "writing," but just as some unified, undifferentiated sphere of visible language, may have a tool of analysis. However, it is a blunt one, which cannot deal with multiplied language.[10] Although here one should remember that this discussion is being conducted in English, and in this language a rather clear distinction is made between "writing" and "printing." But, for example, German has *Schrift* as a common term between writing (by hand) and printing (with a machine). Whereas in English, one speaks of "writing" and of "type" (i.e., words with quite different roots), in German, one speaks just of *Schrift*, or perhaps of *Handschrift* and *Druckschrift*. As if to confirm the distinction that English makes, one can judge typographic innocence in an English-speaker by the extent to which they muddle "writing" and "printing." Thus: "I like the writing [i.e., type] on that record cover." Or: "please print your name and address" (i.e., write in capital letters).

Theorists of spoken and written language cannot divorce their subject from its place and time. Thus Jack Goody's main field of interest has been in Africa and the Near East, and in ancient societies. When Goody touches on European or modern societies, he is alert to the differences introduced by printing; but for the most part he can properly concentrate on written—handwritten—language.

From within the world of typography, Gerrit Noordzij has been a productive and powerful theorist of writing, which he usually takes to include typographic composition of text: "typography is writing with prefabricated letters."[11] This definition is offered as an alternative way of thinking, within the context of a discussion of graphic design and typography as processes of specification and worldly intervention between texts, commissioners, printers, and producers. Noordzij's wish to subsume typography within writing is the purest piece of dogma: an essential item of mental equipment for a master scribe, lettercutter, and engraver, whose main focus is on the minutest details of letters and their production. But here, in this essay, our focus is on the world that Gerrit Noordzij sees when he puts down his magnifying glass and picks up his telephone: the social world of producers and readers. In this domain, typography and writing are essentially different activities.

Typography deals with language duplicated, in multiple copies, on a material substrate. Here we can add in screen displays, and any other means of multiplying text. And to "text," we can add "images" too: the same point applies. The exact repetition of information is the defining feature of multiplied text, and it is what is missing from writing. The historical elaboration of this perception has been made most thoroughly by William M. Ivins in his *Prints and Visual Communication* and by Elizabeth Eisenstein in her *The Printing Press as an Agent of Change.*[12] If printing was not, as Eisenstein sometimes seems to suggest, the lever of change in the history of fifteenth- and sixteenth-century Europe, it was certainly a fundamental factor in the changes that took place then. Printing could for the first time provide the steady and reliable means for the spreading and sharing of knowledge. Science and technology could be developed, ideas could be disseminated and then questioned. With a stable and common text for discussion, a critical culture could grow. Argument had a firm basis on which to proceed.

The emphasis of historians of print culture, such as Eisenstein, has tended to be on books, partly perhaps for the mundane reason that these are the printed documents that survive most abundantly. It is certainly harder for a historian to investigate newspapers or street posters: harder to locate surviving copies, and to consider their effects. Indeed this branch of history has become known as "the history of the book." A book is, most characteristically, read by one person at a time, and often that person will be alone. One can counter this perception by recalling the practice—now declining—of reading aloud, in churches, in schools and other institutions, and in the home. Texts are also read alone-in-public: on buses, in parks, in libraries. So reading often has a visible and apparent social dimension. But its truer and perhaps more real social dimension lies in the reading that happens when one person picks up a printed sheet and turns its marks into meaning. The page—it could be a screen too—is then the common ground on which people can meet. They may be widely dispersed in space and time, unknown and unavailable to each other. Or they may know each other and come together later to discuss their reading of the text. Then the social dimension of the text may become a group of people around a table, pointing to the text, quoting from it, arguing, considering.

A text is produced by writers, editors, and printers. With luck, if they keep their heads down, designers might find a role somewhere here, too. The text is composed, proofed, corrected, perhaps read and corrected further. Then it is multiplied and distributed. Finally it is read alone but in common, for shared meanings. When one starts to think along these lines, the semiology of texts and images doesn't seem to help much. Yes, "signification" can be identified as part of a larger process. And within this small part, what of the "arbitrary link" between signification and signal? Saussure's too-little noticed suggestion that "unmotivated" is a better term than "arbitrary" helps because "arbitrary" is not what typography is about at all.

The juxtaposition that one finds happening in typography is easy to grasp. It is the link between a keyboard and a monitor; between manuscript copy and a laser-printed proof; between information on a disc and on sheets of text on film; and finally, and differently, between the page and the reader. The links between these pairs are, we try to ensure, anything but arbitrary. Correcting proofs, with its attempt to turn "arbitrary" into "intended," can stand as the clearest instance of this defining characteristic of typography.

The argument made here is that deconstruction and poststructuralist theory can't account for the material world. The only material it knows is air, and its foundations are built not even on air, but on the entirely abstract and intellectual.[13] Certainly, when it takes on typography, the huge mistake that poststructuralist theory makes is not to see the material nature of typographic language.[14] Here screen display, because it is indeed so fluid—materially so—probably should be considered separately. But certainly in printing, language becomes real and materially present: ink on paper. Here lies the responsibility of the designer of printed matter: to bring into existence texts that will never be changed, only—if one is lucky—revised and reprinted. The idea that design should act out the indeterminacy of reading is a folly. A printed sheet is not at all indeterminate, and all that the real reader is left with is a designer's muddle or vanity, frozen at the point at which the digital description was turned into material. Far from giving freedom of interpretation to the reader, deconstructionist design imposes the designer's reading of the text onto the rest of us.[15]

This argument against poststructuralism in typography is not directly about style, nor is it about tradition and breaks with tradition. It is a social argument. Saussure's formulation, already quoted, that "the individual has no power to alter a sign in any respect once it has become established in a linguistic community" makes the point firmly. Too firmly, because it seems to leave out the creative aspect of language, of syntax especially, and of the ways in which every one of us mints these signs freshly, with new meanings, every day.

The theme of language as the possession of a community was developed by Benedict Anderson in the course of his book *Imagined Communities*.[16] This book is one of the handful of general works on history and politics that should be dear to typographers because it takes notice of printing; in fact printing is at the heart of Anderson's thesis. In one chapter Anderson weaves together the rise of capitalism, the spread of printing, the history of languages, and the "origins of national consciousness." Arbitrariness is acknowledged. He writes about alphabetic languages, as against ideographic: "The very arbitrariness of any system of signs for sounds facilitated the assembling process." But, unlike the poststructuralists, he does not stop there. "Nothing served to 'assemble' related vernaculars more than capitalism, which, within the limits imposed by grammars and syntaxes, created mechanically-reproduced print-languages, capable of dissemination through the market." But this is not a reductive account of mere capitalist exploitation. Anderson continues:

> These print-languages laid the base for national consciousness ... they created
> unified fields of exchange and communication below Latin and above the spoken

vernaculars. Speakers of the huge variety of Frenches, Englishes, or Spanishes, who might find it difficult or even impossible to understand one another in conversation, became capable of comprehending one another via print and paper. In the process, they gradually became aware of the hundreds of thousands, even millions, of people in their particular language-field, and at the same time that *only those* hundreds of thousands, or millions, so belonged. These fellow-readers, to whom they were connected through print, formed, in their secular, particular, visible invisibility, the embryo of the nationally-imagined community.

This "imagined community" may be difficult for some people to grasp, particularly if they live within the community of one of the dominant languages of the world. But even in the English-speaking metropolis where these words are being written, it can be understood and felt. Greek, Italian, and Irish newspapers are sold at corner shops in this neighborhood, serving their readers here as conductors or lifelines out into the larger sphere of their linguistic-cultural community. This may describe the case for some, probably older readers. For others from those communities, and for us too—the mother-tongue English-speakers—the local weekly newspaper is the place where we come together, where we read the neighborhood. The activity of reading, as Benedict Anderson puts it, may take place "in the lair of the skull," but it has this social extension.[17] We always read in common, with fellow readers.

PLACES AND NETS

Some qualifications need to be made to this argument. I have been stressing the "in-common" element of reading, against the idea that this is a wilful, arbitrary process, without an intersubjective dimension. But as an extreme of "in-common" reading, one thinks of conditions in totalitarian societies. In China at the time of the Cultural Revolution, Mao Zedong's "little red book" became—despite its praise of contradiction and dialectics—the emblem of a society in which an attempt was made at coercion even into feeling in unison. The book was a badge, as well as a manual of "correct thinking." Like the trim, beautifully made jackets into whose breast pockets it slotted, the "little red book" was a model of fitting, unobtrusive design and production; but this uniform became oppressive. The project of complete, totalitarian standardization is inhuman, impossible, and will always eventually collapse. After a while, people rebel.

To the list of the nondeterminable tendencies in reading, we can add that texts age and travel, or their contexts change both in time and place. Each generation, as well as each person, will find different meanings in a text. Much that is fresh in writing and thinking comes through recovery of old texts, and through reading them against the grain of current orthodoxy in an attempt to discover the original habits of thought and language in which the work was written.[18]

Thus among the freshest of recent tendencies in music has been the uncovering of "early music," by the attempt to understand and re-attain its original conditions of production. But, against any idea of static and finally knowable pieces, it is clear that there can only be performances of their time and place. Take the example of J. S. Bach's *Matthew Passion*: "authentic performances" in the 1990s differ markedly from those in 1970s. The most moving and convincing readings are those that—perhaps just through their concentration on "the work itself"—speak more directly to us. This was certainly the case in the recent "performed" version of the work.[19] This production discarded the conventions of the concert performance (white ties, tails, diva dresses, upright posture)—often then uneasily situated in a church—and joined the work instead to the sphere of the everyday reality of the audience (jeans and sweaters, gestures and perambulation). Somehow this helped set free the emotional power in the Passion story, especially for the nonbeliever, for whom the work may otherwise remain a long-distance and largely aesthetic experience. The audience, grouped around the action in stacked scaffolded seating, entered the event more intimately than is usual. The acting-out was quite limited: a touch on the shoulder, a gesture of the head, and not much more. But just in this very constraint it gained in effect. One could point to some historical legitimation for this performance (the work was felt to be surprisingly theatrical and operatic by its first audiences in Leipzig in the 1730s), but this was at most a starting point rather than a complete program to emulate or recreate.

The "reading" that is given before an audience gathered under one roof—or even that is broadcast on television—is, of course, a different matter to the reading that is the concern of this essay. Although, by comparison and contrast, it may illuminate. The director of the performance, in collaboration with others, presents an interpretation, a reading. We the audience receive it and interpret that interpretation, and our attention interacts with and may affect this interpretation. Afterwards, with others who have been there, we consider, discuss, develop, modify, revise our interpretations. These have been different experiences, maybe quite wildly different, if members of an audience bring very different assumptions and beliefs to the event (say, people of different religious beliefs at the *Matthew Passion*). This may be why theater can be so vivid an experience in small communities, where audience members have shared pasts and a sense of who each other is. And it may be why theater in a large city—however technically assured—can be such a desolate experience. Whatever the composition of the audience, there is a common event by which to measure. And the sense of community that may be engendered at such a performance is, of course, what makes the difference between public performance and private reading. But joint reflection over something that has been shared can happen with both these experiences of watching and of reading. Both have public and private dimensions, if in different measures.

"The truth lies somewhere in between" may be a truism, but one that is also true in this case, or in these infinite particular cases of people reading texts. One only has to think of any reader turning the pages, misunderstanding, turning back to see what was said before, sneaking a look at the last chapter, being distracted by a phone call or the demands of a child, perhaps falling asleep and dreaming around the text, and then returning to this business of turning marks into meaning. The process is individual and unpredictable. As if we needed a designer to make this so! And yet the text is there as an irresistible and multiple fact: a common ground. For any writer, the intersubjective dimension of reading comes vividly to life when one hears from a friend that they have been reading something you wrote. Then you may reach for your copy of the text and read it again, but this time in the voice of that other reader, turning the words over, wondering what she or he made of them.

Computer-based means of transmitting texts are no doubt introducing fundamental changes to the model that is here taken as characteristic of reading. Text and images organized as nodes on a network, as in hypertext, or intercut and layered with other information and other kinds of media (animated images, sound)—this provides a different experience from that of reading a printed page. And here the deconstructionist rhetoric about the active reader may have more truth in its descriptions. At least here there really is fluidity and the possibility of change, as there hardly is in printed deconstruction.

Debates over the coming of the "electronic book," at the expense of the printed one, have always seemed a little futile.[20] Futurist visionaries tend to underestimate the dimensions of bodily comfort and cost. Reading cheap small books in bed can still be a great pleasure. The dead duck of "legibility" is hardly the issue here. Much more critical— apart, of course, from content—is page size, weight, openability and flappiness, lighting, temperature of the room, and how many pillows you have. Sitting in an upright chair at a screen brings a more serious air to the processes of reading, and there would be some sense of contradiction in reading a thriller that way. To read an intimate letter sent over the wires to your terminal may also feel a little odd. The present upsurge in this mode of communication must bring large changes. One already noticeable effect is that an informal, unedited style which goes with private communication is spreading into multiplied communication. Electronic mail is fine, but not if this becomes the model for all communication. The formality that multiplication and publication demands of text carries a social function. And the social necessity of "in-common" reading, which was won for us by printing, remains—even if it is now carried by other ways of transmitting text. If this is lost, then we really will all be reduced to "individuals and their families."

An extract from the text originally published as: Fellow Readers: Notes on Multiplied Language *(London: Hyphen Press, 1994).*

Notes

1. Jacques Lacan, *Ecrits* (London: Tavistock, 1977 [original French edition, 1966]), 65. The remark is quoted by Raymond Tallis in his *Not Saussure: A Critique of Post-Saussurean Literary Theory* (Basingstoke: Macmillan, 1988), 58. The clarity, humor, and vigorous argument of Tallis's book will provide welcome relief to those lost in the world of muddy theorizing. A good résumé and extension of the case against poststructuralism is made by Brian Vickers in *Appropriating Shakespeare* (London: Yale University Press, 1993). I read Vickers after completing this essay, with the feeling that the points I make in this first section are accepted wisdom in some quarters. Strong criticism of value-free deconstruction is made by Christopher Norris in *Uncritical Theory: Postmodernism, Intellectuals and the Gulf War* (London: Lawrence & Wishart, 1992). This book is of special interest in showing a former protagonist changing his mind.

2. The English translation quoted from here is that of Roy Harris (London: Duckworth, 1983). This may supersede the translation by Wade Baskin (New York: Philosophical Library, 1959), which has provided the basis for most English-language commentary on Saussure. See also: Roy Harris, *Reading Saussure: A Critical Commentary on the Cours de linguistique générale* (London: Duckworth, 1987).

3. Saussure, *Cours,* trans. Harris, 66.

4. Saussure, *Cours,* trans. Harris, 68–9.

5. "There is no such thing as 'society,' there is only individuals and their families." This is the quotation as made by Stuart Hall, principal analyst of "Thatcherism," in *Marxism Today* (December 1991): 10. Although endlessly quoted, the exact source for the statement is elusive. Russell A. Berman traces connections between deconstruction and Reaganism in his "Troping to Pretoria: The Rise and Fall of Deconstruction," *Telos,* no. 85: 4–16. But in his nice remark that "deconstruction is the restaurant where one can only order the menu . . . Let them eat tropes!" (at p. 10) Berman seems to exaggerate deconstruction's purchase on the material world (of paper, in this case).

6. Saussure, *Cours,* trans. Harris, 42.

7. Saussure, *Cours,* trans. Harris, 24–5.

8. Josef Vachek, *Written Language* (The Hague: Mouton, 1973). A helpful survey here is an unpublished Ph.D. thesis by Robert Waller: "The Typographic Contribution to Language," University of Reading, 1987.

9. See: Jack Goody and Ian Watt, "The Consequences of Literacy," in Jack Goody (ed.), *Literacy in Traditional Societies* (Cambridge: Cambridge University Press, 1968), 27–68. See also these books by Goody (also published by Cambridge University Press): *The Domestication of the Savage Mind* (1977), *The Logic of Writing and the Organization of Society* (1986), *The Interface Between the Written and the Oral* (1987). Goody's work is illuminatingly scanned in the course of Perry Anderson's high-altitude essay "A Culture in Contraflow" in his *English Questions* (London: Verso, 1992), 231–8. I am grateful to Giovanni Lussu for reminding me about Jack Goody's work, in an article that bears on the themes of this essay: "La grafica è scittura," *Lineagrafica,* no. 256 (1991): 14–19.

10. I would include Jacques Derrida here. Reviewers of this essay in its original form remarked that my criticisms of Saussurean thought shared some ground with Derrida, the proponent of deconstruction. But I fail to find in Derrida any extended materialist or worldly concept of language: no distinction between texts that are written and those that are typeset, printed, distributed, and sold.

11. Gerrit Noordzij, *De Staart van de Kat: de Vorm van het Boek in Opstellen* (Leersum: Uitgeverij ICS Nederland, 1991), 12. Noordzij can be read in his own idiosyncratic English in the occasional publication *Letterletter,* published by ATypI (Münchenstein), from 1984, and from 1993 by the Enschedé Font Foundry (Zaltbommel).

12. William M. Ivins, *Prints and Visual Communication* (London: Routledge & Kegan Paul, 1953); Elizabeth Eisenstein, *The Printing Press as an Agent of Change: Communications and Cultural Transformations in Early-Modern Europe* (Cambridge: Cambridge University Press, 1979). The social dimension of printing is more evident in the book that opened up this field of history: Lucien Febvre and Henri-Jean Martin, *The Coming of the Book: the Impact of Printing 1450–1800* (London: New Left Books, 1976 [original French edition, 1958]).

13. This point was first made for me by Sebastiano Timpanaro in his essay "Structuralism and its successors," *On Materialism* (London: New Left Books, 1976 [original Italian edition, 1970]), 135–219. I tried to amplify it in two articles: "Semiotics and Designing," *Information Design Journal,* vol. 4, no. 3, (1986): 190–8; "Notes after the Text," *Information Design Journal,* vol. 5, no. 1 (1986): 75–8.

14. Among more recent essays in this field, see: Ellen Lupton and J. Abbott Miller, "Type Writing: Structuralism and Writing," *Emigre,* no. 15, (1990). In their theoretical preamble, Lupton and Miller misread Saussure's "arbitrary," and then apply poststructuralist theory to typeface design—as if this is what constitutes typography. In a later essay on "structure" in typography, Miller does discuss whole passages of text and their configuration, but to less clear effect: in *Eye,* no. 10 (1993): 58–65. The first essay and material from the second have been republished, along with much else of relevance to these themes, in Lupton and Miller's *Design Writing Research* (New York: Princeton Architectural Press, 1996).

15. Paul Stiff succinctly takes apart the "designer-centred ideology" of deconstructionism in *Eye,* no. 11 (1993): 4–5. [This article is reprinted in this volume as "Look at Me! Look at Me! (What Designers Want)."]

16. Benedict Anderson, *Imagined Communities: Reflections on the Origins and Spread of Nationalism* (London: Verso, 1983). The quotations that follow are from page 47.

17. Anderson, *Imagined Communities*, 39.

18. Here I am thinking especially of the art historian Michael Baxandall in his books *Painting and Experience in Fifteenth-Century Italy* (London: Oxford University Press, 1972) and *The Limewood Sculptors of Renaissance Germany* (London: Yale University Press, 1980). His book on method, *Patterns of Intention* (London: Yale University Press, 1985), discusses these and related themes in ways that design theorists could learn much from.

19. First performances took place in London in February 1993. The production was the initiative of the promoter, Ron Gonsalves, with the support of the conductor Paul Goodwin and the director Jonathan Miller.

20. Among recent works in this genre, Jay David Bolter's *Writing Space* (Hillsdale, NJ: Lawrence Erlbaum, 1991) is of interest here in its deployment of poststructuralist theory to rationalize hypertext.

THE RULES OF TYPOGRAPHY
ACCORDING TO ~~CRACKPOTS~~ EXPERTS

Jeffery Keedy

The first thing one learns about typography and type design is that there are many rules and maxims. The second is that these rules are made to be broken. And the third is that "breaking the rules" has always been just another one of the rules. Although rules are meant to be broken, scrupulously followed, misunderstood, reassessed, retrofitted and subverted, the best rule of thumb is that rules should never be ignored. The typefaces discussed in this article are recent examples of rule-breaking/making in progress. I have taken some old rules to task and added some new ones of my own that I hope will be considered critically.

Imagine that you have before you a flagon of wine. You may choose your own favorite vintage for this imaginary demonstration, so that it be a deep shimmering crimson in colour. You have two goblets before you. One is of solid gold, wrought in the most exquisite patterns. The other is of crystal-clear glass, thin as a bubble, and as transparent. Pour and drink; and according to your choice of goblet, I shall know whether or not you are a connoisseur of wine. For if you have no feelings about wine one way or the other, you will want the sensation of drinking the

stuff out of a vessel that may have cost thousands of pounds; but if you are a
member of that vanishing tribe, the amateurs of fine vintages, you will choose
the crystal, because everything about it is calculated to reveal rather than to hide
the beautiful thing which it was meant to contain. . . . Now the man who first
chose glass instead of clay or metal to hold his wine was a "modernist" in the sense
in which I am going to use the term. That is, the first thing he asked of this
particular object was not "How should it look?" but "What must it do?" and to
that extent all good typography is modernist.

> Beatrice Warde, from an address to the British Typographers' Guild at the St.
> Bride Institute, London, 1932. Published in *Monotype Recorder,* Vol. 44, No. 1
> (Autumn 1970).

Beatrice Warde's address is favored by members of a vanishing tribe—typography
connoisseurs who "reveal" beautiful things to the rest of us (modernists). Such connoisseurs
are opposed to typographic sensationalists who have no feelings about the material they
contain with their extravagance (postmodernist hacks). In short, the typographers with
"taste" must rise above the crass fashion-mongers of the day. Connoisseurship will always
have its place in a capitalist, class-conscious society and there is nothing like modernism
for the creation of high and low consumer markets. The modernist typophile-connoisseur
should rejoice in the typefaces shown here because they reaffirm his or her status as being
above fleeting concerns. After all, if there was no innovation to evolve through refinement
to tradition, then where would the connoisseur be?

Beatrice Warde did not imagine her crystal goblet would contain Pepsi-Cola, but
some vessel has to do it. Of course, she was talking in terms of ideals, but what is the ideal
typeface to say: "Uh-Huh, Uh-Huh, You got the right one baby"? There is no reason why
all typefaces should be designed to last forever, and in any case, how would we know if
they did?

The art of lettering has all but disappeared today, surviving at best through sign
painters and logotype specialists. Lettering is being incorporated into type design and the
distinction between the two is no longer clear. Today, special or custom letterforms designed
in earlier times by a letterer are developed into whole typefaces. Calligraphy will also be
added to the mix as more calligraphic tools are incorporated into type-design software.
Marshall McLuhan said that all new technologies incorporate the previous ones, and this
certainly seems to be the case with type. The technological integration of calligraphy,
lettering, and type has expanded the conceptual and aesthetic possibilities of letterforms.

The rigid categories applied to type design in the past do not make much sense
in the digital era. Previous distinctions such as serif and sans serif are challenged by the
new "semi serif" and "pseudo serif." The designation of type as text or display is also too
simplistic. Whereas type used to exist only in books (text faces) or occasionally on a building
or sign (display), today's typographer is most frequently working with in-between amounts
of type—more than a word or two but much less than one hundred pages. The categories
of text and display should not be taken too literally in a multimedia and interactive
environment where type is also read on television, computers, clothing, even tattoos.

Good taste and perfect typography are suprapersonal. Today, good taste is often
erroneously rejected as old-fashioned because the ordinary man, seeking approval

of his so-called personality, prefers to follow the dictates of his own peculiar style rather than submit to any objective criterion of taste.

Jan Tschichold, 1948, published in *Ausgewählte Aufsatze über Fragen der Gestalt des Buches und der Typographie* (1975).

"Criteria of taste" are anything but objective. Theories of typography are mostly a matter of proclaiming one's own "tastes" as universal truths. The typographic tradition is one of constant change due to technological, functional, and cultural advancement (I use the word "advancement" as I am unfashionably optimistic about the future).

In typographic circles it is common to refer to traditional values as though they were permanently fixed and definitely not open to interpretation. This is the source of the misguided fear of new developments in type design. The fear is that new technology, with its democratization of design, is the beginning of the end of traditional typographic standards. In fact, just the opposite is true, for though typographic standards are being challenged by more designers and applications than ever before, this challenge can only reaffirm what works and modify what is outdated.

The desktop computer and related software have empowered designers and nonspecialists to design and use their own typefaces. And with more type designers and consumers, there will obviously be more amateurish and ill-conceived letterforms. But there will also be an abundance of new ideas that will add to the richness of the tradition. Too much has been made of the proliferation of "bad" typefaces, as if a few poorly drawn letterforms could bring Western civilization to its knees. Major creative breakthroughs often come from outside a discipline, because the "experts" all approach the discipline with a similar obedient point of view. The most important contribution of computer technology, like the printing press before it, lies in its democratization of information. This is why the digital era will be the most innovative in the history of type design.

The more uninteresting the letter, the more useful it is to the typographer.

Piet Zwart, *A History of Lettering, Creative Experiment and Letter Identity* (1986).

Back in Piet Zwart's day most typographers relied on "fancy type" to be expressive. I don't think Zwart was *against* expression in type design as much as he was *for* expression (an architectonic one) in composition. Zwart's statement epitomizes the typographic fundamentalists' credo. The irony is that the essentially radical and liberal manifestos of the early modernists are with us today as fundamentally conservative dogma.

I suspect that what is most appealing about this rhetoric is the way the typographer's ego supersedes that of the type designer. By using uninteresting "neutral" typefaces (created by anonymous or dead designers), typographers are assured that they alone will be credited for their creations. I have often heard designers say they would never use so-and-so's typefaces because that would make their work look like so-and-so's, though they are apparently unafraid of looking like Eric Gill or Giovanni Battista Bodoni. Wolfgang Weingart told me after a lecture at CalArts in which he included my typeface Keedy Sans as an example of "what we do not do at Basel" that he likes the typeface, but believes it should be used only by me. Missing from this statement is an explanation of how Weingart can use a typeface such as Akzidenz Grotesk so innovatively and expertly.

New typefaces designed by living designers should not be perceived as incompatible with the typographer's ego. Rudy VanderLans's use of Keedy Sans for *Emigre* and B. W. Honeycutt's use of Hard Times and Skelter in *Details* magazine are better treatments of my typefaces than I could conceive. Much of the pleasure in designing a typeface is seeing what people do with it. If you are lucky, the uses of your typeface will transcend your expectations; if you are not so fortunate, your type will sink into oblivion. Typefaces have a life of their own and only time will determine their fate.

> In the new computer age, the proliferation of typefaces and type manipulations represents a new level of visual pollution threatening our culture. Out of thousands of typefaces, all we need are a few basic ones, and trash the rest.
>> Massimo Vignelli, from a poster announcing the exhibition "The Masters Series: Massimo Vignelli," (February/March 1991).

In an age of hundreds of television channels, thousands of magazines, books, and newspapers, and inconceivable amounts of information via telecommunications, could just a few basic typefaces keep the information net moving? Given the value placed on expressing one's individual point of view, there would have to be only a handful of people on the planet for this to work.

Everything should be permitted, as long as context is rigorously and critically scrutinized. Diversity and excellence are not mutually exclusive; if everything is allowed it does not necessarily follow that everything is of equal value. Variety is much more than just the "spice of life." At a time when cultural diversity and empowering other voices are critical issues in society, the last thing designers should be doing is retrenching into a mythical canon of "good taste."

> There is no such thing as a bad typeface . . . just bad typography.
>> Jeffery Keedy

Typographers are always quick to criticize, but it is rare to hear them admit that it is a typeface that makes their typography look good. Good typographers can make good use of almost anything. The typeface is a point of departure, not a destination. In using new typefaces the essential ingredient is imagination, because unlike with old faces, the possibilities have not been exhausted.

Typographers need to lighten up, to recognize that change is good (and inevitable), to jump into the multicultural, poststructural, postmodern, electronic flow. Rejection or ignorance of the rich and varied history and traditions of typography are inexcusable; however, adherence to traditional concepts without regard to contemporary context is intellectually lazy and a threat to typography today.

You cannot do new typography with old typefaces. This statement riles typographers, probably because they equate "new" with "good," which I do not. My statement is simply a statement of fact, not a value judgement. The recent proliferation of new typefaces should have anyone interested in advancing the tradition of typography in a state of ecstasy. It is always possible to do *good* typography with old typefaces. But why are so many typographers insistent on trying to do the impossible—*new* typography with old faces?

Inherent in the new typefaces are possibilities for the (imaginative) typographer that were unavailable ten years ago. So besides merely titillating typophiles with fresh new faces, it is my intention to encourage typographers and type designers to look optimistically forward. You may find some of the typefaces formally and functionally repugnant, but you must admit that type design is becoming very interesting again.

Originally published in Eye, No. 11, November 1993.

THE NEW TYPOGRAPHER
MUTTERING IN YOUR EAR
Kevin Fenton

Writers who attempt to discuss typography are in an awkward position: we are simultaneously interested and incompetent. Every published word is filtered through the sensibility of a typographer or a designer acting as a typographer. Writers have a great deal to lose or gain from the choices thus made. Yet even in those places which most actively encourage collaboration between writers and art directors, the specifics of typography remain inaccessible to us. We lack the technical vocabulary or the design aptitude to engage in discussions about many aspects of the craft. When we turn our attention to what might be called the new typography, this feeling, this mix of passion and humility, is particularly strong.

In his introduction to *Typography 15*, Dirk Rowntree of the Type Directors Club provides a useful sketch of the origins of the new typography. He describes an upheaval where, given the new freedom allowed by the computer, "monolithic, centralized authorities that dispense standards of practice are shown to be inadequate, if not entirely irrelevant." The judges of *Typography 15* extended the revolutionary rhetoric. They praised design which "participates in the meaningful dialectic of deconstructionism," "challenges the way we read," and refuses to breathe "the [impoverished] air of consumerism and technology"—thereby "subverting messages and creating alternative readings of a text" and ensuring that "the usual hierarchy of text and design is subverted by its message." Although forms of the word "subvert" were used twice in the passages quoted above, I could not identify what was being subverted other than "the traditional hierarchy of image and text." This, of course, begs the question: what was wrong with the traditional hierarchy? What are typographers subverting and why? You almost get the sense that corrosiveness has become a value in and of itself. But subversion without a discernable purpose seems little more than vandalism.

Ultimately, I believe that what has happened is something more than vandalism and less than revolution. I believe it is a reaction to staleness, a return to a kind of expressionism, an insertion of ghosts into the machine. By introducing more emotion and irony, the new type corrects a tradition dominated by soullessness. The embrace of ugliness and playfulness suggests an openness of spirit. Some pieces make me a little sick to my stomach, which is an appropriate reaction to much of the twentieth century. The displacement of typographers by designers has resulted in some powerful work, work where the emotion that powered the design suffuses the type.

But I suspect that, in the spirit of liberation, the new typography may have gone too far. While it is one thing for a designer to displace a typographer, it is something else for a designer to ignore a text. Without explicitly stating it, much recent discussion assumes that typography is—or can be—a creative act. But because it depends on existing subject matter, the process of selecting and arranging fonts seems more properly described as interpretive rather than creative. Like acting or literary criticism, typography responds to a response to the world. In fact, typography's reliance on existing words is what distinguishes it from other disciplines within design. It assumes a text, which it attempts to interpret as richly as possible. That is why legibility is such a sacred cow. Without legibility, I do not see how typography can exist as typography. It dissolves into illustration.

Although I do not think a typographer can ignore the text, she can sometimes profitably ignore its author. Anyone who has written knows that text can contain meanings that even the most careful writer did not intend. Good designers, like good actors, can discover and highlight those complexities. At times, the interpretation is of such originality and power that it overwhelms the original. It seems to me that these kind of bold, often ironic, interpretations can succeed especially well when the copy is handed down anonymously from a corporate client or when it is little more than the time and place information of most posters.

By the same token, the new typography generally does an injustice to serious literature, which it tends to overinterpret and suffocate. In one of the winning entries in *Typography 15*, Carl Lehmann-Haupt praised design students at the University of Illinois for rendering the first line of Franz Kafka's short story "The Metamorphosis," "perspicuous and alarming." In my mind, the opening of that classic story resonated long before it was manipulated by this particular type treatment. If anything, the intrusive line breaks and the obvious capitalization of "gigantic" (evidently because it means "big") cheapen that wonderful line. I would have liked the designers to have respected Kafka's intentions more. He intended this to be the first line of a piece of prose; it has been treated as poetry, and, to my ear, it doesn't benefit from the attempt at colorization. Writers are not the only ones with areas of incompetence. If designers are going to be as radically interpretive as they have recently threatened to be, one would like to see them become more sensitive readers. Otherwise, the revolution could lead to some very ham-handed interpretations of text.

Nor, as a reader, do I unreservedly embrace the habit of interpreting text by juggling fonts and sizes and leadings. Lehmann-Haupt justified this eagerness to interpret text by arguing that type is not transparent. While that is true, doesn't the act of reading long passages convince us that some type is more effectively transparent than other type, that the known is less intrusive than the new, that constancy is less jarring than change, and, finally, that there is a state which you reach where you no longer are conscious of the words as configurations of ink but as something more ethereal and efficient? In its quickness to interpret, and its occasional expressionistic frenzies, the new typography denies the reader the opportunity to experience the text for himself. It feels like someone is standing over your shoulder while you read, underlining some passages, italicizing others, muttering through yet others.

Designers could not have selected a more inopportune time to obscure meanings and tweak readers. We are less literate and less likely to read than ever before. To speak of "challenging the way we read" seems almost naively optimistic. It would make more sense to challenge the way we don't read. At the same time, we at least seem to have more information than ever before to absorb. For every one book I read, there are three equally interesting books that I don't read. And this sense of falling behind doesn't apply simply to serious literature. Why do typographers feel so self-righteous about confounding my ability to read movie posters, trade ads, party invitations, fund-raising solicitations? Just as the modernists may have overvalued clarity, the new expressionism overvalues ambiguity. For reasons that are themselves sometimes obscure, it promotes obscurity and cultivates a faint sense of menace. It also overvalues irony. The new type can sometimes suffer from weirdness for its own sake, a mere distancing of the artist from the work, a time-wasting peek-a-boo of meanings.

In my most alarmist moments, I fear that what is being subverted may be the language itself. *Ray Gun* declares "the death of print" on its masthead, but what David Carson is killing may not be not print but literacy. Some experiments might be justified on the grounds that they entice jaded readers to engage otherwise dry material, or that they better acknowledge diversity, but this seems neither the effect nor the intent of most of the new work. Even given the value of promoting diversity, aren't there good reasons for conservative typography? We discourage the proliferation of new fonts for the same reason that we discourage the creation of new alphabets or the coining of new languages. Didn't we invent language to mediate diversity? Like language itself, isn't typography inherently communal? Shouldn't it be efficient and stable? Organic and evolutionary? Yes, Western civilization—like most civilizations—has left a great deal of brutality in its wake, and, to some extent, that has been absorbed into its traditional fonts. But isn't the clarity of the best traditional fonts one of the treasures of Western culture? And isn't the alternative to typography that evokes our sometimes bloody history a typography that is even more sterile than modernism?

If nothing else, those who interpret words should be more sensitive to language. I am especially uncomfortable with design commentary that borrows the language of progressive social movements. Dirk Rowntree spoke of "centralized authorities" and "control over production tools." Such language should be reserved for true instances of oppression: the humiliation of slaves by slaveholders, the disenfranchisement of Irish Catholics by the English penal laws, the debasement of women by laws denying them property and suffrage, the annihilation of Jews by the government of Germany, and the betrayal of the citizens of Soviet regimes by their own government. To suggest that designers have been oppressed by typographers trivializes the term.

All of which argues in favor of perspective. Some of the new work is beautiful; much of it is fun; a fraction of it may be profound. As a writer, I am disturbed by the penchant of contemporary typographers for inserting yet more self-expression into an already narcissistic society and for creating confusion in a world which already seems sufficiently confused. I believe that, if it is skillfully used, the new type has the power to introduce us to new feelings, new interpretations, new shades and shadows of thought. That is no small accomplishment. But, at the very least, type shouldn't make us any more stupid than we already are.

Originally published in Eye, *No. 19, Winter 1996.*

LOOK AT ME! LOOK AT ME!
(WHAT DESIGNERS WANT)
Paul Stiff

Graphic designers used to have straight-forward reasons for what they did. Paul Rand, for example, could say, "If it looks terrific, then that's all I care about. After the looks, and strictly of secondary importance, comes client approval."[1] Marcello Minale was equally clear: "The core of our philosophy is that design is based on self-expression."[2]

As these simple credos have come to seem thin, so more complex but equally designer-centered explanations have filled the vacuum. For example, Michel de Boer, of Studio Dumbar, strikes a now-familiar note: "This is at the center of the studio's philosophy—that design should not be too easy, either to do or to see. The receiver of the message should be made to work, forcing them to think about what they see."[3] And if this disciplinarian injunction sounds over simple, then more sophisticated versions are available. Michele-Anne Daupe has invoked "the postmodern condition," and "radical approaches to communication" which "attempted to engage the audience with the text, to make the audience 'work,' and to emphasize the 'construction' of meaning. Radical typography might aim, not to flow seamlessly, legibly, but to halt and disrupt, to expose meaning and language as problematic."[4] Phil Baines, too, is "trying to involve the viewer as an active participant rather than as a passive recipient."[5] Rick Poynor suggests a Paris-Michigan lineage for such apparently radical positions: "The aim is to provoke . . . the reader into becoming an active participant in the construction of the message. . . . The Cranbrook theorists' aim, derived from French philosophy and literary theory, is to deconstruct, to break apart and expose, the manipulative visual language and different levels of meaning embodied in a design."[6]

The visual style associated with these positions could loosely be called "postmodern deconstructed," or pomo for short. The pomo claims seem to be: Reading is passive, uncreative, one-dimensional. Readers are under-challenged, too lazy to discover that meaning is undecidable. Typographers should goad them into work—typically by removing familiar landmarks, by laying obstacles, diversions, and false trails, and by recognizing that "the cry of 'legibility' masks a reactionary attitude against progress, change, or critical intervention."[7]

The tone of these claims—of idlers in need of short sharp shocks—may sound familiar. But they predate both Thatcherism and pop deconstruction, and were made by book artists long before Barthes and Derrida featured in lifestyle pages. Joel Roth, for example, wrote in 1969 of a "new use for typography . . . based on erratic type arrangement which pulls the reader in as an active participant, and makes reading a creative act rather than passive absorption of information."[8]

A variant on this theme is what Sharon Poggenpohl, editor of *Visible Language*, calls "content-responsive typography"; it is preferred in her journal because: "People read less, they obtain more of their information from other media. . . . contemporary readers who are distracted by more dynamic modes of presentation demand . . . more responsive typography."[9]

These assertions deserve a response. First, there is little or no evidence to support them. In fact the evidence about reading points to the contrary: that "reading" is a highly complex set of activities, working on many levels—from the relatively automatic one of eye movements to the intentional levels of navigating, monitoring, sampling, and selecting. When people read they make strategic choices, constantly making inferences and generating hypotheses—about intention, relevance, tone of voice, and so on. Far from being passive and mechanical, reading is typically active and purposeful. (And all this is uncontroversially in line with postmodern theories of signifying practices which argue that each reading is a re-writing.)

Second, when pomos generalize about reading they often hide undeclared assumptions about what kind of readers they have in mind. They are less likely to imagine people deprived of literacy and its promises than a more comfortable fraction of the population favored by designers as "target audiences." (What if readers are old, or visually impaired, or not very good at reading, or poor, or ignorant of their rights?) They rarely describe what kinds of reading form the object of designing, but exclude what Bridget Wilkins calls "sloppy skim reading"[10]—the reading of educational texts, reports, forms, specifications, walkers' guides, catalogues, price lists, reference books, maps, diagrams, food and medicine labels, dictionaries, timetables, schedules, user manuals, and so on. Pomos prefer something bracketed off within a more privileged "literary" or "artistic" category, and take reading as an act of private consumption.

Third, "content-responsive typography"—today justified as a response to the alleged demise of reading—is little more than a new label for a well-worn rationalization. Marinetti's hasty perceptions and screams do not need quotation here, but Vincent Steer may be less familiar: a founder of the British Typographers' Guild in the 1930s, he recommended that "a detective story might read more convincingly in a matter-of-fact typeface like Scotch Roman. A book intended to be read by a doctor or scientist might suitably be set in a precise and pedantic type like Bodoni Book, while a light novel for a holiday maker would call for a more robust typeface."[11]

Fourth, the tale of a lost golden age (once people read, now they watch videos) is here implicated with a competitive account of design in which readers' choices are mediated by the free market. To survive the hazards of that market, messages have to be ostentatiously differentiated to draw attention to themselves, better to encourage readers to discriminate from an array of shopping opportunities.

Sceptics might ask: of all the sources of knowledge about reading and communication (cognitive psychology, ethnography, ergonomics, discourse analysis, feminism, dialectical materialism . . .) why have typographers defaulted to those which neither offer nor require evidence? Those which permit them to "theorize" reading as passive osmosis, to marginalize readers (mere receptacles), and at the same turn to foreground the act of designing (explained as the "challenging" of empty vessels)? Whose interests do such theories serve?

Although typographers may sprinkle their utterances with postmodern fragments (and perhaps, when business improves, the more expansive inflections of management-speak), their reflexes still draw them towards homelier territory. What could be more natural for young prizewinners than to describe their student days in epic terms: "It was very academic . . . and it gave me an incredible grounding in type. But I had to fight to be creative."[12] We know from Hollywood—remember Charlton Heston's *The Agony and the Ecstasy* and Kirk Douglas's *Lust for Life*—that it was ever thus.

Not much has changed. Once, designers just wanted to look good; now they also want theories to justify looking good. To graduate into the creative elite, they must first stamp a visibly personal mark. This designer-centered romance, which pomo designers share with Paul Rand and Marcello Minale, is endorsed by Hermann Zapf, who enthuses that "typographic creativity can be expanded . . . as long as it is controlled by people with knowledge and taste."[13]

Designers' insensitivity to people as readers and users is not confined to typography. Don Norman reviews industrial design: "A good way to find out what the design world cares about is to read the magazines of industrial design. *I.D.* is a fascinating magazine, with clever innovative design. But I detect little interest in making designs usable, functional, or understandable."[14] And Ted Nelson, who put hypertext on our Macs, is unimpressed by developments in design for interaction between people and computers: "It is nice that engineers and programmers and software executives have found a new form of creativity in which to find a sense of personal fulfillment. It is just unfortunate that they have to inflict the results on users."[15]

Critical reasoning about design has always offered alternative—modest but more challenging—forms of explanation. In 1968, the Working Party on Typographic Teaching reported that inadequacies in design education arose mainly from treating the subject as "a form of personal visual expression. . . . Consequently, many unspectacular areas of design . . . which play an important part in our lives are either not designed at all or are designed badly."[16] In 1970, Anthony Froshaug—practicing, teaching, and writing from the margins—reviewed a showcase of "pioneers": "'Modern' typography is not a mode; it consists in a reasoned assessment of what is needed, and of what somehow is done, under certain constraints. When technical and social constraints change the important thing is not to spray a random pattern on the page but to assess the new, with the old, requirements of the text."[17] Two decades later, in a final provocation, Otl Aicher argued that when "typographic signs become mere graphic material used as a kind of formal 'quarry' for symbols and textures . . . then writing is reduced to nothing more than an aesthetic object."[18]

Does any of this matter? Most graphic designers have managed to get by without explanations much more complicated than "just do it." But traditional graphic design—pomo and all the rest—has probably had its day, and is unlikely to survive, except as a "heritage" craft, the more demanding questioning it now faces. The challenge for designers, still, is to explain. "Because I like it this way and hope that other people will too" or "because it expresses my feelings" may be fair explanations for relatively content-free designing. And while wholly inadequate for design tasks which involve active readers with questions and purposes of their own, they at least have the virtue of honesty. What we are offered, in their place, is a new mixture of personal preferences and designer-centered ideology. To elevate this mixture to the status of a theory about design for reading is just another step on a false trail.

Originally published in Eye, *No. 11, 1993, under the editor's title "Stop Sitting Around and Start Reading."*

Notes

1. Paul Rand, cited by James Woudhuysen in "Paul Rand Hates Logos," *Blueprint* (September 1989): 37.
2. Marcello Minale, reported in *Design,* No. 489 (September 1989): 12.
3. Michel de Boer, lecture at Monotype Conference, London, 1991, cited by Graham Wood in "Too Much Legibility," *Desktop Publishing Commentary,* No. 7 (1991): 8–13.
4. Michele-Anne Daupe, "Get the Message?" *Eye,* No. 3 (1991): 4–7.
5. Phil Baines, speaking in STD/CSD debate, London, 1991, cited by Peter Rea in "To Be Clearly Read: Is This the First Consideration of Typography?" *Typographic,* No. 43 (February 1992): 17–23.
6. Rick Poynor, introduction to *Typography Now: The Next Wave* (London: Internos, 1991), 9–13.
7. Michele-Anne Daupe, "Get the message?" *Eye,* No. 3 (1991): 4–7.
8. Joel Roth, "Typography That Makes the Reader Work," *Journal of Typographic Research,* 3:2 (1969): 193.
9. Sharon Poggenpohl, editorial comment, *Visible Language,* 25:4 (1991): 424–25.
10. Bridget Wilkins, letter to the editor, *Design* (March 1993): 11.
11. Vincent Steer, *Printing Design and Layout* (London: Virtue, [no date; around 1932]).
12. Kathy Miller, cited in M. Evamy, "The Miller's Tale," *Design Week,* No. 22 (February 1991), 14-15.
13. Hermann Zapf, *Hermann Zapf and His Design Philosophy* (Chicago: Society of Typographic Arts, 1987), 95.
14. Donald Norman, *The Psychology of Everyday Things* (New York: Basic Books, 1988), 239.
15. Ted Nelson, "The Right Way to Think About Software Design," in *The Art of Human-Computer Interface Design* ed. B. Laurel (Reading, MA: Addison-Wesley, 1990), 127–36.
16. Working Party on Typographic Teaching, *Interim Report* (1968): [fifth page].
17. Anthony Froshaug, "Typography Ancient and Modern," review of *Pioneers of Modern Typography* by H. Spencer, *Studio International,* No. 924, (1970): 60–61.
18. Otl Aicher, *Typographie* (Berlin: Ernst & Sohn, 1988), 118.

FABULOUS US: SPEAKING THE LANGUAGE OF EXCLUSION

Natalia Ilyin

Something is happening to graphic designers: we are losing the ability to make choices. We used to speak to each other in controlled tones about the merits of a Brodovich or the timelessness of a Lustig, as we cleaned our small round glasses or downed the chicken with lemongrass. Now we mumble that every administrative assistant with Quark is going to take all the business and leave us sitting quietly alone and sad, as the wind picks up the dust and scatters it meaninglessly across our archival copies of the American Can Company's annual report.

Up to this time, the language of design was based on exclusionary principles that we, as designers, all recognized. We went to school and learned and taught our clients what tools they needed to understand this language. We all agreed to use these principles, were welcomed to the long house, had a corner on the market of knowledge, and paid the Con Ed bill. It was fabulous us and not-so-fabulous them, and it was our job to keep them realizing that we knew more than they did.

Now that these principles, for which we worked long and hard, are being built into the software on everyone's desktop, designers find themselves displaced, and are scrambling for another code that has value, one they can protect. Clean work is easy. Edgy, inclusive work is unintelligible to those who do not speak the language. Our exclusionary language is now a language of obfuscation, which clients pay money to understand. And they said the computer was just a tool.

Graphic designers, by nature, are in a bind. We need to be individuals, because we spent all that time with painters in art school and, damn it, we're just as sensitive as they are, but we need to create work that communicates a specific idea not of our own choosing. We work for somebody else. This communicative activity, if not handled well, can result in a brush with the mainstream.

We need to feel that what we create is individual, specific, and inspired. But we need to be individual, specific, and inspired in a way that does not get knocked down at marketing meetings. We chafe at the restrictions of client, budget, and lack of vision, but without these restrictions, we are not designers. We need to speak the language of design (that confluence of influences, one-upmanships, and radical egalitarianisms), but we cannot afford to look as though we care about speaking it too fluently. We must constantly reinvent ourselves, because edginess is next to godliness, but we must espouse an appreciation of those arcane universal design principles that we, as individuals, choose to break because we're so radical. Design is a language of exclusion, even though it is, at this moment, a language of exclusion that is trying its best to be inclusionary. And there is the rub.

All communication happens through codified systems, or languages. Design, by nature, is a language about choosing. The choice between that photograph and this one, between Garamond and Interstate, puts a designer in the position of leaving something in and something out. What's left in generally has to do with the designer's spiderweb of educational impressions—eighth-grade teachers, various technologies, what's in *Bikini*. Choices that seem self-generated often depend upon who has been the teacher, on what has been the guide. What's left out is information that the designer finds unworkable: things that don't fit the prescribed boundaries of the set solution, images that don't communicate. In other words, we design along the boundaries laid out by our learned design language. We slice up a problem, organize it into concepts, and make these concepts significant— all because we agree as a group to organize the design of communication this way. Our agreement is never stated, but its terms are absolute.

Many languages develop around objective acts. But our language describes an act that is subjective—that exists only as a decision between what is perceived to be good and what is considered better. The Sapir-Whorf hypothesis suggests that the distinctions encoded in one language are not found in any other language. Over time, as graphic design became a profession, the linguistic act of deciding what's left in and what's left out developed into a specific language unto itself—into a series of codes for various species of designers. Sentences like "It's Vignelli-ish," "She went to Cal Arts," and "He worked for Roger Black" are shorthand descriptions of various design hierarchies. Most of these hierarchies can be traced back to the Bauhaus, to the beginnings of modernism, to a time when design took on the public good as an area of its concern, albeit an often patronizing concern. After years of telling the great unwashed masses what to do, some designers feel as though they must now give popular culture a chance to talk back, and are making a big effort to synthesize backwards and to show the imagemakers of our society the influences that are acting upon them. The language of design now includes a code for those whose design depends upon the codification of a lack of codification.

In the best post-everything tradition, designers are dealing with issues of meaning and nonmeaning in ways that can only be described as pertaining to a dominant style: a style of inclusion. What happens if I put together random images from influential childhood cartoons with wacky Fontographer errors? It's a design hierarchy allegedly based on a leveling of value. And yet that's impossible in the real world. All design is equal, but some design is more equal than others.

Even when inclusion is the style of the moment, the designer is making choices about meaning: there is always some choosing inherent in a design solution, always meanings that escape the designer's consciousness. These meanings happen when the designer's message is received by the person "reading" the work.

After ripping through the arts and literature, postmodernist black magic has seeped into the design world, and with it has come a style based on a leveling of authority. Designers who adopt a position of alternativism, who have read their graduate texts, and who are determined to show the dirty underside of design and its dominance are actually contributing to the very machine of culture they deride.

If the alleged objectivity of modernist design principles is a thing of the past, how do you make choices? And if you are still making choices without a measurement of value, of what value is your work? If objectivity is deemed impossible in our era, subjectivity is making the decisions. Is the opinion of a twenty-two-year-old brand manager just out of UCLA business school really as valuable as the opinion of an art director schooled in the Constructivists, Derrida, Lacan, and the whole nine yards? Inclusivity breeds contempt.

It's an inclusivity based on fear. We're afraid to take a stand because styles change so fast. We're afraid we'll be refuted. We're afraid that our solutions—that our "design philosophy"—will have its moment in the sun, but then languish on the trash heap indefinitely. So we present the elements, albeit ironically, and force the reader to take the burden of putting together the text. It's an old postmodernist trick: throw the responsibility for choice back on the audience. That way, what the audience chooses to see is its own problem.

This approach is starting to get old, just like its progenitors: 1968 can't go on forever. Let's face it. Design is really a mild form of fascism: the fascism of valuing one person's viewpoint over another's. To be unwilling to accept this role of form-giver, reluctant to take a stand on the slippery pile of mush that is popular culture, is to be unable to take the responsibility for choice. This unwillingness signals a breakdown of the hierarchies that are the language of graphic design and an introduction of the elements of a language that describes, but does not choose.

Graphic designers have the opportunity to influence the way average people are informed. This influence affects people, and it involves real responsibility—responsibility that has proved terrifying enough to drive the best design minds of the generation into a tailspin of tangential stylistics. Grappling with the issues confronting our society head-on takes guts. Presenting them airily to a reader already overwhelmed by a cumulative backlog of choices is the easy way out. Playing with the forms of the graphic design language is intriguing, but languages are created to carry meaning, and to deny responsibility for that meaning is to be ironic, elitist, and chicken. We need to stop pretending that we are egoless and egalitarian, and start saying something with our language of exclusion.

Originally published in the AIGA Journal of Graphic Design, *Vol. 12, No. 2, 1994.*

DESIGNING BEAUTY: FROM THE
OUTRAGEOUS TO THE SUBLIME
Véronique Vienne

Major cultural shifts often translate on a personal level as a series of small but significant choices. Recently I came to this realization while buying a bottle of Sublime by Jean Patou. For the same price, I found out, I could either get the fragrance in its elegant yellow and gold packaging or walk away with a promotional gift basket, an opulent arrangement featuring the same flacon and its coffer, plus an attractive satin box, a set of miniature soaps, and a generous array of free samples—the whole thing wrapped in colorful tissue paper and crinkly cellophane. I wanted the freebies, but I could not picture myself leaving the store carrying a huge shopping bag stuffed with this ostentatious bonus, only to trash most of its contents as soon as I got home.

What happened to my sense of wonderment? Nowadays I look at pretty packaging and see a pile of empty cartons, torn cellophane, and wilted tissue paper. Recycling has lost its redemptive power. It seems that only last year I could walk through a cosmetic department and feel an emotional rush from the abundance of glitter, gold trimmings, boxes, and ribbons, and the rustle of tissue paper being stuffed into shopping bags.

Perhaps I have become weary of sorting, collecting, and bundling used shopping bags, boxes, and wrappers. If so, this is good news for the environment. Bette Fishbein, packaging expert for Inform, a nonprofit environmental research organization, explains that eliminating packaging—what she calls *source reduction*—is far more effective than recycling. "Packaging accounts for a third of our municipal solid waste—more than 200 million tons a year," she says. "If we want to make a real difference, we must start at the beginning, not the end, of the process."

The "greenest" country on this front is Germany, where protesters have been known to march through stores, tearing off packaging and leaving cardboard and paper wrappings strewn among the aisles. Currently, waste reduction is legislated in Germany, and industries are responsible for managing packaging to the end of its life cycle, including the costs of collecting, sorting, and disposing of it after consumers discard it. This "polluters pay" principle forces up the price of packaged goods and discourages extravagant overwrapping. Department stores are expected to provide recycling bins for customers to discard excess cardboard and paper as they leave the premises. In cosmetic departments, it's not unusual for salespeople to open boxes and throw them away before handing the products to their customers.

In the self-regulated U.S. beauty business, cosmetic companies are voluntarily streamlining their packaging and investigating new ways of lessening its burden on the environment. Bob Luzzi, senior vice president of creative design and advertising for Estēe Lauder, explains how his team managed to discard 30 percent of the bulk of the packaging. "We took all our products, pulled out the guts, and looked at what was there—a huge pile in the middle of the room," he says. "For starters we got rid of two pieces of future landfill—the cellophane wrapping and the corrugated filler, then we eliminated the pattern printed inside the carton. Too much ink is bad for the environment." Next year sun-protection products will be sold with a hangtag only, devoid of their boxes. Plastic inserts that hold lipsticks and mascaras in place will be banished. And the skincare-line packaging will no longer be film laminated—a process that gives boxes their shine, but leaves them non-biodegradable. Estēe Lauder chose not to advertise its waste-reduction campaign. "Boasting about our efforts would simply create more paper," says Luzzi.

At Prescriptives, the success of All You Need Action Moisturizer, which is shrink-banded rather than boxed, has prompted the company to evaluate the cost-effectiveness of extending the no-packaging policy to its entire line—a monumental undertaking.

Some of the most creative packages, coming from companies such as Stila, Face, and Kiehl's, are in fact so small that they have trouble fitting the information stipulated by FDA regulations; and the bar code is sometimes bigger than the manufacturer's label—or the product itself. To accommodate these smaller companies, department stores have begun to waive the electronic ticketing process that keeps track of sales.

Stila cosmetics, available at Barneys New York and Fred Segal, are presented unboxed, in demure little black cardboard cases. Jeanine Lobell spent two years developing the line. "As a makeup artist, I was handling products all day long. I couldn't stand all the plastic—it drove me crazy," she says. "I craved products I'd want to touch. Familiar yet new."

Martina Arfwidson, president of the Swedish makeup line Face Stockholm, finds traditional packaging aggravating. Face's 150 eyeshadows and custom-blended bases and powders are merchandised in plain, refillable plastic or glass. Yet Arfwidson estimates that, at present, only 5 percent of customers return for refills.

For her spicy new fragrance, Comme des Garçons, Rei Kawakubo has designed the most unlikely and improbable package to date: a bottle that does not stand but lies flat on its side, like a pebble full of water. It comes vacuum-packed in a plastic bag stuffed in a plain box whose focal point is the bar code.

Ostentation may be out, but glamour is on the offensive. Joël Desgrippes, who designed the bottle for Patou's Sublime and, more recently, the extravagant Jaïpur perfume bracelet by Boucheron, is a firm believer that a beautiful package, if it creates a pleasurable emotional response, is never wasted on a woman. "The recycled look is gimmicky—so is the minimalist trend," he says. "In France we try to cut down on costs and waste without diminishing the glamour. Take the Boucheron line: all items are carefully designed to be luxurious; yet, at the same time, most are refillable." In the United States there is a new element to the glamour equation, says Marc Gobé, Desgrippes's partner in New York. "Traditional glamour was color coded—gold stamping for prestige and lacquered black for sophistication. The new glamour is sensualistic and texture oriented."

Modern luxe appeals to the sense of touch as well as to the eyes and the nose. "Consumers always wonder if it's going to feel the way it looks," says Marc Rosen, a designer whose clients have included Lagerfeld, Halston, and Elizabeth Arden. But today even indulgence is grounded in reality. Most new upscale fragrances combine fantasy with practicality and give potential customers an ecological incentive to overcome their environmental scruples. Gaultier's new scent, presented in a Madonna-inspired corseted female shape, is crated in a recyclable tin can. Glass-cartridge refills are now available for the new L'Eau d'Issey brushed-metal purse spray. Money-saving recyclable refills in generic containers are available for both Tocade by Rochas and Annick Goutal fragrances. Twice a year on a promotional basis, Goutal scents can be refilled at the counter. Thierry Mugler's Angel was one of the first fragrances in America available for refilling at the counter on a regular basis. The refillable Angel was dreamed up by Saks fragrance buyer Earl-Rodney Holman and Ben Gilliken, general manager, Thierry Mugler Parfums. It was inspired in part by customer demand: why should they have to throw away their beautiful bottle every time they use up the fragrance? And there is a charming precedent. Refilling bottles was once the rule in Paris at small perfume boutiques like Guerlain, but the motivation was not "green." Rather, it was a practical issue in a time before mass-produced bottles.

Next to eliminating paper and cardboard packaging, refilling is probably the most responsible environmental measure. After eight refills, returnable glass bottles can save up to 78 percent in energy expenditure—which means less air and water pollution. Bringing empty containers back to the counter, a policy encouraged by companies like Kiehl's and Origins, is equally beneficial. According to industry sources, 20 percent of Origins' customers take the time to do so, while 70 percent of the remaining group recycle at home.

To satisfy the need for modern luxury, package designers are now searching the globe for environmentally responsible textures and materials—handmade papers, pearlescent films, soft vegetable dyes, biodegradable plastics, colored glass, and matte-finish paints. Aveda, known for its virtually petrochemical-free cosmetics, is seeking to introduce a new packaging material made of plant-derived biodegradable fibers.

Daniel Rachmanis, who represents the famed French glass company Saint Gobain Desjonqueres, knows how his perfumer clients think. "The trend is toward less bulk—but more weight. As the carton shrinks, the bottle gets heavier. If the package feels good when they lift it, customers think it's beautiful."

"But packaging is more than the package," says Fabien Baron, *Bazaar* creative director, who worked on the packaging for CK One. "You can never eliminate it. Get rid of a box and you'll find another box inside. Packaging is how a product is photographed in ads, shown on television, and seen by people in every situation. Packaging is total perception."

Originally published in Harper's Bazaar, *December 1994.*

IT MAY BE WRAPPED BUT WILL IT WARP?

Jon Wozencroft

It is too early to predict how, exactly, the conversion from analogue to digital forms will affect human communication and interaction on an everyday level. Already, it is possible to send computer files down a telephone line; we will soon all be able to publish our own faces on videophones hooked up to all corners of the globe; magazines with the wherewithal can retouch photographs to make smiles flash on full beam. Yet the full potential of new technology is still beyond our means; the cutting edge is never accessible, and by its very nature it never will be.

Fundamental changes in the process of transmitting language create fundamental changes in its expression. To have any chance of understanding the impact of digital forms of communication on the way we use language, we are, paradoxically when dealing with such a modern invention, forced to pretend that we are in a precondition rather than a "post" state. The reduction of words and images to a system based on the binary code is not simply a sophisticated "techno/logical development": it necessitates a revolution in the way we perceive any information.

In effect, we have two choices: to go along with it blindly, or to reconsider everything. And if we return to the origins of our language, to phonetics, hieroglyphs, embryowriting, and early alphabets, looking for clues or for archetypes of linguistic change, this is also a form of futurology, but retrodivination. There are drawbacks: we color the past, lose sight of the present and fall subject to "the disease of tomorrow." And all the time we are compelled to weigh up whether or not anything is obvious anymore. Education systems are not working, every individual holds "views" but few are in a position to make themselves heard. Acronyms, euphemisms, jargon, and catchphrases are used to such excess that a direct statement either leaves us speechless or is dismissed as another piece of advertising.

Having mastered the technique of building superstructures and shopping malls, we have forgotten how to build homes. So it is with language. In order to communicate, we designate our thoughts and feelings into prearranged compartments. To articulate means that we fill a space and hope to connect. We agree that an owl is not an elephant, but that is as far as it goes—in the main, we navigate a way through broad generalizations. Words, spoken in the first person, are primarily sonic devices with endless possibilities for personal pitch change—nuances and gestures that cannot be recorded on disk or tape even if they have been registered in real time.

The spoken word is standardized to keep pace with new modes of transmission. It becomes another format that can be captured in time and space; as Goebbels noted, "the spoken word is more 'magnetic' in its effect than the written one." The chaos of communication has to be kept tidy, thus as soon as human encounters cease to be either original or impromptu (which is to say, relatively early on in the day), codes are developed to hold fast the compartments (here a parallel can be drawn with the fate of RMS *Titanic*). As the population and diversity of voices increases, so must the codes be made more rigid. Until communication, driven by mass media forms which expressly rely upon the concept of hidden (if not invisible) information, consists only of codes . . . then codes of codes of codes. Tabloidish, pastiche, and self-referential terms become our staple diet—"garbage in, garbage out," as the saying goes. And we shout to make ourselves heard.

In the best of all possible worlds, nothing needs to be recorded because the experience is always available. When a civilization devotes its energies to upholding (and thus redefining) its "heritage," a storage problem arises—just like the housing crisis. As soon as the exposure and availability of any item or idea is restricted by the need to control the amount of people who wish to be exposed to it, the need to capture this information and to replicate it results. Words and ideas, like cities, become overpopulated. In this way, communication is no longer guided by the desire to emancipate, but the need to edit. The notion that, in today's marketplace, any product or message has to be "commercial" in order to achieve "a high profile" is often the kiss of death as far as meaning is concerned (and as for irony?!). This is the age of convenience, no matter what the cost. And the computer screen's *caveat emptor*—"what you see is what you get"—legislates the illusion of substance, when any content can only be quantified in terms of *amount*.

Since different peoples evolve different solutions to their societies' needs for information storage, codes are as old as written language. In the beginning, everybody knew them—we presume. And if they did not, does this mean that language has always involved exclusion? Who knows? In spite of the fact that DNA research can now tell us more about the origins of man than ever before, we really have not got a clue. So rather than speculate, we can at least say that all forms of writing are a means of information storage. Anything stored needs to be codified. Is there an essential difference between early man, who made knots in a length of fabric as a mnemonic device, and modern man, who types letters on a keyboard and saves them on a hard disk?

As a noun, the first meaning of "code" is a legal one. The word then develops to refer to a system or collection of rules of any sort. The lines you are now reading are, of course, in code, yet those of us who fall within the demographic range of the Roman alphabet and the English language have, from an early age, been instructed in its use and thus rarely inspect the cargo; its tradition as a common denominator determines that we would never consider it to be cryptic (from the Greek *kryptos,* "secret"). Following this line, nor can Chinese/Arabic/Russian be assigned such a status, yet their alphabets are so unfamiliar to us that any written messages presented in these languages might as well be cryptographic.

At what point does a language become a code? Perhaps the dividing line is simply based on familiarity, and we have been misled by too many postwar spy films into thinking codes to be the privy of James Bond, Smiley's People, the government, the military, and *The Prisoner,* and that to gain access to these codes would involve our crawling through a ventilation shaft, hoping that the guards will not be roused.

To press further for a distinction, the idea that all information in the public domain must be made familiar in style in order to appeal to a specific ("target") audience, and judicial, state, and military information be encoded and "made classified" creates a class system based on the relative ability of the reader or audience to receive and interpret the coded information. Codes are like camouflage: they are founded on the twin precepts of display and concealment. The distribution, the SEND, is all important. The method or process of disseminating information, the "reaching out," the lying that is part and parcel of this process, demands that there be codes; and if this form of containment is insufficient, more direct forms of censorship can be called upon.

There is so much information vying for our attention that, inevitably, techniques are used to compress it into smaller loads, using codes to replace what may seem to be excess, complex, or redundant wordage. This compression is also regulated by time: deadlines, clearance, desk space, the available slot. The transmission of information must be made *efficient* to enable it to attract the right target audience. In the same breath, the world's information is increasingly articulated in one language—electronumerical U.S. English (itself a hybrid)—so that every message becomes one that begs to be deciphered and then relocated and renewed using another code. Ours is a translation game.

The game has more losers than winners. The pressure of codification makes ("amateur") users of language turn (or retreat) to metaphors to "fill out" and rebuild their flattened mental environment. The reduction of complex ideas to basic dimensions demands that we juggle signs around, twist them, and redecorate. Then we wonder why and how we became confused.

The need to conceal and guard information is an ancient one. An early example A.D. is the so-called Caesar Alphabet, a basic method of transposing letters so that A becomes D and B translates to E. This, to be exact, is not a code but a cipher. A code works on complete words or phrases, and a cipher upon individual letters; there are two principal techniques—transposition and substitution. ("Cipher" comes from the Arabic *cifr,* meaning the arithmetical zero, and in this sense it has passed down into English to mean "a mere nothing, a worthless person"). As for the word "code," it now strikes us most often in its cybernetic sense (and is thereby better termed as a *formula*). This meaning did not enter the language until 1946. Accordingly, the noun merges with its verb. This linguistic shift is closely related to the progressive emphasis during the twentieth century on the use of codes in wartime—a hijack performed by the military. Just as Alan Turing's improvised techniques cracked the German Enigma code, so was his later prototype for "intelligent machines" adapted to compromise peacetime.

The very ability to mechanize message sending and receiving creates the capacity for "total war." In turn, the possibility for artificial intelligence makes real life artificial. The apparent need now to define words in almost any context, from essays to ad campaigns to multimedia presentations, is proof enough that as far as our language is concerned, we are still in the dugout.

> **5.** *Cinemat. and Television.* The end of a session of filming or recording.
>
> **1974.** M. AYRTON *Midas Consequence* I. 63 Other cars are heard starting up out of shot and the lights on the pergola go off so I assume it's a wrap and the crew is listening to the director saying something consequential and busy about tomorrow's call. **1980** J. KRANTZ *Princess Daisy* xii. 191 "Right . . . it's a wrap." . . . The large lights, cameras, sound equipment and other tools of the trade were quickly stowed away. **1983** *Listener* 23 June 18/2 The Director says: "Cut! Thank you, Ben, that's a wrap—there is no more filming."

This article was published in Communicating Design, *1995, and adapted from it's original publication in* Fuse 6: Codes.

DISCOVERY BY DESIGN
Zuzana Licko

Can new design—like new science—discover phenomena that already exist in
the fabric of typographic possibility? If so, who owns a discovery?
Ellen Lupton, *The 100 Show: The Sixteenth Annual of the American Center for Design*

Although science and design are both based upon experimental investigation, the comparison is not altogether straightforward; science investigates naturally occurring phenomena, while design investigates culturally created phenomena. But if such a parallel is to be made, then we might replace a falling tree by a typographic possibility and thereby ask the question "does a typographic phenomenon exist if no one recognizes it?"

Potentially, if every graphic and typographic possibility already exists, and each is waiting to be discovered, then we need only create an appropriate context in order to bring life to any of them.

For example, consider the twenty-six letters in our alphabet and how they are combined to form words. There is a finite number of combinations, or words, if we limit ourselves to words of a certain length; say, five letters. Then, for ease of pronunciation, let's omit all words that contain a string of three or more consecutive consonants. Even with these restraints to give some "meaning" within our understanding of words, there will be many words that will have no meaning to us. Does this mean that these are not words? Does a sequence of letters not form a word when we do not recognize its meaning?

It is important to note here that the meanings of words are not intrinsic to the words themselves; the meanings are arbitrary, since the same word may have different meanings in different languages. In fact, the entire concept of using twenty-six letters is an arbitrary one. We could just as well have used twenty letters, or thirty letters, or thousands of ideograms like the Oriental cultures. Although these systems of communication and meanings are arbitrary, once they are established, they serve as the foundation for the creation of new meanings, and therefore do not appear to be as arbitrary as they really are.

As another example, consider the grid of a computer video display, or that of a laser printer rasterizer; each point on the grid can be on or off; black or white. Given a fixed resolution, again, there is a finite number of combinations that these on/off sequences will compose. If a computer is programmed to run through all of the possible combinations, some will appear to us as pure gibberish, while others will be recognized as something that we already know or might be interested in getting to know better. Even though all these compositions are randomly generated, only those few that fit into our preconceived notions of context will have meaning. Therefore, it is the meaning, and not the form itself, that has been created.

New design is the creation of new meanings; that is, new contexts for typographic possibilities. However, new meanings must be linked to existing ones. Even that design which "pushes the envelope" must build upon existing preconceptions. For unless a critical portion is understandable, the entire piece will be dismissed as complete nonsense. On the other hand, if no portion of the design is new, then it will appear so uninteresting that it might result in boredom and therefore be equally dismissed. Intriguing consumers with just the right amount of unrecognizable information spurs their interest. By initiating these changes of meaning, design educates the consumer to the changes in culture. Thus, design is a very powerful component in controlling our collective consciousness. However, design is also a subconscious process, and it is therefore nearly impossible for a designer to intentionally alter a specific cultural concept.

This process of reassimilation and adding or changing of meaning with each step creates an environment in our popular culture that is conducive to the assimilation of particular ideas. As this environment changes, it makes certain ideas ripe, or "ready to be liked."

In this manner, meanings change, and over time great shifts take place. Since the creation of new meanings usually results in the replacement, displacement, or change of older meanings, we may also wonder if some meanings become obsolete. We may ask, "does obsolescence exist in design, and can we plan obsolescence?"

It is possible to engineer the components of a car or refrigerator to break down after a certain duration of use, thereby defining the product's obsolescence. But is it possible to do this with a design style, typeface, or typographic form? Unlike industrial products that have a physical life, the lifespan of a typographic possibility is purely conceptual. Designs become obsolete as they are consumed by our culture, and subsequently forgotten in favor of other ones. Yet what was obsolete years ago is often revived from obsolescence to be reassimilated or expanded upon as appropriate to fit into new cultural meanings. This process repeats itself again and again, making obsolescence a temporary state in the world of design possibilities.

Because this ongoing change is affected by many different forces from numerous directions, it is impossible to predict what will happen next, or even how long- or short-lived any particular design idea might be. Since the life, or lives, of a design idea are dictated by its appropriateness for currently accepted ideas, it would be impossible to specifically plan the longevity of a design without also controlling these forces of style.

This evolution of meanings is also unpredictable over time. Some meanings change very quickly, like the second hand on a stopwatch; others change so slowly that we don't even see them change, like the hour hand on a grandfather clock. These slow changing ideas are seen as timeless, while those that change quickly are perceived as being timely. The words "timeless" and "timely" often have very strong negative or positive connotations, though neither is good nor bad, per se. The value of either of these qualities lies in the appropriateness of use, and appropriateness is usually a question of efficient use of design resources, or financial viability.

For example, if it costs millions to change the signage in an airport or subway system, then a timeless design is appropriate. However, if a design can be changed every time it appears on, say, an interactive television platform, and especially if such change will stimulate interest and add levels of meaning to the audience, then a timely design would be appropriate.

However, more often than not, it is timelessness that is seen as most valuable. Timeless creations are seen as the result of the process of refinement, and give us the impression that we are always working towards an ultimate goal of perfection, independent of the whims of fashion. This may appear so because history is told as a logical and progressive development. However, histories are composed in hindsight; actual events do not occur with such twenty-twenty vision. For example, once we identify a design idea as being fully developed, historians then work to explain its development by referring to the appropriate chain of events. However, this process also involves the filtering out of inappropriate events: events that nonetheless occupy the same time line. The inevitability of design ideas is therefore never so apparent when we're standing on the other end of the time line.

Although each development can be explained as an outcome of any number of preceding factors, this does not mean that any particular course of development is therefore inevitable. The sometimes arbitrary choices that are made along every step subsequently become a foundation for future developments, but there are usually many parallel, equally viable paths not taken.

So, who owns these design discoveries, if we are facilitating their existence through the appropriate contexts? It may be true that all designs exist in the fabric of typographic possibility. However, since not all possibilities can exist at the same time, there must be some way to choose intelligently those possibilities that will have meaning; that intelligent force comes from designers.

The discovery of a design possibility is therefore largely a matter of the designer being in the right place at the right time. However, it is the designer's ability to recognize the opportunity, the talent to apply the idea to a specific creative work, the willingness to sometimes go out on a limb, and the perseverance to convince others that the idea has validity, that deserves claim to ownership. Because, in the end, it is the expertise to communicate new ideas to others that gives credibility to the designer's existence.

Originally published in Emigre, *No. 32, 1995.*

ELECTRONIC TYPOGRAPHY:
THE NEW VISUAL LANGUAGE
Jessica Helfand

In 1968, Mattel introduced Talking Barbie. I like to think of this as my first computer. I remember saving up my allowance for what seemed an eternity to buy one. To make her talk, you pulled a little string; upon its release, slave-to-fashion Barbie would utter delightful little conversational quips like "I think mini-skirts are smashing" and "Let's have a costume party." If you held the string back slightly as she was talking, her voice would drop a few octaves, transforming her from a chirpy soprano into a slurpy baritone. What came out then sounded a lot more like "Let's have a *cocktail* party."

I loved that part.

What I loved was playing director—casting her in a new role, assigning her a new (albeit ludicrous) personality. What I loved was controlling the tone of her voice, altering the rhythm of her words, modulating her oh-so-minimal (and moronic) vocabulary. What I loved was the power to shape her *language*—something I would later investigate typographically, as I struggled to understand the role of the printed word as an emissary of spoken communication.

Twenty-five years later, my Mac sounds a lot like my Barbie did then—the same monotone, genderless, robotic drawl. But here in the digital age, the relationship between design and sound—and in particular, between the spoken word and the written word—goes far beyond pulling a string. And don't be fooled by voice recognition software: The truth is that the computer's internal sound capabilities enable us to design *with* sound, not in imitation of it. Like it or not, the changes brought about by recent advances in technology (and here I am referring to multimedia) indicate the need for designers to broaden their understanding of what it is to work effectively with typography. It is no longer enough to design for readability, to "suggest" a sentiment or reinforce a concept through the selection of a particular font. Today, we can make type *talk*: in any language, at any volume, with musical underscoring or sci-fi sound effects. We can sequence and dissolve, pan and tilt, fade to black, and spec type in Sensurround. As we "set" type, we encounter a decision-making process unprecedented in two-dimensional design. Unlike the kinetic experience of turning a printed page to sequence information, time becomes a powerful and persuasive design element. Today, we can visualize concepts in four action-packed, digital dimensions.

Multimedia has introduced a new visual language, one which is no longer bound to traditional definitions of word and image and form and place. Typography, in an environment that offers such diverse riches, must redefine its goals, its purpose, its very identity. It must reinvent itself. And soon.

Visual language, or the interpretation of spoken words through typographic expression, has long been a source of inspiration to designers, artists, and writers. Examples abound, from concrete poetry in the twenties to "happenings" in the sixties, and in graphic design, dating as far back as the incunabula. Visual wordplay proliferates, in this century in particular, from F. T. Marinetti's *Parole in Libertà,* to George Maciunas's Fluxus installations, to the latest MTA posters adorning the New York subway walls. Kurt Schwitters, Guillaume Apollinaire, Piet Zwart, Robert Brownjohn—the list is long, the examples inexhaustible. For designers, there has always been an overwhelming interest in formalism, in analyzing the role of type as medium (structure), message (syntax), and muse (sensibility). Throughout, there has been an attempt to reconcile the relationship between words both spoken and seen—a source of exhilaration to some and ennui to others. Lamenting the expressive limitations of the Western alphabet, Adolf Loos explained it simply: "One cannot *speak* a capital letter." Denouncing its structural failings, Stanley Morison was equally at odds with a tradition that designated hierarchies, in the form of upper- and lower-case letterforms. Preferring to shape language as he deemed appropriate, Morison referred to CAPS as "a necessary evil."

Academic debate over the relationship between language and form has enjoyed renewed popularity in recent years, as designers borrowed from linguistic models in an attempt to codify and clarify their own typographic explorations. Deconstruction's design devotees eagerly appropriated its terminology and theory, hoping to introduce a new vocabulary for design: it was the vocabulary of signifiers and signifieds, of Jacques Derrida and Ferdinand de Saussure, of Michel Foucault and Umberto Eco.

As a comprehensive model for evaluating typographic expression, deconstruction proved both heady and limited. Today, as advances in technology introduce greater and more complex creative challenges, it is simply arcane. We need to look at screen-based typography as a *new language*—with its own grammar, its own syntax, its own rules. What we need are new models, better models, models that go beyond language or typography, per se—models that reinforce rather than restrict our understanding of what it is to design electronic media. "What we need," says design and new-media consultant Wendy Richmond, "are extreme and unusual metaphors."

Learning a new language is one thing; fluency, quite another. We've come to equate fluency with literacy—another outdated model for evaluation. "Literacy should not mean the ability to decode strings of alphabetic letters," says Seymour Papert, director of the Epistemology and Learning Group at MIT's Media Lab, who refers to such a definition as "letteracy." And language, even to linguists, proves creatively limiting as a paradigm. "New media promise the opportunity to offer a smoother transition to what really deserves to be called literacy," says Papert. Typography, as the physical embodiment of such thinking, has quite a way to go.

The will to decipher the formal properties of language, a topic of great consequence for communication designers in general, has its philosophical antecedents in ancient Greece. "Spoken words," wrote Aristotle in *Logic,* "are the symbols of mental experience. Written words are the symbols of spoken words." Today, centuries later, the equation has added a new link: what happens when written words can speak? when they can move? when they can be imbued with sound and tone and nuance and decibel and harmony and voice? As designers probing the creative parameters of this new technology, our goal may be less to *digitize* than to *dramatize*. Indeed, there is a theatrical component that I am convinced is essential to this new thinking. Of what value are bold and italics when words can dance across the screen, dissolve, or disappear altogether?

In this dynamic landscape, our static definitions of typography appear increasingly imperiled. Will the beauty of traditional letterforms be compromised by the evils of this new technology? Will punctuation be stripped of its functional contributions, or ligatures of their aesthetic ones? Will type really matter?

Of course it will.

In the meantime, however, typography's early appearance on the digital frontier doesn't speak too well for design. Take e-mail for example. Gone are the days of good handwriting, of the Palmer Method and the penmanship primer. In its place, electronic mail—which, despite its futuristic tone, has paradoxically revived the Victorian art of letter writing. Sending electronic mail is easy and quick. For those of us who spend a good deal of our professional lives on the telephone, e-mail offers a welcome respite from talking (though it bears a closer stylistic resemblance to conversational speech than to written language). However, for those of us with even the most modest design sense, e-mail eliminates the *distinctiveness* that typography has traditionally brought to our written communiqués. Though its supporters endorse the democratic nature of such homogeneity, the truth is, it's boring. In the land of e-mail, we all "sound" alike: everyone speaks in Monaco.

Oddly, it is laden with contradictions: ubiquitous in form yet highly diverse in content, at once ephemeral and archival, transmitted in real time yet physically intangible. E-mail is a kind of aesthetic flatland, informationally dense and visually unimaginative. Here, hierarchies are preordained and non-negotiable: passwords, menus, commands, help. Networks like America OnLine require that we title our mail, a leftover model from the days of interoffice correspondence, which makes even the most casual letter sound like a corporate memo. As a result, electronic missives all have headlines: titling our letters makes us better editors, not better designers. As a fitting metaphor for the distilled quality of things digital, the focus in e-mail is on the abridged, the acronym, the quick read. E-mail is functionally serviceable and visually forgettable, not unlike fast food. It's drive-thru design: get in, get out, move on.

And it's everywhere. Here is the biggest contribution to communication technology to come out of the last decade, a global network linking an estimated 50 million people worldwide, and designers—communication designers, no less—are *nowhere in sight*.

Typography, in this environment, desperately needs direction. Where do we start? Comparisons with printed matter inevitably fail, since words in the digital domain are processed with a speed unprecedented in the world of paper. Here, they are incorporated into databases or interactive programs, where they are transmitted and accessed in random, nonhierarchical sequences. "Hypertext," or the ability to program text with interactivity (meaning that a word, when clicked upon or pointed to, will actually do something), takes it all a step further: by introducing alternate paths, information lacks the closure of the traditional printed narrative. "Hypertextual story space is now multidimensional," explains novelist Robert Coover in a recent issue of *Artforum,* "and theoretically infinite."

If graphic design can be largely characterized by its attention to understanding the hierarchy of information (and using type in accordance with such understanding), then how are we to determine its use in a nonlinear context such as this? On a purely visual level, we are limited by what the pixel will render: the screen matrix simulates curves with surprising sophistication, but hairlines and idiosyncratic serifs will, to the typophile, inevitably appear compromised. On a more objective level, type in this context is both silent and static, and must compete with sound and motion—not an easy task, even in the best of circumstances. (Conversely, in the era of the TV remote, where the user can mute at will, the visual impact of written typography is not to be discounted.)

To analyze better the role(s) of electronic typography, we might begin by looking outside—not to remote classifications imported from linguistic textbooks, or even to traditional design theories conveniently repackaged—but to our own innate intelligence, our own distinctive powers of creative thought. To cultivate and develop adequately this new typography (because if we don't, no one else will), we might do well to rethink language altogether, to consider new and alternative perspectives. "If language is indeed the limit of our world," writes literary critic William Gass in *Habitations of the Word,* "then we must find another, larger, stronger, more inventive language which will burst those limits."

In his book *Seeing Voices,* author and neurologist Oliver Sacks reflects on sign language and looks at the cognitive understanding of spatial grammar in a language that exists without sound. He cites the example of a deaf child learning to sign and describes in detail the remarkable quality of her visual awareness and descriptive, spatial capabilities. "By the age of four, indeed, Charlotte had advanced so far into visual thinking and language that she was able to provide new ways of thinking—revelations—to her parents." As a consequence of learning sign language as adults, this child's parents not only learned a new language, but also discovered new ways of thinking as well—*visual thinking.* Imagine the potential for multimedia if designers were to approach electronic typography with this kind of ingenuity and openmindedness.

William Stokoe, a Chaucer scholar who taught Shakespeare at Gallaudet College in the 1950s, summarized it this way: "In a signed language, narrative is no longer linear and prosaic. Instead, the essence of sign language is to cut from a normal view to a close-up to a distant shot to a close-up again, and so on, even including flashback and fastforward scenes, exactly as a movie editor works." Here, perhaps, is another model for visual thinking: a new way of shaping meaning based on multiple points of view, which sees language as part of a more comprehensive communication platform—time-sensitive, interactive, and highly visual. Much like multimedia.

Addendum: In gathering research for this article, I posted a query on Applelink's typography board. I received the following response:

> As a type designer, I am sort of surprised to find myself NOT VERY CONCERNED with how type is used in the fluid context of multimedia. In a way, type is as flexible as photography or illustration in a mm context . . . i.e., it's a whole new ballgame for everyone.

Though my link-pal claimed not to be concerned, he did take the time to respond. And as I read his reply, I realized how important it will be for all of us to be concerned: not merely to translate the printed word to the screen, but to transcend it.

Then I found myself wondering: what would Stanley Morison have thought of all those CAPS?

Originally published in Print, *May/June 1994.*

THE POLITICS OF STYLE
Philip B. Meggs

Amerika is a vast and pluralistic country; it should be capable of accommodating a diverse range of graphic design sensibilities. Yet leaders of each generation or faction of graphic designers seem compelled to attack design approaches that veer from their own. The literature and folklore of design are filled with challenges to work that breaks with a prevailing approach.

In 1940, T. M. Cleland, a key designer in the revival of Renaissance type and ornaments in the first half of the century, launched a furious attack—a lecture later published as a hardbound essay titled "Harsh Words"—against the modern design movement that was making inroads in America.

"Embraced with fanatical enthusiasm by many architects and designers is the current quackery called 'Functionalism,'" Cleland fumed. He dismissed functionalism's "gladsome gifts" ("concrete boxes with holes in them for buildings, chairs of bent pipe with no back legs, glass fireplaces, beds of cement blocks joined by structural steel, the queer agglomeration of unsightly edifices we call the World's Fair and many other specimens of stark and forbidding claptrap") as "mass vulgarity."

Noting that laymen "accurately" call sans-serif types "block letters," Cleland said, "they bear the same relation to roman letters as would an engineer's drawings for a trolley track. . . . They are supposed to represent the spirit of our day like the noise of riveting hammers in a modern musical composition."

Typeface designer Frederic Goudy concurred. In his 1938 lecture to the Advertising Typographers Association of America, "Why Go Modern?" Goudy noted, "The modernist prefers sans-serif types—bolder, blacker, and more erratic forms . . . usually the whole arranged with a studied disregard for charm or beauty. . . his types contain nothing of romance or sentiment, and his arrangements follow no known law of order or beauty." (One wonders if Goudy may have had Cleland's elaborate ornaments and borders in mind when he said, "When printing for industry becomes too elaborate and too fanciful, its vulgarity of display becomes impertinent indecency which I resent.")

Paul Rand—who, as an emerging leader of the American modern design movement in 1940, often used the sans-serif types that Cleland believed "simplify the traditional forms of type as you might simplify a man by cutting his hands and feet off"—a half century later aimed his own fire at the design renegades of the 1990s. Wrote Rand in 1992, "Today the emphasis of style over content in much of what is alleged to be graphic design and communication is, at best, puzzling. *Order out of chaos* is not the order of the day . . . the qualities that evoke this bevy of depressing images are a collage of chaos and confusion, swaying between high tech and low art, and wrapped in a cloak of arrogance."

Rand's *order-out-of-chaos*-is-not-the-order-of-the-day comment is eerily similar to Cleland's attack on Rand's generation: "The order of the day, it seems, is disorder."

Why do changing design styles evoke such angry responses? Why is peaceful coexistence so difficult for some of the most creative designers?

The seeds of design conflict are often rooted in simple economics: who gets to do the work. The classic example of a radical "changing of the guard" occurred in the early 1960s, when photography replaced illustration in print advertising. Advertisers were anxious to coordinate print ads with their television commercials, while a new generation of art directors, embracing a modern, "total design" approach, preferred photography's neutral, objective images. The advertising designer, rather than the illustrative artist with a subjective and personal style, gained control of the medium. Paper, photographic technology, and four-color process printing were improving and permitted better photographic reproduction. These and other developments combined to cause advertising illustration virtually to disappear. Its collapse was so total that New York's Cooper Studios, which employed more than two hundred illustrators, was forced into bankruptcy.

Many illustrators who had enjoyed lucrative and productive careers found themselves either leaving the profession or shifting to layout and paste-up work.

In a lecture I attended in Washington, D.C., in the mid 1970s, the late Herb Lubalin launched into a denunciation of "Swiss" design, also referred to as the International Typographic Style. He lambasted the sameness and uniformity of the work emanating from the Swiss-oriented design studios. Lubalin often competed with these Helvetica-and-grids studios for projects. By pointing out the deficiencies of the competition, he was merely doing what any salesman does when trying to make a sale. In this case, the politics of style was about competing for commissions.

But the politics of style go far beyond economic considerations. Persons with strong aesthetic or philosophic viewpoints are frequently intolerant of other positions. Deeply held convictions can actually lead individuals to view so-called deviant styles as degenerate or corrupt. Nazis and communists were so fanatical in their beliefs that they actually believed art that did not support the official dogma was deranged.

In the case of Cleland—as of Rand—I believe passion motivated his critique of new design directions. As a deeply committed designer who strove for excellence in everything he did, he was unable to countenance work that defied his aesthetic dicta. Cleland believed in symmetry and ornament every bit as much as Rand believes in sign and symbol expressed through elementary form and color.

In matters of aesthetics, unfamiliarity often breeds contempt. The computer has unleashed a swirl of experimentation with unprecedented typographic arrangements and forms, provoking outcries of condemnation. The arrival of Futura type, asymmetrical layouts, and extreme weight contrasts caused a similar uproar sixty years ago. Even John Baskerville's typefaces were denounced as illegible by English readers of the 1750s who were used to less stroke contrast and the stubbier serifs of Caslons and Dutch romans. Rudy VanderLans was correct when he observed not long ago that readers read best what they read most.

Those who dismiss style as something superficial are as myopic as those who see it as the most important aspect of design. Form (style) and communication (message) have a yin-yang relationship. Each should be formed by, and reinforce, the other. Style becomes part of the message: it can declare a generation, an attitude, or even a lifestyle. Radical shifts in graphic style often signify that times are changing. Art nouveau probably seemed pointless as Europe swirled into the abyss of World War I; expressionism and a gritty naturalism came to the fore. Modernism was accepted by Americans in the 1930s after being rejected in the 1920s. Ornament and decoration seemed out of place, almost obscene, when millions were unemployed, while modernism's stripped-down functionalism evoked an appropriate economy and restraint.

Clashes between design factions represent nothing more than a struggle for the heart and soul of a culture. Along with music, drama, and fine art, design is a manifestation of the values, concerns, and fantasies of a time and place. Ultimately, graphics belong not to the designers who bring them into being, but to the audience they are aimed at and the society at large. After their day has passed, graphic designs quickly become cultural artifacts signifying an era. Perhaps when designers criticize other schools of thought, they are seeking control of their society's cultural direction.

In the face of the cataclysmic changes that have come to characterize our century, denial is sometimes used as a defense in a desperate attempt to avoid being left behind. The politics of style can become very fierce, a death struggle between generations.

Originally published in Print, *March/April 1995.*

EMIGRE COMES OF AGE
Michael Rock

Getting a new *Emigre* magazine can be an exhausting experience. It may be the closest thing we have to a graphic design fashion magazine and it operates with the same brutal combination of cheerful fantasy and the dissatisfaction of perpetual change. So when a review copy of the *Emigre* retrospective book landed on my doorstep it was jarring to realize the champion of the new just turned ten years old.

Who could have guessed back in 1984 that two young Berkeley grads would parlay an obscure art and culture tabloid—obsessed with the unlikely theme of "What Is Legibility?"—into an international presence and, in turn, lend a name to a whole genre of typography? While circulation hovers around seven thousand, the magazine's modest readership belies a far-reaching influence; the echoes of *Emigre* style are everywhere. Zuzana Licko is the most imaginative and knocked-off type designer of her generation, and her husband, Rudy VanderLans, is one of the most (in)famous art directors working today. In addition, exactly how you feel about that last statement has become a benchmark of sorts, the line in the sand in a whole range of arguments.

But controversy aside, successfully churning out twenty-eight consecutive issues of anything—especially with limited staff, money, and distribution—is ample excuse for a little celebration. In that spirit, VanderLans, Licko, and Company have published *Emigre: Graphic Design into the Visual Realm* (New York: Van Nostrand Reinhold), a ninety-six page retrospective covering a decade of publication. The title page image of a brimming slide carousel foreshadows the portfolio show that follows: sample spreads from every issue, font specimens, professional projects, and a color section featuring posters, promos, and a complete set of magazine covers. The pictures are cut with short quotes from VanderLans and Licko explicating the *Emigre* philosophy together with a running text outlining the magazine's brief history—self-authored but cast in the third-person plural, giving it a somewhat unsettling, authoritative tone.

While it may be hard to imagine someone writing something like, "the strength of their work lies not in the graphic design alone, but in the way that they have combined type design, writing, graphic design, and publishing into one, much like it was done before the days when moveable type was first invented by Johann Gutenberg in 1476," about themselves, it's easy to overlook the superlatives, it's easy to sit back and admire the pictures; the work speaks for itself. But *Emigre* has drawn so much vitriolic criticism and hyperbolic praise over its short life that it is impossible not to reread this retrospective in search of the values underlying the couple's "experiments, ideologies, designs, and their commercial implementation," and, in turn, re-examine the romantic notion of the emigre.

Emigre was born amidst the typographic implosion of the early 1980s—sparked by Punk and New Wave and fanned by the introduction of desktop publishing—that fractured the unified front of rational functionalism. (It is not coincidental that *Emigre* and the Macintosh were introduced the same year.) In time *Emigre* has come to symbolize the entire diverse movement of new typographies. While supporters denounce this over-simplification—all labels are stereotypes, after all—that hasn't diminished the usefulness of the symbol in design discourse. And though the work published in *Emigre* cannot be reduced to a single style, it does share some common quality, attitude, or aura; if it didn't, the magazine would have no identity or consistent audience.

In fact, *Emigre* has not only developed a consistent audience, but it is also constructing a whole new generation of devotees weaned on their editorial ideology. In the introduction to issue No. 28, guest editor Gail Swanlund breathlessly disclaimed, "This is the magazine I've followed, read, studied, and copied shamelessly, and now I'm writing for it. . . ." The *Emigre* ideology is open but structured on a few basic principles: (1) Legibility is a function of reading not typography; (2) New forms should be infused with the spirit of the day and their means of production; (3) New technology should be embraced and expended, not forced to replicate antique forms; (4) Idiosyncratic and iconoclastic goals are superior to objective and universal ones (which in themselves are fantasies).

While this ideology has drawn mean-spirited criticism from typographic conservatives and professionals predicting some cataclysmic dissolution of good taste, no one has attacked more virulently than Massimo (we-only-need-five-good-typefaces) Vignelli. "It's the difference between the culture of obsolescence and the culture of refinement," Vignelli asserted in the *Los Angeles Times*. "In the cult of refinement, you don't need to come up with the junky typefaces they're coming up with today. They're junky because they have no style, no background, no depth, no elegance, no history." For his stand, Vignelli has been both lionized as a protector of high culture and pilloried as the model of intolerance. But while I disagree with both the content and spirit of his totalitarian grumblings, there may be a kernel of insight buried within them.

In the constant search for the edge of acceptable design practice, *Emigre* does, perhaps inadvertently, promote a kind of "culture of obsolescence." In an earnest introductory essay entitled "Graphic Designers Probably Won't Read This But . . ." Jeffery Keedy posits designers as "the 'scouts' of visual culture, looking ahead of the pack," sending dispatches back from the creative wilderness for the stuffy metropolitans to do with what they may. The design activity, in Keedy's vision, is one of discovery, not implementation. It is only after the rigors of that cultural plundering have exhausted them that designers "collapse into a 'timeless' stasis or retreat into nostalgia."

This commitment to a kind of visual colonization fits neatly into traditional capitalist themes involving the expansion of the frontier. After all, conquering new territory always ends up profiting somebody. Keedy's metaphor of the unbridled Californian working outside the conservative strictures of the New York establishment relies on the figure of the Westerner as cultural maverick and libertarian escaping from the suffocating history of the East. (It is reminiscent of Frank Lloyd Wright spending his final years in the liberatory exile of Taliesan West on the border of civilization and the desert.) All of which in turn reinforces the myth of the modern emigre artist, severed from the oppression of bourgeois society, seeking fortune in a new world.

Those libertarian tropes of uncharted territory courageously cultivated by the loner willing to work outside of conventional cultural boundaries, promote ideals that equate value with novelty. (Remember, *Emigre* is "The magazine that ignores boundaries.") Those ideals fit perfectly into a business set up to manufacture and market a product ruled by the dictates of changing taste, i.e., typefaces. A sense of currency based in experimentation— or visual exploration—becomes a highly effective force; it's a form of planned obsolescence, like tail fins or designer colors. *Emigre* has been able to coalesce all aspects of product development and marketing: a) the construction of an anti-establishment ideology promoted through the magazine's content; b) a manifestation of that ideology in a recognizable visual identity, i.e., "the signature *Emigre* style"; and finally c) the commodification of that message in a saleable product—a Postscript format typeface or even a collection of Ed Fella's doodles, list price $59.

This endless cosmetic variation as an engine of commerce was exactly what the socialist, protomodernist designers and critics like William Morris envisioned overcoming. Now vilified as elitist fantasies, ideas of timelessness had their origins in early attempts to break the burgeoning cycle of Victorian consumerism. The early modernists naïvely imagined "well-designed" objects existing outside the frenetic cycle of fashion, obliterating the need for constant re-invention and acquisition. In design, postmodernism may actually be a victory of market economy over socialist utopianism.

In that light it is difficult to say whether *Emigre* and the ideology of the new is radical or conventional. What is fascinating is the way that the avant-garde impulse parallels deeper patterns of mainstream consumer culture. In both systems, the wild will always be captured, surveyed, developed, and cultivated. In order to keep it all running, new territory must continuously be claimed, new markets tapped.

It would be unfair to categorize *Emigre* as merely a glorified mail-order type catalogue. The magazine has played perfectly to its audience and served as an alternative voice, at once serious and lighthearted, printing thoughtful articles and intriguing interviews. One of my only complaints about the retrospective is that, despite all of Mr. Keedy's introductory harping about designers that don't *read* the magazine, not one of the original articles or interviews are republished; this is a book primarily about the formal evolution of page layouts and typefaces. This is especially disappointing as few libraries collect the magazine and back issues can be expensive or unavailable.

Perhaps the most inspiring aspect of *Emigre* is the drive, perseverance, and generosity of spirit Licko and VanderLans have maintained over the course of their project. They have unapologetically pursued their work on their own terms and shaped the debate in the process. And in the end, their work has succeeded tremendously; *Emigre* has effectively infiltrated the host culture.

"When the visual trappings have reached the point of half-hour episodic TV," observed cinematographer John Bailey, "then a genre truly is a carcass." *Emigre* may be quickly reaching that level of cultural penetration: Licko's font Variax graces the Arrid Teen Image deodorant ads, and Barry Deck's now-ubiquitous Template Gothic, first introduced and licensed by *Emigre,* made it all the way to Wall Street via the financial pages of the Time-Warner annual report. With neighbors like that, *Emigre* may have to light out anew in search of a virgin frontier.

Originally published in I.D., *May/June 1994.*

DESIGN IS HELL
Steven Heller

For about a decade a small war has raged in the design press. The outcome could determine whether or not the ideas of a young generation will supersede that of an older one, and whether so-called theory-based graphic design born in academic hothouses is really a viable alternative to the more or less dominant practice. But since it takes two to skirmish, the war made enemies out of kindred spirits. The *designosaurs,* as Jeffery Keedy calls the enemy, are the representatives of the archetypal twentieth-century design ethic that held sway after World War II. With its Eurocentric ideals, rationalist dogma, old boy affiliation, corporate association, and fading mythology, modernism and its aging proponents neatly represented the generational divide.

War is hell. And this was a hell of a war. But despite the rhetoric, the fundamental wedge between young and old is not ideological, philosophical, or even methodological. The generational rift has simply been recalcitrance on the part of a few remaining "missionary" moderns to open their arms and warmly embrace unconventional work. Despite some undiplomatic—though beneficially provocative—remarks about cultural garbage and a few critical ripostes about illegibility, chaos, and ugliness, the anticanonicalists have never been prevented from mounting their challenge; pursuing their outlets and audiences; having their work showcased in magazines, competitions, and annuals; or, for that matter, developing magazines, competitions, and annuals of their own. Ultimately, of course, clients determine who get the assignments, so viability in the marketplace has little to do with whether one design generation is embraced by another. Therefore, without diminishing the intellectual importance of the new design discourse and its component parts, a sober analysis might place the conflict on the par of Canada going to war against the United States over the pronunciation of "about" (or is it aboot?).

The rift is not as wide as one might believe. The fact is, vocal minorities have a natural tendency to alter public awareness and perception. And the young generation's deconstructionist, poststructuralist, postmodernist, neodigitalist, and distinctly individualist approaches were destined to earn serious critical attention (and a share of acolytes) once the early proponents went public. Which is exactly what happened in the mid 1950s, when Push Pin Studio received kudos (and jobs) for providing an eclectic alternative to what at the time was an even more entrenched corporate modernism. Push Pin did not, however, declare war; it simply published a promotional periodical, *The Push Pin Monthly Graphic,* that influenced a shift in attitude and style through its revivals of passé graphic forms, prefiguring the postmodernist penchant for pastiche. This appealed to specific markets and media (books, records, editorial) where modernism (particularly Swiss modernism) was deemed inappropriate, cold, or impersonal. Although Push Pin's borrowing of historical styles was antithetical to "art-must-be-of-its-time" modernism, by the late fifties, such orthodoxy had already begun to disappear. While some moderns clung to dogma, the influence of new styles forced many others to veer towards more eclectic forms. Indeed the tension between modernism and eclecticism gave rise to what might be called "late modern," notably the expressive approaches exemplified by Herb Lubalin's photo typography in which he conceptually weds letterforms with images. In the mid 1960s, *Avant Garde* magazine became the bible of this unique typographic approach.

While no formal peace accord has yet been signed (and it's been reported that sniper fire could still heard at last fall's *Fuse* conference in London), the recent hostilities appear to be evolving into a more fundamental debate about design criticism and academic versus professional practice. Nevertheless, modernism is a casualty of this war that must be cared for. While it served well as the straw dog against which the new alternatives could be contrasted, its legacy should not be regarded simply as a bankrupt establishment ideology. Before we forget the historical relevance and contemporary influence of modernism, the time has come to reconcile the similarities between this venerable ethic and progressive contemporary practice.

In "On Overcoming Modernism" (*I.D.* magazine, September/October 1992), Lorraine Wild argues, "The influence of modernism on American graphic designers may have originated in the work of the European futurists or the constructivists or the designers of the Bauhaus, but the social utopianism of the aesthetic that accompanied early modernism never reached the United States. Indulging in sloppy thinking, fake history, and romance, we attribute a fantasy of ethical accomplishment to modernism as a reaction against the uncomfortable unknowns of postmodernism."

This statement is a critical exaggeration in the attempt to debunk modernist mythology by recasting it as corrupted, and, by extension, suggesting its exponents are poseurs. The truth is that modernism was fraught with contradiction from the outset, but that's what gave it breadth. Modernism evolved from its original utopian guise of making the industrial world a better place to live into its post-war functional role of making the industrial world clean and sanitized. The ideal of "the universal," as proffered in the late 1940s by the Swiss, girded by rules and strictures, ultimately became inflexible. But despite its catechism, modernism did not begin as an all-encompassing ideology rooted in art and design, but rather as a confluence of progressive ideas that more or less attempted to reflect and mediate the radical changes in politics, society, technology, and economy that faced European industrial nations between the world wars. When it was finally adopted in the United States ten years after its beginnings in Europe, modernism was no longer the radical experimental language of design school teachers and students practiced at the Bauhaus and Vhekutumas, but a codified form language of commercial art. Even in its experimental context it was intended for commercial application. The unconventional typography of Italian futurist Fortunato Depero, Bauhaus master Herbert Bayer, *Merz* meister Kurt Schwitters, Russian productivists Alexander Rodchenko and Lazar El Lissitzky, and others in the pantheon of early modernism, were applied to commercial advertising and packaging. They may have had a loftier mission, but for their "clients," these were not utopian messages.

Modernism was introduced to Americans as a bridge between art and commerce; a tool in the retooling of the American economy. It did not come neatly packaged in formal art history books (which virtually ignored modernism at the time), but rather was advanced in the late 1920s and early 1930s advertising trade magazines and layout manuals that provided templates for the modernization of word and image. Its theoretical base was all but ignored by its enthusiastic acolytes. Although pure utopianism was removed from modernism when it was clear that Europe was surging headlong toward dystopia, nevertheless the *symbolism* of social change remained fixed. For American practitioners, modern design did not signal a classless society, but it did rebel against stodgy convention. And so in the hands of its pioneers it was every bit as confrontational as the postmodern methods of today.

After seeing the first examples of Bauhaus work in a 1928 issue of the British *Commercial Art* magazine, a young Paul Rand was one of the few who appreciated the theoretical underpinnings of this method and embraced modernism not as novelty, but as a viable alternative to the saccharine, copy-heavy, overly stylized graphic art that was being pumped out in ads, packages, and magazines. Here was a chance to bust cliché through the marriage of modern art and rational design. Rand saw modern graphics as the print equivalent of jazz; while rooted in theories that redefined the nature of harmony and balance, modernism allowed considerable room for unique and varied impromptu interpretation, as his conceptually exciting covers for *Direction* magazine attest. He further incorporated aspects of modern theory—cubist, neoplasticist, constructivist—into advertising and editorial work. Harnessing abstraction as a means for conveying messages was another radical accomplishment in a commercial art field based on hard sell techniques. While never resolutely Bauhausian, constructivist, or futurist, Rand synthesized the key avant-garde theories into an applied arts language that through his force of will and vision pushed the boundaries of anonymous commercial art into the realm of authored "visual communications."

That is the real legacy of modernism.

But American modernism has nevertheless suffered its share of false expectations based on its ethical precept to make the world a better place. Sure, its adoption by corporations suggested that any similarity between modernism and utopianism was purely vestigial. But it's ridiculous to think that modernism could ever sustain the moral high ground in a field that is ultimately a service to commerce, although those who practiced it tried their best. By the 1950s, modernism had been transformed from an ideology into a methodology—corporate modernism—where integrated systems replaced ad hoc practices. But even in this incarnation, modernism broke ground by insisting that graphic design could relieve the chaos and confusion that existed in most communications. In the days when chaos and confusion reigned, simplicity and organization were radical concepts. But even in visual economy, there was an exquisite complexity, as Ladislav Sutnar proved through his meticulous, yet graphically adventurous, industrial catalogues. Likewise the most innovative results of the rational revolution—pure typographic systems devised by the likes of Rudolph DeHarak, Brownjohn, Chermayeff & Geismar, Lester Beall, and others—signaled a significant shift in the status quo.

Even in its most synthetic, minimalist, or functional state, modernism's most audacious practitioners experimented with how to expand the range of visual communication, from transparent to multileveled. In addition to refining typography, these researchers looked towards the big idea or how to make diverse graphic forms including photographs, illustration, collage, etc., as comprehensible as written language. Aaron Burns, type director of the Composing Room in the late 1950s and later, in the early 1970s, cofounder of International Typeface Corporation, produced a series of experimental booklets published in 1961 that allowed Gene Federico, Lester Beall, Brownjohn, Chermayeff & Geismar, and Herb Lubalin the opportunity to intuitively and intellectually play with hot metal type in ways that had never been tried before, such as touching and smashing letters, overprinting color combinations, and exploring levels of transparency, and otherwise expressing meaning through the form of type. The results were certainly comparable, at least in spirit, to the earliest deconstructivist exercises in which multiple typefaces and weights at various readings tore apart the traditional Swiss grid. As experiments, they were both admired by those who sought new means of expression and criticized by those who saw no reason to tamper with convention. In the end, however, technology altered the practice of design and the thinking behind it, and today these experiments appear tame. But in their day they influenced a generation of editorial and advertising designers.

Modernism ran out of steam more than a decade ago. But at its core is an ethic—the responsibility that a designer has to contribute actively to, indeed enhance, the social, political, and cultural framework—that continues to inform even the most diehard postmodernist. Now that the recent generational war is coming to a close, it would be prudent to reassess, and even reappreciate, the breadth of modernism and the complexity of its leaders. The fact is, it's foolish to deny that anyone who seriously explores the outer limits and inner soul of visual communication is not in some way a modernist. Or as *Pogo's* Walt Kelly said: "We have met the enemy and he is us."

Originally published in Emigre, *No. 33, Winter 1995.*

ON TEACHING
AND
LEARNING

BUILDING BRIDGES BETWEEN THEORY AND PRACTICE

Rick Poynor

For a non-American looking across at America, the future—our future—ceases to be matter of wholly untestable speculation. At least one possible version of it is already happening in the United States. This is as true of graphic design as it is of diet crazes, plastic surgery, and television. To anyone who keeps a weather eye on the climate changes of international graphics, the American scene is fascinating because the issues that will shape the future course of the discipline become apparent earlier and they are thrown into higher relief. The American graphic design community is exceptional for its edgy mixture of self-confidence and doubt and its up-front willingness at conferences, in competitions, and in the pages of the professional magazines to keep asking itself what exactly it should become. In the 1990s, this introspection shows signs of maturing into a practice founded in critical reflection.

The generational rift runs deeper than might at first have been supposed, and there is no going back. The younger radicals still talk as though they were beleaguered, marginalized, and misunderstood—and for a long time they were. But while the fundamental changes that are occurring may not yet be fully reflected in mainstream practice where the power, money, and professional kudos are concentrated (and may, in fact, be antithetical to it), when it comes to the argument itself, the passion, tenacity, and intellectual conviction of the new guard is winning the day, even if the curmudgeons of modernism have yet to wake up to it. The new guard's victory finds symbolic expression, at an institutional level, in the recent redesign by Lisa Naftolin of the *AIGA Journal*. Even as Rudy VanderLans was excoriating the old design as "amateurish, tasteless, and bland," the journal was outfitting itself in funkily serious, unmistakably 1990s garb.

In the nineties, once radical and transgressive digital styles have burst their subcultural boundaries (design school, music scene, art gallery catalogue) and infiltrated the mainstream, and while the stylistic details will evolve and change and double back on themselves, the rule-breaking pluralism is here to stay. For me, chairing the American Center for Design's "100 Show" this summer, one of the most unexpected and telling entries was *SAY* magazine, designed by Johnson & Wolverton of Portland, Oregon, for Amnesty International. Here was the fractured idiom of West Coast youth culture magazines like *Ray Gun, Blur,* and *Plazm* applied with undeniable power, though debatable taste, to the hugely sensitive issue of human-rights abuses. If this seems unremarkable, no more than you might expect these days—and if it does, that is exactly my point—it may be worth mentioning that Britain's equivalent newsletter is a piece of sober, conventional, up-and-down desktop publishing.

Most promising for the development of American graphics in the coming years is the gradual emergence of a new spirit of critical inquiry and reflection. The critical discussion fostered in the pages of *I.D., Print,* the *AIGA Journal,* and *Emigre,* the "100 Show" book, and at Steven Heller's "Modernism and Eclecticism" symposium is helping to create a profession with a more sophisticated sense of its history, its practice, and the function of its products in society. It is perhaps a sign that real progress is being made that such strong dissatisfaction is now being voiced about the nature and aims of this criticism: is there enough of it, who is it for, and what is it about? Andrew Blauvelt, currently setting up a graduate program at North Carolina State University, argues that journalistic criticism's main shortcoming is that it fails to make its assumptions explicit. Blauvelt believes we need a more rigorous form of criticism, closer in its methods to the literary kind, in which critical positions are clearly stated and defended. Such a criticism would build a "bridge between theory and practice." Its goal, he told *Emigre* recently, would be to function as a form of research and development—"to drive the profession."

To some degree, perhaps in a less systematic way than Blauvelt envisages, this is already happening. Some of the most challenging new design is being forged at the controversial interface of theory and practice, education and the profession. Designer-educators such as Katherine McCoy (Cranbrook), Jeffery Keedy and Lorraine Wild (CalArts), and Michael Rock (Yale) combine design work, teaching, and critical writing. The future of Cranbrook's design department may be uncertain with the departure of the long-resident McCoys, but it has created a legacy of critically minded graduates—including Keedy, Wild, and Blauvelt—now in positions of influence. The critical fusion of media and methods is nicely summarized in the name of the New York studio founded in the eighties by Ellen Lupton and J. Abbott Miller: Design Writing Research. Design fuels reflection and the process of research and reflection, in turn, feeds back into design. As a result of this process, "critical positions" evolve.

Designers who wonder what any of this has to do with the daily realities of commercial practice may doubt that there is much to be gained. In American graphic design, as elsewhere, there is a manifest tension between the pragmatics of the studio and the academy's more speculative flights. There is a real danger, if the critical process takes a wrong turn and becomes too inward-looking and insistent on its own theoretical agenda, that it will be rejected by the wider design community as the narrow concern of a minority of design school-based initiates, a useful source of provocative new styles, but nothing more. Such a development at this crucial moment would rob the profession of one of the most obvious and valuable benefits of the new criticism—its critical insight and judgment.

What American graphic design needs now more than ever is to establish new grounds for making assessments of effectiveness and value. With the old consensus of what constitutes "good" graphic design in tatters and professional standards in free-fall, the problem of quality has become one of the central dilemmas faced by designers. Is there such a thing as good graphic design any more? And how do we decide what it is?

Few graphic designers, despite the mood of uncertainty, will answer "no" to the first question. Anyone struggling to keep up with the pace of change can see that the need for evaluative criteria has not only not gone away, but it also has become more acute. It is a matter, as much as anything, of professional definition. If all graphic design is equally good, and one response to a brief has no more to recommend it than any other, then graphic designers can make no claim to provide anything other than a technical service. While this may be the implicit promise of a "democratizing" technology and the breaching of craft's closed circle, no self-respecting designer with several years of hard-won education (or self-education) and many years of experience believes it is that simple.

Learning how to use a page layout program does not in itself make you an editorial designer. Design for multimedia's coursing stream of words, sounds, and images requires great sensitivity and skill. As a matter of urgency, designers need to convince clients with computers loaded to the gunnels with cheap fonts that they have special talents to offer.

Developing new evaluative criteria is another matter. American graphic design is fragmenting. As it moves toward the millennium, the new pluralism is a necessary response to a multicultural society which, if the profession is to remain relevant, it must more fully reflect. "We need more graphic design particular to the tribes," says Lorraine Wild, "not less." Or to put it another way: design that talks to diverse groups in specially made visual languages each group will understand. A handful of well-worn professional yardsticks with claims to universalism, evolved in simpler times, will be of no help in judging the effectiveness of such work. Instead, a new set of critical yardsticks is needed for the new diversity of applications—many of them still emerging from new media with, as yet, no established conventions. It will be a slow process of trial and error that will mean abandoning our comfortable preconceptions ("this typeface is ugly") and responding to the particularities of context ("does it communicate here?"). And if, as observers and critics, we fail to understand the context, because it falls outside our experience or sphere of expertise, we will have to leave it to those who do understand it. The accepted standards of one sphere will not necessarily apply in another.

But talk of tribes raises a larger dilemma and it is here, perhaps, that graphic design's thorniest problem lies. For, despite regular handwringing and a torrent of platitudes, the "tribes" themselves are still hardly represented at all at the heart of the successful design community. This is as true of the group now assuming the mantle of influence and leadership as it was of their predecessors. The new leaders are in the main white, middle-class alumni of a small group of highly visible, vigorously self-promoting graduate schools. They are diverse, but nowhere near as diverse as American society. Only the increasing proportion of women in their ranks suggests anything is really changing as the baton is passed, and some would dispute even this. Nevertheless, the profession's "underground matriarchy" of women designers (to use Ellen Lupton and Laurie Haycock Makela's phrase) has been in recent years, and remains, the source of many of the most original and constructive ideas.

Now, to build on this progress, the profession must reconcile demands which, though not ultimately incompatible, can often find themselves at odds with each other. It needs to be more inclusive, more genuinely multicultural, while at the same time maintaining the highest educational, conceptual, and technical standards. It will be a difficult task, but the best hopes for achieving this necessary evolution lie in the spirit of critical reflection, energy, and vision that are transforming the theory and practice of graphic design in the 1990s.

Originally published in I.D., *November 1994.*

GRAPHIC DESIGN EDUCATION AS A LIBERAL ART: DESIGN AND KNOWLEDGE IN THE UNIVERSITY AND THE "REAL WORLD"

Gunnar Swanson

Although this essay concentrates on issues of graphic design education, my arguments also pertain to education in other areas of design; most apply to arts education and many are relevant to post-secondary education in general. I assume a university setting, though many of the ideas presented in this essay apply equally to art schools. Finally, just as the essay calls for a broad view of design education and a broad context for design, I hope it will be read in a broad context and the arguments applied wherever appropriate.

FOREWORD

With all of the pressures on higher education and all of the questions facing graphic designers and design educators, why reconsider the basic premise of graphic design education? Since inertia tends to discourage basic change, why not concentrate on excellence within the current system?

The answers to those questions center on both fairness and survival. Ask most graphic design teachers what happens to their students who do not become graphic designers and you will get the same silence or lecture that you hear from basketball coaches when someone asks about players who don't go on to the NBA. Not just the reaction is comparable, the whole situation is. Measuring the success of college sports by the number of players that go on to play professionally often leads to players' being cheated out of a real education and a chance for a satisfying life. We need to consider whether our attitudes toward "professionalism" in design education do the same.

GRAPHIC DESIGN EDUCATION

Though hardly homogeneous, the vast majority of graphic design programs, whether in vocational schools, art schools, or universities, are, at least in concept, vocational training programs.

The Bauhaus, which was grounded in craft ideology and stressed intuitive solutions to design problems, provided the model for much of modern design training.[1] Hannes

Meyer, the architect who became the director of the Bauhaus after Walter Gropius, brought in experts from other disciplines as speakers, but his tenure was too short to have established a design theory at the Bauhaus. When László Moholy-Nagy formed the New Bauhaus in Chicago in 1937 (which later became the Institute of Design at Illinois Institute of Technology), he included lectures by philosophers and scientists.[2] Since then, various other programs have introduced semiotics, literary theory, etcetera, to their curricula, and there is a growing recognition that a wide-ranging education is needed for a synthetic and integrative field such as design to progress.

By "synthetic" I mean that design does not have a subject matter of its own—it exists in practice only in relation to the requirements of given projects. The path of progress for the field is not defined by the next great unsolved design problem. Design is "integrative" in that, by its lack of specific subject matter, it has the potential to connect many disciplines.[3]

Even while some design programs are strengthening their liberal studies requirements, the tendency toward professional rather than general education at colleges and universities has been growing for the past two decades. Graphic design programs are, on the whole, doing well. Students and parents alike seem to be impressed with the idea that there will be a job waiting at the end of four years of study, and at many schools graphic design has made up for declining enrollments in traditional fine arts programs.

As the estimated two thousand graphic design programs in the United States pump out more graduates than there are jobs in traditional graphic design firms and corporate design departments, the natural tendency may be toward entrenchment of professional training. Each school would reason that in fairness to its students it must do a better job of providing entry-level job skills so its graduates have a chance in this competitive job market.

In light of this tendency toward professionalism, it may seem counterintuitive that I suggest that we not only increase the augmentation of design training with more liberal studies, but also reconsider graphic design education—as a liberal arts subject.

THE HISTORICAL CONTEXT OF THE LIBERAL ARTS

The concept of liberal arts was first delineated by Aristotle. He characterized liberal studies as those studies fitting for the education of a freeman. He made "a distinction between liberal and illiberal subjects," the latter being those that would "make the learner mechanical . . . [and] make the body, soul, or intellect of freemen unserviceable for the external exercise of goodness."[4]

Aristotle defined the liberal arts as having four points. First, they are not mechanical. Second, they are not utilitarian, i.e., they have intrinsic value; even if extrinsically useful, their pursuit is useful in and of itself. Third, if an area of study is undertaken as a liberal study, there must be no specializing that would restrict the mind. Finally, liberal arts study must be undertaken for its intrinsic value, not merely to earn a living or to impress others. (Thus intrinsically valuable studies undertaken for the wrong reasons would be disqualified as illiberal.)

It would be easy to dismiss this classical view of the liberal arts as a product of and for a society where routine work was left to slaves. Although the distinction of liberal versus illiberal studies came to light in that cultural context, the development of reason, moral grounding, and pursuit of truth was a prerequisite for citizenship in the fullest sense. Despite their primary interest being intrinsic, Aristotle recognized their utility in building a democratic society. Since our conception of democracy is broader based and more inclusive than that of the ancient Greeks, the current cultural context does not argue for the reduction of liberal studies, but rather for broadening their influence.

It is not clear what subjects Aristotle considered liberal, but the Greeks and later the Romans came to agree on seven liberal arts: the trivium of grammar, logic, and rhetoric and the quadrivium of arithmetic, geometry, music, and astronomy. In medieval times, reason was subordinated to revelation until St. Thomas Aquinas harmonized Christian doctrine and Aristotelian philosophy with the addition of theology—reason leading to the knowledge God had revealed. The humanism of the Renaissance rediscovered Aristotelian liberal education through the rediscovery of classical literature and came to equate liberal education with literary studies.

It was not until the nineteenth century that various concepts of liberal education akin to Aristotle's theories were reintroduced (reconsidered, of course, in the light of modern knowledge). Cardinal John Henry Newman's views are seen as more-or-less purely Aristotelian, but practical values played some part. In his lectures during his tenure as rector of the Catholic University of Ireland in the 1850s (published in 1873 as *The Idea of a University*), Newman claimed: "when the Church founds a university, she is not cherishing talent, genius, or knowledge, for their own sake, but for the sake of her children . . . with the object of training them to fill their respective posts in life better, and of making them more intelligent, capable, active members of society . . . ,"[5] but his main emphasis was on purely intrinsic value. According to Newman, the university's "function is intellectual culture. . . . Intellect must have an excellence of its own . . . the word 'educate' would not be used of intellectual culture, as it is used, had not the intellect had an end of its own; that had it not such an end, there would be no meaning in calling certain intellectual exercises 'liberal,' in contrast with 'useful,' as is commonly done. . . ."[6]

During the nineteenth century, English critic Matthew Arnold modified Aristotle's view that the pursuit of knowledge is intrinsically worthwhile and the fulfilment of man's rational nature. Arnold concentrated on *building* rationality—in his view, knowledge is important in that it allows one to develop abilities and live a harmonious natural life.[7]

The value of the liberal arts, however, was not universally assumed. Harvard instituted the elective system in 1883 with the purpose of allowing students to move in the direction of their future careers. Johns Hopkins University was founded in 1876 as the first research institute in the United States. In 1890, the Harvard Graduate School of Arts and Sciences was established in much the same mode. Its main purpose was, and still is, the production of college teachers with doctoral degrees, while producing scholarly research that is, at least in the ideal, not solely utilitarian.

A movement for "liberal culture" in opposition to both utilitarianism and research was significant enough that, in 1909, Charles William Elliot, who instituted both the elective system and the graduate school, was replaced as Harvard president. Within a few years the debates over educational philosophy died down. Most universities soon accommodated utilitarianism of one sort or another and the liberal arts.[8] The notion that professional training, general education, and research were incompatible lost most of its voice in the early part of the twentieth century. This accommodation of multiple approaches continued, expanding the nature(s) of the university. By the mid 1960s, Clark Kerr, then president of the University of California, coined the term "multiversity," comparing the "idea of a university" to a village with its priests, the idea of a modern university to a one-industry town with its intellectual oligarchy, and the idea of a multiversity to a city of infinite variety.[9]

In such a "city of infinite variety" that provides the football team for local and national entertainment, the hospital where babies are born, as well as scholarship, professional training, continuing education, and a multitude of other services to diverse publics, Kerr recognized that "there is less sense of purpose than within the town but there are more ways to excel."[10] The clarity of Cardinal Newman's goals may be lost, but the opportunities are more numerous and varied.

COLLEGE EDUCATION TODAY

It may be that universities have survived by being, to a large extent, all things to all people. Higher education has largely escaped serious damage from parallel charges of elitism and abandonment of traditional standards, eggheadedness and mundaneness, or impracticality and bourgeois debasement by maintaining a wide variety of virtues, thus maintaining support of an eclectic plurality.

However, attempting to be all things to all people has produced some paradoxes. For example, the same psychology course may be a start toward the understanding of human behavior for one student, a "breadth" requirement for another, and an introduction to what will be a specialized field of study and research for a third. An art history course might add spiritual enlightenment to the psychology class's list of aspects; an English class might also provide remedial communication for native speakers and, increasingly, language training for foreign students.

Largely because standards of excellence and paths of career progress are more clear within the research/publishing/specialization path than they are in a teaching/personal enlightenment/broad education one, the liberal arts have become less an approach to integrated learning and more of a list of fields defining "broad education." Even though the vast majority of students have no intention of specializing in a given academic subject, classes tend to be preparatory for graduate study and thus preprofessional education.

Although there may be careerist tendencies, the system of students with traditional subject majors assumes preparation for life as well as vocation. Philosophy teachers, for example, do not measure their success based on whether the majority of their students become philosophers. Likewise, the goal in literature is not only to create producers of literature or literary critics, but also to create literate people. By contrast, ask teachers of graphic design about students who don't make careers in design or a related field. Most often, those students are seen as failures. There is little feeling that graphic design has prepared the student for life or a career other than design.

On the whole, design schooling has not helped students become broader thinking people who can help shape a democratic society. The tools for analysis and insight of many disciplines have broad extradisciplinary application for understanding the world. The tools of graphic design do not seem to serve much purpose beyond a graphic design career. Graphic design education is not, for the most part, education. It is vocational training, and rather narrow specialized training at that.

VOCATIONAL TRAINING FOR A CHANGING VOCATION

It has become a cliché of career counseling to point out that most of today's jobs won't exist in fifteen years and most jobs that will exist in fifteen years don't exist now. Certainly the changing names of programs—commercial art to advertising design to graphic design to visual communication and sometimes back to graphic design—testify to the fact that, though there may be graphic designers in fifteen years, graphic designers will likely be doing something very different from the present vocation of graphic design.

Most four-year graphic design programs try to teach something beyond "entry-level skills," but preparing students for their first job is often seen as "practical education." It is questionable whether such job training could rightly be called education or even if it is rightly deemed "practical." If simulating a "real world" environment is the best preparation for a designer, design training should take the form of apprenticeships—what could be more "real" than the real world itself?

The entry-level jobs of the past were largely in production. Since paste-up artists are largely a thing of the past, courtesy of small computers, many programs now struggle to produce computer operators. It is only faith that makes us assume that upward mobility will be available to the nineties version of the often trapped (and now largely unemployed) paste-up artists. The Quark XPress®, Adobe Illustrator®, and Photoshop® jockeys, today's electronic paste-up artists, may soon find their skills obsolete in the next technological revolution.

Design teachers should teach basic principles of form and communication, but are, by teaching what *they* were taught, teaching the graphic designers of the twenty-first century how to be mid-twentieth-century graphic designers. Educators can and should examine trends (we know, for instance, that electronic communication will increase and become more flexible than it is currently) and try to prepare themselves and their students for the future. There is only one thing, however, that we really know with precision about the future—it will be different from today. Therefore, the best thing we can do for design students is to make them adaptable.

GENERAL EDUCATION AND ADAPTABILITY

The correlation between general education and adaptability makes a belief in general education for designers widespread, though hardly ubiquitous. This belief is often tempered by a distinctly anti-intellectual streak in design teachers. In the mid 1970s, an industrial design teacher of mine told me I was "too articulate" and that great design happens when designers have no other way of expressing themselves than with form. Paul Rand, perhaps the best known living graphic designer and design educator, recently wrote that a "student whose mind is cluttered with matters that have nothing directly to do with design . . . is a bewildered student."[11] Clearly many design teachers and many design students see "academic" classes as time stolen from their true purpose—the design studio.

Rand's denial of "matters that have nothing directly to do with design" places design education clearly in the realm of vocational training. In addition to his questionable assumptions about the separability of form from meaning, Rand's statement assumes that any current list of subjects that "have nothing directly to do with design" will apply in the future.

Institute of Design at IIT professor Sharon Poggenpohl argued well for the opposite stance.[12] She adopted the term "contrarian" from Wall Street where long-term players, recognizing the cyclical nature of the stock market, determine what everyone else is doing and then do the opposite. I believe design educators must be contrarians and look at the fact that "practical education" is neither practical nor education and move beyond, as Charles Bailey puts it, the present and particular.

GRAPHIC DESIGN AS A LIBERAL ART

What would graphic design as a liberal art entail? It would, no doubt, take a variety of forms. Certainly the current trend toward history and theory would be an element, but the switch to "liberal" design will require a change in outlook. We must begin to believe our own rhetoric and see design as an integrative field that bridges many subjects that deal with communication, expression, interaction, and cognition.

Design should be about meaning and how meaning can be created. Design should be about the relationship of form and communication. It is one of the fields where science and literature meet. It can shine a light on hidden corners of sociology and history. Design's position as conduit for and shaper of popular values can be a path between anthropology and political science. Art and education can both benefit through the perspective of a field that is about expression *and* the mass dissemination of information. Designers, design educators, and design students are in a more important and interesting field than we seem to recognize.

DESIGN AND SCHOLARSHIP

What form the new liberal field of design would take is unclear. Currently there is no clear role for design scholarship. Unlike most traditional fields of scholarship, design has no subject matter of its own, so it is hard to find models for this new approach. Design, in practice, exists primarily in response to an externally generated need or situation. Richard Buchanan, head of the Department of Design at Carnegie Mellon, pointed out that the "subject matter for the designer is an indeterminate problem, made only partly determinate by the interests and needs of clients, managers, and the designer."[13] This contrasts with the more clearly defined subject matter found in other academic fields.

At present, design scholarship largely takes the form of historical analysis or criticism. Although there is a place for the history of design in and of itself, (just as in the histories of science and many other academic fields), it would be absurd to suggest that *any* field abandon itself wholly to the contemplation of its own past. Design in any full sense will, of course, involve methodology and the creation of designed objects.

Clearly most design programs would include a significant concentration on skills. This would hardly be unique to academia—language programs do not hesitate to have students conjugate verbs; chemistry students learn laboratory procedures; and there are professional aspects to social science classes. Technique will probably be a large part of any design program, but the meaning of techniques will take on more importance.

Buchanan has suggested rhetoric as the closest available model for design.[14] Rhetoric, as a field of study, is both the practice of verbal persuasion and the formal study of persuasive verbal communication. Design may be seen as the visual counterpart to rhetoric. Buchanan is quite persuasive in his argument that through designed objects, "designers have directly influenced the actions of individuals and communities, changed attitudes and values, and shaped society in surprisingly fundamental ways."[15] Buchanan writes primarily of what is usually called product design or industrial design, but the case for graphic design as a parallel to rhetoric is more obvious.

Graphic design, more than other design areas, is usually directly about persuasion: intellectual, logical, aesthetic, and emotional. Thus the balance of practice and analysis of rhetoricians clearly makes sense for graphic design. This is not to say, however, that the formal procedures of rhetorical study should be applied to graphic design to the exclusion of all others. Grammatical, semiotic, theatrical, anthropological, psychological, physiological, philosophical, and political perspectives also need to be considered.

DESIGN AS A LIBERAL ART VERSUS DESIGN PLUS LIBERAL ARTS

Mark Salmon and Glenn Gritzer argue for integration of liberal arts, in general, and social sciences, in particular, into the professional design curriculum.[16] They reject the strategy of art faculty introducing social science material because of lack of academic preparation on the part of faculty, and that of team teaching with social scientists because of assumed lack of willingness on the part of faculty. Salmon and Gritzer advocate parallel content, where social science courses that correspond to the design curriculum are offered. For instance, interior design students would study courses on marriage and family, sociology, and occupations, while their design courses covered domestic design, office design, etc.

Such courses are to be encouraged, but, while parallel disciplines are the basis for understanding the context of design, we can hardly expect a real examination of design issues by nondesigners. Research into issues of typography and understanding, for instance, generally misses the questions a designer would ask. (Broad categories, such as sans serif typefaces, are often assumed to be homogeneous, alternative design solutions are rarely considered, etc.) Other fields can provide a framework for basic consideration of some design issues, but we cannot rely on them to advance design any more than medicine can rely solely on the work of biologists. The concerns of design will not be directly addressed by academia until it *becomes* an academic subject.

BALANCING SKILLS AND UNDERSTANDING

A primary task of design education is to find the balance between skills training and a general understanding that will benefit students, the field of graphic design, and working professionals. Bailey charts his ideal balance of skills and knowledge in British elementary and secondary education. Under his scheme, students in the earlier grades will be primarily involved in learning "serving competencies" or skills. Later, social sciences and other "inquiries into goings-on themselves manifestations of intelligence," will share the stage with, and ultimately take over from natural science and the like, or "inquiries into goings-on *not* themselves manifestations of intelligence." Bailey acknowledges that his allocation applies only to "a liberal and general education. Nothing is said [about] specialist training."[17] If for no other reason, Bailey's particular division cannot be applied directly to graphic design education because it ends at an age before most design training begins. It does, however, offer an analytical framework for considering components of an education.

It is too early to assign the activities of students in the hypothetical liberal field of design, but it is interesting to observe that the present pattern of education is often the opposite of the most common forms of professional training. At the risk of overcategorizing, most professional education begins with general knowledge, moves on to an overview of the profession's underpinnings, and concludes with specialized activity.

As a general pattern, design training runs the opposite direction. Although usually preceded by a "core" class, common to many of the arts, undergraduate training tends to be specialized design skills. It is only in the upper division, if at all, that undergraduates are introduced to history, theory, or a broader perspective on design. Early postgraduate work is often remedial skill enhancement, and it is only at the level of MFA study that many design programs introduce what resembles the abstract overview provided a freshman in an introductory social science course.

IS DESIGN IMPORTANT?

Designers and design educators spend much time and energy talking about developing public awareness of design and how to gain recognition for design. Victor Margolin points out that arguments over legal theory and even literary theory appear in popular magazines because people can see the importance for their lives, but design remains unnoticed.[18] Can studying design be of general, not just professional, interest? Can the study of design inform other areas of study? We assume that a design student would benefit from studying anthropology; we need to consider whether an anthropology student would benefit from the study of graphic design. Do we really have anything to offer outside of the sometimes questionable promise of a job?

Even a field as abstract, specialized, and self-referential as cosmology recognizes that its activity, in addition to its intrinsic value, ultimately matters because of its relation to general knowledge. In *A Brief History of Time,* Stephen Hawking writes:

> What would it mean if we actually did discover the ultimate theory of the universe? . . . In Newton's time it was possible for an educated person to have a grasp of the whole of human knowledge, at least in outline. But since then, the pace of the development of science has made this impossible. . . . Seventy years ago, if Eddington is to be believed, only two people understood the general theory of relativity.[19]

Hawking noted that relativity is now widely understood, at least in outline, and an ultimate theory of the universe could be absorbed by nonphysicists. The real importance of the goal of cosmology for the world's best known cosmologist seems to be that philosophers could understand science as they did in the eighteenth century. Hawking bemoans the fact that science has become so technical and mathematical that only specialists can understand and philosophers' scope is reduced from the great tradition of Aristotle and Kant to Wittgenstein's statement that "The sole remaining task for philosophy is the analysis of language."[20] A unified theory of the universe could be understood by everyone, Hawking writes:

> Then we shall all, philosophers, scientists, and just ordinary people, be able to take part in the discussion of the question of why it is that we and the universe exist.

If we find the answer to that, it would be the ultimate triumph of human reason—
for then we would know the mind of God.[21]

The point is that, although each branch of study may be an end to itself, the
progress of each field is doubly validated as it contributes to general knowledge. The
revolutions in physics that Hawking seeks to surpass would not have come about without
previous breakthroughs in mathematics. The revolution in literary criticism of the 1970s
and 1980s would not have come about were it not for previous breakthroughs in linguistic
theory.

In light of those linguistic and literary revolutions, I should point out that I don't
share Dr. Hawking's disdain for Wittgenstein's goal of language analysis, though I do agree
that a single task for any field might represent a too-narrow viewpoint. If the word
"language" is used in the broadest sense, then language analysis is at the core of much of
the humanities and social sciences. Design, and graphic design in particular, is in the position
to be at the center of this study.

Design's past failure to have carved a proper academic niche for itself may, in the
end, be one of its saving graces. Design as a professional practice has often bridged fields
as diverse as engineering, marketing, education, and psychology. Design as an academic study
can do no less.

Originally published in Design Issues, *Vol. 10, No. 1, Spring 1994.*

Notes

1. For a discussion of the development of modern design education, see Victor Margolin, "Design Studies and the Graphic Designer," *Proceedings of the Graphic Design Education Association, 1990 Symposium,* 56–62.
2. Margolin, "Design Studies and the Graphic Designer," 60.
3. For an expanded discussion, see Richard Buchanan, "Design as a New Liberal Art," *Papers: The 1990 Conference on Design Education,* Industrial Designers Society of America, 15–16.
4. Aristotle, "Politics" in *Aristotle on Education,* John Burnet translator (London: Cambridge University Press, 1903), 107–109.
5. John Henry Newman (Cardinal), *The Idea of a University* (Garden City, NY: Image Books, Doubleday & Co., 1959), 9.
6. Newman, *The Idea of a University,* 149.
7. Paul Hirst, "Liberal Education," *The Encyclopedia of Education,* vol. 5, Lee C. Deighton, ed., (New York: The Macmillan Company & Free Press, 1971), 505–509.
8. Louis Menand, "What are Universities For?" *Harpers,* 283, 1699 (December 1991).
9. Clark Kerr, *The Uses of the University,* (New York: Harpers, 1966), 39–40.
10. Kerr, *The Uses of the University,* 41.
11. Paul Rand, *Design, Form, and Chaos,* (New Haven, CT and London: Yale University Press, 1993), 217.
12. Sharon Poggenpohl, "A Contrarian Approach to Graphic Design Education," *GDEA Proceedings 1990,* Graphic Design Education Association.
13. Buchanan, "Design as a New Liberal Art," 15–16.
14. Richard Buchanan, "Declaration by Design: Rhetoric, Argument, and Demonstration in Design Practice," *Design Discourse, History, Theory, Criticism,* ed. Victor Margolin (Chicago: University of Chicago Press, 1989), 91–109.
15. Buchanan, "Declaration by Design," 93.
16. Mark Salmon and Glenn Gritzer, "Parallel Content: Social Sciences and the Design Curriculum." *Design Issues* (Fall 1992).
17. Charles Bailey, *Beyond the Present and Particular: A Theory of Liberal Education* (London: Routledge & Kegan Paul, 1984), 114.
18. Margolin, "Design Studies and the Graphic Designer," 73.
19. It is said that, shortly after Einstein published his theory, Sir Arthur Stanley Eddington was asked it if were true that only three people really understood relativity and that he was one of them; he replied that he couldn't think who the third person might be. See Stephen Hawking, *A Brief History of Time,* (New York: Bantam Books, 1988), 167–168.
20. Hawking, *A Brief history of Time,* 174–175.
21. Hawking, *A Brief History of Time,* 175.

BUILDING BRIDGES: A RESEARCH AGENDA FOR EDUCATION AND PRACTICE

Andrew Blauvelt and Meredith Davis

It is difficult, if not impossible, to imagine a program of graphic design education that is not in service to current definitions of professional practice. After all, what purpose does the education of a graphic designer serve without the presumed need to practice what has been learned? The assumption has always been that the field "demands" and schools "supply" according to the prevailing definition of professional practice.

But if we place common sense aside for the moment, can we imagine what the education of a graphic designer might encompass, particularly for graduate study and as we approach a new century? We contend that it is important for the field of graphic design to assess its relationship to education through a mental uncoupling of the theory/practice (i.e., school/work, thinking/doing) model that currently exists by critically reappraising the role of graduate studies in the field. We define the field of graphic design in the broadest, most inclusive sense, as involving a variety of activities: professional practice, teaching, criticism, and research, among other things.

We advocate the development of an expanded research agenda that connects the activities of graduate study with practice and that anticipates the demands of the field. The added dimension of a research culture for the field seems timely in the wake of major changes in and challenges for the practice of graphic design.

THE CHANGING PROFILE OF GRADUATE STUDENTS

Formal programs in graphic design education began in theUnited States shortly after World War II and borrowed heavily from European curricular models and modernist design theories. These programs served the burgeoning design needs of a post-war commodity culture (i.e., the design and promotion of new consumer goods and services). Graduate education in graphic design was created largely to cater to the graphic design interests of students whose previous study was in other disciplines. Only recently do we find students with undergraduate degrees in graphic design, or with comparable professional practice experience, applying to master's degree programs in graphic design. Today, it is common to find a significant number of students with undergraduate degrees in graphic design continuing their study at the master's level, the acknowledged terminal degree in the discipline. Given this circumstance, what can we expect graduate education to give these students and what contributions can they make to the field that are not attainable through undergraduate study?

THE CHANGING TECHNOLOGICAL SCENE

Not only has the typical educational profile of potential graduate students changed, so has the professional practice of graphic design. Now faced with a future made uncertain by its demystification—which devalues technical skill by making design available to anyone with a personal computer—graphic design places its hopes on the world of electronic media, the very source of its current professional decline. As graphic designers scramble to secure their places in the cross-disciplinary practices of multimedia and interactive design, questions arise about the organizing principle of a design education when technical skills and knowledge become available outside professional education.

Along with increased public access to the technical means of visual message production and distribution come changes in the nature of information and its interpretation. The concepts of "writing" and "publishing" take on new meaning as the relationships between source, message, and audience are redefined through electronic technology. The assumptions about human cognition and mass communication upon which graphic design decisions were based have been challenged by audiences raised in a reconfigured, highly experiential information environment. At the same time, information is produced faster and faster, outpacing our ability to model it and audience capacity to use it, spawning design concepts such as "visualization" and "information management."

THE CHANGING SOCIAL CLIMATE

The social backdrop against which graphic design has operated is also different from the past. Largely because of the cultural consciousness engendered by the successive social movements of the 1960s and 1970s (e.g., civil rights, feminism, gay and lesbian rights, nationalism, and so on), the constitution of both graphic designers and audiences has changed. We have witnessed an influx of women into the field; this, along with an increasing ethnic diversity, has produced challenges to many of the premises of a white, male, European approach to design education and practice. Simultaneously, there have arisen an increasingly tailored approach to message construction and a narrowing of audience definition along cultural lines, challenging the simplistic models and outdated theories of communication based on reaching homogenous "masses" or "average" consumers,

How will design education respond to the erosion of its technical service function, fundamental shifts in the nature of information, and changing social constitution of designers and audiences? We believe graduate programs in graphic design must adapt to evolving definitions of professional practice and the shifting demographics of the field, with particular attention paid to developing bridges between theory and practice. We believe that developing a research culture for graphic design represents such a bridge and constitutes an agenda shared between academia and practice that is responsive to the challenges facing the field.

DEVELOPING A RESEARCH CULTURE FOR GRAPHIC DESIGN

What is research in graphic design? While many designers see design research in practice as limited to conducting marketing studies and informing themselves about their client's subject matter, the definitions are more confusing in the academy.

For the most part, the notion of graphic design research in college and university programs is the legacy of the discipline's basis in the visual arts. Graphic design's historic residence in art departments shapes the kind of research that has been encouraged for professors and graduate students. We usually equate such design research, often referred to simply as "art," with visual experimentation without a client, but not necessarily without an audience. This type of research is useful for professional practice mainly as stylistic fodder to enlarge the range of acceptable forms, or it is dismissed because its research findings are not measurable in an empirical sense, explainable in linguistic terms, or exportable in practical applications.

A second, more recent area of design research concerns the development of bodies of knowledge. Known variously as "scholarly" or "theoretical" research, it is most clearly identified with academia for obvious reasons. Historical research in graphic design serves professional practice by legitimizing its current definition through a representation of the past that progresses toward and confirms the present. The unearthing of history also expands the range of visual forms available to certain designers, who de- and recontextualize these forms for present-day applications. Analytical research in graphic design attempts to define broad conceptual frameworks for message creation, production, distribution, and consumption. Such research influences the field by revealing and critiquing the implicit values and theoretical assumptions in these frameworks and the outcomes of their adoption.

A third area of research is more typical of other design disciplines, such as industrial design, and is pragmatically driven and contextually specific. It is action-oriented and often involves a case study of specific design problems. One developing subset of this type of research in graphic design involves the communication problems associated with electronic information displays and their human users: tackling problems such as navigating through multimedia presentation programs, facilitating people's use of programmed options, or the integrating of motion and sound into audiovisual environments of computer displays, for example.

Because the discovery of new knowledge is the founding principle of graduate studies in other disciplines, as well as the basis for the awarding of an advanced degree, it is important to develop initiatives for all of the aforementioned types of research. For us, the role of graduate education is particularly suited to such an endeavor, using the educational and job experiences of potential students without presenting graduate education as solely the refinement of technical and formal skills, which we consider the basis of undergraduate education.

DEVELOPING ANTICIPATORY CURRICULA FOR GRADUATE EDUCATION

Graduate curricula in graphic design are decidedly responsive to current definitions of professional practice. We advocate that, as graduate studies grow to include research, design education can take on an anticipatory role—one that might predict emerging practices rather than reflect the current state of the field.

In conjunction with the development of a research culture, we foresee changes in the pedagogical strategies and theoretical premises of graduate programs. The shifting nature of our social and cultural landscape, as reflected in both designers and audiences, demands a more responsive approach in how we foster the critical-thinking skills that a research climate requires. A critical, pedagogical strategy that emphasizes alternative approaches to conventional problem-solving paradigms would include both problem-seeking initiatives and problem-posing inquiries. In this way, we could foster many well-formed questions and myriad contingent solutions rather than the singularity of answers found in so much problem-solving.

A crucial element of critical pedagogy is the recognition, not the dismissal, of students' social experiences and cultural affiliations, which serve as lenses through which they experience the world and are a reflection of the audiences we attempt to reach. This awareness means the classroom represents the intersection of different voices, many of which are absent from most programs and educational philosophies, as well as from many successful design offices.

THE INTEGRATION OF INTERDISCIPLINARY ACTIVITIES

The teaching of graphic design focuses increasingly on collaborative efforts, a phenomenon that reflects the scale of contemporary problems, the reality of design offices, and the nature of projects that require expertise outside graphic design for their resolution. The spread of technical graphic design knowledge beyond the profession necessitates a shift in the function of designers.

The professionalization of the field since midcentury effectively segregated the production of design, with the eventual splintering of tasks into conceptual development, visual direction, and technical production. The advent of desktop publishing fostered the reintegration of tasks (whether for better or worse), collapsing the distinct activities of designer, typesetter, and printer. The ability of the digital environment to make fluid (through one machine) the activities of writing, designing, and publishing further blurs the boundaries. Thus, the synthesizing potential of the digital realm rejoins many previously discrete tasks, suggesting not only the problem of increased knowledge and skill, but also the potential for designers to entertain notions of authorship and entrepreneurial independence. Such demands for greater skill and knowledge will not be thought of as the burden and sole responsibility of the designer (a romanticized version of the "Renaissance Man"); instead, experience and knowledge will be gained through work and commu-nication with others outside our discipline while activities such as "creation," "production," and "distribution" become more fully integrated.

GRAPHIC DESIGN AS A CONTEXTUALLY BASED FIELD OF STUDY

Advanced studies in graphic design should examine graphic design in all modes of its existence. While most educational curricula focus on the creation and production of graphic design, we envision an expanded notion that encompasses distribution and audience reception in a cyclical mode of influence. This more holistic viewpoint aids all forms of research in graphic design. As the focus of graphic design itself expands, it comes in contact with ideas from other disciplines, fostering a demand for interdisciplinary study and knowledge. The use of theories and practices of other fields requires an integrative approach, interpreting and synthesizing ideas within the particularity and materiality of graphic design. The growing need for working relationships with other disciplines and for designers of different disciplines to collaborate on large-scale projects suggests a shift away from independent programs and schools of art to larger academic institutions with access to multidisciplinary libraries and diverse faculties. Schools will collaborate in large electronic networks that facilitate the sharing of resources, especially in an era of so-called downsizing.

As we approach the end of the twentieth century, graphic design education must reconsider the role of graduate studies. The likely outcome will be program specialization among schools reflecting diverse philosophical and research postures. Graduate education will provide a valuable component of research needed for the profession while contributing to the growing body of knowledge the discipline demands. The technological and sociological challenges that currently confront the field can be seen in a more positive light than has been suggested by the popular design press. To adopt this vision requires that we entertain notions previously ignored by the field that affect how we teach and practice graphic design into the next century.

Originally published in the AIGA Journal of Graphic Design, *Vol. 13, No. 1, 1995.*

REFLECTING ON A STONE
Philip C. Repp

My clenched hand inside my coat pocket discovers a smooth, rounded stone left there from my summer vacation to the shores of eastern Lake Superior. The beaches of Lake Superior are rocky and cobbled with billions of wave-worn stones, which are so plentiful that they soon become unremarkable to the eye. But months later, walking over the flat and gray-green Indiana landscape with its appliqué of utility poles, highway signage, and concrete interstates; the stone seems different. I rub it between my index finger and thumb. It feels comfortable—flat and smooth—the smoothness coming from caressing waves slowly polishing the stone. The stone strikes me as unique. I see a streak of feldspar and flecks of quartz reflected in the dull winter sunlight. I notice a small gouge that has been rendered smooth by the watery waves of time and wonder how many decades it took the lake to polish the silky stone. The small gouge—is that where the stone was attached to a bigger piece of granite? I remember giving little thought to the billions of stones while standing on a Lake Superior beach months ago, using them more for target practice against breaking waves than as a rosary prompting quiet reflections. Yet the stone from my coat pocket has become an unique object compelling examination. The single stone has become a metaphor for the power of a single thought. But to recognize

that isolated thought among billions of pulsating bits of information, a quiet must overtake
the mind. I realize that a pause for reflective silence is what design education is rapidly
leaving behind as we wrap ourselves with the informational and technological force that
is enclosing our profession. Design education has forgotten the ingredients of the learning
process and, most importantly, the vitality of a single thought when unfolding knowledge
and understanding.

To suggest what is missing, let me examine a portion from Alfred North Whitehead's *The Aims of Education*. Whitehead criticized "inert ideas"—those that become facts
which are unused or tested by the mind. Even during the 1920s he warned his readers, "not
to teach too many subjects," fearing that knowledge would become useless to the mind
if it were inundated with too much information. He believed that every student should
experience the "joy of discovery." Whitehead states:

> Culture is activity of thought, and receptiveness to beauty and humane feeling.
> Scraps of information have nothing to do with it. A merely well-informed man
> is the most useless bore on God's earth.[1]

Whitehead stated his premise decades before the "information age" of the late
twentieth century where the transferring of information bits is becoming a global industry
involving billions of dollars. We have taken to an extreme the Jeffersonian tradition of an
educated citizenry, in which one of the objectives was, "to give to every citizen the
information he needs for the transaction of his own." Thomas Jefferson never envisioned
the power of CNN.

Most institutions of higher education have had to wrestle with integrating the
processes of technological information exchange into their teaching programs. Phrases such
as "computer literacy" and "technologically competent" dance across the pages of
curriculum documents and memoranda, with little discussion or debate regarding their
impact on learning and the mind. The number of elective hours required for an undergraduate degree has gradually eroded to allow room for courses that will better enable
students to handle more information. We keep improving the tools in order to speed-up
our ability to process the information, then, conversely, add to the information we need
to transfer to our students as they process it faster. The complexity is enriched with each
step we take forward. A microcosm of technology's impact on higher education can be
found in design education. Let me digress to expand upon this point.

On my desk are two books of opposite points of discourse, *The Poetics of Space*, by
Gaston Bachelard, and *Design Management: The Handbook of Issues and Methods*, edited by
Mark Oakley. The former is an essay on the ethereal quality of imagined poetic space, while
the latter focuses on the pragmatic control of design decisionmaking. Well written and
clearly conceived, the Oakley book describes systems to control the flow of data in any
design scenario. Books of this genre help us to analyze and present data in diagrams and
charts, which reassemble the information into new sets of facts to investigate. Such
recapitulation makes our minds perform like the dull and constant whirl of machines with
constantly firing synapses. We have forgotten our genesis from a natural order where highs
and lows, pauses and starts, better describe our mode of processing information. Instead,
we try to mirror the machine, engaging in continuous factual review. In our rush to analyze
information, we seek to prepackage it in numerous shrink-wrapped units, losing in the

ingredients the diversity, richness, and uniqueness that the world has provided. As Bachelard states:

> One must be receptive, receptive to the image at the moment it appears; if there be a philosophy of poetry, it must appear and reappear through a significant verse, in total adherence to an isolated image; to be exact, in the very ecstasy of the newness of the image.[2]

Can we be receptive with so much information pounding at our senses?

I remember in graduate school reading and supporting the premise of an "electronic village"—information and technology would empower people, decentralize their decisionmaking, and make them more autonomous. Ideas that appeared noble to me fifteen years ago have, today, raised more questions than answers. I live the "electronic village" life. Daily, I engage in the process of acquiring information to make decisions. But not only do I need new information every day, but also the technology that helps me arrange my information changes too. Some information transactions require me to update myself by constantly reading manuals and software upgrade READ ME files. Likewise in the design profession, information and technology have exploded, resulting in manuals, codes, data, charts, graphs, and other technological displays. I don't think much about what I read anymore; I just apply it to my "database" and include it in my teaching and approach to design. Consequences of each design decision become unrelated among all my design projects. What applies to one project doesn't apply to the next. I have become like the computer that sits on my desk: a transferrer of bits of data with little thought to context and consequence. I no longer engage in reflective thought about my design decisions. Instead, I have become efficient and linear when handling thoughts, managing them as informational nodes along a pathway to an optimum solution. I wonder where all this started for design education and where we are going with this informational-processing paradigm?

I know where it started for me. When I was an undergraduate at Bowling Green State University in the early seventies, my studio professor showed the Charles Eames film, *Powers of Ten*. The multiple layering of information and the speed at which it described the mathematical concept of exponents was intoxicating. Eames felt that we could process large amounts of information through the correct visual display by using selective visual, auditory, and graphic redundancy. The film was short, but visually powerful and, for me, an introduction to the visual video montage that has made MTV famous. Eames and the author/architect George Nelson collaborated on a number of projects that involved the idea of information and its transfer. Through this collaboration they explored several ideas and projects. But most of these projects focused on how we see the world. Nelson, in an article published in *Interiors* during the 1960s entitled "The Enlargement of Vision," stated that an "atomistic" view of the world led to a static view of problems. He added that what was really needed was a more "dynamic" view. He wrote:

> The modern way of seeing things starts with the assumption of a dynamic rather than a static situation, and it proceeds from this assumption to a growing understanding that relationships can take us closer to the truth about things than the things themselves.[3]

Eames and Nelson are still my design idols. Their impact on the design profession has been profound and progressive. But, now in my fifteenth year of teaching, I begin to take exception to one of their ideas. The film, *Powers of Ten,* and the article, "The Enlargement of Vision," seem to promote the search for answers by adding to the complexity. In their view, the single notion or single idea, because of its simplicity, lacks meaning; more information is needed, and with more information comes the desire to process it faster; and somehow, by the amount of information collected and displayed, truth will be closer. The single object or thought, it seems, holds little insight into the world.

Designers are adding to the confusion. Density and complex layering appear to be the working concepts in design. Words are made illegible in video and printed materials under the pretense of postmodern typography. Designers justify the confusion as a response to the phenomena of social and cultural alienation and the need to develop a more personal design vocabulary that reaches across cultures. The designs of products and buildings are buried under program documents thick with issues of environmental sustainability, behavioral data, postoccupancy evaluations, and marketing studies that are to integrate the environment's and user's needs with the artifact created. The quality and power of a single thought is lost in the informational expansion we undertake in design. All we do is confuse the message, unable to probe beyond the surface of an idea or thought. In the age of globalness and thickly layered design messages, a response that listens to smallness and the single thought will be more in tune with what is needed.

Information and technology have their part in the design process, but we should remember to stop once in a while and listen to the movement of a single idea. I tell my students to listen to the stillness; maybe I'll have them turn off their computers and tap on keys while they press a smooth stone from the eastern shore of Lake Superior between their fingers.

Originally published in Design Issues, *Vol. 11, No. 3, Autumn 1995.*
Copyright 1995 by the Massachusetts Institute of Technology.

Notes

1. Alfred North Whitehead, ed. Rena Foy, "The Aims of Education," in *The World of Education* (New York: Macmillan Co., 1968), 58.

2. Gaston Bachelard, *The Poetics of Space* (Boston: Beacon Press, 1969), 1.

3. George Nelson, "The Enlargement of Vision," in *George Nelson: Problems of Design,* 4th ed. (New York: Whitney Library of Design, 1979), 67.

CHANGING
PARADIGMS

FACING UP TO THE REALITY OF CHANGE
Rob Dewey

Graphic design, as it is currently practiced, is an anachronism. Despite its pretensions to scholarship and professionalism, its structures and change mechanisms remain firmly rooted in its craft origins. The practice of graphic design has been dominated by modernist notions of rational problem solving and the search for objective, universal forms. Yet the basis of modernism has been undermined by large-scale social change which has resulted in uncertainty about our values and a loss of consensus, both real and imagined. We live in a complex, pluralistic society. Rather than homogeneity, there are now multiple and multicultural audiences which are often in conflict. The ideals and methods of modernism have been rejected by many of graphic design's visionaries, inciting the establishment to launch attacks on the new ideas. Like a spoiled child, graphic design has not come to terms with the realities it faces.

Graphic design is undergoing a crippling identity crisis, as evidenced by the pathetic hand wringing at design conferences and in publications such as this. Such forums have been dark places of late, full of fear and uncertainty about graphic design's role in our brave new world. Ironically, this crisis comes at just the time when graphic design has perhaps the most to offer society. The cultural and technological changes we have witnessed in the last decade offer unprecedented opportunities for those whose responsibility it is to connect message providers and consumers.

Graphic design's survival as a profession may rest on its ability to redefine itself in the eyes of its publics. But what should its new definition be? Should it focus on creativity or on contributions to client success? How can graphic design gain professional respectability without selling itself short? A broader definition of the discipline as a mediator of meaning, integrating all elements of the communication process, suggests a possible way out of the current malaise.

Graphic design shares special qualities with other creative disciplines. As a result, it does not fit into traditional models of discovery and knowledge. In *The Structure of Scientific Revolutions*, science philosopher Thomas Kuhn outlines an idealized model for professional activity. Through ongoing research and experimentation, scientists reveal new truths which are then disseminated through the community of professionals, leading eventually to a shift in the paradigm within which professional activity takes place. Change under this model is an inexorable trek towards an immutable truth.

According to sociologist Donald Schön, professionalism is based on "technical rationality," which he defines in his book *Educating the Reflective Practitioner* as the idea that "practitioners are instrumental problem solvers who select technical means best suited to particular purposes. Rigorous professional practitioners solve well-formed problems by applying theory and technique derived from systematic, preferably scientific knowledge." While many graphic designers have embraced these models as ideals, neither is wholly adequate for the particularities of the profession.

The problems to be solved in real-world design practice do not present themselves as well formed, but as messy, indeterminate situations. Moreover, graphic design is holistic in that it ideally involves the integration of rigorous analysis and creative intuition. In an attempt to position itself as a professional activity, however, graphic design has emphasized analysis over intuition, minimizing the importance of creativity for its own sake. An accomplice in this process has been our computer-based design, typesetting, and print production tools. The marketers of these products have led their customers to believe that with the right hardware and software, they too can produce well-designed documents in no time and at minimal cost. The value of graphic design has been diminished in the minds of many potential clients, and the profession has been unable to offer a meaningful response.

How could it, when it lacks even the most fundamental level of self-awareness? Graphic design's professional organizations are weak; they enrich the field through their activities, but are parochial in their scope, redundant in their programming, and unrepresentative of the field. It is estimated that there are as many as 250,000 professionals working in something that could be described as graphic design in the United States, yet the combined memberships of America's three largest design organizations is less than 13,000. In the United Kingdom, there are at least 30,000 graphic designers of whom approximately 2,000 are members of the leading professional body.

Graphic design lacks all but the most basic mechanisms for disseminating new ideas within its professional community. Little formal analytical, descriptive, or historical research is conducted, and there are few journals or other vehicles in which to make available what research does take place. Instead, new ideas are typically generated from experimentation and the development of a personal voice; they travel through the field primarily via professional publications, competitions, and, ultimately, style appropriation.

The trepidation underlying the current discourse about the fate of graphic design flies in the face of the new social context in which it is practiced. While some commentators have recognized this and challenged the profession to change, their prescriptions have lacked specificity and substance. But if we define graphic design as the mediation of meaning, we can look to several old and new sources of meaning to suggest a way out of the desert. I will suggest just a few: language, culture, complexity, and technology.

Perhaps the most thoroughly developed area of graphic design research is the application of literary and language theories such as rhetoric, deconstruction, phenomenology, hermeneutics, structuralism, and reception theory to visual communications. While this work has been published and debated, it is not widely understood. Scholars have long used these analytical tools, but their ideas have seldom escaped the cloistered confines of their own circles. As new and ethnically diverse audiences emerge and language changes in response to social pressures, these theories have much to offer graphic designers trying to address deep structures of meaning. In turn, designers who understand and use these tools have much to offer their clients.

Our awareness of the relationship between design and culture has been enhanced in recent years by the work of several thoughtful curators. Yet the fundamental connection between our material reality (of which the product of graphic design is such a large part) and the culture that shapes our identity has not been dealt with in professional practice except in the most superficial way: through the easy application of trendy visual forms to wholly inappropriate projects. If, as Ellen Lupton suggests, "there is no rigid boundary between private life and mass culture, personal memory and public record," then the graphic design profession occupies a privileged and responsible position which it has neither recognized nor attended to.

The sciences of complexity, such as information and chaos theory, also suggest new applications for graphic design. These areas of investigation were developed to help us to understand the nature of such complex systems as language, biological organisms, ecosystems, weather, communication networks, and human society. Once a system reaches a critical level of complexity, scientists have discovered, its description becomes more complicated than the system itself. Complex systems require a vast number of qualitatively distinct variables to describe their behavior. It has been shown, however, that some complex systems have an underlying simplicity whereby a few key variables largely determine the behavior of the system as a whole. Such ideas can help graphic designers to communicate complex messages, help their audiences to operate complex equipment, or their clients to manage complex organizations.

Another increasingly important source of meaning is technology. The most prevalent computer-human interface paradigm, on which the Apple Macintosh and Microsoft Windows operating systems are based, was developed more than twenty years ago at the Xerox Palo Alto Research Center. Hierarchical file management systems and windows, icons, and pointing devices are likely to be eclipsed by new tools and metaphors as the power of desktop computers increases. Voice recognition and synthesis, video teleconferencing, decentralized computing, wireless telecommunications, handwriting recognition, gesture recognition, media integration, intelligent agents, and virtual reality all offer intriguing new possibilities. But in spite of these advances, computer science and engineering are still driving the development of computer-human interfaces, which in almost every recent case suffer from poor design.

Rather than wallow in self-pity, graphic design must embrace the new world if it is to survive. While its history is central to its identity, the models of the past are no longer adequate. Educational institutions must broaden their curricula and become centers for research and new ideas. Professional organizations must prepare their members for the future by disseminating those ideas and not let themselves be ruled by a small, established elite. And designers must engage their clients on a more substantial level and educate them about graphic design's potential. The world has changed and graphic design, if it is not to become increasingly irrelevant, must change to keep pace.

Originally published in Eye, *No. 14, 1994.*

WHERE THE DEAR GOD LIVES
Robin Kinross

So everyone—real estate agents' secretaries, refugee-center information officers, technical writers in electronics multi-nationals, editors in sleepy publishing firms, subsidy-seeking dairy farmers, primary-school kids, and architects—now designs texts for multiplication, and sometimes even typefaces too. Everyone is their own PageMaker™, their own Fontographer™. Is there any place left for the professional typographer? Shouldn't we bow out gracefully, glad that the people are in charge of their own print and multimedia destiny?

In this brief discussion I want to shift the terms of the argument as it has developed over the past few years by raising some questions over just what it is that typographic designers have been doing. This may, I hope, provoke some embarrassment. But honest self-examination will help us to find ways forward, and I think that in the present great democratization of text and image production there are new roles for the professional typographer to play.

A glance at the history of Western typography reminds us that the profession of typographer has suffered an ill-defined, precarious, and brief life. The story starts properly only in the mid 1920s in Europe and the United States, when a few thoughtful and articulate practitioners began to try to bridge the gap that had opened between the old printing-trade workers and the new machines. Into this widening crevice, taste and style were dropping—and disappearing. The matter is usually put in aesthetic and visual terms, but at least half of this historical complex has to be understood otherwise: as an issue of human ambition, commercial and technical constraint, social struggle, and labor relations.

This process can be seen clearly in typeface design: a special domain within the larger field of typography. In sixteenth-century Europe, design and production of punches (the male forms that shaped the female matrices from which masculine type was then made) was undivided work. It lay entirely in the hands of punchcutters (all men, as far as we know). In this realm of the miniature image, drawing for production wasn't necessary or possible. Gradually, the making of type was brought into a larger system of manufacture by the type foundries. Then at the end of the nineteenth century with Linn Boyd Benton's invention of the pantographic punchcutting machine, typeface design was split off from production and routinized. The way was open for the "artist"—who could merely draw letters—to design typefaces. Production lay in the hands of technical managers and drawing-office functionaries. So although the artist-designer might supply a nicely finished set of letters inked on board, the translation of his desires—the final forms of the letters, and, crucially, the space around the letterform as it sat on its "body"—was then in the hands of the women (as they often were, certainly at Monotype in England) in the drawing office.

In the early to middle years of the twentieth century, this system resulted in some marvelous things. One thinks of typefaces such as the Akzidenz Grotesks from Berthold in Berlin; or Franklin Gothic and News Gothic from the American Type Founders company in Jersey City; Imprint and Plantin from the English Monotype Company; the Janson and Garamond typefaces made at the Stempel Foundry in Frankfurt. One can find authors for some of these great works: most notably, ATF's house-designer, Morris Fuller Benton— son of Linn Boyd Benton. But really they are company typefaces.

Meanwhile these companies were beginning to enter into more or less fraught dealings with artistic advisers and freelance designers. These designers drew the best they could and fired off pleading memos from the sidelines of production. But execution of their designs was out of their hands, and often they seem not to have quite understood, or were anyway out of sympathy with, the processes and ethos of the company drawing office. Notable among these frustrated men were Stanley Morison at Monotype in England and Jan van Krimpen at Enschedé in Holland. The Americans tended to be of more open-minded and robust disposition. The shining example here is W. A. Dwiggins, who was happy to engage in dialogue with the technical staff of the Mergenthaler Linotype company. Frederic Goudy, who started out as a simple artist, became "art adviser" to the Lanston Monotype company, and later resorted to making matrices and casting type himself.

Outside this rarified zone of typeface design, one could make the same sort of commentary for the typographic designer proper: the person who tried to design and coordinate whole pages of text and image. However precise their layouts (and often they were far from exact), final control lay in the hands of the compositor at the machine keyboard and in the hands of the men (few women entered these fumy, inky, light-industrial workshops) who made up the pages, ran the presses, guillotined the sheets, sewed and stuck them (yes, that work was reserved for nimble-fingered, ill-paid women). As with the typeface designers, I think one would also tell a rather sarcastic story of artist-designers trying to get their dreams turned into reality, hoping for the best in processes they didn't quite understand, with lots going wrong on the way, and saved—if the designer was lucky—by compositors and printers who, after long years of apprenticeship and induction into a literate and proud trade, really did know their business.

In the 1960s, this young and unstable system began to unravel. Here again there was a complex of factors at work: the end of metal typesetting and letterpress printing; the introduction of computers into the processes of text composition; the end of the post-1945 economic boom; the end of job securities: of wide economic margins and social quiescence. The details of typesetting, which the compositor had known sometimes just tacitly—the space around punctuation marks, where to break words, good form in a paragraph of unjustified text, how to make up columns of text, and so on and so on—now began rather dramatically to be exposed: by suddenly not being tended to. Typographers had always had these details decided for them by compositors. If a typographer had ever thought about this state of affairs, he or she had usually been glad that it was so. Only the more hardened and obsessed of them had tried to instruct compositors in this microdomain. But now text composition and printing began to be done by people without the old skills, and trade boundaries and protections began to collapse. Or this work was done by frustrated and fed-up old compositors on new machines and with new materials whose constraints had been determined by engineers ignorant of semantic detail: that rich web of meaning that it had been possible to create on a Monotype or Linotype machine. I am thinking here of things such as small capitals, nonlining numerals, ligatures, alternate dashes, and the diacriticals and nonstandard characters that are necessary for setting all the world's languages, except English.

The 1970s were in text composition, as in some other areas of human endeavor, a time of shame and despair. Certainly this was so in Britain. Books might be set in a single master typeface, ripped off by engineers from a mid-twentieth-century imitation of an eighteenth-century model, and justified without word breaks. One of these books I've kept for the record. It is called *Principles in Design,* and was published in 1979 in London by the Design Council.

Since the mid 1980s, this process of the dissolution and dispersal of production out of trade hands has intensified with the introduction of what we know as desktop publishing. The compositor is now almost extinct; the printer has become someone who runs presses to multiply from materials (discs, film) usually made elsewhere. But this pattern of drifting apart has its aspect of coming together too. Thanks to the invention of a common page-description language (PostScript), out of the ruins of the old printing trade there has come the chance for designers to take command of these processes, as they haven't been able to before. Or not since, perhaps, the sixteenth century in Europe. This is true of both the areas I have distinguished: the design of typefaces and of the overall configuration of text and image.

In the last ten years some designers—those that are honest and serious—have admitted that indeed we never did quite know all the skills and subtleties of the compositor. So we have to think, examine, and articulate these things to ourselves, to our desktop publishing programs, and, via templates and standard procedures, to the lay people with whom we may be collaborating. It would be a delusion to pretend that designers were ever in possession of some higher wisdom that was taken from us by technological development. And anyway, designers never really had much power. With computerization, the center of power moved from the printing trade to the designers of the software. But now, maybe, if we are lucky, these more primary designers, the software writers, will begin to realize the potential of their languages. Their problem is to resist the pressures to load applications with baffling, baroque excesses, and rather to design intelligent and intelligible features. Multiple Masters and TrueType GX have yet to prove themselves, but at least they are signs that we are truly over and out of the black hole of the 1970s and have a chance to enter new realms of sophistication and control.

We haven't reached these realms yet. Most of Latin-alphabet desktop-publishing humanity still does not know what an *fi* ligature is and why it might be good to have this little thing in text. This despite the fact that in taking care to search and replace ligatures there is only increased expenditure of time in production and no measurable gain for the reader. But the dot of an *i* is where the dear god is to be found. Small capitals and nonlining numerals remain a zone of confusion: look at how Canadian and British postcodes are typeset.

But then the setting of more than one line of text remains a dodgy business in all the desktop publishing programs I have encountered. The space between words and between letters, where words get broken: there is no program that does it well, as if by magic. Even the best-set preferences result in text that has then to be checked over by a thinking, literate human being. And then there is the work of making up columns of text into pages. Some printers used to know, but hardly ever articulated this notion, that it was good to enable columns either to run short or to extend by a line or two, in order to configure lines and paragraphs in ways that made the best sense: avoiding headings cut off from the text that follows; or avoiding a short line (the "widow") at the top of a page, which then looked more like a heading than the last line of a paragraph. You might think that all this is just the manners of another age and part of that dreaded "crystal goblet." I think it's more like basic visual syntax and semantics.

The realm of detail remains stubbornly out of reach of the theorizing and polemic that has surrounded recent typography. Ligatures and word-breaks can't be grasped by big, single-tack ideas about the death of the human subject, the end of grand narratives, the terrors of the Enlightenment, the tyrannies of Western metaphysics. Such details are just too small, too mundane, too material, too much just a matter of keyboard layouts and pixels. The kind of theory that matters for word-breaks is not poststructuralist semiotics, which hopes to describe pretty much everything in the universe, but rather what is useful here is the workaday grammar and etymology of a particular language. Where does it make sense to split words? According to sense or sound, or a bit of both? With some understanding of German, for example, you know why an *fl* ligature would be wrong in the word *Auflage,* and why it's good to break after *f,* or maybe, if pushed, between *a* and *g.*

One bad upshot of the craze for poststructuralist theory seems to be that we are getting classloads of postgraduate designers who might be well versed in Foucault, Barthes, and theories of discursive space, but who can't place a heading so that it belongs unambiguously to the text to which it refers or scale a picture when the scanner breaks down.

So there is still work for a typographer to do. It is modest work, but essential. This isn't a nostalgic view. "Golden ages" of printing lose their splendor when you come to ask just what was golden about those cramped workshops or those smudged pages. And I don't think that the troubled profession of the typographer ever really occupied the ground that some of us are now trying to lay claim to. It is rather that gaps have opened up to reveal ground that no one ever quite described before, which no one ever quite knew was there, and which it is important to try to be articulate about and to intervene in.

Originally published in the AIGA Journal of Graphic Design, *Vol. 12, No. 1, 1994.*

Some of the ideas here were prompted by an article by Paul Stiff, "Instructing the Printer: What Specification Tells About Typographic Designing," in Typography Papers, *No. 1, 1996 (pages 27–44), a publication from the Department of Typography, University of Reading, England.*

THE PLACE OF ORIGINALITY IN THE INFORMATION AGE
Paul Saffo

D oes technology extinguish creativity and originality, or does it expand them? The history of technology and creativity over the last few centuries suggests that the answer is less bleak than today's information-age fears might indicate. Our response to a given new technology typically repeats a pattern of initial resistance, followed by uneasy accommodation and eventual acquiescence. Ultimately, we achieve a seemingly irreversible integration of the new technology into our creative lives, as once-offensive tools become seamless extensions of artistic reach and creativity. Be it bulldozer, chain saw, or laser printer, each new technological threat has been tamed into a useful tool for creative expression.

Three centuries of mechanical innovations have insinuated themselves into virtually every corner of physical creative expression. We have made a reluctant peace with the artifacts of the industrial revolution. The machine has extended the power of the hand in precision and speed, making the scarce common and the dear cheap—often at great aesthetic cost, but also creating newer wonders never possible before. Could a scrivener's unaided hand have delivered to us the photo-mosaic of earth shot from space by the Apollo astronauts that so reshaped our 1960s consciousness and influenced the environmental movement?

Above all, the machine has created an astonishing abundance. We live in an age of profligate reproduction, a world of enabling, multiplying machines, their output exceeding the wildest dreams of nineteenth-century industrialists. The machine breakers of Lyons feared deprivation of wealth and security from loss of work and of expression from being reduced to mere machine tenders. But mechanization has been so complete that we no longer tend the spinning frames—they tend themselves. As it has always been with technological revolutions, the present danger is that we will be done in by the success of our inventions, creating more subtle and insidious forms of servitude than the machine breakers ever imagined.

The engines of profligate reproduction have also drastically altered our notions of creativity and originality. Technology has made precision in multiplication the province of the machine, forcing the essence of human creativity to retreat slowly from the hand to the head. The merits of this retreat are fertile grounds for debate. But the debate is also something of a red herring, for the most important issue of all may lie in an unexamined assumption that seems to be shared by technophile and technophobe alike: no matter how precise our machines become, the familiars of the industrial revolution will never invade the last sanctum of creativity, the human mind. This smug, industrial-age assumption is blinding us to more fundamental shifts in much the same way that fear over becoming machine tenders blinded our predecessors to the impact of technology on consumerism.

This time, the transforming agents are the microprocessor and the communications laser. These and the artifacts of the information revolution are not simply extending the means of profligate reproduction; something utterly new is afoot. The machine age of profligate reproduction is yielding to an information age of infinite recall. This shift will do more than redefine design. It will cut to the very heart of what we mean by "creativity" and "originality," and it will do so by invading the once-exclusive province of the mind.

Human culture has been shaped by a dance of two opposing forces: memory and forgetfulness. Memory gives us context while forgetfulness provides an opening for invention and originality. Successful creativity occurs when the two are balanced and originality is set within the larger context of tradition.

Memory was once the exclusive domain of the intellect. Homer and his contemporaries carried epic poems and culture in their heads. The result was captivating, but transmission was laborious and imperfect. On the bright side, the process conferred an imprecise patina to culture that itself encouraged and enabled further creativity. On the down side, though, the sum total of human knowledge that could be preserved was limited to what could be recalled from frail memory and stored in one human lifetime. Every information innovation since then has nibbled away at the margins of memory. In his *Phaedrus,* Plato expressed the fear that writing would make human memory lazy. In fact, the "memory arts" became the central tool of scholarship until well after the invention of the printing press, a response to the human need to deal with burgeoning paper-based information.

Gutenberg's invention of movable type in the mid 1400s triggered a newer revolution that extended and complexified human knowledge and thought yet further. But it, too, merely augmented memory, making the mind more important than ever. The advent of printing as a medium triggered a shift from the use of the mind as storage to the mind as processor of print-based information. These advances all enhanced creativity. Aided by the press and the book, the creative mental horizons of our ancestors grew by leaps and bounds.

Each of these information innovations also triggered fundamental shifts in cultural world views. Writing set us on a path of history. The formal memory arts led to a systematic though static medieval world view, while the press added a radical new Renaissance dynamism, setting us also firmly on the path of acknowledging individual originality and creativity. The press was the first industrial replication machine, with its pieces of type amounting to standardized parts centuries before the idea occurred to the captains of the industrial revolution. As a replication machine, it was also a star-making machine, for the notion of authorship barely existed before the multiplication of texts invented the audience. The book and its replication led to a cult of the individual and of individual originality unprecedented in human history.

Now we are on the verge of an information revolution that is so great as to amount to a difference in kind. A triad of information technologies—communications, processing, and memory—is reshaping both the real and the symbolic world. We are entering a hyperdynamic world of connections, relationships, and abstracting tools that help us make sense of the information flooding about us. Already, the dominant form of information storage in our society has ceased to be either the fragile and forgetful patterns of memory or yellowing paper and aging books. Today, more information is stored in digital form than in all the libraries of the world combined.

But this is much more than a memory revolution. We are in the earliest stages of creating in a world of infinite recall, where all can be stored and nothing can be forgotten, no matter how profound or banal. This digital shift to infinite recall will upset the apple cart of originality forever. For starters, the line between original and derivative works will blur as link-building information systems relentlessly identify the origins of ideas that perhaps the originator and creating designer had forgotten or never known. We may one day critique art the way the IRS conducts tax audits. What seems like luck, inspiration, and risky happenstance at the moment of creation could take on the aspect of plagiarism and fraud when viewed in perfect unblinking twenty-twenty digital hindsight.

Imagine clients routinely demanding an affidavit of originality from designers. Indeed, plagiarism itself could become a profoundly relative sin, differing only by degree from more venial derivations, and the causality of plagiarism might be determined more by happenstance and not by the original designer's intent.

Will the act of creativity be reduced to assembling old ideas like so much digital clip art, as the once-sustaining web of tradition becomes a suffocating blanket of electronic recall? In *Choruses from "The Rock,"* T. S. Eliot articulated a very modern fear: "Where is the wisdom we have lost in knowledge? / Where is the knowledge that we have lost in information?" To this we might add, "Will vast memory and infinite recall leave room for invention and creativity at all?" Of course, this coming world of infinite memory and recall is not without its advantages. Think of the fruits of creative labor lost when the library of Alexandria was torched in the seventh century by Muslim invaders, or when Spanish padres burned the Mayan codices in the 1600s. Even modest recall and reproduction can preserve ideas from the ravages of foolish contemporaries who would censor what their descendants may see.

Now, in an age of digital storage, duplication is so facile and storage so cheap that the notion of a single original will all but disappear. For, as the music industry has discovered to its alarm, digital technology makes each copy of every copy equal in quality to the initial master. Just as digital reproduction and replication extend rather than extinguish the original, I wonder if the coming new world of infinite recall will be more likely to extend and redefine originality than to eliminate it. "Origin" is defined as that from which anything derives its existence, source, or cause. The mechanical age, with its profligate replication and reproduction, turned origin into a point, leaving us with an obsessive illusion of individual creativity. And history became a pattern of multiple points of originality with patterns of copying and duplication fanning out from them.

This, however, is a myth. I think plagiarism has become so devilish an issue today because true, strict originality is vanishingly rare. We swim in a sea of culture, of memories old and new, and all our acts flow out in response to what we experience. In the coming age of infinite recall, I think we will rediscover a preindustrial fact: origin is not a point but a continuum, and the process of originality is much more linked than we imagine. For a world of infinite recall is a world of infinite unity, of deeply interconnected relationships. In this new world, originality is going to be recognized as an additive and transformative process, with multiple paths and forks along the way, as new and old divide and recombine in infinitely intriguing complexity. And this new understanding will lead us to realize that creativity and originality are much stranger and scarcer than we ever assumed, and much more precious than ever.

Eventually, we will look back on the closing half of this century and realize that we suffered from something of a cult of originality. And as the cult subsides, perhaps the litmus test of individual creativity will cease to be originality above all. Instead, the test will be passion—passion, surprise, and insight. The growing emphasis in the design industry on collaboration is evidence that the shift is already under way. We worry about working together today as a team. Perhaps we will come to value as well vertical collaborations with thinkers long dead and with visionaries yet unborn.

Of course, nothing is new. You can reach back to the caves of Lascaux or the century-long process of building a medieval cathedral to see this kind of multigenerational collaboration taking place. With luck, perhaps the deep interconnections revealed by the coming age of infinite recall will also turn back and recombine into a new power of vision that will help us bring sense and control to the existing industrial forces of infinite replication. That, I think, would be the most welcome and creative act of all.

This essay is based on a talk presented at the 1991 International Design Conference in Aspen, and was first published in the AIGA Journal of Graphic Design, Vol. 12, No. 1, 1994.

FROM ETERNITY TO HERE
Karrie Jacobs

The obvious topic for this talk is print versus electronic media. I imagine what I'm expected to discuss is the future of print, whether we will continue to have books, newspapers, maps, and money printed on paper or whether it will all be electronic.

In "The Man in the Clunky Helmet," a talk I gave in 1989, I offer a view of a world after paper, in which a virtual reality device allows the wearer to read electronic simulations of books in three-dimensional space. Here's how I described this device:

> The Bookman is a virtual reality suit—the helmet and gloves—now available at Uncle Steve's for $29.95. And what you see on the tiny TVs inside the helmet is something that looks just like a book. If you are reading, say, *The Catcher in the Rye,* what you see is a reproduction of the first edition, a very fifties-looking book, framed by a view of a fifties living room. Peek around the corner of a page and there's a starburst clock on the wall and an amoeboid coffee table in front of you. The edge of one of those scooped-out George Nelson Coconut chairs—the chair

you're sitting on—is visible on the periphery. To turn the page, you gesture with
the thumb of your data glove. In fact, this gesture of gloved hands is as commonplace in 2010 as the twentieth-century Walkman gesture, the drum solo, was back
when people still knew how to drum. In the twenty-first century all drumming
is virtual.

Already, in 1995, the man in the clunky helmet has become something of a fixture.
I have gone to trade shows, looked out across the sweeping landscape of the exhibition
hall, and seen dozens of people wearing these things—these high-tech blindfolds—looking
like models in some weird bondage magazine, swaying, ducking, or waving their arms in
response to unseen stimuli, reacting to the little pictures they see on the screens before
their eyes. I remember a businessman dressed in Brooks Brothers, his eyes obscured by a
headset, uninhibitedly acting out the part of the cue ball on an electronic pool table. There
he was, up on a raised platform, completely oblivious to the crowd that had gathered,
bumping and grinding like a dancer at a rave, high on ecstasy. This man's whole being was
truly immersed in some other reality.

I made a point of memorizing the scene. If twenty or thirty years from now I'm
interviewed for some oral history project about what things were like before the turn of
the century, I'll know what to tell them.

Of course, we all know that a headset is not really required for total immersion
in electronic space. Anyone who's spent an evening chatting on line will testify to the
gravitational pull of the flat screen. Anyone who designs or writes in front of a screen knows
how sucked in it's possible to be. At the same time, the immersion doesn't appear to be
determined by the content, but rather by the activity.

This is something that the people at Sega and Nintendo know well.

Content is, however, migrating to electronic media. Voyager publishes Shakespeare
and Gloria Steinem on floppy disk and CD-ROM. Many publishers have launched, or are
in the process of launching World Wide Web magazines. Still, the Web is more potential
than reality. Most of us don't have the right sort of connections to the Internet to reach
the Web, and our modems are way too slow to make surfing it any fun. If you've surfed
the net with a typical modem, you know what I mean. If not, imagine what flipping
through the channels with your remote control would be like if you had to wait a minute
or two for each channel to come up on screen. You would get so frustrated that you'd stop
surfing and watch something—maybe even the *MacNeil Lehrer Newshour*—all the way
through.

Although endless amounts of print have been dedicated to the new electronic
media, the salient point is that there is still print to dedicate. For now.

Having said all that, I'm not really interested in arguing print versus electronics.
I think there's a deeper issue.

I spent the better part of last year doing nothing but talking and thinking about
technology, and decided that the hardware isn't so important. What matters is the way we've
been influenced by the culture of computers. We've been seduced into thinking about
ideas—the intangible stuff that comprises our culture, our mental universe, our home-
grown organic virtual realities—as information. We've been seduced into thinking of ideas
as software.

We are making a mistake. It's a mistake we've made before. One we seem destined to make again and again. We are being defined by technology when we should be doing the defining.

There's an idea that is as crucial to people like you, designers—creators of intellectual property—as it is to people like me, writers—also creators of intellectual property. Our survival is not tied to our skills with a particular medium. Our survival does not hinge on our literacy in a given technology. It hinges on how much we value the work that we do. It hinges on whether we see ourselves as producers of information or as interpreters of information, whether we are smart enough to understand that information is our raw material, not our end product.

I believe that the deeper issue isn't print versus electronics, but long-term versus short-term. Or eternal knowledge versus ephemeral knowledge.

There's a theorem I'd like to put forth: as the speed of change accelerates, the value of newness diminishes. (Someone else will have to plot the curve. I don't have the right software.)

As the world around us becomes more virtual and less real, more transitory and less stable, the trick won't be knowing what's hot and what's new, it will be knowing what is of value. What's good. What's worth holding onto.

Let me read you a passage from a document called "A Magna Carta for the Knowledge Age":

> The dominant form of new knowledge in the Third Wave is perishable, transient, and customized: the right information, combined with the right software and presentation, at precisely the right time.

The paragraph continues:

> Unlike the mass knowledge of the Second Wave—public good knowledge that was useful to everyone because most people's information needs were standardized—Third Wave customized knowledge is by nature a private good.

New knowledge! Great. It sounds like a laundry detergent.

What they're saying here is that we're going from Timex to Swatch. Everyone gets a watch that expresses their very own personality. (More work for designers.) Except they're not talking about wristwatches. They're after big game.

"The Magna Carta for the Knowledge Age." You may recall that the original Magna Carta was issued in 1215 by King John, who had spent the better part of his reign losing battles. He lost Brittany and Normandy to the French. Then he was excommunicated by the Pope. By 1215 the barons, the feudal lords of Britain, had King John's back to the wall. It was as if his party had been trounced in the mid-term elections, but worse.

And so he issued the Magna Carta, which said that the king could not encroach on the privileges of the barons. The document also guaranteed the freedom of the church and afforded some rights to the king's subjects. The document has generally been regarded as a forerunner of democratic constitutions. However, it has also been argued that the Magna Carta was mostly about reinforcing the power of the feudal barons. So some people see the Magna Carta as the beginning of public-spirited government, and others see it as a declaration of the power of private enterprise.

Interpretation, you'll note, has a way of customizing public knowledge and turning it into private knowledge.

The authors of the new Magna Carta include Esther Dyson, the computer consultant whose mission in recent years has been wiring Eastern Europe; George Gilder, who, in the Reagan era, was the intellectual force behind trickle-down economics; and futurist Alvin Toffler.

It was issued by an organization called the Progress and Freedom Foundation, which is the futurist adjunct to Newt Gingrich's GoPac. You should know that in Toffler-speak, the First Wave is agriculturally based society, the Second Wave is industrial, and the Third Wave is . . . knowledge.

"The central event of the twentieth century is the overthrow of matter," begins the new Magna Carta. "In technology, economics, and the politics of nations, wealth—in the form of physical resources—has been losing value and significance. The powers of mind are everywhere ascendant over the brute force of things."

This, the authors announce, is the "Knowledge Age." Bureaucratic power and central governments are passé. The authors single out for immediate extinction those parts of government that regulate the cable and telephone industries. They also argue for the elimination of copyright and patent protections for intellectual property. Here they cite the cowboy poet of cyberspace, John Perry Barlow, who has suggested that authors, designers, and other creators be remunerated as actors or lecturers are, on a per performance basis.

In Barlow's words:

> One existing model for the future conveyance of intellectual property is real-time performance, a medium currently used only in theater, music, lectures, stand-up comedy, and pedagogy. I believe the concept of performance will expand to include most of the information economy, from multicasted soap operas to stock analysis. In these instances, commercial exchange will be more like ticket sales to a continuous show than the purchase of discrete bundles of that which is being shown.

I guess this means you collect a royalty every time someone clicks on your Web site. Or something. Such a system might also mean that somebody somewhere (or rather, some computer somewhere) keeps track of what each and every person reads, of what each and every person looks at.

Here's Barlow again:

> The other model, of course, is service. The entire professional class—doctors, lawyers, consultants, architects, etc.—are already being paid directly for their intellectual property. Who needs a copyright when you're on a retainer?

Barlow, before he became a traveling salesman for cyberspace, was a songwriter for the Grateful Dead. He may well have been on retainer. He might not have needed the nickels and dimes ASCAP brings in.

There's already a comparable situation. It's called work-for-hire. It's where you do creative work and your boss owns it. It's not a very innovative or utopian scheme.

In the "Knowledge Age," as envisioned in this document, knowledge itself has been devalued, downgraded into a commodity. Embedded in this Magna Carta is the idea that owners and builders of telecommunications systems—the John Malones and Rupert Murdochs of the world—should have even more power, and the creators of the intellectual property that will, presumably, be zipping around cyberspace should have even less.

That's my interpretation.

The new Magna Carta's argument seems to be that ownership of intellectual property is superfluous because such property will have the longevity of a fruit fly. The assumption seems to be that ideas take on the characteristics of the medium that conveys them: instantaneous, immediate, ephemeral.

God, remember when we used to think of paper as ephemeral? Well, as some guy once said, "the medium is the message."

But maybe it doesn't have to be.

Certainly the medium does a great deal to structure and shape the message. But it could be a mistake to allow the nature of a medium, the nature of a technology, to determine the nature of our culture, of our thoughts, of our beliefs.

Isn't it kind of fatalistic to assume that because print is the medium of lasting knowledge and electronics are the media of meaningless blips—of Trident gum commercials and interactive on-line Schnapps ads—and because we are moving inexorably, blindly toward electronic media, that our culture must consist of meaningless blips?

Have we ever considered the possibility that we don't have to be getting dumber?

After all, it's smart people who create the dumbness in the first place. These people are producers, directors, engineers, writers, and—of course—designers.

Then other smart people analyze the dumbness and pay homage to its brilliance. These people are critics.

Recently, a graduate student from Yale's graphic design program sent a draft of his thesis project for me to critique. The student, David Israel, wrote an excellent, coherent paper in defense of fragmented culture. I offer it as an example of a very smart defense of dumbness.

He begins the paper by proudly declaring, "I don't read books, I skim. Entirety is not of interest: a chapter, a sentence, a detail, someone else's highlighting are all of more importance."

Israel continues, "I thrive on fragments, half-finished thoughts, and important quotations. This strobe-effect universe is all that I have ever known, and I am happy."

He is discussing the habit of designers, artists, filmmakers, musicians, and even writers to make works that are essentially collages of elements from other works, other media, other disciplines, other eras. Recontexualized, as the theorists like to say, these bits and pieces take on new meaning. In this vein, Israel makes a strong case for channel surfing.

"My remote control has always been an integral part of the viewing experience," he writes.

In fact watching TV without the remote in hand is like being a passenger in a car whose destination I cannot imagine, a car out of my control. Through the genius of this palm-size appliance, a mere half-hour sitcom slot takes on the qualities of a nonlinear narrative art film, as scenes from the *Brady Bunch, The Jetsons, PM Magazine, An Afterschool Special,* and *Donahue* blend into one coherent

whole. Taking charge of our viewing experience, we have destroyed the linear
television narrative, leaving a viewing environment composed of fragments. The
viewer has evolved into editor, creating unique montages and juxtapositions
beyond the control of the television networks.

Israel's paper is fascinating and well stated. However, there is a flaw in his logic—
something troubling about the notion that one can construct a culture of fragments, of
ideas that are no bigger or more significant than dust motes.

Israel says he wants to use fragmentation in design that can actually look deep and
be deep. In that case he will have to wrestle with some issues that he didn't quite address
in his paper. He'll have to decide whether his fragments possess meaning of their own or
whether they derive meaning from some other source.

For instance, would channel surfing work if there weren't, at any given time, fifty
or more conventional narratives from which to steal a few seconds? Would a snippet of
the *Brady Bunch* have any significance at all if there wasn't a thirty-minute linear episode
(one of dozens in a series) behind it, if the *Brady Bunch* didn't have a history? Doesn't
meaning diminish as fragments are used over and over, as they are further and further
removed from their source?

And, by the way, if new knowledge is so perishable, how is it that the *Brady Bunch*
lives on and on? Does this mean that the *Brady Bunch* qualifies as old knowledge? If the
Brady Bunch refuses to go away, is anything truly ephemeral?

It seems to me that the only thing that allows fragments to be meaningful is that
they are pieces of something larger. Once upon a time someone constructed a narrative,
or lived a life, or created a symbol imbued with enough meaning that even the leftovers—
crumbs of imagery, crusts of catch phrases—have the ring of truth. Or at least of familiarity.

For there to be an X baseball cap, for example, there had to have been a Malcolm
X, both a real life and a Hollywood movie. The cap is a fragment, but its significance springs
from something substantial and whole.

The connections have to be there. A culture of fragments is like a city of mobile
homes. Not being rooted is fun until heavy weather hits.

We have global reach. We can fly anywhere. Go anywhere. Contact anyone. If we
do it via the Internet, we don't even have to pay long-distance telephone rates. Our reach
is infinite. Our grasp, however, is weak.

We have somehow engendered a situation in which everyone has a voice—on line
we are all authors—but no one pays much attention.

Everyone has a voice, but no one says anything particularly important.

Demassification. Fragmentation. It comes naturally, like entropy. Technologically,
it's easy. Whether computers are being used in the editing, design, and distribution of an
ink-and-paper publication, or whether a publication exists only in electronic form,
computers are the instruments of individualization. We get subscription copies of *Time*
magazine in which our very own names have been inserted into the ads. We can send our
measurements electronically to a pants factory and have jeans cut to fit us. We will, in the
near future, be able to configure our own newspapers and advertisements by using an
intelligent agent to scour the net for the things it knows we like.

These agents will learn by observing what we actually bother to read and give us
more of the same, limiting what we could possibly learn to what we already know.

I have a nightmare. It isn't one in which paper has given way to electronic media. Rather it is one in which everything I have contact with is tailored just to me. I imagine the intelligent agent as the Stepford Husband, the one who becomes more and more like me as time goes on, the one who gets better and better at catering to my needs.

I have a nightmare. It is that we are shrinking. We can have access to everything but we understand none of it. Our reach is infinite but everything slips through our fingers like sand, little tiny grains of sand.

So I ask, can eternal knowledge be carried by an ephemeral medium? That is to say, if we decide to value something, can we keep it, medium be damned?

What, for example, is more ephemeral than a dinner party? A group of people show up, they eat, they drink, they tell jokes, they go home. The whole thing lasts on average three or four hours. Once the dishes are washed, there is no trace that the thing has occurred. It is, as the new Magna Carta authors would say, perishable, transient, and customized.

I'm thinking of a specialized dinner party. I'm thinking of the Seder, the ceremonial dinner that marks the beginning of the Jewish holiday Passover.

Here's how it works. A group of people gather. Before dinner a story is told, that of the Exodus of the Jews from Egypt into Canaan—an event that may have occurred in the thirteenth century B.C.E., or more than three thousand years ago. The event was celebrated as a holiday, perhaps for the first time (I'm not a clever enough scholar of Hebrew history to be sure) some six hundred years later. Up until the destruction of the Second Temple in Jerusalem in 70 C.E. (or A.D., if you prefer), the Passover celebration revolved around the sacrifice of a lamb. After that time, without a temple, the sacrifice was no longer practical and something cleaner and more manageable was devised.

In Jabneh, a city on the Mediterranean where the Romans held Jewish prisoners who had surrendered to them, rabbis and scholars worked out a new ceremony. Writes one historian, "The order of the Passover eve (which in the course of time came to be popularly referred to as the Seder) was given a new image."

It was redesigned, so to speak.

I participated in a Seder a few weeks ago. It was a good one, led by a friend's father. Into the story of the Jews' flight from Egypt he inserted his experiences in the Spanish Civil War and his opinion of Newt Gingrich. During this Seder, I saw in the arrangement of symbolic objects on the table something at once quite familiar and disorientingly strange.

"How old is this ritual?" I wondered in the car on the way home. I looked it up. I was amazed to discover that the present form of the Seder has survived for almost two thousand years. And it made me wonder about what has happened to the human brain. Given the capacity we now have for storing information, what makes us think that new knowledge is fleeting knowledge? Why don't we believe that we are capable of creating ideas that will still be meaningful two thousand years hence? Who benefits from short-term thinking that appears and disappears without a trace?

I began thinking about how the Seder might have been invented. I imagined a meeting.

I picture Rabbi Gamaliel sitting at the head of a conference table with all the brightest first-century scholars gathered round.

"Sacrificing a lamb, now *that* was a ritual," says the rabbi. "That was something, but we can't do that anymore. The temple is gone. The Romans are everywhere. There's a diaspora in progress. People want something faster. Cleaner. More convenient. Yet, I think it should still be distinctive, elegant, timeless."

A scholar at the far end of the table held an object aloft.

"Yes, Yitzhak, what is it?" asked the rabbi.

"Rebbe, I have the solution. It is a bone from a lamb, a shank bone. It's smooth and white, with clean lines. Very modern. Very futuristic. *Very* second century. It is the essence of the lamb (the one whose blood was placed on the doors of the Jewish homes in Egypt so that the angel of death would pass over) without the lamb. Think of the lamb shank as a symbol, a logo."

Another scholar, Joshua, jumped up and said, "Rebbe, I think it is a mistake to use a lamb shank, which only serves to remind people of the sacrifice we no longer get to make. It's depressing. It's a downer. It'll turn people off of the whole ritual. I suggest making this roasted egg the focus of a new ceremony. How simple it is, but yet it's laden with meaning. Not only is it the sort of offering a pilgrim to Jerusalem might have made in the old days—so there's the nostalgia angle—but it's a symbol of resurrection. It's upbeat. It's about birth, not death. About regeneration."

Joshua continued breathlessly, "It is a springtime holiday after all. In fact, if you're not interested in using the egg concept, I'm going to shop it to the Christians who, I'm told, have brought in some people to brainstorm on the resurrection theme."

And so on.

The rabbi, being a wise leader—but a bad client—came up with a compromise: a Seder plate containing five different iconic objects. The shank bone and the egg, plus a mixture of apple and nuts (blended with a dash of Manischewitz) that symbolizes the mortar used by the Israelites to build for their Egyptian masters, some horseradish symbolizing the bitterness of slavery, and some greens, usually parsley, that are dipped in a bowl of salt water during the ceremony, a reminder of the tears of our ancestors.

We're talking about a ritual devised some 1,700 years ago to tell the story of something that occurred perhaps 1,400 years earlier. At the center of the ritual, at the center of the Seder table are a group of icons. Symbolic souvenirs of a journey made long ago.

A diagram of the plate is found in many Haggadahs, as the Passover prayer book is called. I bring all of this up because I marvel at how a body of knowledge, a story about events that took place very long ago, can travel across time. There is, in this, a certain amount of magic. And while the text, the written word is central to Judaism, I don't think the magic is in the Haggadah. I think it is in the ritual itself, which acts as a template. As long as the key elements are intact, other things can be freely added. Interpretations come and go.

I prefer to see it as evidence that if you value something enough, if you work hard enough to preserve it, you can use any medium to convey your meaning. A communion wafer. An egg, hard-boiled and roasted, or dyed pink and painted with polka dots. Even a sprig of parsley.

Religion, of course, is all about the preservation of knowledge over time. It is the opposite of technology. But I think it's important to understand that religion is also language, one way of describing how the world is made and how it works. Art is also such a language. So is design. So is technology.

When I started looking at diagrams of Seder plates they reminded me of something. But what? Then I realized that the use of symbols is like something I see every day.

Behold the desktop as represented on the little screen of a Sony personal digital assistant. It is a reminder of when we were slaves in a windowless office on the thirty-fifth floor, before we were led by—who was it, Stephen Jobs? Bill Gates? Jay Chiat?—to the land of milk, honey, and telecommuting. Here is the telephone icon, symbol of what was once our primary mode of communication with those at a distance, a reminder of how we once toiled with our voices. Here is the Rolodex icon, a reminder of the way we laboriously stored our telephone numbers, writing each one by hand. Here is the postcard icon, a reminder of the ink and paper greetings that pilgrims once sent to those they left behind. . . .

I don't think the issue is whether or not print will survive. It will, for some purposes, in certain forms. I think that there will still be readers who prefer books to screens. They may be marginalized, much like audiophiles who prefer LPs to CDs and hang on at the fringes of the music industry, patronizing their own specialty shops, reading their own magazines, posting on their own computer bulletin boards.

I think the issue is whether we define the media or whether we let it define us. So far the media is winning.

Knowledge isn't being customized. We are. We're learning to think in blips, to design in blips, to write in blips, to hunger for blips, to resent anything that isn't a blip.

We seem willing to accept the idea that, because electronic media makes it possible for everyone to be a publisher and, soon, a broadcaster, we don't need any shared sources of information, that there doesn't need to be a newspaper of record, a newscast of record, an official version. There will just be 250 million of us expressing ourselves. Or six billion of us.

We seem willing to accept the idea that all is ephemeral. It's understandable that people in the computer business believe that nothing lasts. In the world of electronics, rapid change is the only bankable currency. Obsolescence comes so fast that one could scarcely have time to plan it. Nothing is valid for more than a moment. However, this protean quality is generated by the technology and is an illusion valid only when you are playing by technology's rules.

Words and ideas—printed on paper, painted on canvas, embodied by a sprig of parsley—they can sit immobile and unchanged for an extraordinary period of time and still be fresh. Words and ideas have a very long shelf life.

And we cannot have a society without sharing certain documents and certain values. Not everything can be demassified. In a demassified society, one with no central government, no central documents, in which knowledge is a private good, everyone is marginalized. If everyone is an artist, no one is an artist. If everyone is a writer, no one is a writer. If everyone is a designer, no one is a designer. If all knowledge is customized, every audience is an audience of one.

There is a sentence in the penultimate paragraph of the new Magna Carta that says, "Next, of course, must come the creation of a new civilization, founded in the eternal truths of the American Idea." I thought it was a little odd coming from people who'd thrown out the concept of eternal truths—or eternal anything—five thousand words earlier.

But this new Magna Carta is basically a political document, about moving money and power—as well as knowledge—to the virtual world. It was issued by an organization with strong ties to Speaker of the House Gingrich, and it's agenda is the Right's agenda couched in New Age future speak.

On the other hand, a similar agenda comes from the Left, where anarchists, hackers, and nice counterculture organizations like the Whole Earth Foundation promote the idea of on-line utopia. A similar agenda also comes from Al Gore.

When so many disparate political voices agree on something, it must be good, right? I'm not so sure.

I just know that a lot of print publishers are taking their publications on-line because they don't want to be left out in the cold. They don't want to be left stranded in reality. Even Time Warner, with its sophisticated World Wide Web interface, winds up creating pale electronic imitations of real magazines because they don't spend the time to figure out what else they could do, or why they're there.

So the Net, and most particularly the Web, has become a dazzling theme park of highly disposable information products. What are all those publishers doing on line? They're practicing a self-fulfilling prophecy. They're helping to ensure a future in which new knowledge is perishable, transient, and customized. They are demonstrating that a culture obsessed with change can't make ideas that last.

Does it have to be that way?

Maybe. After all, most of our cultural output today—whatever the medium—is pretty ephemeral stuff.

I'd like to suggest, however, that if we learn to use the qualities of interactive electronic media to create works of substance, works that are visually and editorially rich, we might be able to use this most mercurial media to make things that last and are worth saving.

I'd also like to suggest that we move beyond the notion that absolutely everything has to be electronic. I'm hoping that once we get past the novelty stage—once we get past the idea that pointing and clicking is a satisfying form of interaction—our appetite for the new will be sated and we'll start thinking about what's good.

A talk originally given to the Chicago chapter of the AIGA in May 1995.

THE FUTURE OF THE BOOK AS
VIEWED FROM INSIDE A TORNADO
Timothy Barrett

The maelstrom of developments in the world of information access is as disorienting as it is exciting. Spinning in the middle of the vortex, like Dorothy and Toto, we aren't sure where we've been or where we're going. It's getting more and more difficult, amid the flying debris, to keep the traditional book and paper arts in our field of vision. In a recent PBS special on the future of libraries, Stephen Jobs, cofounder of Apple Computer, described a study comparing the efficiency of locomotion of different species.[1] The capabilities of various creatures were plotted on a graph of energy expended versus distance covered. "Human beings performed poorly compared to other species," says Jobs, "and the California condor beat them all. But in a related study published in *Scientific American*, data gathered on the capabilities of a human being on a bicycle put humans completely off the chart. "The computer," concludes Jobs, "is a bicycle for our minds."

It is not hard to appreciate what Jobs is suggesting. We barely get comfortable with our new state-of-the-art laptop and we're hearing about machines coming down the pike that have substantially improved capacity and performance. We promised ourselves that the speed and capacity of our present machine would keep us happy for a long time, but within weeks of its arrival, we become impatient with delays of only a few seconds or with the lack of space for new megabyte-hungry software. We lust after a new computer, and we can't help it.

We become enthralled by the concept of worldwide information access through the Internet and other commercial interactive systems coming on line. Even if we don't have time to use the information or a need for it to begin with, we love the idea of assorted libraries and databases at our fingertips. Like the home library of old, we confuse having access to the information with having the knowledge in our heads. Access isn't knowledge, but it is the next best thing, and the immediate and near-future possibilities are intoxicating.

If we make the crucial assumption that we won't destroy ourselves first by ignoring our place in the ecosystem, by a sudden manifestation of thermonuclear war, or by some other calamity initiated by humans, then the future of computers is open territory. Letting one's imagination run wild is a frighteningly safe way to go. From my own perspective, the wafer-thin, eight-and-one-half-by-eleven-inch, half-pound, cellular-modem, satellite-interfaced personal terminal is right around the corner. With it, information will become as available as daylight. Stretching a bit, I imagine three-dimensional holographic technology is not far behind, allowing live-action tableaus atop our wafer-thin readers. It is not a leap at all from there to life-size figures.

Where in the midst of all this are the traditional book and paper arts going to end up? Not an easy thing to call, but I'm going to make some predictions. First we have to remember that we are right in the middle of a tornado, which makes understanding what is happening around us difficult. But some things seem clear, and the more we understand about what is transpiring now, the more we can play a role in what happens next in the world of the book.

At this juncture in the discussion I propose to set aside the topic of artist's books. By their very definition, they can head in any imaginable direction, bounded by traditions and precedents only to the extent the artist wishes it. There is much fertile territory for artist's books in the future; the possibilities are without limit and most promising.

It seems clear that books and paper are losing their original role as information storage modules. As is readily apparent, computers do this much better. Cross indexing, "find" commands, and keyword search capabilities make possible quick retrieval of information from widely diverse and distant sources. Written financial bookkeeping (receipts and invoices) and printed currency are giving way to elegant computerized "money"-handling systems and electronic home-shopping capabilities.

But when it comes to the thing itself, *the information*, we will continue to want to hold *it* in hard copy form, to be assured of its existence, for a long time to come. This is partly because of a mistrust of the electronic media born of home computer crashes, dysfunctional automated tellers, urban power brownouts, and revelations about the brief lifespans of magnetic tape and disk media. But our uneasiness comes also from the fact that electronic information on the oxide surface of a disk or running down a fiber optic bundle or flying through the air is almost imaginary until it's captured and translated into letters on a screen or printed out on paper. We know this, we feel it in our bones, and no matter how elegant the computer becomes, for a long time we're going to want the assurance that we can press a button and get hard copy on paper at any time.

Human beings also know from experience that books are real, that they're instantly accessible, and that they last. Some last longer than others, but we have a simple basic trust in the traditional book "thing." Whatever cataclysmic event might halt access to our elegant information superhighway (major solar flare, nearby lightning bolt, or laptop fall from our desk), we know that in the midst of the resulting chaos, the old copy of *Huckleberry Finn* will still be on the shelf, fully accessible, ready for reading.

But why, other than mistrust of the electronic media, do so many people show an inclination toward the book? One reason is that unlike the electronic book, which is two dimensional if not dimensionless, the traditional book is three dimensional. So is paper. We tend to think of them as devices that carry information on a two-dimensional planar surface. But in our hands they are far from flat. We can feel them; we know by touch how far we are in the text. The paper makes a sound when the leaf is turned and accentuates our experience of the three-dimensional thing. Our entire world is three dimensional; one might speculate that the mind itself is probably a three-dimensional construct. We feel much more comfortable with a three-dimensional thing we can hold, manipulate, and read without any intervening device save a lamp and eyeglasses. Purely because of their user friendliness, books will continue to exist in their traditional form.

Finally, and perhaps most intriguing, the transition to storing most information in electronic form makes books and paper, quite suddenly, powerful icons. Without ever having thought about it before, we finally begin to appreciate what book and paper have meant to us. They are quickly losing their functional roles as purveyors of knowledge, power, and wealth, and gaining stature, in the same instant, as eerily powerful icons for the same things.

So where does this leave those of us who love books and paper, and, in particular, those of us who make books and are in the midst of teaching others to do the same? Is there really any future in it? My guess is that there is, and that it may be a comfortable one, if not a rich one.

A crucial question is at hand, one this generation of bookmakers should take time to consider carefully. Before the tornado overtakes the entire culture and electronic information surrounds us, we need to have a firm grasp on the essence of the book. What makes the book special, precious, worth preserving? This generation of bookmakers, readers, and booksellers is at the interface between the book as we know it and an entirely open-ended definition of "book" in the future. Those of us with bookmaking skills have the opportunity to help shape that future. The window of opportunity is small. If we blink our eyes, it may disappear, lost in the mad rush to adopt new electronic formats. The question deserves our full attention if we feel the book as we have known it embodies something worth preserving for future generations. To succeed, this generation of bookmakers needs to identify and make manifest the heart and soul of books as it has never been done before.

The essence of the book. What is it that we love about it? Why are we frightened by its possible demise? It is too easy to say there are as many responses to these questions as there are book lovers. What I am interested in are convictions about the essence of the book that we share *in common*. There will be different viewpoints, different perspectives, but I am convinced that there are truths about books we share that are well worth clarifying for ourselves and future generations.

Let me offer, as a point of departure, my own take on the essence of the book. I choose, for starters, the model of the manuscript or hand-printed book, that is to say, the pre-nineteenth-century book that has served as a model for all subsequent books, machine made or handmade. This model, I would argue, embodies the essence of the book of the past, but the points below are phrased in terms of what are likely, in my view, to be the most enduring and successful books of the future.

1. The thing will be handmade. There are many excuses for cutting corners or making hybrids that are partly handmade, but when we encounter an object that embodies and epitomizes what the book has meant through the majority of its existence, very likely it will have been made by hand. This is important, not so much as a matter of principle, or philosophy, but because the thing made by skilled talented hands exudes the presence of its makers in subtle but powerful ways. The ability to emit this presence, this authenticity more than any technical attributes is what makes the handmade thing unique and precious.

2. The materials used to make the thing will originate from natural materials and hand processing. Along with the hand assembly of the book, that is what gives the final thing its integrity, its connection with the earth and with life.

A few comments on items 1 and 2 before proceeding:

I am not advocating that the only way to make a real book is to produce a manuscript entirely by hand from materials manipulated from nature. But that is indeed square one. We move from there to the printing press, polymer plates, computer-generated type fonts, holographic watermarks, and a full range of twists on the book we cannot yet envision. All the while, however, we must note how far we are ranging from one-hundred percent hand work and natural materials manipulated toward machine-generated text or images and machine-made physical book components. The more we move toward the latter, the closer we get to an entirely machine-made object.

Books can and will take many forms, and should, and many book hybrids using the latest technology will be made for enthusiastic audiences. But the test of any classic future book icon is how well it expresses our humanity and our connection with nature and the cosmos around us. The first books did this elegantly and honestly. We can argue that our humanity is more and more defined by the machine and machine-made things, and less and less by hand work and our relationship with nature, and that we should welcome a machine-based identity and let go of the latter. We have no choice but to work with machines; our physical survival may depend on it. But the survival of our collective human soul, and our connection with nature and the cosmos, depends on our continuing to work our minds and our hands together with materials provided by nature.

Future books may look nothing like early manuscript books. But the best, most coveted ones will require a similar amount of time and skill to make, and they will be made from materials that have similar histories. The more we move toward machine-made books or book components, the less soul, the less authenticity a book will have. Perhaps more important, the less effectively it will serve as icon and mythological symbol of our past— a primary source of success, I predict, in books of the future.

3. Inventive design. The book will be visually attractive and pleasing to read or view (if text gives way to imagery). Its contents will be well designed and effectively rendered so the reader can partake of what the book has to offer. It will work well mechanically as it is used and carried or stored. User friendliness will be one of the most sought-after qualities in books of the future.

4. The book will be a tactile, three-dimensional experience as well as a reading or viewing experience.

5. It will contain valuable and important text or imagery. Some would reasonably argue that this should be the first item in our listing. On this point our future book reaffirms its old, traditional role as information-storage module.

Before the reader offers suggestions for how this listing should be changed, I should emphasize that what we are after is not so much strictures for what all future "true" books must be, but instead, reference points for what the essence of the book is or was or should be in the future. Variations on the theme are expected. All traditions were once innovations. The questions are: what is central about the book? what gives it life from generation to generation? what makes it timeless? The points above are a beginning.

Still, you are anxious to make changes. Good, fine. That's exactly the discussion I am after, but let us assume for the moment we are in agreement thus far, that these are useful working guidelines to pass on to future bookmakers. Then the questions are: who in the world is going to buy these books? and will there be enough of them to support people making a living at the book trades? That depends entirely on demand, and here is where the electronic information age becomes, ironically, the savior of the book rather than the destroyer.

For future generations, I predict traditional books will have a mythical almost talismanic quality in a culture gone fully holographic. A library filled with old books will become a cross between a museum and a church.[2] In this cultural atmosphere, I predict we will find future "commonplace" books stuffed in the pocket of the same person carrying around the wafer-thin satellite-connected computer. Onto its handmade pages, our counterparts in 2095 will set down favorite passages and ask their friends to sign their names, write messages, and make drawings.[3] Surrounded by their fully electronic world, they will leave marks by their hands alone, sans electronic interface, records of themselves that will have great value to the owners of the books.

I predict that the most elegant form of hard copy will be authentic hand-printed or hand-lettered text, not done often and only when the highest form of attention or honor is required. The literary press of old may reappear in university towns to print those items someone has decided deserve special attention. In the future, when people are honored by their peers, they will get not wrist television communicators or holographic wall plaques, but books or blank commonplace books or calligraphic works on handmade paper. In a fully electronic world, my guess is that the handmade book, pamphlet, letter, and image will become much more highly prized and respected than they are today. The argument that these things will cost too much to produce is valid only to the extent that they will have little value. I predict that they will have great value in the midst of a revolution second only to the Industrial Revolution.

Wishful thinking? Perhaps, but I think not.

Some contributors to the conversation will argue that, like it or not, the book will go the way of the radio and be overwhelmed by new media. Each new generation, they will point out, will become less and less familiar with the handmade book and less and less interested in it. In a sense, radio went through such a demise, overshadowed by MTV, film, and home videos. My father grew up listening to the radio with his family, but I grew up watching TV with mine and could have cared less about radio.

That is, until one Saturday evening when I bumped into "The Prairie Home Companion" on public radio and began listening. To my surprise, all my normal mental distractions began to fade as I was drawn more and more into the monologue by Garrison Keillor. I became totally absorbed by the images and feelings the man's voice brought forth. In large part due to the effect Keillor's show had on me, slowly but surely, radio has become one of the more important information and entertainment media in my life. And I know there are a great many TV-generation people who have had a similar experience.

Keillor, I would argue, has taken the time to know the essence of radio. He and his colleagues clearly understand what makes radio special, and every Saturday night they work it for all it is worth. We have to do with the book what Keillor has done with radio.

All this optimism may be way off the mark. It may be naive to suggest that far-future generations of young people, who have had no contact with books whatsoever, will have any interest in books, in any form. Indeed, the book may die off completely, and sooner than I think. But my guess is that human beings are going to continue to find that making things with their hands, from materials drawn from nature is somehow linked with their sense of what it means to be human, with how they fit into the cosmos at large. When future bookless generations realize the need to make such objects, I predict utilitarian, user-friendly, handmade book-like objects will be reinvented, if they do not persist tenaciously from here on out.

Originally published in Bookways, *No. 15 and 16, Summer 1995.*

Notes

1. *Memory and the Imagination: New Directions at the Library of Congress.* This is an excellent one-hour program produced by KQED in San Francisco.

2. The intriguing image of libraries becoming museums of books in the future was first suggested to me by Tom Taylor (the publisher of *Bookways*), but, as he has made clear in a recent letter, it is not a new idea; the Morgan Library in New York has explicitly modeled itself that way, almost since its inception.

3. Iowa City artist David Dunlap has been doing this with small books for many years as an ongoing project.

ADVERTISING: MOTHER OF GRAPHIC DESIGN
Steven Heller

The word "advertising," like "commercial art," makes graphic designers cringe. It signifies all that sophisticated contemporary graphic design, or rather visual communications, is not supposed to be. Advertising is the tool of capitalism, a con that persuades an unwitting public to consume and consume again. Graphic design, by contrast, is an aesthetic and philosophical pursuit that communicates ideas. Advertising is cultural exploitation that transforms creative expression into crass propaganda. Graphic design is a cultural force that incorporates parallel world views. Advertising is hypnotically invasive. Graphic design makes no such claim.

Although graphic design as we know it originated in the late nineteenth century as a tool of advertising, any association today with marketing, advertising, or capitalism deeply undermines the graphic designer's self-image. Graphic design history is an integral part of advertising history, yet in most accounts of graphic design's origins advertising is virtually denied, or hidden behind more benign words such as "publicity" and "promotion." This omission not only limits the discourse, but also misrepresents the facts. It is time for graphic design historians, and designers generally, to remove the elitist prejudices that have perpetuated a biased history.

In *Layout in Advertising* (Harper Brothers, 1928), William Addison Dwiggins, who coined the term "graphic designer" in 1922 to define his own diverse practices of book, type, lettering, and advertising design, wrote that, "for purposes of argument, 'advertising' means every conceivable printed means for selling anything." This suggests that advertising is the mother of almost all graphic design endeavor, except for books and certain journals. In fact, the majority of commercial artists from the turn of the century until fairly recently—from anonymous "sho card" renderers to celebrated affichites—were engaged in the service of advertising of one kind or another. Despite the common assertion that graphic design began with seventeenth-century Italian printing, modern graphic design is the result of the transition in the late nineteenth century from a product to a consumer culture. The move from producing (or bartering for) goods to buying mass-produced consumables created a need for printed advertising that quickly developed into a huge, dedicated industry.

Dwiggins' manual is not the only one to assert that graphic design was invented to put "an advertising project into graphic form." Jan Tschichold's *Die Neue Typographie*, also published in 1928, was a seminal handbook for the practitioners of *Gebrauchsgraphik*, or advertising art. This book and Tschichold's subsequent *Typographische Gestaltung* (1935), which became the basis of the modern canon, were focused not on some idealistic notion of visual communications in an aesthetic vacuum, but on dynamic new possibilities for advertising composition in an archaic and cluttered print environment. In *The Art Director at Work* (Hastings House, 1960), Arthur Hawkins, Jr., describes how such ideas influenced American advertising design: "As competitive pressure squeezed the innocence out of advertising, [art directors] became rougher and tougher. They were usually paste-up boys . . . who had picked up a certain facility with a 6B pencil. Somehow, they discovered *Gebrauchsgraphik* magazine and the Bauhaus School. Their future was paved with Futura."

By the 1920s, graphic design was synonymous with advertising design. In Germany, France, and Italy, agencies and consortia extolled the virtues of the well-designed advertising image. Lucian Bernhard and others associated with the Berliner Plakat group, under the management of printing salesman and advertising agent Ernst Growald, invented artful ways to identify and announce new products. Even the cultural avant-gardes—futurism, dada, surrealism—created design forms for advertising that expressed their particular visions and ideologies. Russian constructivism's most notable graphic achievements were advertisements for films and products. The productivists Alexander Rodchenko and Lasar El Lissitzky developed ways of composing typecase design elements on an advertising page that eventually influenced layout trends in capitalist nations. In Germany the Ring, a close-knit association of radically modern designers including Kurt Schwitters, Willi Baumeister, and Piet Zwart, attempted to sell to an expanding industrial clientele a "new advertising" based on the New Typography.

For the avant-garde, producing advertising for technologically progressive corporations, which incidentally often sponsored artistic innovation, was such a modern idea that they proudly referred to themselves as "artists for industry" or "advertising engineers." Since advertising was at once the medium of progressive graphic expression and a growing industry, many of the most influential graphic design trade journals of the late 1920s and 1930s had names with advertising in their titles: *De Reclame* (the Netherlands and Germany), *Reklama* (Russia), *Gebrauchsgraphik* (Germany), *Werbung* (Germany), *Publicité* (France), *Pubblicità d'Italia* (Italy), and *Advertising Arts* (United States). Even those trade magazines that focused on printing and other aspects of commercial art featured many articles on advertising.

ICONS OF PROGRESS

"Today it is difficult to recapture the intoxicating feeling of aesthetic possibility that once surrounded national advertising," writes Jackson Lears about the American experience of the 1920s (*Fables of Abundance,* Basic Books, 1995). "But for a while, especially during the early years of the courtship, it seemed to many artists as if advertising embodied exhilarating energy, rather than merely impoverishment of spirit." As the modern movements sought to redefine the place of art and the role of the artist in society, advertising was seen not only as a medium ripe for reform, but also as a platform on which the graphic symbols of reform could be paraded along with the product being sold. Within this scenario, layout (or craft) was replaced by graphic design as an artistic endeavour, the engine of *style.* Lears points out that during this period, advertising art "became detached from the product to which it referred. 'Advertising design' became a value in and of itself, without reference to the sales that design was intended to generate." Design still served, but was no longer a slave to copy-driven campaigns.

American advertising agencies gradually shifted their preference from "capitalist realism," or unambiguous if mythic representation, to surrealistic imagery that imbued the commodity with a fantastic aura. Refrigerators floating in space signified the abstract notion of progress as well as the fantasy of an ethereal, modern home. Industry became the totem of the American Century and advertising extolled its monumentality through modern and moderne graphic forms. As in the Soviet idealization of the industrial state, factories, smokestacks, and gigantic bearings and gears were heroicized as icons of progress. Advertising not only sold, but it also told a tale about America's aspirations.

American advertising had traditionally been dominated by hard-sell copy, and the shift in emphasis from words to art and design did not occur overnight. But it did change precipitously thanks to Earnest Elmo Calkins, founder of the Calkins & Holden advertising agency in New York. Calkins became interested in design reform in about 1908 and instituted his new ideas by engaging some of the most widely admired magazine illustrators, including James Montgomery Flagg and J. C. Lyendecker, to render ads for common products. Later he led the field in the introduction of modern art (cubism and futurism) into advertising. He wrote profusely in trade journals and design and poster annuals and was a frequent contributor to London's *Commercial Art* annual. In articles in general magazines, such as one titled "Beauty the New Business Tool" (*Atlantic Monthly,* August 1927), Calkins expounded on the need for dynamic new design to help communicate the marketing innovation that became known as programmed or forced obsolescence.

Calkins, whom Jackson Lears calls the "apostle of taste" and "corporate connoisseur of artifice," introduced the consumerist idea that all products—from coffee tins to automobiles—should regularly shed their surface styles as an inducement to consumers to toss out the old and purchase the new. This pseudoscience of style engineering—a kind of design-based behavior modification—forced American industrial design to shift from its quaint Victorian ornamentalism to machine-age modernism, and so encouraged the retooling of American industry. As Terry Smith states in *Making the Modern: Industry, Art, and Design in America* (University of Chicago Press, 1994), "Advertising's parentage of U.S.– type industrial design is traceable not only to their common economic purposes, but to the histories of the individuals who shaped the design profession. Most . . . spent the 1920s as advertising artist-illustrators. Joseph Sinel, John Vassos, Raymond Loewy, and Walter Dorwin Teague are the outstanding examples."

These pioneering practitioners are rarely cited in graphic design histories. Likewise Calkins, who is arguably the single most important figure in early twentieth-century American graphic design, makes no more than a few cameo appearances in such significant accounts as Philip B. Meggs's *A History of Graphic Design,* Richard Hollis's *Graphic Design: A Concise History,* and R. Roger Remington and Barbara J. Hodik's *Nine Pioneers in American Graphic Design.* Yet thanks to Calkins's promotion of European modern and modernistic design, along with his invention of the creative team of copywriter and designer, graphic design grew by leaps and bounds as a service to advertising in the late 1920s, prior to the Great Depression. During the 1930s it developed into a field with its own integrity, canon, and luminaries. Although Calkins did not invent contemporary design standards, he codified them and urged their adoption. Advertising design influenced modes of editorial and institutional design until World War II; afterwards editorial design surpassed advertising in originality.

GRAPHIC DESIGN AS ART

The 1950s saw the beginnings of a schism between graphic and advertising design. Modern graphic design veered from mass advertising towards corporate and institutional communications and evolved into a rarefied practice decidedly more sophisticated than advertising design of the same period. Some advertising artist/designers were celebrated for individual achievement, but as Terry Smith writes, "advertising designed primarily by an individual artist was becoming rare enough in the United States to be remarkable, exceptional, and expensive." Over time such advertising luminaries as did exist—E. McKnight Kauffer and A. M. Cassandre being the prime examples—were detached from the history of advertising and made into heroes of graphic design.

A kind of sociocultural stratification began to distinguish the advertising designer from the graphic designer. Today, a common view among advertising people is that graphic designers simply "do letterheads," while graphic designers scorn their advertising counterparts for being ignorant about type. Job or class distinctions have driven a wedge between graphic designers and advertising designers and graphic design history has perpetuated the schism. While cultural scholars, consumer theorists, and media critics have done considerable work on the social, political, and psychological role of advertising in American culture, their writings are rarely cited in graphic design literature, as if issues of consumerism and marketing have no bearing on the "art" of graphic design. This omission can be traced back to formal prejudices.

THE FORMALIST LENS

If advertising is the function, then graphic design is the form. As Dwiggins pointed out in *Layout in Advertising,* "The advertising piece is not an end-product; it is an intermediate step in a process. The end product of advertising is not [design]—it is sales." Yet selling is an ignored aspect of the story contemporary graphic design historians choose to tell—after all, graphic designers are not salespeople but form-givers, which is perceived as a more culturally significant activity than being a mere advertising huckster. The problem is that an advertisement must be analyzed as a collaborative endeavor involving considerably more than just its graphics. So to avoid having to admit that graphic design has a subordinate role, the historical discourse has built up around graphic design as a formal endeavor. As if in art history, graphic designs are removed from their contexts, placed on pedestals, and examined under the formalist lens. Like the annual design wysiwyg competitions in which work is judged entirely on how it looks, graphic design history more often than not focuses attention on style, manner, and structure rather than on the success or failure of a piece of work in the marketplace. The audience, which is rarely considered in formalist critiques of fine art, is likewise ignored in favor of aesthetic and sometimes philosophical or ideological considerations. This not only denies the public's role, but the client's as well.

In the first important historical text published in America, *A History of Graphic Design* (Van Nostrand Reinhold, second ed. 1992), Philip Meggs skirts the role of advertising. In his discussion of graphic languages in a chapter entitled "A New Language of Form," he writes: "A spirit of innovation was present in all the visual arts, ideas were in the air, and by the end of World War I, graphic designers, architects, and product designers were energetically challenging prevailing notions about form and function." Where in this litany does the advertising designer fit? In the chapter entitled "The Modern Movement in America," which should focus on the advertising designer, Meggs asserts, "graphic design in America during the 1920s and 1930s was dominated by traditional illustration. However, the modern approach slowly gained ground on several fronts: book design, editorial design for fashion and business magazines catering to the affluent, and promotional and corporate graphics." By subsuming advertising under the term "promotional graphics," Meggs presents an inaccurate picture of the forces that brought about modernism's ascendancy. In the chapter "The New York School," he further snubs advertising when introducing New York City, the advertising and publishing capital of America: "New York City assumed [the role of Paris] during the middle twentieth century. It may have been that these cultural incubators nurtured creativity because the prevailing climate enabled individuals to realize their potential. Or, the existing climate may have been a magnet that attracted individuals of great talent."

In Meggs' otherwise painstaking historical account, advertising is portrayed not as the mother of graphic design, but as a midwife. While scant attention is given to the economic forces that forged the practice, certain key individuals who were nurtured by advertising are highlighted. Thus discussion of advertising is used merely to push the great master narrative along until the individual emerges from the birth canal as a graphic designer.

The problem is not that advertising cannot be read from a formalist viewpoint, but that history demands that its function and outcome be equally scrutinized. This turns the focus away from graphic design, and in order to refocus attention on their discipline, graphic design historians tend to treat advertising simply as a matter of surface. For instance, when one of Alexey Brodovitch's advertisements for the New York department store Saks Fifth Avenue is put under the historical/critical microscope, we learn about the typeface, lettering, and illustration, but not about how it functioned as a piece of advertising in a newspaper. Does consideration of its function diminish its artistic—or graphic design— value? By referring to it as "advertising," does the work shrink in stature from a paradigmatic piece of graphics to kitsch?

In *Nine Pioneers in American Graphic Design* (MIT Press, 1989), R. Roger Remington and Barbara J. Hodik marginalize Brodovitch's early advertising design when they write that he "increasingly specialized in poster design between 1925 and 1930 and devoted himself to experimentation with new techniques with the goal of producing intelligible images through good graphics." The fact that the posters under discussion were advertisements is overshadowed by formalistic concerns in such statements as: "He learned how to simplify the subject through analysis of the Purist painters. His posters for Martini, now in the Museum of Modern Art in New York, are among the major products of this fruitful period." Nowhere do the authors acknowledge this work as advertising, even when they report that Brodovitch was invited to create a program in advertising design at the Philadelphia School of Industrial Design. With rare exceptions, when advertising is included in graphic design history, it is as an incidental part of the consideration of individuals and artifacts. In my own *Graphic Style: From Victorian to Postmodern* (Harry N. Abrams, 1988), the advertising artifact is treated merely as a vessel for style, not as a model from which to examine functional attributes.

Remington and Hodik do, however, take a step towards integrating advertising and graphic design in their selection of Charles Coiner, art director of the Philadelphia-based ad agency N. W. Ayer, as one of their pioneers. Coiner brought modernity to America's oldest advertising agency, introducing fine art to the repertoire and hiring some of America's leading graphic designers, such as Leo Lionni and Alexey Brodovitch, to conceive and style print ads. The authors give him full credit for his contribution to his firm's success: "Ayer clients received forty-one awards during the first nineteen years of exhibitions by art directors . . . Ayer pioneered the production of 'beautiful' ads through campaigns for Cannon Mills, Caterpillar Tractor, Climax Molybdenum, French Line, Marcus Jewelers, DeBeers Diamonds, and Capehart." Yet their text—the only contemporary study of this significant advertising pioneer (a profile appeared in *Portfolio* in 1950)—reads more as a list of achievements than an analysis of advertising's, and by extension Coiner's, role in the larger culture. Advertising is used as a backdrop to his endeavor rather than a lens through which consumer culture can be explored. Despite Coiner's inclusion, advertising remains marginalized.

Yet *Nine Pioneers* provides a key insight into how graphic design began to break from advertising during the war and how advertising designers emerged as creative forces afterwards. "During the war, very few goods were available for consumer purchase. Advertising had nothing to sell. When the war ended, the scene changed dramatically to a buyer's market. Designers finally had the opportunity to express their ideas in the spheres of advertising and communications." That wartime austerity offered other creative challenges to the advertising industry that were consequential to graphic design is conveniently overlooked.

Of the histories discussed here, only Richard Hollis's *Graphic Design: A Concise History* (Thames and Hudson, 1994) openly addresses the role of advertising. "In the 1930s, it had been art directors who had established graphic design, mainly in advertising and magazine layouts." Hollis concisely argues the importance of the "New Advertising"—the integrated design—and concept-driven campaigns of the late 1950s and 1960s. He focuses on the key art directors—Paul Rand and Gene Federico—and campaigns such as Doyle Dane Bernbach's for Volkswagen, explaining this work as important because it made the spectator active, not passive. But Hollis's brief discussion avoids the broader implications of advertising, focusing instead on iconoclasts who are soon positioned in his narrative as graphic design exemplars.

This is the inevitable paradox of graphic design history. Since advertising is marginalized, the few acknowledged advertising design leaders must somehow be presented as graphic design leaders.

For instance, the majority of work by Lou Dorfsman, the former art director of CBS Radio and Television, is institutional and trade advertising, through which he not only set new typographic standards, but also increased business. Although the success of his ads is sometimes cited anecdotally in references to his career, Dorfsman is usually presented as either a typographer or an art director, rarely as an advertising man. Likewise Herb Lubalin, the art director of Suddler & Hennesy before branching out into editorial and type design, is routinely discussed as a typographic pioneer who, incidentally, broke new ground in pharmaceutical advertising. Analyzing such figures' design as a milestone in the marriage of type and image avoids the stigma of it being advertising. Gene Federico and George Lois, both of whom owned ad agencies, are presented as creative forces who transcended the advertising field. Federico was a great typographer, Lois a brilliant art director, and, for the purposes of design history, they achieved their status in spite of their profession.

UNHEROIC ARTIFACTS

Graphic designers have distanced themselves from advertising in the same way that children put as much space as possible between themselves and their parents. And indeed, graphic design did develop its own characteristics. American advertising was originally copy-based and unresponsive to design, and though reformers like Calkins (and later Bill Bernbach) encouraged the seamless integration of words, pictures, and design, the copy, slogan, and jingle have been the driving forces. From the turn of the century, would-be journalists and novelists were recruited as copywriters, giving the field a certain *faux*-literary cast. Eventually, advertising developed its own stereotypical professionals, who even today are distinct from graphic design professionals.

The tilting of the scales towards the copy-driven "big idea" is one reason why advertising histories veer away from extensive analysis of graphic design. Another issue is quality as defined by the two fields—a great advertising campaign may not be exceptional graphic design, while a superb piece of graphic design may mask a poor advertising campaign. The history of advertising is more interested in how Marlboro cigarettes tested a variety of trade characters before stumbling on the Marlboro Man as a symbol of manliness. While graphic design appears negligible in the cultural analysis of this campaign, understanding the relationship of this symbol (which is graphic design in the broadest sense) to the larger mythology provides insight into how the American myth was perpetuated.

As important as this long-running campaign is (and not just as an example of politically incorrect thinking), it has never been analysed in graphic design history for its symbolic connotations. Although the Lucky Strike package designed by Raymond Loewy and the Eve Cigarette package designed by Herb Lubalin and Ernie Smith are featured as design artifacts, the advertising campaigns that sold the designs have been ignored. Graphic design historians are prudishly selective in what they discuss. They base decisions on ideal formal attributes—what is inherently interesting from a design perspective. They write as though consumerism is wicked—us (the canon) versus them (the mass) underscores graphic design history. Yet by eliminating advertising, design history loses rich insights into visual culture.

One of the touchstones of inclusion in graphic design histories is whether or not a work broke the stranglehold of commercial convention. Paul Rand's advertisements for Orbachs, for instance, have become part of the canon not because they were effective advertising, but because they assaulted antiquity. But this criterion is not the only way to read advertising design. Like some of the European modernists before him, Rand introduced principles of modern art into advertising, bringing the rarefied avant-garde to ordinary citizens. In *Advertising the American Dream: Making Way for Modernity, 1920–1940* (University of California, 1985), Roland Marchand describes the mainstreaming of the avant-garde as a significant marketing ploy that both introduced and made it frivolous. This important aspect of graphic design history can only be told if certain unheroic artifacts are included in the narrative. To refer to or reproduce only billboards, posters, and other aesthetically acceptable tokens of advertising is not enough.

In the 1930s, the distinction between advertising art and graphic design was virtually nonexistent. While typography was often written about as a separate aesthetic field, it was also addressed in terms of its function in advertising. Moreover, whether discussing a book jacket, record sleeve, poster, brochure, magazine, or any other form of graphic endeavor, the word "advertising" was not regarded as derisive.

Today, advertising is not totally ignored—many trade magazines cover it—but it is rarely integrated into the broader analysis of graphic design. While certain aspects of advertising—marketing, demographics, and other pseudosciences—are less important to graphic design history, considerably more consumerist theory, media criticism, and even perceptual psychology would be useful in understanding the form and function of graphic design through the advertising lens. Likewise aesthetic theories can be applied through the lens of design to put a visually bereft advertising history into clearer focus.

During the past decade there have been calls to develop new narratives and to readdress graphic design history through feminist, ethnic, racial, postcolonialist, post-structuralist, and numerous other politically correct perspectives. There are many ways to slice a pie, but before unveiling too many subtexts, it is perhaps first useful to reconcile a mother and her child.

Advertising and graphic design have more in common than even the postmodern trend for vernacularism (or the aestheticization of timeworn artifacts) reveals. Advertising and graphic design are equally concerned with selling, communicating, and entertaining. To appreciate one, the other is imperative. But more important, if graphic design history does not expand to include advertising and other related studies, it will ultimately succumb to the dead-end thinking that will be the inevitable consequence of being arrested in a state of continual adolescence.

Originally published in Eye, *No. 17, 1995.*

HOW LONG HAS THIS BEEN GOING ON?
HARPER'S BAZAAR, FUNNY FACE, AND THE CONSTRUCTION OF THE MODERNIST WOMAN
Susan Sellers

Suddenly we stopped using the word "bourgeois" . . . we were very interested
in houses and things: chairs, tables, silverware. We went to the Museum of Modern
Art to study furniture and displays of modern architecture, and bought our first
possessions—Eames chairs, a blond free-form sculptured Noguchi dining table,
and a Herman Miller couch day bed with a plain tweed-covered mattress and
bolsters, so modern, so different from the overstuffed tufted davenport at home.[1]
—Betty Friedan

In 1956, the same year Alexey Brodovitch retired as art director of *Harper's Bazaar,* Hollywood released *Funny Face,* a film musical depicting the intricate machinations of *Quality,* a fictionalized double of *Bazaar,* and its editor, art director, photographer, and star model. *Quality* is a magazine, in the words of its strident editor Maggie Prescott, "for the woman who isn't interested in fashion, the fashion magazine for the woman who *thinks.*" She imagines a new kind of literary household helpmate, one designed to elevate the woman reader from the drudgery of domestic chores and suburban isolation to the rarified pleasure of high taste and urbane culture.

For the design historian, *Funny Face* sheds an alternate light on a familiar story; the incorporation of Eurocentric modern design in *Harper's Bazaar* and the meaning of that incorporation in the context of a publication produced for women. In addition, *Funny Face* offers a prescient glimpse into the way in which the fashion magazine was understood in the mid 1950s as both a purveyor of fantasy and cultural capital and as a coercive medium, eight years before the release of Betty Friedan's *The Feminine Mystique.* In the opening passage, Friedan implies that in the late 1940s the modernization of domestic furnishing seemed to represent a structural reformation of domesticity. In a similar vein, the modernization of the fashion spread suggests a female consumer liberated from the overstuffed constraints of Victorian femininity. In deconstructing fashion images—that is in revealing those seamless images to be constructions—*Funny Face* seems to overturn those modern utopian ideals, replacing social reform with a more conservative vision of feminine destiny.

The film's thinly veiled caricatures illuminate *Bazaar's* creative troika: editor-in-chief, Mrs. Carmel Snow; photographer, Richard Avedon; and art director, Alexey Brodovitch. *Funny Face* depicts a highly mythicized design process dramatizing the complex negotiations that exist between producers and consumers of the modern fashion magazine, focusing on two distinct feminine characters: the hard-boiled, masculinized woman editor and the resistant woman consumer in the form of Audrey Hepburn, "the woman who isn't interested in fashion." In witnessing the transformation of Hepburn at the hands of the *Quality* design team, the film forces us to reconsider the effects of Brodovitch's visual innovations and the ultimate site of his modernist experimentation, the female body.

ALL EYES ON EUROPE

The primary plot of *Funny Face* centers on *Quality* editor-in-chief Maggie Prescott's orchestration of her newest model, Joe Stockton (Audrey Hepburn), and chief photographer Dick Avery (Fred Astaire as Richard Avedon). Avery discovers Stockton during a chance encounter in her dank workplace, the Embryo Concepts Bookshop in Greenwich Village, center of the Beat universe. An unexpected kiss from the presumptuous photographer draws the androgynous Joe to reveal her embryonic sexual identity in a cloying rendition of Gershwin's "How Long Has This Been Going On?" The scene prefigures Joe's transformation from "a thinker" and "a talker"—sheathed in black turtleneck and slacks, the masculinized uniform of the young beatnik—into Prescott's model of femininity, the *Quality* woman, drifting away in a brilliant white wedding gown in the closing shot.

As a budding intellectual, Joe scorns the fashion magazine as "an unrealistic attitude toward self-impression and economics," yet she is lured to model as the *Quality* woman with the promise of a trip to Paris and a meeting with her academic idol, the famed professor Emile Flostre, "father of empathicalism."[2] She accepts her compromised role as "a means to an end," though the ultimate result is not what she had anticipated. Although the voyage is invariably madcap, it yields several key revelations: Emile Flostre, the archetypal European aesthete, is a lecherous sham; her unacknowledged femininity has real power;

and her own intellectual pretensions mask her intuitive desire for conventional feminine rewards: beauty, love, and marriage.

On the most basic level, this neat formula falls in line with Hollywood's postwar imperatives to restore traditional values of home and hearth. This process turns on the privileging of intuition over rationalism, desire over knowledge. Metaphorically, it suggests the fate of European modernism which accepted the strictures of the nascent mass media "as a means to an end." It seemed inevitable that modernist graphic materialism assume its *natural* place in the product world of postwar America. Formal strategies such as surrealist defamiliarization and Bauhaus simplicity, functionalism and constructivist reflexivity—the foundations of graphic materialism—were wedded to industrial capitalism. Modern design found a life-partner in corporate capitalism, the union of commerce and culture.

Coming at the end of the tenure of Carmel Snow and Alexey Brodovitch at *Harper's Bazaar,* the film's rejection of European cultural superiority seems to close a curtain on a project thirty years in the making: the domestication of European modernism. Maggie Prescott's insatiable appetite for novelty apes Carmel Snow's dedication to the tenets of modernization. Prescott imagines herself a general leading faithful troops of hapless American women though the labyrinths of a (necessarily) European taste and culture. Snow noted that her readers followed *Bazaar* "because they are fascinated by the new (in styles, in photography, in art, in writing), because they are eager to train their taste, and because they depend on the editors to present the best in every field."[3] Prescott's mission—like Snow's—is not only to dress the women of the world, but to instruct them in the ideology of progress.

By the time of her retirement, Carmel Snow was an internationally recognized authority of sorts; a paradigm of the high fashion maven, equally at home in the salons of Paris and New York. *Life* included her image alongside other "headliners": Eleanor Roosevelt, Martha Graham, Georgia O'Keefe, Grandma Moses, and Claire Booth Luce.[4] But even as an assistant editor working her way up the ranks of the fashion industry, she was an early and ardent promoter of the budding aesthetic movements and contradictory avant-garde activities now gathered under the general heading of modernism.

It is important to emphasize that many forms of aesthetic modernization were prevalent by the time Carmel Snow adopted the mantel of European modernism in the name of *Harper's Bazaar* and "the well-dressed woman with the well-dressed mind." After the Paris *Exhibition des Arts Decoratifs et Industriels Modernes* in 1925, the terms "modern," "modernistic," and "modernist" were bandied about intermittently in the pages of prescriptive literature and home-furnishing magazines like *House Beautiful* and *House and Garden.*

Modernism often referred to the stylized forms derivative of modern art: i.e., cubism, futurism, etc. Its primary aim was the interpretation of chaotic reality, "lived Nature."[5] Startling incongruity was produced through the juxtaposition of heavy organic forms with wildly angular patterns capturing both angst and laughter. These stylistic attributes were apparent in illustrations by eminent artists like Erté and A. M. Cassandre, window displays by industrial designers Norman Bel Geddes and Raymond Loewy, and the interior decoration of large department stores.[6]

It was suggested by some editors that the modernist impulse was motivated by a surfeit of tradition, an unlikely ailment in the United States, a country with such a short history. The logic followed that a young nation was bound to be conservative, protecting and nurturing what little tradition it possessed. In 1933, *House and Garden* editor Richardson Wright noted the foreign nature of the modern movement:

> For over a decade the modern taste had been creeping into all lines of designing in America. It did not spring up here. It was imported from abroad. It has come from the faubourgs of Warsaw, Vienna, Berlin, Stockholm, and Milan, and gradually like a slow moving mist it has coated the taste of the people.[7]

Another writer, explicating "The 'New Simplicity' in Modern Typography," warned of the alien nature of modern style, "One of our greatest dangers is in copying too literally European typography," and went on to promote an American version of the new typography befitting American taste.[8]

The widely variable meanings and styles gathered under the rubric of modernism had, by the 1930s, been streamlined to refer to the work of the Bauhaus, Le Corbusier, and the International Style. Avant-garde strategies like defamiliarization were replaced by functionalism as the official expression of modernism in American intellectual circles, in part, through the efforts of cultural institutions like the Museum of Modern Art and through the writings of critics such as Philip Johnson and Henry Russel Hitchcock.[9]

As assistant to the editor at American *Vogue,* Carmel Snow was introduced to the modern aesthetic in graphic design by Russian-born art director Mehemed Fehmy Agha and photographer Edward Steichen. Agha, who emigrated from Berlin in 1928 with an invitation from Condé Nast, "was trained in the new European style of layouts, which was a complete departure from the static, stilted look of all American magazines at the time . . ." Snow recalled that "Dr. Agha wanted bigger photographs (vigorously supported by me and Steichen), more white space, and modern typography."[10]

In a 1930 issue of *Advertising Arts,* Agha recognized the fracture between the modern qualities in form and content when he queried: "What makes the magazine modern?" Agha was disheartened with the American attachment to a nationalist style embodied in Americana, typified by elaborate surfaces of figurative ornamentation drawn from an eclectic array of historical movements: "The change in women's fashion, in a direction precisely opposite to that which every self-respecting modernist would advise, is a terrible blow to the faith which was built on the creed of simple clothes—simple interiors—simple art—simple typography—etc." This disjuncture was apparent in the contradiction of developing a grammar of "eternal artistic units out of elementary and 'timely materials.'"[11]

Well-known for her competitive spirit—and presumably ready to top *Vogue* at its own game—Carmel Snow sought a new art director for *Bazaar* upon her appointment as editor-in-chief in 1934. After attending an exhibition of advertising art sponsored by the New York Art Director's Club and curated by Brodovitch, Snow wrote:

> I saw a fresh new concept of layout technique that struck me like a revelation: pages that "bled," beautifully cropped photographs, typography and design that was bold and arresting. Within ten minutes I had asked Brodovitch to have cocktails with me, and that evening I signed him to a provisional contract as art director.[12]

In hiring Brodovitch, Snow advanced the aesthetic ideals of a European-based modernist movement through the editorial, sartorial, typographic, and photographic forms of *Bazaar*. *Bazaar's* success and distinction in the vast marketplace of women's magazines were tied to its close association with the European fashion industry. Brodovitch would serve as Snow's conduit to the European avant-garde, felicitating the transformations she envisioned in both the magazine and its audience. For Brodovitch, *Harper's Bazaar* and models like Dovima—Snow's paradigmatic *Quality* woman and Avedon's "real" girl—would serve as the canvas for his formalist vision of the world as a montage of rhythms, sequences, light, and color.

THE REAL GIRL AS CANVAS

Four years before Carmel Snow "discovered" him, Brodovitch had sailed to New York to coordinate a "design laboratory" at the Pennsylvania Museum School of Industrial Art. Fundamental to the foundation of this program was Brodovitch's fascination with new forms and production techniques. He was particularly devoted to photography, which was to become his acknowledged contribution to the profession of graphic design and the development of the fashion magazine. Students report his favorite exhortation was "Astonish me!"—reportedly an affectation borrowed from Diaghilev—which fell in line with an aesthetic ideology more closely aligned with the surrealists than the Bauhaus. His article from the British journal *Commercial Art* (1930) entitled "What Pleases the Modern Man?" supports this assertion:

> Blinking lights of a city. The surface of the revolving phonograph record, the fantastic reflection of the red tail light and the tread of an automobile tyre on the wet pavement, the heroism and daring in the silhouette of an aeroplane. The rhythm of the biographical or statistical diagram. . . . In the monotony and drudgery of a work-a-day world, there is to be found new beauty and a new aesthetic.[13]

The tendency toward novelty and the fascination of defamiliarization that drove the modernist movement coincided perfectly with the capitalist need to expand markets. "Admitting it is odd that such a 'radical, eccentric art form should have been embraced by the most conservative element of the American community, i.e., business, the unassailable fact is,'" a 1944 *Newsweek* article confirmed, "'surrealism Pays' . . . its very weirdness seems to present a high potentiality for attracting attention."[14] The fashion magazine's devotion to the modernization of the domestic landscape—and the fashion industry's inexhaustible need to invest old products with new meanings—accommodated Brodovitch's fascination with visual innovation. Both functionalism and surrealism were aesthetic devices that could reinvest everyday images with intrigue and the mystique of high culture.

The contrasting nature of surrealism and functionalism would come to be an essential feature of the Brodovitch redesign of *Bazaar*. His typography tended toward the stark and unadorned, setting off vivid, often surprising, photographs. Before his arrival at *Bazaar,* text was paramount, the clothing represented through illustration. Words and pictures were not closely allied and the text was determined by a grid of symmetrical proportions reminiscent of traditional book design. Drawings and photographs were contained within the text area in conventional frames.

In contrast, a spread from the October 1934 issue, the first Brodovitch designed, foreshadowed the changes ahead. On the left-hand page is a photograph by the surrealist Man Ray. The elongated shape of the model leans dramatically to the right—most likely a distortion performed in the darkroom—its edge bears the trace of the camera aperture which mirrors the tilt of the silhouette. On the right-hand page, two skewed columns of text, a distortion of a traditional typographic grid, are set in a sans-serif font of different weights composed to mirror the photographic composition.

The extreme excess of white page and simple, asymmetric typography are emblematic of the Brodovitch style. By the early fifties he had eliminated almost all ornamentation and depended completely on typographic composition to express values of currency. White space was the key to graphic materialism. Its successful manipulation distinguished clear typographic hierarchy without the use of rules and bars vestigial of printing technology prior to the introduction of offset lithography. A focus on technical production and qualities inherent in materials purported to liberate the consumer from the deceptive facade of fashion. It was the typographic equivalent of the architectural theory that espoused open-plan design, exposed structure, and natural materials that projected a kind of formal "honesty."[15]

Brodovitch employed his powerful white space to counterpoint the full bleed photograph and facilitate a seamless, "cinematic" layout which flowed uninterrupted from page to page. The art director turned away from fashion illustration, long the staple of women's magazine, and like *Life,* adopted grainy black-and-white images to signify a kind of visual immediacy. Early photographs not only represented the featured sartorial accoutrement, but also often encapsulated a dreamlike narrative in a single frame. Carefully arranged sets and location photography set the stage for fantastic dramas. In later years, Brodovitch applied the same graphic principles to his art direction as his typography; the surrealism of the earlier issues increasingly gave way to a kind of photographic formalism. He reduced his models to formal abstractions. The Brodovitch image was as much about form/counterform, rhythm, and contrast as the Dior gown or the Chanel suit.

Of all his photographers, none captured his vision like Richard Avedon. Brodovitch described Richard Avedon's photographic panache as a "vacation from life," which was tremendously appealing to war-weary Americans.[16] Avedon's father had owned a women's shop, Avedon's Fifth Avenue. In his early work, he aimed to capture the carnivalesque glamour of the department store, just as he recreated his childhood world of the women's shop on his bedroom walls in a haze of clipped photographs by photographers such as Edward Steichen, George Hoyningen-Huene, and Martin Munkasci. His interest in capturing the invisible or aberrant has been characterized by historians of fashion photography as realistic in the tradition of Munkasci, a Hungarian sports-photographer who preceded him as chief photographer at *Bazaar.* Avedon had admired the flecked surface of Munkasci's images, the spontaneous texture of rhythm of color captured on film as if by accident.[17]

Avedon came to prominence photographing the collections of the most exclusive European designers, especially Christian Dior. "Dior's New Look," writes Lesley Jackson, "was reactionary and an anachronism, making women once more subservient to their clothes, but it caught the public imagination, seeming to promise women exhausted and depressed by the war everything they thought they wanted."[18] Avedon wrapped what was perceived as a regressive style of almost caricatured femininity and material excess in a new form of photography that emphasized color, movement, and carefree, incidental gesture in blurred or out-of-focus images. In this way, he managed "to suggest freedom and spontaneity even when [his] subject matter was corsetry."[19]

One of the most interesting of Avedon's techniques—often exploited by Brodovitch—was his use of the silhouette, the empty form waiting to be filled. The silhouette suggests a certain filmic identification, the form compels the reader to insert herself into the magazine narrative, to become the "Beautiful Individualist." Famous for his single-minded attachment to a particular model—Dorian Leigh, Suzy Parker, Dovima—Avedon cast his various fantasies on one woman at a time.[20] Each model became the consistent backdrop for a series of successive transformations. As Avedon was a key consultant to *Funny Face,* it is not surprising that the film focuses on a photographer's unyielding devotion to the transfiguration of his newest star.

In *Funny Face,* the photographer Avery rewrites Joe's body. Summoned to *Quality* headquarters by Prescott, Joe is assaulted by a bevy of stylists eager to reconstruct her fashionless façade. Repelled by the swarm of cosmeticians—and pursued by Prescott wielding a mammoth pair of shears—she escapes to Avery's darkroom where she finds the photographer in the process of enlarging her image: a detail captured in the background of a frame from the bookstore session. The ensuing sequence commences Joe's refiguration: from gamine to woman, from obscurity to stardom, from funny to classic, from seeing to seen.

Avery develops a large print that he lifts for Joe to behold. She is momentarily transfixed by her own transfiguration. Her face, small and nondescript, is covered by the exaggerated image Avery has fabricated. Through the *magic* of photography her face is transformed from funny to a thing of beauty. The scene concludes with her face framed in the easel under the bright white light of the enlarger. Her positive image has replaced the negative, as Avery's hand steadies her head.

Joe's face is just a trace of its original. Through the mystery of the photographic process, Avery has stripped the face of specificity. She becomes the raw material of "woman," on which an excessive femininity will be mapped through the *masquerade* of fashion. As with magazine art direction, it is not through the naturalistic, indexical aspect of photography that the manipulation takes place, but rather in its ability to be distorted, cropped, and changed. It is through the perversion of the object that the *Quality* woman is manufactured. Joe had castigated Avery for promoting superficiality—dismissing his pursuit of a "synthetic beauty at best"—but confronted with her new image, she is seduced by Avery's vision. In justifying her complicity in the plot as "a means to an end," Joe adopts the masquerade as a form of positive image, a method to employ the structures of advertising for her own devices.

Emptied of her specificity, Joe is ready to assume the litany of guises that constitute the magazine's construction of "womanliness." Joe's presumed masculinity is not so much erased, as coated with layer upon layer of assumed meanings. "Womanliness," notes film critic Mary Ann Doane:

> . . . could be assumed and worn, both to hide the possession of masculinity and to avert the reprisals expected if she was found to possess it—much as a thief will turn out his pockets and ask to be searched to prove that he has not stolen goods. The reader may now ask how I define womanliness or where I draw the line between genuine womanliness and the "masquerade." My suggestion is not,

however, that there is any such difference; whether radical or superficial, they are the same thing.[21]

The photoshoot sequence in *Funny Face* is segmented into metonymic melodramas encapsulated in ten brief scenarios on location for the *Quality Woman* collection. In these segments, Joe is transformed time and again into varying images of femininity. Avery's photo narratives evoke the Avedon women that "laughed, danced, skated, gamboled among herds of elephants, sang in the rain, ran breathless down the Champs-Elysées, smiled, and sipped cognac at café tables. . . ."[22] Each shot involves Joe's composition and inclusion in a mythic narrative contained within the film still. The process from real time (twenty-four frames per second) to still photograph to printed page is represented in a rapidly edited montage at the end of each story in which the captured image is frozen, reversed, separated into color plates, cropped, and framed.

In each brief segment Joe is *developed* and *fixed* by her photographer. Joe's femininity is formed through the eyes and apparatus of the photographer. Avery's development of Joe is more than a little self-serving; in classic Pygmalion fashion, he forms the object of his own desire. (Avery counters Joe's "means to an end" with "or perhaps a means to a beginning," implying their impending love affair.) Perhaps his fabrication of an un-ambiguously feminine Joe Stockton serves to assure the audience of Astaire's masculinity and unoccluded position as her Professor Higgins. The bifurcated structure in which an audience is both constructed and courted is central to the strategy of the fashion magazine that shapes readers to be the kind of women that read fashion magazines.

In this way, the film is ultimately self-reflexive. *Funny Face* is one media's explication of another, employing the magazine as a metaphor for its own formal structure. Thus the key characters of the fashion magazine—the art director, the editor, the photographer, and the model—illuminate the popular roles of the director, writer, cinematographer, and star. The film demonstrates the manner in which the magazine fantasy is constructed, and Hepburn is the canvas on which each narrative is painted.[23] Although masquerade is proffered as a form of resistance or "a means to an end," it is ultimately bound by the larger strictures of a mass-mediated femininity. Joe's transformation from obscurity to celebrity, which parallels the alchemic metamorphoses of the undiscovered actress into a movie star, is, in effect, the development of her exchange value.

THE ORGANIZATION WOMAN

While *Funny Face* foregrounds the more traditional love story developing between Avery and Stockton, it is Maggie Prescott who serves as the true sexual foil to the reluctant Joe Stockton. Prescott presents another image of femininity selected from the roster of masquerades available to women in the white collar world of the 1950s. She is representative of a distinct caste of highly paid, hard-working women who emerged in the nascent mass-market fashion industry in the early century and who were ridiculed as "the Brahmins of the ready-to-wear store world," and "lady buyers." "She laughs too much, she argues too readily. She's used to getting her way. She is Success."[24] In *Funny Face*, Prescott is clearly masculinized, linked to the sterile modernist office of the managerial landscape: a cool white, minimalist stage ringed with a series of identical doors marked by color. Her entrance is underscored by a drum tattoo. Her mission: to clothe the American Woman. Over an intercom she calls—with a bellowing "Now hear this!"—the *Quality* magazine staff, a brigade of homogeneous, nameless women, to order.

The troops emerge from the colored doors—which come to signify myriad packaged tropes manufactured at *Quality* magazine—to the tune of the *Light Cavalry Overture,* a succession of commodified fantasies, each a stereotype of the fashionable individual completely undistinguished from her workmates. The women speak in unison: "Oh no, Miss Prescott, you mustn't say that," just as the consumers of her magazine are expected to respond to her nationwide directives on the appropriate behavior for the fashionable set.

In a musical number, "Think Pink" performed by Prescott and a chorus of troopers, the narrative is frozen in a series of still photomontages evoking magazine spread layouts: advertisements for clothes, shoes, toothpaste, cars, modern art, film. The frozen images reflect the American graphic designer's fascination with mechanical techniques of the historical avant-garde,[25] such as montage and the stylistic applications of surrealism and modernism. It is the manifestation of Prescott's power disseminated through products and the artificial construction of difference. Prescott urges her readers to "Try pink shampoo." Her original idea ("to turn the whole world pink") is transformed into a commercial attraction.

Essentially, the location photoshoots, the darkroom scene (in which Avery makes Joe's face into the image of *Quality*), and the "Think Pink" number clarify the central question of the movie: how is femininity constructed through aesthetic device, in this case, modernist design? As Prescott elaborates this master narrative, she hands a small fetish of pink crinoline to each of the women circling her, each donning "the New Look" at *Quality,* the little pink suit. Prescott, on the other hand, prefers gray flannel. She is not subject to the vagaries of fashion; she creates them. She fabricates the spectacle of femininity, turning everything pink from the *Quality* TWA jet to her troopers' uniforms. When art director Dovitch—the film double of Brodovitch—questions: "But what about you?" she retorts, "I wouldn't be caught dead." Prescott is director of production; pink bags, pink toothpaste, pink shampoo are the indices of her control. The proliferation of *pink*—an obvious signifier for mass-mediated femininity—through everything from shoes to shampoo exposes the acculturation of an advertising campaign that markets that particular brand of femininity.

Avedon believed Carmel Snow unconsciously imagined herself "a dictator over women—a general, maybe."[26] Snow was frequently characterized as hard and uncompromising, a stickler for detail, for which she was loved, mocked, and despised. Perhaps the most frequent word used to describe Snow was "uncompromising" and yet the masculinization of Prescott reveals the sacrifices women like Snow made for a life outside the femininity they helped to manufacture. Avedon elaborated on Snow's tendency to view herself outside her sex:

> She made a strange slip of the tongue at the last collection we went to together.
> She talked through the collections, always out of the corner of her mouth, and
> sometimes she'd say, "now if I were a society woman, I'd choose that dress, or If
> I were a secretary, I'd take that." This time she said, "If I were a woman. . . ."[27]

Maggie Prescott is all exception, as was Snow presumably, in that as a woman, she controlled the production around her. "She was Success." She had authority in spheres that routinely excluded women: the office, the boardroom, the corporate headquarters.

Modernism was a man's game for the most part, reserved for the space of the city center, the factory floor, the efficient office. As corporations grew increasingly diversified and multinational, abstract modernism, the International Style, was adopted as the official corporate language. Writing in 1954, Russell Lynes attributes the spread of the modern in the corporate landscape to the failure of the program at the domestic level. Suburban men, he contends, did not take to the idea of their homes mimicking their offices:

> The modern house was unrelenting in its demands for an orderly life. . . . It seemed an unlikely place for a man to come home to, throw himself down, put his feet up and shut out the world of work and neighbors. . . . He insisted it was not for him and never would be. Modern was damned nonsense and he wanted no part of it, and neither (except in the kitchen) did his wife.[28]

Men preferred the solace of tradition after a hard day in the world of corporate modernism, and the wives were expected to play along.

But perhaps Lynes misread the wife's rejection of modernism and, in turn, this accounts for the success of Brodovitch's redesign of *Harper's Bazaar*. The wife, isolated in the suburbs, surrounded by the modernistic efficiency of her hygienic kitchen, could not have access to the cold rationality of the corporate office. *Bazaar* brought the visual language of museum and the boardroom into women's homes. Elegantly spare, white space shaped by sedate columns of Didot type and the svelte arms of an Eames chair, *Bazaar* bore the mark of "good design," showcasing modern products amidst the models. In relegating all advertising to the front and back sections of the magazine, Carmel Snow afforded women the luxury of negotiating their path through the magazine—their path to art and culture—without passing through the kitchen, the home, the suburb, or the representational worlds portrayed in the unrelenting advertising that had assailed readers in earlier decades.

Bazaar sold women "upward mobility" through the pleasure of knowledge rather than pecuniary advantage; it produced a kind of high cultural consumerism. Thus "the New Look" was interleaved with the words, images, and portraits of renowned novelists, painters, photographers, architects, dancers, and actors. "Carmel Snow's Paris Report" sat neatly between a short story by Carson McCullers and a photographic journey to José Luis Sert's modernist Piazza. The Little Black Dress was admirably ensconced between an essay by Aldous Huxley and an interview with curator of the Museum of Modern Art René d'Harnoncourt, not coincidentally, the architect of its "good design" agenda.

As fashion and marketing turn on the construction of difference, the shift from the suburban landscape to the environment of culture and art democratically advanced through the mass-cultural form of the magazine forged a devoted constituency. In 1933, *Bazaar's* advertisers had ranged from Budweiser (beer) to Heinz (tomato paste), Canon (towels) to Hachmacher (suits). By the early fifties, new advertisers were almost exclusively department stores and fashion accessories with the exception of a few discrete beauty items. *Bazaar* delivered a new consumer market forged from the "Career or Would-Be Career Woman,"[29] the emerging class of women disinterested in traditional notions of domesticity, who, like Betty Friedan, were suddenly "very interested in houses and things: chairs, tables, silverware."

In contrast to the scientific homemakers in streamlined kitchens of the 1910s and 1920s, *Bazaar's* women were abstract, cool, formal. The happy homemakers and the smiling wives were conspicuously absent in the pages of the magazine. Modernism represented women as connotative of elegance and cultural sophistication, outside the messy realities of everyday life. The modernist style was another representational layer laid over the framework of femininity. Industrial designer Raymond Loewy had defended the superficial quality of streamlining, asserting that the external shield "accomplishes something, and it becomes functional, the specific function being to eliminate confusion."[30] In this respect abstract modernism, or functionalism, shared that role. Just as streamlining had served to hide complex machinery inside its sleek casings, the rational, ordered surface of modernism smoothed over the confusing workings of a socially constructed femininity.

HOW LONG HAS THIS BEEN GOING ON?

The complex machinery of Joe Stockton's masculinized intellectual identity is neatly occluded under the abstract other of the "New Look." But Joe's initial rejection of Prescott's and Avery's advances gives us a hint of at least one form of resistance, that of the enlightened beat, savvy to the manipulation of the fashion machine. Prescott offers another vision of the masquerade: the woman resistant to the proffered models of womanhood in the 1950s, one who conquers the man's world of management and power.

Joe Stockton is not without motives when she finally gives way to Avery's proposal. The false consciousness of the *Quality Woman* is not entirely forced upon her: her acquiescence is more aptly an exchange. A trip to Paris seems a fair trade for "a few silly pictures." Tellingly, Joe is lured to femininity with the *promise* of authentic—European, masculine, intellectual—culture. As a caricatured young beat from the Village, she is drawn to the realm of *authentic* intellectual thought, necessarily European, and into the schemes of both Prescott (as sales tool) and Avery (as sexual object). Joe accepts the formulaic image of womanhood proffered through *Quality* in order to gain access to high culture, "the best that has been thought and said."[31] Ironically the film turns that notion on its head by exposing the intellectual culture of Joe's dreams as a sham and lionizing the common-sensical, folk truth associated with the spheres of marriage and unambiguous femininity.

Through her Faustian deal with *Quality* magazine, Joe penetrates the elite circles of Dior and Noguchi, but perhaps, more importantly, she comes to have insight into the aesthetic *production* of the fashion magazine and, so follows, the social production of femininity. In her complicity with *Quality,* one might argue, Joe attains a perspective on culture not so much in Matthew Arnold's sense but rather more in line with Raymond William's definition as a "particular way of life which expresses certain meanings and values not only in art and learning, but also in *institutions* and *ordinary behavior* [my italics]."[32]

This new perspective, however, does not save Joe from the wedding dress at the end of the film. She is unable to link her intimate knowledge of the fashion industry with her own gendered role. The film suggests a deep fulfillment at the level of traditional femininity; Joe gets the man in the end, not to mention a lovely new wardrobe. *Funny Face* suggests the complex relationship that existed between women and media in the mid fifties, a wary standoff that belies typical images of suburban bliss. As Joe was making her peace with American capitalism—throwing off the vaguely socialist ideals of her youth—the idealistic proponents of modernism were completing a similar pact. The intellectual and socially engaged utopianism of European modernism quietly disappeared as modernism and American capitalism marched down the aisle and set off on a honeymoon that would last the next thirty years.

Originally published in Visual Language, *Vol. 29, No. 1, 1995.*

Notes

1. Betty Friedan, in Susan Ware, *Modern Women: A Documentary History* (Chicago: Dorsey Press, 1989), 293.

2. Emile Flostre is an obvious parody of Jean-Paul Sartre while "empathicalism" stands in as depoliticized existentialism.

3. Carmel Snow and Mary Louise Aswell, *The World of Carmel Snow* (New York: McGraw Hill, 1962), 117.

4. *Life* magazine (December 1956).

5. Richardson Wright, "The Modernist Taste," *House & Garden* (October 1925): 77–79.

6. For a fascinating account of John Wanamaker and the development and uses of modern aesthetics in early department stores see William Leach's *Land of Desire* as well as Neil Harns's "Designs on Demand: Art and the Modern Corporation" in *Cultural Excursions: Marketing Appetites and Cultural Tastes in Modern America,* (Chicago: University of Chicago Press, 1992).

7. Richardson Wright, "Will Our Ancestors Shudder at Modernist Architecture?" in *House & Garden* (October 1933): 30.

8. Alice Beeson Ecke, "The 'New Simplicity' in Modern Typography" in *Advertising Arts* (July 9, 1930): 25–26. For an account of the role of *Advertising Arts* and other trade journals instrumental in the promotion of modernism in America see Lorraine Wild, "Europeans in America," *Graphic Design in America: A Visual Language History* (New York: Harry N. Abrams, Inc., 1989), 152–169.

9. Karen Davies, *At Home in Manhattan* (New Haven, Connecticut: Yale University Art Gallery, 1983), 12. For an account of the early institutional promotion of modern design, particularly in the decorative arts such as furniture design see "Promoting Modern Design," 83–101.

10. Andy Grundberg, *Brodovitch* (New York: Harry N. Abrams Inc., 1989), 67.

11. M. F. Agha, "What Makes a Magazine Modern?" *Advertising Arts* (October 13, 1930): 17.

12. Snow and Aswell, *The World of Carmel Snow,* 90.

13. Alexey Brodovitch, "What Pleases the Modern Man?" in *Commercial Art* (August 1930): 60.

14. "Surrealism Pays," in *Newsweek* 23, No. 56 (January 1944).

15. Modern designers seemed to overlook that their honest aesthetic might not be read as they intended. For instance, Russell Lynes critiques the excessive white space used in a contemporary DeBeers Diamond advertisement as the hypocritical expression of "understated quality," which was in fact ostentation, a sign of conspicuous waste. Russell Lynes, *The Tastemakers* (New York: Harper & Brothers, 1954), 294.

16. Nancy Hall-Duncan, *The History of Fashion Photography* (New York: International Museum of Photography/Alpine Book Company, 1979), 136.

17. Hall-Duncan, *The History of Fashion Photography,* 136–144.

18. Lesley Jackson, *The New Look: Design in the Fifties* (London: Thames and Hudson, 1991), 120.

19. Grundberg, *Brodovitch,* 84.

20. Winthrop Sargeant, "Profiles: Richard Avedon," *The New Yorker* (November 8, 1958): 64.

21. Mary Anne Doane. "Masquerade Reconsidered," *Femmes Fatales: Feminism, Film, Theory, Psychanalysis* (New York: Routledge, 1991), 34.

22. Sargeant, "Profiles: Richard Avedon," 49.

23. "[T]he face of Audrey Hepburn," remarked Roland Barthes in 1957, "is individualized, not only because of its peculiar thematics (woman as child, woman as kitten), but also because of her person, of an almost unique specification of the face. . . ." Roland Barthes, *Mythologies* (New York: Hill and Wang, 1957), 57.

24. William R. Leach, *Land of Desire from the Department Store to the Department of Congress: the Rise of America's Commercial Culture,* (New York: Pantheon Books, 1993), 312.

25. Peter Bürger, *Theory of the Avant-Garde* (Minneapolis: University of Minneapolis Press, 1984). The "historical avant-garde" specifies the term "avant-garde" as a moment and movement in the history of art rather than as an attribute connoting stylistic innovation.

26. Snow and Aswell, *The World of Carmel Snow,* 207–208.

27. Snow and Aswell, *The World of Carmel Snow,* 207–208.

28. Lynes, *The Tastemakers,* 247.

29. Betty Friedan, *The Feminine Mystique* (New York: Norton, 1963), 206–230.

30. Raymond Loewy, *Never Leave Well Enough Alone* (New York: Simon and Schuster, 1951), 219.

31. Matthew Arnold quoted in Dick Hebridge, *Subculture: The Meaning of Style* (London: Metheun, 1979), 7.

32. Raymond Williams, *The Long Revolution* (London: Penguin, 1965), 8.

DESIGNERS AND VISIBILITY:
DESIGN—NOT BIOLOGY—IS DESTINY
Véronique Vienne

L ast year in this column, Moira Cullen wrote a piece on gender and design in which she proposed Hillary Rodham Clinton as a role model—a risk taker willing to spark controversy in order to cut across gender, class, culture, and party lines. Today, in spite of her high visibility (or maybe because of it) the wife of the president is fighting an image battle she apparently cannot win. An exemplary woman by all accounts, she is treated by the media like just another celebrity, not like the hard-working public advocate she is.

In contrast—and in retrospect—Jackie Onassis could do no wrong. When she died she seemed to have only admirers, no detractors. Unlike Hillary, who is a powerful player, a savvy communicator, and an accomplished speaker, the former Mrs. Kennedy had no political voice, was obsessed with privacy, and spoke softly, almost inaudibly. So why did the popular press lionize her to the point of idolatry?

Jackie seemed to have a natural affinity with the printed page. Paper was her natural element; ink was her true medium. She was simply a living icon. While her consistent two-dimensional image was a visual treat, Hillary's ever-changing hair, makeup, and wardrobe style has become a press joke. Every new attempt at defining her image only adds to the confusion. Ubiquity is not synonymous with visibility. The eye is an editing device: we only see what we recognize and we only recognize what we already know. Design—not biology—is destiny.

Ellen Shapiro, a New York graphic designer who makes her high profile clients even more visible (American Express, Goldman Sachs, Paine Webber, just to name a few), once tried to challenge the known content of a universal image. "I saw this mother and child in the subway," she tells. "The baby was dressed in pink, with matching ruffles, bonnet, socks, and booties. On impulse, I wondered what it would be like to ask the mother if her baby was a boy or a girl." She never found out—questioning some of our shared assumptions is simply unthinkable. Confounded by the irrevocable character of her perception, she realized that gender is first and foremost a powerful optical illusion.

Right from the start, little girls are imprinted with the concept of "femininity"—and with the color pink—in the same way young birds are imprinted at birth with the sight of their mothers. Gender is so confusing it must be colorcoded. In our Western culture, the female of the species learns at an early age to associate pastel colors with infantile helplessness and its maternal response. Did you ever wonder why the sight of a baby in

pink prompts adults to make cooing sounds? Eye-catching pink, still the bestselling color
for doll packaging, magazine covers, ice creams, and lipsticks, triggers in most teenage girls
a sense of utter vulnerability combined with a vague anxiety regarding their sex. Later,
remembering that they must be seen but not heard, women will dutifully seal their lips
in shades of coral, mauve, rosebud, and peach.

You never forget that first pink dress. My mother wrapped mine in tissue and gave
it to me. I just have to look at its faded silk, hand-sewn smock embroidery, puffed sleeves,
and apron ties to remember what it was like to wear it. I must have been eighteen months
old. That's the tallest I ever felt. By the time I had outgrown the dress, I was on the road
to becoming a woman—someone who associates pleasant visual clues with a need for
approval, protection, and love.

No wonder female designers later in life have trouble sorting out their feelings
about colors, patterns, shapes, and textures. The blank page reminds them of the pristine
dress they cannot soil; bright colors suggest forbidden toys; sharp angles signal the edge
of the comfort zone. The visual world is charged with potential transgressions and personal
visibility is fraught with dangers.

"I didn't want to become a woman; I wanted to be a boy," says Rebeca Mendez.
"At first, designing made me feel dead inside. I couldn't find the person behind the design."
Like so many other designers, she hates being objectified, or rather adjectified, as a "woman"
designer. She says she was reconciled with her gender—and with her professional choice—
when she realized that design had little to do with "visibility," and everything to do with
what's below the surface. A rather shy Art Center College of Design graduate student with
a slight Mexican accent, she is today considered one of the newest and freshest voices of
her generation. Her approach to design is internal, not external. "Paper represents the skin,"
she says. "I am interested in what we can see beneath—veins, tendons, skeletal structure."
Her work shows intricate layers of translucent surfaces that overlap and intersect, revealing
delicate emotional and physical connections between graphic elements.

For many designers born with XX chromosomes, coming out as a "woman"
designer seems to be a critical step in the creative process. "It's important to realize that
women have very different lives from men," says Ellen Lupton, curator of contemporary
design at Cooper Hewitt, a writer-designer who became a household name when her book
and exhibition *Mechanical Brides: Women and Machines from the Home to Office* won national
acclaim. "We are tempted to reject the term 'woman' because it is disenabling and we don't
want to be perceived as victims. But we won't be truly successful until we accept the fact
that, as women, we can gain ground and lose ground, all at the same time."

Neither victims nor goddesses, women are in possession of one of the most
powerful forces of nature: they can create new life. The "fe" in *fe*male is derived from "dhe,"
an ancient Indo-European prefix that replicates the sound of sucking. Also found in *fe*cund,
*fe*rtile, *fe*tus, *fe*ed, and *fe*el, "fe" suggests a movement inward, into the body. For a woman,
the act of creation is preceded by the act of gestation. While the idea of visibility is, for
male designers, obvious and primary, for female designers it is only secondary. Birth is what
happens "after."

With a massive injection of estrogen, the field of visual communication is
undergoing a major transformation. The design process is *feminized*—literally "sucked"
inside. The structural grid is slowly sinking below the surface. The division between image
and type is being blurred. The page is acquiring more depth. The text, this symbol of male

authority according to deconstructionist theories, is progressively losing its readability. References to the body abound. Hands, eyes, lips, organs, x-rays, footprints, and human shadows are turning up as icons. No longer a reflecting mirror, the graphic surface is now a threshold. Instead of looking at, readers are invited to look in.

April Greiman was one of the first designers to freely incorporate images of her own body in her work. "The personal and the professional agenda should be integrated," she says. "I am interested in the metaphorical properties of femaleness and look for kindred clients to match my own needs." Resolutely feminine, she is not a feminist, but a universal female role model for both men and women designers. "Fame and visibility came only recently," she notes, "thanks to the support of the men who, I am proud to say, have been inspired by my work." Neville Brody, Rick Valicenti, Scott Makela, David Carson, and Rudy VanderLans are some of her champions. Still, she is weary of the limelight. "I respond visually, not verbally to praise," she says. "When people ask me to talk about my work, I look at my watch and mutter something about having to go back to work."

Less ego-directed than men, women are more self-involved: they unbashfully bring a personal dimension to their work. Margo Chase, a former medical illustrator who is known for her trend-defining album covers, masterfully handles the most intricate designs with the dexterity of a surgeon. She has been accused of being "feminine, ornate, and decorative" because she always incorporates elegant and lyrical semi-organic forms in her work. Instead of becoming defensive, she turned her biology degree into a unique trademark. Chase's typographical approach to problem-solving is zooidal—the result of a progressive cellular division of simple design elements. "I used to be invited to lecture because I was a woman designer, but now people call me because they are intrigued by my slide show on the subject of design germs," she says. If you don't want to be treated like a token, try impersonating a female bacteria.

Personal commitments are often an integral part of the creative process—but sometimes they co-exist without mixing. Pat Gorman, who with her partner Frank Olinsky, came up in 1981 with the original MTV logo, now prides herself on being both a discreet designer and a good acupuncturist. She is known for her refreshingly primitive graphic approach and for her caring concern with AIDS, cancer, and heart disease patients. "Problem solving means helping people solve real problems, not trumped-up ones," she says. "I'll turn down a lucrative album cover for a rock group in order to design an unglamorous poster for the rain forest." The music business seems to foster nonconformity. "I have grown used to living in terror of making a fool of myself and being found out," she adds candidly, verbalizing what many women designers secretly fear the most. "I guess I am not a big supporter of the good-taste mentality," she concludes.

Sylvia Woodard, who teaches graphic design at Yale Graduate School of Archi-tecture, remarks that more and more of her female students are "interested in issues, and learning to communicate them—not in serving corporate America and being members in good standing in men's institutions." The real story—the late breaking news, she says—is that more and more designers are opting out, not opting in. "They want to find new ways of working with each other—be inventive and stay on the edge."

Male or female, the next generation of graphic designers will be entrepreneurs, not managers. As the economy slows down and the technology speeds ahead, they can look forward to being thrown into the vortex. Less time and fewer dollars will be left to enter competitions, attend conferences and network over lunch. People will have to opt out just to stay in the game. "I am starting to say no to things that don't contribute to my well-being," says designer-writer Fo Wilson. "One of the most important skills I have learned is not to be concerned with success." This sentiment is expressed by women coast-to-coast.

"I learned from Chuck Anderson and Joe Duffy to promote myself," says Sharon Werner in Minneapolis, "but I am not quite as aggressive as they are. I do not try to put on airs. What works for me is to be up front and honest." She speaks plainly and her typographical style is unceremonious, candid, surprisingly witty. She is representative of a rare breed of talented designers who know how to deliver the message and throw it away. The woman behind Werner Design Werks Inc., she makes the work of her former bosses, Duffy and Anderson, look overworked, fussy, and almost "feminine" in comparison.

In Chicago, Jilly Simons keeps Concrete, her design office, purposely small. "I do very little marketing and never look for new business; I just design promo pieces from time to time." She wants every project to have a one-of-a-kind feeling, and, as a result, her work looks crafted rather than designed. "I don't think that I could achieve the same level of quality and the same level of pleasure if I let it get blotted," she says of her four-and-a-half-person operation.

In San Francisco, Linda Hinrichs, who left Pentagram after being for years its first and only female partner, now has her own design office, Powell Street Studio. "I admire women designers who manage to be successful in a city where, unlike New York, Los Angeles, or San Francisco, the cost of living is not exorbitant. These small-city pioneers are redefining success for all of us and making it possible for other women to think of design as a profession where one can keep a balance between business and personal life."

Women's genuine lack of interest in traditional ego perks—or at least their genuine unwillingness to pay the price for them—could turn out to be a major cultural influence. Already the emotional gap between mothers and nonmothers is slowly closing. "It's not easier, but at least it's OK to have a family now," says Hinrichs, who has a teenage son. "You don't have to be a closet mother anymore; you can even turn dropping out into an opportunity." Kirin Hibma, married to Michael Cronan, worked for years as his business partner. A couple of years ago she started a direct mail sportswear operation, The Walking Man, in order to juggle her creative talent and her personal ambition with her two kids' schedules. "As a creative director, Michael reports to me for the clothing business," she explains, "and I report to him as business manager of Cronan Design." Maternity is no longer a dirty word. "I love the design business," she says, "because it's a *midwiving* process."

For her new book, *Silenced Partners: Women of Modern Design,* Virginia Smith, author of *The Funny Little Man,* is exploring the complex relationship between men and women partners in the design profession by researching early modernists like Varvara Stepanova who was married to Alexander Rodchenko and Lilly Reich who was an early collaborator of Ludwig Mies van der Rohe. "Traditionally, women were perceived as bringing a sense of domesticity to the workplace," she says. "Femininity used to be equated with babies, home, decoration—not design." Women will be the first to admit that it is still the case. The truth be told, diapers and design deadlines don't mix. Terrible twos and clients' tantrums don't mesh. School schedules and airlines schedules don't coordinate well. Giovanna Di Paola, who started with her husband Michael Jager a prolific Vermont design office that produces some of the most serendipitous graphics, brochures, and catalogs for the snowboarding industry, says, "My three-year-old child is a new focus in my life, and I had to reduce my involvement with clients. There is a price tag to pay for being a mother.

Although I am still growing as a designer, I had to give up my visibility. Forget judging shows or attending conventions . . . I am maxed out."

For many women, graphic communication represents a chance to develop a powerful voice without having to speak up in public. Hillary Rodham Clinton would not make a good graphic designer. Edison, not Gutenberg, is her patron saint. She does not "read" well in the press because she's more interested in the context than the text, the substance than the form, the message than the print media. Hillary does not need another makeover—just a small injection of ink in her bloodstream.

"Behind the veil of the printed word, women can find their voice," says Cindy Jennings, a corporate communication designer who is working on a master's degree at North Carolina University. "The graphic expression is less demeaning than standing on a podium, *taking* everybody's time." And making everyone yawn! The main criticism women had of the Miami AIGA design biennial, besides that it was male-dominated, was that it was excruciatingly boring. "We talk to each other at conferences as if we were each other's clients," remarks Jennifer Morla, a leading San Francisco graphic designer whose intensely personal work has broad universal appeal. "We are locked into a trade mentality and fail to share our real experience."

Access to the printed word gives graphic designers an aura of authority. While men in the communication field are quite comfortable with this state of affairs, women tend to be critical of speakers who do not take advantage of this fortuitous situation to address important environmental, social, or community issues. In Los Angeles, Lorraine Wild, founder of the award-winning firm ReVerb, a four-women-one-man "consensus," wonders if getting recognition from peers means anything anymore. "The system is designed to support one particular version of the history of graphic design. Just like everything else attached to design, 'seeing' and 'being seen' has become more sweaty and obvious, more competitive, too time consuming—and somehow less fabulous," she remarks. "Our goal is not to win more awards, but to keep growing without stagnating."

San Francisco graphic designer Lucille Tenazas, a meticulous and articulate speaker and one of the most visible new leaders, has given a lot of thought to the responsibility of the designer as spokesperson. "I never repeat myself and never give the same lecture twice," she says. "I dissect my subject matter into fragments to encourage the process of questions and answers. I empathize with my audience—what they think and feel is not different from what I feel and think." For her, a speaking engagement is a chance to articulate her guests' concerns as much as her own.

Well-known women designers—Paula Scher, Sheila Levrant de Bretteville, Nancye Green—are living legends, but not role models to a new generation. Today, less visible contributors to the communication field—teachers, department heads, art directors, writers, artists, curators, or clients—are more likely to inspire awe. People like art director Ruth Ansel, with her long list of art directing prestigious magazines from *Harper's Bazaar* to *Vanity Fair*, says, "I never thought of myself as having a career." Or Michelle Barnes, a Denver-based illustrator who organized WIG (Women Illustrators Group), a networking salon for isolated artists who make a living meeting publishing deadlines, but seldom get a chance to actually meet and share ideas. Or Jeri Heiden, vice president of creative services and chief art director at Warner Brothers Records in Los Angeles, who consistently supports the work of women designers without ever ghettoizing their contribution. Or editorial design consultant Mary K. Baumann, who is exploring, with her husband Will Hopkins, the fuzzy frontier between printed matter and virtual design, and who remarks, "I am getting progressively less visible as I go deeper into cyberspace, but it does not bother me." Or Kati Korpisaakko, a magazine art director at Condé Nast who has given many now-famous fashion photographers their first assignments, but says, "I would feel very silly to be written about."

The list of female mentors is long, and drawing it is a thankless task: you cannot give credit to people who don't want credit for themselves. Susan Slover, principal of Susan Slover Design Inc., in New York, says it best: "Individually, we're all good at what we do. But together, we're even better."

Looking back at the last decade, Laurie Haycock, former design director at the Minneapolis Walker Art Center, noticed that the greatest influence in graphic design were the silent brokers who "created a scenario for others to make permissive design." She mentions Sheila Levrant de Bretteville, Katherine McCoy, April Greiman, Lorraine Wild, Lucille Tenazas, Zuzana Licko, just to name a few. But she goes further. "We should also include the people who organized the lectures, wrote the comments on the entry forms, and edited the articles," she says. "Focusing on the text is a masculine thing. There is a new underground matriarchy in graphic design; its mandate is interactivity, not authority."

Originally published in Communication Arts, *September/October 1994.*

UNDERGROUND MATRIARCHY
Laurie Haycock Makela and Ellen Lupton

The role of women in graphic design is consistently marginalized or overlooked. This dialogue, written across fax lines between New York and Minneapolis, focuses on American women who have had a profound impact on the profession, not only through the projects that bear their own signatures, but also through the creativity of others, women and men, working in their midst. They represent not a closed canon of matriarchs, but an open set.

LAURIE HAYCOCK MAKELA: During a pivotal period in the mid 1980s, the insistence on something called "subjectivity" forced an opening in the tight rightness of "good" design. The radical efforts of renegade modernists such as April Greiman, Sheila de Bretteville, Lorraine Wild, and Katherine McCoy, however different from one another, added up to a powerful underground matriarchy that upended formal constraints and validated personal content and gesture. Ten years ago, "good" design meant objectivity, obedience, cleanliness, and correctness; into that impossible modernist environment, these women placed subjectivity. Messy, permissive, full of idiosyncratic logic, and essentially feminist in nature, subjectivity is at the heart of the explosive avant-garde in American graphic design today.

ELLEN LUPTON: Important design emerges from contexts that encourage innovation and experimentation. Good design is not simply the product of individuals graced with a miraculous talent—designers are stimulated by schools, clients, companies, studios, colleagues, competitors, and other social networks. The danger in mapping out an underground matriarchy is that we will replace the old boys' network—which for so long has excluded women, younger designers, and people working at the margins of the professional mainstream—with an equally exclusive new girls' network, defined by its own personal ties and ideological biases. For me, to chart the family tree of an underground matriarchy is not to recast the traditional pantheon of individual genius with a new set of shining stars, but to shift the focus of design journalism from the individual as creator *ex nihilo* to the individual as actor in a social context.

The word "matriarchy" invokes the values associated with feminine culture— gathering as opposed to hunting, cultivating as opposed to conquering, nurturing rather than self-promotion. These values are not strictly tied to sexual identity but have been linked in our society to women. As the design profession—and public life in general—becomes more inclusive, these values are increasingly shared by both sexes. Sheila de Bretteville, Muriel Cooper, Carol Devine Carson, and Mildred Friedman have contributed to the evolution of contemporary design both by producing their own work and by creating contexts in which innovation can flourish.

LHM: When I was in high school, Sheila de Bretteville created a poster called "Taste and Style Aren't Enough" for the then-new CalArts in Valencia. Its low-tech, vernacular look was a deliberate commentary on the high-finish corporate aesthetic celebrated by most of her colleagues. In 1980 at the University of California at Berkeley, I was a student in her senior studio, where we were given projects in which design served only as a formal language for expressing personal values. De Bretteville's encouragement of self-reflective subject matter connects the student to the content and the content to the form. From the early 1970s she has consistently conveyed to her students the sense that their content is worthy, with the result that their forms resonate with personal choice. She has increased the value of plurality, interpretation, and collaboration in design, values that inspire my current role as design director at the Walker Art Center, Minneapolis.

EL: De Bretteville became chair of the graphic design program at the Yale School of Art in 1990. In addition to encouraging her students to draw on their own experiences, she believes that designers should interact with their audiences and should consider the social consequences of their practice. According to de Bretteville, producing design in collaboration with one's audience is a feminist act because it makes use of values of intimacy and cooperation associated with women's culture. She and her students have studied the ways the media marginalize groups with certain sexual, ethnic, racial, and class identities, and have produced projects with communities in New Haven, the harsh urban setting from which Yale has traditionally stood aloof as a bastion of privilege.

LHM: The success of her approach depends on keeping a distance from style-related design trends. Her students shun competitions as irrelevant beauty pageants. She distrusts pure formmaking without commitment to a larger issue.

But for some designers, the bigger issues can only be expressed in abstract, formal terms. April Greiman—often criticized for creating an "empty" kind of beauty—wraps her talent around global themes: the overlapping of science, technology, and spirituality. Greiman exhibited her Space Mats (designed with Jayme Odgers) at our design gallery at Berkeley at a time when I was doing a typographic poem about my menstrual cycle for an assignment for Sheila. The place mats were produced without a client and captured an erotic and exotic hyperdimensional vision. Greiman found a glamorous, funhouse, Zen-like center to the practice of design: she threw the Swiss grid on its back and lovingly fucked it with color and wild imagery. This was a galactic brothel compared with the retentive, methodological aesthetic of corporate design.

To this day, Greiman will tell you she is not a feminist. But I believe her visual seductions are motivated in part by an emotional freedom undiscovered by her male colleagues at the time. Katherine McCoy has said that "the modernist design paradigms of objective rationalism are typical of a male sensibility, safely disengaged from emotional involvement." Greiman's work depicted volumes of passion: when that passion turned to technology, she gave the future a beautiful, sensual, and bright new aesthetic.

EL: Greiman's work is a painterly and personalized response to digital technology. As the progenitor of a distinctive signature style that has been widely imitated, she is a legendary star who has helped fuel—inadvertently or not—the cult of personality cherished by many graphic designers. Her work is an exquisite revision of the formal languages of modernism; her approach to technology is often suggestive and metaphorical rather than structural, engaging the mythology of the machine rather than the revolutionary potential of electronic media.

A very different exploration of technology is found in the career of Muriel Cooper, who in 1975 founded the Visible Language Workshop (VLW), part of MIT's Media Lab. While Cooper's untimely death in May 1994 is a profound loss to designers, her work will be carried forward by the institution she created and the people she inspired.

The VLW has treated digital typography not as a tool for designing printed graphics, but as a unique medium with its own properties and possibilities. Most graduate programs concentrate on the making of complete, self-contained works: books, posters, installations, and other objects whose "signature" status is modeled on the products of painting, sculpture, and photography departments. The VLW's focus has been different: Cooper worked to build an electronic language that will *support* the work of future designers, helping them to make complex, malleable documents in real time and three-dimensional space. Cooper gave concrete functions to such principles as layered information, simultaneous texts, and typographic texture—visual structures that are familiar as expressive, personal gestures from the "New Typography" of the 1970s and 1980s. While many designers working at the stylistic edges of contemporary typography have approached technology in terms of impressionistic imagery—the territory traditionally reserved for graphic design—Cooper aimed to restructure the language of design in four dimensions.

Many women today are excelling in the fields of interface design and electronic publishing, including Red Burns, Jessica Helfand, and Loretta Staples. While men are the visible mouthpieces and economic leaders of such companies as Voyager, Microsoft, Apple, and Whittle Communications, women are playing important roles in crafting environments for the new design media. Perhaps "interface" is an electronic counterpart to realms of culture that have traditionally been feminized—an interface, like a housewife or a secretary, provides a gracious, comfortable setting for the performances of others. Many tasks known as "women's work" in the twentieth-century office involve *mediating* technologies. From answering phones, transferring calls, and taking messages to typing letters and making copies, female office workers have formed a human link between male managers and their machines. Women have served as bodily extensions of communications equipment. The contemporary ideal of the user-friendly electronic environment reflects the continued desire to humanize technology.

LHM: An interface is also like a teacher. As cochair of the Cranbrook Academy of Art's design program, Katherine McCoy shepherded dozens of students through the school's now-notorious formal experiments. In the mid 1980s she allowed some of the first debates about deconstruction to surface in critiques of graphic design. I use the word "allowed" because though she may pursue a more conservative course in her own work, her critiques were a free zone for new thinking about design. She was willing to take the heat and the glory for staking out the potentially unbeautiful aesthetic manifestations of literary deconstruction, or, if you will, postmodernism.

Women seemed particularly well equipped to grapple with the decentering of the times, or at least to be a center for decentered thinking. McCoy found her students aggressively rejecting traditional approaches to visual communication and encouraged their private dialogues, their strange and cultish works. The intellectual comfort of the formal exercises that teach abstraction was abandoned at Cranbrook. This new turn in design education was psychoanalytic and difficult to control, but it was a perfect antidote to the depersonalized endpoint of modernism that many young designers of the time experienced. Cranbrook became such a powerful cult because people came for refuge, and the McCoys ran a foster home for design addicts. They have recently decided to retire after twenty years, now that those weird Midwestern lab experiments have grown to be a powerful influence on international design trends.

EL: The exemplary matriarchs that we have discussed so far have come mostly from the academic world, a place where women have found visible and influential positions over the last twenty years. Perhaps the institutional support and clear structures for advancement that schools offer have made academic settings more penetrable by women than large-scale design studios where vast numbers continue to hover in midlevel positions. The academic world can put designers in the ambiguous position of producing both marginal and official culture: marginal because academia provides a place outside commercial practice where experiment and opposition can be safely expressed, and official because schools are charged with articulating principles that young designers will take with them into the marketplace and which will, in turn, inform much of the professional community's dialogue.

Carol Devine Carson has had a tremendous impact on contemporary design, working not from an academic post but from a major publishing house. Arriving in New York from Nashville, Tennessee in 1973, she was an outsider to both the city's design establishment and to the academic/modernist vanguard. Since she became art director at Alfred A. Knopf in 1987, she and her design staff have transformed bookstore shelves with their strange and sinister jackets. The principal designers at the Knopf Group have been with Carson from the beginning: Chip Kidd, Barbara de Wilde, and Archie Ferguson. The fact that this amazingly productive (and now widely imitated) team has stayed together for so long reflects the strength of the imprint's management. Knopf has brought visually challenging graphics to a broad public—these are not esoteric art catalogues or posters for design events, but mainstream consumer products displayed in shopping malls across the country.

Like colleges and universities, major publishing houses are large, bureaucratic institutions with defined hierarchies; for most employees, the field's cultural prestige is countered by relatively low wages. According to Carson, the book business traditionally has made a place for women. "We have always done a lot of the real work in this industry. The difference in the past fifteen years is that it's more common for women to be rewarded for the work they do."

Before Carson's arrival, art director Bob Scudelari was corporate vice president of Random House and design administrator for all the company's imprints, including Knopf and some dozen others. Carson became vice president, art director in charge of the Knopf Group in 1991, and now directly controls design within the imprint and supervises work at Pantheon and Vintage. In the old system, Scudelari was the chief spokesman and the art directors were kept relatively cloistered from editors and authors. Now Carson has direct contact with these forces (as well as with the meddlesome marketing department), giving her more control over the process.

LHM: I was teaching at CalArts when Lorraine Wild arrived from Houston in 1985 as the new chair of the visual communications program. Soon afterwards, two more Cranbrook graduates—Jeffery Keedy and Edward Fella—joined the faculty. Within a year, the fires were set. The four of us taught a graduate seminar whose students included Barry Deck, Barbara Glauber, and Somi Kim. Informed by theory and history, Wild set a tough standard for critiques that often mocked conventional notions of metaperfection and problem solving. The students' formal and critical skills developed within an authentic and radical contemporary art environment. The rigorous exchange between Cranbrook and CalArts and the emerging influence of *Emigre* magazine (and Zuzana Licko's typefaces) all helped to create a dizzying centrifugal force, a virtual supernova in design evolution.

In this extreme environment, Wild attempted to respond to brutally incongruous demands: in addition to directing the program, she wrote articles, gave lectures, maintained international contacts, designed books, and taught a design history course that kept the interest of even the most informed. Sharing an office with her for several years, I witnessed countless moments between a student's tears and an emergency faculty meeting when she would look up with a pained smile and say, "Why are we doing this?"

The answer, of course, is that if we are to make a difference in the design field, we need to reinvent the setting for design education. For Wild, there was an element of disgust at what she had been exposed to in the New York studios, so she approached the CalArts program with a furious intensity, which she has recently redirected towards creating ReVerb, through which she has launched a constructively angry response to the objectivity and patriarchy that pervaded her training. Her design work speaks for many cultural institutions of our time in alternating fits of elegance and anarchy.

But men still dominate the profession—even at its avant-garde fringes. Women seem to spend more time underground, gaining collective recognition and regenerating the field in intangible ways. Simply put, the efforts of this matriarchy has made possible the kind of permissive, wild, personal, and pluralistic form-language that so many men are becoming famous for. As our "fathers" stood at the front door, firmly protecting the rules of the house, our "mothers" quietly unlocked the back door, freeing the children to act upon their natural impulse to personalize what they make.

EL: The modernist design establishment has never been a solid edifice—it was always threatened from without by consumerism and mass culture and pressured from within vanguardist obsession with individualism and novelty. In recounting the rise of subjectivity in design, it is important to remember that men as well as women opened the back doors of the discipline. Wolfgang Weingart, Dan Friedman, and Gert Dumbar fueled the unleashing of typographic form in the 1970s and 1980s, often working side by side with the matriarchs heralded here. The current fascination with radical personalities (male and female) continues a long line of avant-garde confrontations led traditionally by men.

My primary identity is as a curator and writer, working for Cooper-Hewitt, National Museum of Design in New York. Because I am a curator first and a designer second, I feel obliged to look beyond my immediate circle of mentors. But I have "mothers" too. Mildred (Mickey) Friedman has been a role model and colleague. As design director of the Walker Art Center from 1970 to 1991, she set an international standard for exhibitions and publications. In 1989, she curated the first large-scale museum survey of graphic design in the United States; while her strong vision provoked anger from designers, the exhibition probably did more to raise public knowledge of graphic design than any event in history.

LHM: In my first few months as design director at the Walker, I discovered that I had inherited unbelievable resources in the form of curators who embraced quality design and publishing and audiences who had come to expect design to be part of contemporary arts programming. These attitudes were nurtured by Friedman during the twenty years that she edited *Design Quarterly* and produced exhibitions at the Walker, creating a place for educated dialogue about design when few existed.

"Masculinity" and "femininity" are cultural constructions historically tied to the biological differences between the sexes. An important goal of feminism is to make the values traditionally associated with the world of women into values recognized across the social and sexual spectrum: to nurture, to include, to respond, to support, to enable. As the influence of women continues to grow in the coming decades, such skills may no longer be regarded as distinctly feminine or as the exceptional product of women's achievement. Design competitions must begin to include new categories—such as lectures organized or given, exhibitions curated, new curriculum planning, and special research in areas such as cultural iconography. In this way, we will be in a better position to acknowledge all levels of accomplishment—from the surface of the page to the underground of the community.

Originally published in Eye, *No. 14, 1994.*

THE POLITICS OF CULTURAL OWNERSHIP
Fath Davis Ruffins

While people often suffer the conse-quences of being legally or socially defined as belonging to an ethnic group, they have no legal right to own or even control how their culture is portrayed or exploited. Individuals, corporations, and even state and local governments can own trademarks and copyright ethnic portrayals, such as the Washington Redskins, yet cultural groups do not have such legal authority. There is no single definition of the term "cultural ownership" that would be universally accepted across the various disciplines of art history, anthropology, or political science. However, in light of the complicated social history of the United States, the main issues in the concept of cultural ownership have to do with longstanding contradictions between cultural definition and cultural control. "Cultural definition" involves being identified by oneself (and by others) as belonging to a distinctive cultural group. "Cultural control" involves members of a specific cultural group exerting social, economic, and/or political influence over laws, issues, and representations of that group.

The contradiction between cultural definition and cultural control has been apparent since the early years of the republic. However, such conflicts became particularly contentious when the rise of mass media and mass marketing collided with the growing political power of the modern civil rights movement. Movies, radio programs, and mass-marketed product advertisements were key ways in which humorous, sentimental, satirical, and stereotypical attitudes about American ethnic groups were portrayed, perpetuated, and transmitted to new generations and incoming immigrants. Efforts to resist prevailing negative portrayals have occurred since the Civil War era, but protest efforts gathered speed in the early twentieth century. While no group has the legal power to control its portrayal, some groups have grown more effective in using political and economic tactics to protest offensive imagery.

In 1915, two unrelated events occurred that galvanized certain American commu-nities. The innovative but deeply racist film *Birth of a Nation,* directed by D. W. Griffith, was released. Shown to an adoring public, given a White House viewing by President Woodrow Wilson, *Birth of a Nation* is still remembered for its technical innovation and the pathological depth of its racist portrayals of African-Americans, especially men, and its images of rapacious and corrupt white Yankees. The NAACP, then four years old, made strenuous efforts to boycott, picket, and disrupt the showings of this film, more or less in vain. In the era of silent film, it became the first major success, characterized by such technical innovations as outdoor and long panoramic shots along with a cast of thousands. Also in 1915, the Atlanta merchant Leo Frank, a Jewish man whose grandfather had fought for the

Confederacy, was lynched. He had been convicted of the murder of an Irish girl working in his factory. Although he was clearly railroaded, and the governor of Georgia had pardoned him, Frank was eventually taken from his jail cell and hanged before a jeering crowd of hundreds of white Georgians. The anti-Semitic propaganda stirred up by his sensationalist murder trial and wrongful death spurred the founding of two different important Jewish organizations: the American Jewish Committee and the American Jewish League. Each in distinct ways immediately began to protest the portrayals of American Jews in a variety of popular media, with little success until the Cold War era.

These two examples can demonstrate the earlier difficulties of counteracting virulent stereotypes, even those with murderous consequences. Yet much changed in the years following World War II. Economic boycotts such as the Montgomery Bus Boycott of 1955-1956, which brought the Reverend Dr. Martin Luther King, Jr., to national attention, began to reveal the buying power of heretofore ignored ethnic groups. The development of new outlets, such as the publications empire of John Johnson, produced new ways for advertisers to reach a certain segment of the African-American community. After World War II, the NAACP targeted the entertainment industry, especially movies and television, to change the portrayals of African-Americans in these media. The popular TV show *Amos 'n' Andy* was pulled off the air in the early 1960s because of these protests.

Perhaps an even clearer example of the assertion of cultural identity issues had to do with the elimination of a rather successful character, the "Frito Bandito," introduced by Frito-Lay (a part of General Foods) in 1968. Sales of Fritos were reinvigorated by the introduction of the animated Bandito character, who "stole" Fritos from other characters on television and in print. As described by a journalist, the Frito Bandito "was a sneaky 'toon, part Speedy Gonzalez, part *duende*, that got into people who munched on Fritos and made them grow pencil-drawn mustaches" (Enrique Fernandez, "Ay Bandito!" in the *Village Voice,* October 13, 1992). Although the character had a very high rate of recognition among the public, Frito-Lay dropped it in 1971 in response to the protests of Hispanic groups, including the Mexican American Anti-Defamation League, founded, among others, by Ricardo Montalban, the noted screen and TV actor. Over the last twenty-five years, many large-scale American companies have been forced to pay attention to the interests, sensibilities, and consumption patterns of groups of Americans who had routinely been stereotyped in earlier product advertising.

Each of these examples illustrates the growing power of various interest groups to assert both economic and political desires. In recent years, Quaker Foods has redesigned Aunt Jemima to make her more like an African-American suburban matron, consulting with Dorothy Height, the longtime chairman of the National Council of Negro Women (NCNW). Such changes point to the durability of images that companies knew demonstrated extremely high consumer recognition. At the same time, the death of the Frito Bandito and Sambo's restaurant chain indicate the susceptibility of companies to consumer reaction. But are such instances examples of "cultural ownership"?

While it is undoubtedly positive that ethnic groups are now better able to protest stereotypes of their culture and effect change, the question of cultural ownership remains problematic. With the exception of certain native American tribes, most "cultures" still have no legal definition in the United States. Many ethnic groups now contain watchdog organizations that focus on the various aspects of politics and the media. Yet problems of consensus inevitably arise within the group: who is a "legitimate" spokesperson? who appointed that person or group to "represent" the feelings of all Arab- or Japanese-Americans? Such issues become much more complicated when well-known members of the group take dissenting or even opposing positions on such questions. Should there be different rules when the owners of the advertising agency, film production company, or recording studio are themselves members of the ethnic group being portrayed? Perhaps the most vehement differences of opinion on this topic concern the images and lyrics of gangsta' rap music. In the name of communicating the realities of ghetto life, black rappers have presented controversial images that certainly would be considered racist if created by whites.

Arguments over substance and style, content and form, are raging in contemporary American society, and the idea of cultural ownership per se is not that helpful in guiding us through the ethical thicket raised through the commercial use of ethnicity, or in analyzing the meaning of patterns of imagery. Regardless of the aesthetic choices that designers, agencies, or companies make, they must inform themselves about the history of that imagery. Individuals may feel that particular ideas or images have emerged directly from their own unconscious, with no intention of offending anyone, but run into major opposition when those ideas become public. For example, the Italian company Benetton prudently withdrew some of its magazine and transportation ads in the United States when protests were mounted. Advertisements showing an African-American woman suckling a white child, or models dressed in Catholic nuns' habits, played in the European market but were too offensive in the American context.

The long development of American (indeed, international) consumer culture means that many, many images have an earlier history. That history is not only aesthetic, but also contains the racial and ethnic pieties and conflicts of earlier generations. Before an image goes before the public, it is imperative that its creators research its sociopolitical history as an image as well as its aesthetic appeal.

Those responsible for selecting imagery operate in an environment in which "cultures" may not "own" images, but can assert the power of their historical interpretations of imagery and use their socioeconomic power to force changes in commercial presentation. Knowing the social and cultural history of ethnic imagery could easily prevent key errors (and lawsuits) in this era of tremendous visual sensitivity. Researching the history of a particular image can prevent a company from muddying its commercial presentation by introducing visual elements associated with prejudicial attitudes unrelated to its contemporary commercial purposes. Intentional efforts to draw attention to previous stereotypes need to be produced in a clearcut manner, probably more suitable to documentary presentation than direct advertising. In any event, the complicated history of visual imagery in the United States cannot be ignored as one of the key elements in choosing a final design or company presentation.

Originally published in the AIGA Journal of Graphic Design, *Vol. 14, No. 1, 1996.*

IS THERE LEGAL PROTECTION
FOR CULTURAL IMAGERY?

Rosemary J. Coombe

Graphic designers work in an environment shaped by intellectual property laws that commodify, protect, license, and regulate the use of the imagery upon which they draw. The laws of copyright, trademark, and publicity rights (which prohibit the use of celebrity images or likenesses), however, are as routinely violated as they are enforced. Moreover, not all imagery is legally protected from unauthorized use, and this, I will suggest, may be a matter of particular concern for many cultural minorities.

Laws of intellectual property are based upon liberal, individualist principles born of Enlightenment certainties and legitimated by Romantic ideologies. The Eurocentrism of these (purportedly universal or neutral) premises often serves to devalue creative expressive forms produced collectively, inter-generationally, or in unfamiliar media—often produced by those with non-European cultural traditions. As a consequence, although much imagery may be legally available for public use, unauthorized usage may offend the sensibilities and norms of the people who originate the imagery. The ethics and politics of appropriating imagery from other cultures are indeed complex, and will increasingly demand the attention of graphic designers as new forms of communications media make imagery from ever-farther corners of the globe readily available for adaptation and inclusion in graphic works.

Laws of copyright protect the creative products of individual authors (in copyright law, all creators are deemed "authors"), pictured as autonomous individuals whose creations are solely the products of the originality of an unfettered imagination. Through the imprint of the authors' unique personalities, expressions that originate with their activity and are fixed by their material form are deemed to be their property. The law assumes that "ideas" are always available for appropriation, but "expressions" are the property of those who inscribe or imprint them. Through their labor, authors make these "ideas" their own; their possession and control over the "work" is justified by this expressive activity. As long as authors do not copy another's expressive works, they are free to find their inspiration, ideas, themes, motifs, and design elements anywhere they please, and to incorporate these into their own work. Any restriction upon their ability to do so is viewed in liberal democracies as an impermissible restriction on freedom of expression. Possessive individualism and liberal democracy are thereby mutually affirmed.

The Romantic individualism that permeates this law has certainly been criticized, especially by those influenced by anthropology, sociology, Marxism, and poststructuralism.

Critics argue that all expressive forms are produced in social contexts, that genres, themes, motifs, and design elements are conventionally defined, that "art" is only recognized as art in certain social conditions. Many forms of expressive activity are not recognized as resulting in "artistic" works, even though they involve significant creativity (certain kinds of food preparation, quilt designs handed down and modified through the generations, ritual tattoo motifs, and collaborative fashionings of ritual costumes are a few examples). All ideas, critics suggest, come to us through the medium of "expressions" and it is the circulation of such expressions that provides the very wellspring of creative inspiration. Creativity, these critics assert, must always involve the reworking of those cultural forms available to us.

Copyright laws attempt to preclude artists from reproducing the work of others, making many "arts of appropriation" open to potential lawsuits. On the other hand, the legal emphasis upon individual expression and the requirement of a permanent fixed form leaves many products of artistry unprotected and thus available for incorporation into the work of designers. Although it is tempting to view this aspect of the law as a space of freedom, for many it results in perceived exploitation and expropriation. Creative designs produced by collectives, in ritual contexts, over generations, or not fixed in recognized forms (such as the imagery of the sweat lodge or the sun dance, for example) may be ripped out of sacred, ancestral, and secret contexts to be incorporated into the works of others. A woman in India, for example, may create an elaborately wrought design in the clay in front of her home on a daily basis, using patterns and skills passed down from mother to daughter over the generations. By midday, the design will have disappeared. Should a visiting artist happen upon the creation, sketch or photograph the design, and later use it on the cover of an annual report or as the basis for a textile print, he or she will be deemed its "author." Such activities may produce intense feelings of violation in certain communities, where creative forms may serve distinct purposes, may be understood to be appropriately used only in clearly defined contexts, and may be seen as integral to the identity of a lineage or the heritage of a people. The law enables the expressions of some people to become available as "ideas" for the appropriation of others and may protect the appropriator when the expressions are incorporated into an expressive "work" that is legally recognized.

Trademark laws pose other dilemmas. A trademark is an image, logo, design, brand name, or any other symbol capable of distinguishing one's goods or services in the market. A trademark cannot simply be descriptive; for example, one could not obtain exclusive rights to use the term "sweet" for pears or candies. Instead, the law requires that a mark be suggestive, arbitrary, or fanciful, like Smarties for candy or Sweet for tires. Such marks are legally deemed "distinctive." Once a manufacturer establishes legal rights to a mark through extensive use in marketing and consumer recognition, it can prevent others from legally using the same or a similar mark, on the basis that it will be confusing to the public, or that the distinction of its mark will be "diluted" by the reproduction of the mark in unauthorized contexts.

In their quests for distinction in competitive markets, it is not surprising that designers of trademarks have looked to ever more exotic locales and to other cultures to find signifying forms that are not already in commercial use. This practice may be viewed as an invasive violation by those whose cultural forms become commodified and invested with alien meanings. Imagine the consternation of the Sioux, for example, when a beer manufacturer used the name of their revered ancestor Crazy Horse to market malt liquor. Given the devastation wrought by alcohol in many Indian communities, it was intensely insulting to have a great leader's name used in such a way. Many native people experience great pain when they see the hard-earned, ritually endowed feather headdresses of their ancestors mass-produced as stereotypes to market everything from beer to insurance.

For graphic designers, the trademark field presents two potential sources of ethical dilemma, particularly when design trends move away from abstract symbols to designs derived from vernacular sources. On the one hand, to the extent that trademarks are ubiquitous in the visual culture of commercial societies, they are widely recognized and carry great symbolic weight. It is tempting to incorporate existing marks into new designs because they are so instantly recognizable. Many artists, however, have been threatened with litigation when they have attempted to use trademark forms in new visual contexts (for example, the famous Crayola crayon package used as the basis for a novelty soap presentation). Some artists have deliberately decided to flout the law, using the trademarks of powerful corporations in transgressive works that comment critically upon corporate activities; they take legal risks when doing so.

Another dilemma arises for the designer who is asked to produce graphic trademarks for use in commerce; the legal freedom one has to use motifs, designs, images, and visual signs drawn from other cultures presents the artist with an ethical quandary. Without knowing anything about the traditions, lifeways, and political struggles of those with whom the imagery originates, graphic designers may produce works that are innocuous or merely insensitive. However, these appropriations may also be experienced as insults if not serious affronts to people for whom these expressive forms have histories and traditions that serve important continuing social and political needs. Our legal traditions are based upon particular premises that may not do justice to the values, norms, and aspirations of others.

Originally published in the AIGA Journal of Graphic Design, *Vol. 14, No. 1, 1996.*

DESIGN
AS
STRATEGY

THINK FIRST, DESIGN LATER
DK Holland

Intelligent, effective communication tools have never been more needed as we seek to establish a healthy global economy. Research is the meat on the bones of marketing, and it is often through marketing that we are able to develop a successful communication tool. Yet marketing is the dirtiest word in the dictionary to many graphic designers; designers who view marketing as a restriction rather than a way to open doors to a better design solution. *Webster's* defines marketing as "all the commercial functions involved in transferring goods (or services) from producer to consumer."

In some areas of design, such as package design, solid marketing is absolutely essential. JoEllen Nielsen, an industrial designer and group leader in package design at Kraft General Foods observes, "Before we start the design process, we understand the consumer's vocabulary; what shapes, words, and images give the correct message in the package design; what people understand when they see the package. For instance, if we put a food product in packaging that 'reads' as motor oil to our audience, that package has a big image problem.

"When there's a change in leadership, there's a tendency to act subjectively and scrap the work of the old leadership in favor of developing something new, to make it their own. We think of it as the ownership syndrome. Research is an anchor, a way to avoid reinventing the wheel."

To develop the most appropriate research, Nielsen has turned to Cheskin & Masten, one of the oldest and most respected research companies that firmly believes in the first-things-first approach. "Most research on design is done after the creative process is complete. We call it a disaster check. It's usually a disaster because there is a lack of a clear design strategy," Darrel K. Rhea, a graphic designer and president of Cheskin & Masten in Redwood City, California, says. "The whole point of doing research on design is to empower designers to create breakthrough designs and to give the client the confidence that the designs will achieve their communication objectives. The technology is here, today, to do this quickly, efficiently. We are interviewing a quarter of a million consumers a year on design-related issues on behalf of the leading corporations of America. Those designers who are not familiar with design research had better wake up."

Paula Scher, partner in Pentagram and designer of several award-winning package design systems, says that in reality, "Focus groups are killers. This kind of testing forces the consumer to make a knee jerk reaction, so it shouldn't be surprising that test results are usually reactionary. What's worse is corporate opinioneering. Group opinions in corporations are based on fear of change. Design firms often pander to this by not creating change, but creating consensus. Nothing significant is produced and it's a relatively dishonest process." Corporate opinioneering may be defined as research run amuck in the mire of politics and self-interest. Bill Drenttel, also a principal in a graphic design firm, has additional insights about why designers dislike market research. "Half the problem is that the word itself—research—is loaded with fears and expectations. There's a tendency to think that research is a killer of innovation. We simply want to work with people who are comfortable trusting their own instincts. Listening to people you can look in the eye is the kind of research we like." Designers can't design using meaningless averages. Many designers feel squeamish about marketing because they see it as manipulative and dishonest. And research is often criticized when it reflects the twisted two-and-a-half-members-in-a-household statistical approach.

Graphic design can learn from its big sister the advertising industry, which often uses research—what they now refer to as planning—as a foundation for the development of major campaigns. Solid planning clearly establishes parity between the agency and client. The positioning, based on research, is a rational judgment agreed upon by agency and client prior to the creative process. Everything from then on supports the position and subsequent strategy. It's important to differentiate the product or service in a way that establishes its value to the audience. The positioning, usually a paragraph, provides a jumping-off point for the creative process.

It's hard to talk design to a client. They can discuss ideas, but they're out of their element when it comes to type, color, form, taste. It's the same with focus groups. "I wouldn't dream of letting a focus group judge the value of a design. They simply look at the concept, the content and respond to that," Rich Silverstein, creative director and principal in the San Francisco-based advertising agency Goodby Berlin Silverstein says, "The one exception was the Royal Viking Cruise Line campaign. I felt very strongly about the ad designs, but the client was skeptical that the audience would be able to read the typography. So we tested the ads and I was right. Normally, however, I'd say that designs that break new ground are too scary to focus groups. Letting them be the arbiters of taste could be tantamount to throwing cold water on hot new designs." Some of the recent highly acclaimed campaigns—including Royal Viking, NYNEX Yellow Pages and *TV Guide,* both by Chiat Day, and Nature Made by Hal Riney & Partners—have concepts that are firmly (and happily) rooted in planning, yet all are innovative designs.

Planners are the consumer's advocate. They often go so far as to live with the consumer on the consumer's own turf, absorbing the essence of what it is that thrills or chills them about a type of product or service. Then they sum it all up in succinct, objective phrases that help establish a tone of voice for the designer. This has proven very useful in some agencies, where a typical team used to be limited to the client, account executive, and creative director. The planner grounds the project in reality.

On the other hand, graphic design is often based on fluff, not ideas, strategy, or research. In these cases, only pure style and emotion are expressed through the design. We respond to it or we don't. But there is no concept to discuss with the client, nothing substantial to judge. It's hit or miss.

"It's ego that makes designers think that they need not look further than themselves for a solution to a design problem," says Ann Willoughby, graphic designer and principal of the design firm, WRK in Kansas City. "Independent planners and researchers, such as Art Katz and Leslie Westbrook in Kansas City and Moira Cullen in New York, are examples of professionals who can provide guidance to maximize the results of the design process.

Art is currently working on the development of research for a global brand in the lawn care category with us. He's conducting focus groups through our London, Brussels, and U.S. offices to add depth to our cultural perspective. The point is that we are involved as a team and the design results will be better for it."

RESEARCH HELPS FERRET OUT PROBLEMS

One striking example of the power of research in support of design is the success of the new identity for Columbus Regional Hospital. The seventy-five-year-old hospital is in Columbus, Indiana, a small town often called a living museum of contemporary architecture. Although the official renaming of the hospital was not part of the brief, the hospital wanted the design firm to become involved. Pentagram was selected as the design firm, and they had placed a high value in their proposal to conduct research prior to starting the design process. Pentagram partners and graphic designers Colin Forbes and Michael Bierut, along with research specialist/writer Moira Cullen, conducted a range of face-to-face interviews, including discussions with the chief of staff of the hospital, the lab technicians, even the mayor and his wife. A written report of their findings and recommendations, including results of visual and collateral audits, was presented to the identity committee and the board of directors. The hospital had commissioned several outside research studies prior to Pentagram's involvement. The results had been inconclusive and the conflict over the name had become emotional and political. Cullen recalls, "We had advised the committee that our research process would clarify the naming options and indeed it did. Our report documented the candid voices representing all sides of the issue and concluded with a strong argument and strategy in support of the hospital and the city's highly valued tradition of civic and professional excellence. The name was unanimously approved." Cullen observes that, in general, "Research is the listening, a willingness to understand the other that weaves design into the context of today's social issues and concerns. The knowledge gained in the process builds a powerful platform that allows designers to seek out opportunities beyond the solution of immediate problems."

While design firms too often wish to stay within their own comfortable universe of design solutions when tackling a client project, one simple question put to the client, "do you have any existing research we should look at before we start to design?" would shed a whole new light on many projects. For one thing, if the answer is no, the dialogue may start to address the next question, "would this project benefit from research?" This, of course, requires two things: a budget approved by the client and the ability on the part of the design firm and/or client to conduct meaningful research. Either barrier can be a killer. Clients who have previously not allowed for this expense have a hard time digging deeper to find the resources to pay for it. In the end the adage, "the most expensive suit you own is the one you never wear" can be translated to "the design that doesn't work for you is too expensive." Research is an insurance policy. But even if funds are made available, many design firms and clients have no concept what a thorough research process entails.

BASIC QUESTIONS TO CONSIDER WHEN CONDUCTING
RESEARCH FOR A CLIENT PROJECT

A professional planner or researcher isn't a necessary ingredient to every project. It's irrelevant to some straightforward, less significant projects. And most design firms probably ask some of the following questions even if their firm isn't oriented toward research and marketing. It's just common sense.

1. Can the market (i.e., target audience, age, sex, cultural background, geography, education level) be defined?

2. What are the features and benefits of the product or service? Features are attributes and benefits are the positive results of using the product or service.

3. What is the competition for this product or service? Are there existing materials that should be reviewed from the competition? How does this product or service "stack up" against the competition and the competition's materials? What do you believe your reputation to be within your own industry? Is it different from what you'd like it to be?

4. What is the target audience's attitude about this product or service? What's the appeal? What are potential objections?

5. What does the target audience want from this product or service?

6. What are the legal regulations, if any, that affect this product or service?

7. What are the long- and short-term goals of the client for this product or service? What is the overall image of the client? Does it affect the product or service?

These questions can result in a verbal or written comprehensive report.

The writing is on the wall for design firms that wish to be competitive. "As design matures as a profession, intelligent research will become increasingly necessary in order to develop creative strategies and win the attention of better clients," Moira Cullen cautions. "The race is on. Dentsu, Japan's advertising giant, has already established a separate research division dedicated to human studies; a global information search designed to monitor worldwide preferences, trends, and lifestyles."

TAKING THE QUANTUM LEAP FROM DECORATOR TO DESIGNER

Many designers who shun research and marketing may also be the ones who wish their clients took them more seriously. "Designers tend not to like to have their ideas censored. And, in fact, there's nothing preordained that a designer has to have good research in order to come up with a good creative idea," says Stephen A. Greyser, a professor who teaches consumer marketing at Harvard Business School. "Certainly there have been brilliant package designs and ad campaigns that clearly were not based on research. But you will increase your odds with research. And you'll answer some key questions like, 'is anybody interested? does anybody care?'"

LIMITS ARE OUR FRIENDS

Do designers fear the answers to those questions because they just want to do their own thing, simply to express themselves or to decorate? The graphic design industry is still evolving, struggling to be recognized as a profession. And design students are expected to have much different skills when they graduate in 1993 than around the time when graphic design got its name. For instance, learning how to conduct research is a requirement in some graduate schools now. Christian Simms, who teaches graduate students directed research in preparation for their theses in the communications/package design graduate department at Pratt Institute, says that while his course is one of the most popular in the department, it is also one of the most difficult. "I've seen students faced with a research project for the first time actually break down in tears of frustration and anxiety." Learning how to think analytically and strategically was not what they had in mind when their high school counselor pointed them in the direction of art school. Simms, who is also a graphic designer and principal of The Creative Alliance in New York, thinks, "It's a mistake for a student to enter a design curriculum thinking that, although he or she is a fine artist at heart, he or she can become a designer. The student wants the acceptance of peers and parents, and fine art may not be seen as a career and design is. But the fine artist may not have what it takes to be a designer." It's estimated that there are between 100,000 and 350,000 graphic designers out there in the job market. How many of them are actually qualified to be graphic designers?

The designer must be both analytical and intuitive when problem solving. It's the designer who learns to think first and design later who learns to control; it's the designer who doesn't learn to think and analyze who is doomed to be controlled. Research is a key to the control designers so greatly desire.

Originally published in Communication Arts, *January/February 1993.*

CERTIFICATION FOR GRAPHIC DESIGNERS?
A HYPOTHETICAL PROPOSAL
Ellen Shapiro

The other night I was standing in line for a movie. The guy in front of me was talking with his date: "What d'ya do? she asked. "I'm a graphic designer." "J'learn that in school?" "Nah, got a computer last summer and I'm learning as I go."

Yeah, I thought, then I'm a nuclear physicist.

Somehow, at that moment—on a Saturday night when other things should have been on my mind—the words "accreditation" and "certification" popped into my head.

Those two words have been much bandied about in the design community in recent years, and are almost always accompanied by impassioned debate. An accredited educational program meets standards set by an official body, such as a state or governmental agency; an individual who is certified to practice a profession or trade at a particular level has passed a test or otherwise proven that he or she is qualified.

Although most graphic designers seem to agree that since the advent of computers as design tools standards have fallen, or at least gotten fuzzy, and they don't know what to do about it. I recently polled a nationwide sampling of design firm principals and educators and the results indicate that more than 60 percent feel that there's no accurate way to tell if a job candidate is really qualified—or for a client to tell if an independent designer really has the training and skills to manage a complex project.

Yet the idea of certification has continually been met with skepticism, if not outright dismissal. Jack Summerford, principal of Dallas-based Summerford Design, reports that when he joined the board of the American Institute of Graphic Arts (AIGA) two years ago, certification was brought up at every meeting, and the debate always ended the same way: no progress. Steve Liska, of Liska and Associates in Chicago, agrees that the myriad arguments pro and con have been "discussed a billion times," and says he doubts that it can effectively happen.

Many designers, however, will complain that, "Every yo-yo with a Mac who does a flyer for a bake sale thinks he's a graphic designer." There is a real fear that jobs are being lost to the new army of desktop publishers and "paradesigners" who have taken a layout course at an adult education program. They will express some kind of longing for a solution. Then they will reflect for a moment on their fantasy of what the world would be like if we all had to prove our qualifications, most likely by taking a big stupid multiple-choice exam. And ultimately, of course, they will veto the idea.

CERTIFICATION, A DUMB IDEA

No wonder. There are many good reasons why a certification program for graphic designers is a dumb idea.
- A test will be a royal pain to develop and administer.
- It will cost a lot of money.
- The profession is too functionally diverse to reach a common standard.
- No one wants more bureaucracy.
- Everybody hates tests.
- You can't test for creativity, anyway.
- Some superb designers who've been in the business for years might do poorly, or even flunk.
- Some terrible designers will figure out how to pass.
- Certification could provide a veil of professionalism for the unscrupulous.
- The problem is really in the design schools, and it doesn't make sense to go back and try to fix it this way.
- No one has been hurt or killed by a graphic design, yet.

CERTIFICATION, A SMART IDEA

On the other hand, there is one reason why a certification program for graphic designers is a smart idea.
- We need it.

Ed Gold, professor in the publication design department at the University of

Baltimore and author of *The New Business of Graphic Design,* maintains that the certification process will automatically raise professional standards. "We've been trying for years to convince clients that design does something valuable, but we've failed. Clients buy design because they have to; they can't put out a product that isn't designed," he says. "But the decision is usually made on the basis of pure ego, pure taste. Nobody's suggesting that people won't look at portfolios and awards anymore, but let's at least have something they can use to judge who's got the right skills."

Massimo Vignelli, of Vignelli Associates in New York, believes that people would work hard to meet the standards, and that clients who are interested in quality work would be more likely to hire certified designers, who might even be able to charge higher fees. "Certification is inevitable," he said at last May's AIGA chapter retreat, pointing out that at one time architects and physicians didn't have professional standards either, and that "now is the time for us."

I knew as little as you about this issue two years ago. And frankly, I cared even less. Then I was assigned to research and write an article on the subject, which appeared in the *AIGA Journal* (Volume 10, No 1.), as, "The Accreditation Debate: Give It Up or Give It a Try?" Since then, I have spoken to many colleagues as well as to representatives of the accreditation and certification bodies of the architecture, interior design, and business communications fields—our closest siblings. I have conducted a fax poll of design firm principals and educators, and led a rather messy discussion among thirty-five AIGA chapter representatives and board members. And I have come to the conclusion that *even though all the reasons we shouldn't do it have some merit,* we need it.

Before you moan and groan and turn the page (or curse me for bringing up the subject), I want you to suspend your skepticism for a few moments. Let me walk you through a concept—perhaps a flight of fancy, perhaps an attainable goal—I hope it will make some sense.

THE CONCEPT

The concept has six major points. Read through them. Think about them. Think about what this could mean to the profession.

1. Certification should be individual and voluntary.

2. It should be granted to graphic designers on the basis of a combination of education, experience, and testing.

3. Taste and style should have nothing to do with it.

4. Professional certification should determine whether an individual has attained the level of skills required to serve a client independently—or to open his or her own office.

5. Certification must not depend upon membership in any organization, nor should membership automatically be granted upon certification.

6. The test should be developed and administered by a neutral organization in concert with the nation's leading graphic design associations.

1. Certification should be individual and voluntary. Unlike architects, who must be licensed by the states in which they practice in order to engage in their occupation, graphic designers will never be required to pass a state licensing exam. Designer certification must be strictly voluntary. Career or business doing well? Satisfied boss and/or clients? Level of professional knowledge up to the task you are doing—or would like to do? No problem. No pressure. However, for those who want to learn more, to challenge themselves, to move to the next level, to measure themselves against the best, or for a host of other reasons to attain certification, the opportunity should be there. If a program is administered correctly, the qualifications will be fair and comprehensive. And people will be interested in learning the material, meeting the standards, preparing for the test, making sure they're ready to practice the profession in a serious way.

There are too many design-firm business failures. Dan Wefler, of Wefler & Associates in Evanston, Illinois, which publishes the *Design Firm Directory,* estimates that there are approximately eight thousand U.S. graphic design firms that work directly for clients. His educated guess—there are no accurate government statistics—is that approximately 10 percent of them go out of business in a typical nonrecession year. Perhaps this happens because the principals open their own offices before they're ready; they simply didn't know what they needed to know in order to succeed.

Rather than viewing certification as a bureaucratic nightmare, it should be looked upon as an opportunity to learn everything you need to be a qualified professional; what you weren't taught in school or that you didn't have the opportunity to pick up on the job.

Ron Martin, vice president for employee communications at American Express Company and a past chairman of the International Association of Business Communicators (IABC), which has a well-established certification program, says, "Certification means that you're more than a narrow specialist. It means, here's a well-rounded professional who can serve senior management." Martin notes that many IABC candidates find that the learning that takes place when going through the process itself—taking professional development seminars and participating in informal study groups—is one of its key benefits.

Melanie Roher, principal of Roher Design, Inc. in Ardsley, New York, recalls that there came a moment of truth in her career when she realized that she would have to improve her professional and project management skills. "I took a two-year entrepreneurial business course," she says. "If I'd been working toward a graphic design certification, I might have been able to avoid the trial-and-error route."

2. It should be granted to graphic designers on the basis of a combination of education, experience, and testing. Everybody knows a fabulous designer who majored in biology or who never graduated from college. Jilly Simons, of Concrete, the Chicago design firm she heads, worries that she'd "hate to lose those great designers/thinkers/practitioners with no formal design education." Not to worry. The mandate is to develop a program that makes sense for our profession, that reflects the way things really are. There need not be a formal education requirement, for example, for someone who can demonstrate professional competency through a portfolio or in other ways.

Likewise, everybody also knows someone with an MFA from an esteemed design school whom they think would have better success as a biologist—or as anything but a designer. Just as professional standards in graphic design are "all over the place," so are educational standards. Graphic design is taught primarily by oral tradition. College teachers impart what they know, with their own personal bias. For example, in more than five years of teaching both undergraduate and graduate typography and corporate design courses at two of the leading design schools in the New York area, no one told me what my classes should cover, what it was expected that graduates should know. I created my own curriculum as I went along—as many of my colleagues do. And as design educator Ed Gold points out, graphic design is increasingly seen as a "cash cow" by lesser colleges that are cranking out graduates with minimal training by a not-very-talented faculty. According to one design educator, there are more than 850 programs—from community colleges through universities—that graduate many thousands of graphic design majors every year.

Given the unregulated and uneven nature of design education, a degree is not enough by itself. To assure true professionalism, a valid certification examination should be offered only to people who have practiced in the field for a specified number of years. Experience and a portfolio must be key ingredients. And because everyone's professional experience is different, the test will most likely require exposure to and study of areas that one might not encounter in day-to-day work. If your boss doesn't know anything about signage standards, information design, or Security and Exchange Commission requirements for financial statements, chances are you won't either. But studying for the exam would give all candidates a chance to expand their knowledge and very likely to prepare themselves for new or higher-level positions.

There is much to be learned from the standards required of interior designers. All U.S. and Canadian interior design organizations subscribe to the impressive testing program administered by the National Council for Interior Design Qualification (NCIDQ). To be eligible to take the test, an interior designer must have at least six years of combined educational and practical experience. This includes combinations such as: a four-year degree in interior design plus two years of professional experience; a two-year certificate plus four years of experience, etc. Based on a comprehensive survey of the graphic design field, we can devise our own realistic eligibility requirements.

3. Taste and style should have nothing to do with it. "If professional standards are regulated by licensing architects and interior designers, why do we still have so many ugly buildings and offices?" asks John DuFresne, principal of Pig's Eye Design in St. Paul, Minnesota. Like most of us, DuFresne questions whether an aptitude for aesthetics can be tested.

Well, we shouldn't even try. Whether you like hot pink or cool gray number 3, Helvetica or Bernhard Modern, is up to you—and the employers or clients who hire you. The test must measure knowledge and skill, not taste. It's not whether you favor certain colors, it's whether you know how to specify color so that a printer understands your directions. It's not which type fashions you prefer, it's whether you can spec type accurately. A meaningful, valid test would ascertain if you have what it takes to handle a job from the moment you meet the client through supervising the delivery of the final product. The test must be a test of professional capabilities, not preferences or prejudices. It should not be solely a production test. Far from it. It should test those senior-level skills—problem solving, analysis, organization of information, communication, and presentation—necessary to work with management to produce specific effects and achieve desired goals.

The NCIDQ test can be a paradigm for graphic design qualifications. An instructive 326-page book, *Interior Design Reference Manual,* reviews the subject matter and provides sample test questions.

Here are highlights of the contents:

I Theory. *Elements and principles of design, such as color systems and spatial perception.*

II   Programming, Planning, and Predesign. *A checklist of the client interview—determining space and volume needs, circulation patterns, and methods of cost estimating.*

III Contract Documents. *Construction drawings, specifications, and bidding procedures, including the duties, rights, and responsibilities of the owner.*

IV   Furniture, Fixtures, and Equipment. *Types, selection, and standards.*

V   Building and Interior Systems. *Construction of partitions, doors, ceilings, and cabinetry; finishes; lighting; mechanical and electrical systems; acoustics.*

VI   Communication Methods. *Types of drawings—axonometric, isometric, etc.*

VII Codes and Standards. *Building codes, exiting, and barrier-free design.*

VIII Business and Professional Practice. *Owner-designer agreements; ethics; insurance; business management; and public relations.*

IX   Project Coordination. *From coordinating and directing, changes in the work, to progress payments.*

X   History. *A timeline of periods and history in art, interiors, and architecture.*

Test questions range from multiple-choice, based on written information and graphic materials ("Which is the correct symbol for a duplex outlet?") to written answers ("What are the most important questions you need to ask the client in such-and-such a situation in order to plan a small medical office?"). The candidate then has 2½ hours to complete a "practicum/scenario" that evaluates ability to interpret a written program and develop a floor plan. He or she is given an architectural plan with perimeter walls, position of elevator bank, wet column, etc., and the client's program requirements. The challenge is to develop and draw correctly an interior scheme that includes all required spaces, adjacencies, circulation, furniture groups, lighting. Whether the wallpaper is floral or striped—or there is no wallpaper specified at all—is irrelevant. The manual warns, "Remember that the jurors are not looking for award-winning innovative solutions, just proof that you can respond to a program and integrate design principals and lighting into three-dimensional volume."[1] Several different solutions that would be given high marks are illustrated.

Imagine how this can be applied to graphic design! In my mind, the question is not what can we possibly put in a test for graphic designers, but what we will have to leave out. Merely the equivalent of parts I and II—the production stuff—has to include process and flat color, principles of typography, tile printing and bindery processes, paper grades and specifications, and on and on.

Michael Weymouth, of Weymouth Design, Inc., in Boston, can reel off a whole list of technical material he would like to see covered: when should you use short-grain paper? what constitutes a mailable envelope? should you reference coated or uncoated ink swatches for matte-coated stock? "I am very big on exploring the content," he says. "I hate to see things done wrong, like a double-saddle-wire job that's bound wrong, with a big gap in the middle."

4. Professional certification should determine whether an individual has attained the level of skills required to serve a client independently—or to open his or her own office. The design firm principals I asked tend to agree that it's difficult to tell from a portfolio whether a candidate is qualified for a job. They rely on résumés, interviews, "chemistry," and especially on references. Many report that they're only too aware that plenty of good-looking stuff in portfolios was done by a supervisor, perhaps the art director, or was the result of a group effort—and that dishonest references have helped nonqualified people get jobs from which they had to be fired. Joe Feigenbaum, of The Design Office, Inc., in Irvington, New York, says, "I've seen some 'great' portfolios where 'the designer' basically completed mechanical production." Feigenbaum thinks the most valuable benefit of certification might be encouraging design schools to offer more complete curricula and forcing lesser schools to improve or disband their programs. Steve Liska adds, "Schools graduate designers who can't conceptualize, 'problemsolve,' or functionally do much." He suggests that if an accredited core curriculum were developed to teach a broad spectrum of craft and concept, our industry would be healthier. "It would appear that the whole issue is a reflection of our disappointment in our education system and the students it produces," adds Kenneth Cooke, executive vice president and creative director at Siegal & Gale in New York, who indicates that if schools were accredited it would, "help separate the cosmetics from the knowledge."

To assist in hiring, a brief entry-level or junior designer test could be developed to be administered in the office during interview situations. This would be a helpful tool for employers, and could serve as a guide for design schools that—in the hopes of producing better-qualified graduates—might endeavor to add the content to their curricula.

However, the type of professional certification I'm proposing here is something quite different indeed. It is intended to determine whether an individual has attained the level of skills required to serve a client independently and without supervision—or to open his or her own office. If it's difficult for design firm principals who've worked in this business for an average of twenty years to tell if someone is really qualified, imagine how it is for clients. And they're the ones we should be concerned about. They want to know that you—the designer—know what you're doing, that you're not a flake, that the thousands of dollars they're investing in a project are going to be managed properly from start to finish.

Four areas should be covered: design theory and history, the design process itself (problem solving and visual communication), professional and business practices, and production. Kenneth Cooke, who recognizes that, "a creative idea from the mind of a noncertified designer is worth more to a client than a pedestrian idea from a merely competent but certified designer," has developed a detailed list, a body of knowledge that he believes every senior or practicing designer should have mastered. It also includes marketing, client relations, and environmental responsibility.

All this cannot be learned in school. Some of it is not academic material, it is professional, on-the-job material. Like many of my colleagues who teach, I believe that design school is the place to get a good foundation in theory, then to experiment, to solve the crazy impractical problems, not to be constrained by the realities of the business world. Wouldn't it be awful if during those precious four years of learning the liberal arts and art history, and taking design theory and studio classes, you had to sit through lectures on contracts and proposals? Although good business practice can—and should—be introduced, perhaps in a senior-year portfolio class or a graduate-level seminar, in reality it is only learned through experience, years of experience. I have owned and managed my own business for eighteen years and I'm still learning. But how I wish I had had the opportunity to prepare for a certification program like the one I'm describing before I opened my first business in 1976. What mistakes and calamities could have been avoided!

The IABC test, as an example, makes the assumption that you will be serving senior corporate management at the highest levels. The oral portion of the examination asks, "How would you advise the CEO to proceed with a communications program in such-and-such a crisis situation?" The NCIDQ test makes the assumption that you, the interior designer, will get this commission: a restaurant, a neonatal intensive care unit, retail shop, building lobby, whatever. And you will do it all by yourself. You will have no boss watching over your shoulder, no team to cover for your deficiencies. It will be done correctly, to the client's satisfaction, meeting all programming requirements, documents in order, construction supervised properly.

As a graphic designer—whether you work at a corporation or a design office or head your own firm—only when you can demonstrate the ability to earn that level of trust should you be able to put the initials that indicate professional certification (whatever initials they turn out to be) after your name. Like other certified professionals, you would have to apply, submit a portfolio (not to be judged on taste and style criteria!), and take oral and written examinations that would be offered on a quarterly or biannual basis in selected cities around the country.

Will there be economic benefits to certification? The design firm principals I spoke with were equally divided on the question of "will certified designers be able to charge higher fees?"—50 percent said no and 50 percent maybe. However, some people do see a distinct advantage. "I do look at it from a competitive point of view," says Mike Weymouth. "At a certain level you want people who aren't qualified to be weeded out. You want to have the edge on them."

What do clients think about certification? I spoke to about half a dozen experienced "design buyers," and to report that they're keen on the idea is an understatement. Once they understand the concept, which admittedly takes some explaining, they love it. They say—with the caveat that the credentials must be genuine, not awarded to unqualified people and not passed off as a substitute for talent—that it would really make a difference. "If there were a directory of certified designers, I would limit the people I work with to that group," vows Jane Shannon, manager of human resources communications for Citibank, the global financial services giant. "Business people tend to romanticize designers, as in, 'they're *artistes*, they don't really do this for a living,'" Shannon notes. "Certification might raise respect for the profession and help put an end to unethical practices like asking five designers to come up with ideas and then giving the best one to the in-house guy with a PC."

Mary Durkin, manager of creative services at the headquarters of Big Six accounting firm Deloitte & Touche in Wilton, Connecticut, reviews more than fifty portfolios a year and works with six or seven design firms at a time. She says that the recent proliferation of desktop people who are unqualified to function as project designers has been driving her crazy. "You can't say everyone who's a board-certified surgeon is an equally good doctor, but it sure gives you a field from which to choose," she states. "There's so much involved in designing something, even if it's a one-page flyer, people underestimate the knowledge and the skill that's required." Durkin says that if she had to make a decision between two portfolios of equal quality, she would definitely choose the certified designer.

In Philadelphia, at the Institute at Pennsylvania Hospital, Jane Friedman Century, assistant director of marketing services who was trained as a designer and is now responsible for working with designers on a range of publications, says that the business community needs help. "Your basic businessperson doesn't know a font from a food chain," she remarks, noting that she would probably choose certified designers because she'd be more confident that they'd have more business savvy and wouldn't operate "purely from the gut." Century believes that keeping up the certification entitlement through continuing education should be an intrinsic part of the program.

"Everybody's so cost-conscious these days," notes Citibank's Shannon, "It would be great to have two levels of certification, more junior and more senior, so that we could choose the level appropriate to the project."

5. *Certification must not depend upon membership in any organization, nor should membership automatically be granted upon certification.* If you're with me this far, you're probably wondering, who's going to do all this? *Association Management* magazine cites 151 national, state, and local organizations that have education and certification programs for their members, beginning with Alabama Concrete Industries Association and ending with Wyoming Trucking Association. Forget it! I am opposed to any requirement that is dependent on membership in a particular organization. Sure, an association can, if it chooses, set up self-serving, hollow qualifications and try to make sure all its members pass. Many organizations initiate a grandfather clause, which means that all current members are automatically certified on the day the program goes into effect. But what value would that have? Would clients have to wait until the current generation dies off to have a meaningful situation? And, like the International Association of Business Communicators, whose accreditation program is otherwise admirable, some organizations require that "successful candidates retain their accreditation as long as they are members and continue to pay the annual maintenance fee."

There are a couple of good reasons why graphic designer certification must not depend upon any particular affiliation. First of all, the Federal Trade Commission (FTC) will not approve a certification program that requires nonmembers to join an association before they are allowed to seek certification. Secondly, the AIGA, the oft-cited example of the "right" organization to do this for us, is a national nonprofit organization that promotes excellence in graphic design—as an art, as a profession. If the AIGA got into the business of saying yea or nay to the qualifications of individual members, that, in my opinion, could very likely hinder its mission. Chris Jenkins, an associate director at AIGA national headquarters in New York, explains, "Although we are studying the appropriateness and feasibility of developing a certification program, our mission is to promote the field of graphic design, not to promote individual designers."

And if certification were granted to members of one graphic design association or another, what about the printers, photographers, and illustrators who are members? Would they be granted different status? Could they no longer join? Quite simply, granting certification would be a tricky business for a design organization to be in.

6. *The test should be developed and administered by a neutral organization in concert with the nation's leading graphic design associations.* Seven design organizations are represented in the National Council for Interior Design Qualification. These include the American Society of Interior Designers (ASID), the Institute of Business Designers (IBD), Interior Design Educators Council (IDEC), and so forth. All assist—in conjunction with the Educational Testing Service in Princeton, New Jersey—with the development, constant update, and

revision of the NCIDQ's tests. All participate in the review of education and practice requirements, research, surveys, analysis, question development, grading, and jury procedures.

Doesn't this make sense for the graphic design profession? Why not, as a start, invite the AIGA, American Center for Design, Design Management Institute, Corporate Design Foundation, Graphic Artists Guild, and perhaps the International Council of Graphic Design Associations (ICOGRADA) to form a similar alliance and create certification board. Representatives of each organization, in concert with each other and with a panel of design educators and practicing designers, could compose the basic outline and procedures, amass the funding, and oversee the inception of the program. Rather than grant acceptance to— or reject—individual members, these organizations could use their expertise to advise, define, guide, set standards, and update; in short, to ensure that the program is developed and administered in the best interests of the entire profession and all its practitioners.

Loren Swick, executive vice president of the NCIDQ, says that the interior design profession is as broad and diverse as graphic design, and that developing its program—it was founded in 1972—was a daunting challenge. "But that now the research and results speak for themselves." He acknowledges that in the early days there was skepticism among interior designers, too. "People don't like to subject themselves to rigor and to possible failure," he says. "But when you have a benchmark to measure yourself against, a standard to rise to, it all pays off."

Originally published in Communication Arts Illustration Annual, *1993.*

Notes
1. Taken from the *Interior Design Reference Manual*, David K. Ballast (Professional Publications, Inc., 1992). Used with permission of the publisher.

THE CASE AGAINST CERTIFICATION
Gunnar Swanson

With the advent of personal computers, more people are able to deal with the mechanical basics of graphic design. Jobs that might have been given to graphic designers in the past can be done by clerical workers with a Mac. Because the physical process of assembling graphic materials is less mysterious than it used to be, and because there has been a boom in design education, the small fraternity of graphic design is overcrowded. Untrained newcomers are increasingly seen as threats to "real" graphic designers.

In the last few years, graphic designers have gone from complaining that nobody has ever heard of graphic design to complaining that everyone claims to *do* graphic design. We got over having to explain that we weren't "commercial artists" (debased small-time painters selling their souls to the bourgeoisie), but "graphic designers" (manipulators of type and image, communicators, problem solvers) only now to have to say, "These other manipulators of type and image aren't real graphic designers."

We would love to have "graphic designer" be more than a job description. It should be an honorific, a recognition of our central position in commerce and culture. This is, of course, impossible if we cannot distinguish ourselves from the great PageMaker unwashed—that growing legion of wannabees calling themselves graphic designers. The changed business climate—lower budgets, new demands, more competition—is about as much as a graphic designer can take. Insult is added to injury by our collective good name being usurped by every clown with some stolen software and the price of a Macintosh lease.

Enter certification of graphic designers. What better way to distinguish "Us" from "Them"? As *certified* graphic designers, we might be able to regain our honor and the business that is rightfully ours. What could be wrong with that?

Although talk of certification for graphic designers has been around for some time, it was always vague mumblings until Ellen Shapiro wrote about the subject in the *AIGA Journal of Graphic Design* (Vol. 10, No. 1, 1992, and Vol. 12, No. 2, 1994) and in *Communication Arts* (No. 241, July 1993). In talks and articles, Shapiro describes certification as individual and voluntary, granted on the basis of education, experience, and testing. Taste and style would have nothing to do with it, she says. Certification would be assurance of a designer's ability to serve a client independently. It would not depend on membership in any organization and the test would be administered by a neutral organization.

Even though Shapiro's articles bounce back and forth between issues of certification and accreditation, sometimes mentioning licensing, these are not interchangeable ideas. Certification would affirm an individual designer's skills. (There is currently no large-scale certification of graphic designers in the United States.) Accreditation would signal the quality of a school, its staff, and its curriculum. (Schools are accredited by a variety of agencies. The most common for graphic design programs in the United States is the National Association of Schools of Art and Design—NASAD.) Licensing is state testing and registration of practitioners. Licensing laws make it illegal to practice without state approval. (Licensing is reserved for those who affect the public safety and well being, such as architects, engineers, doctors, and barbers.)

Certification of designers would give potential clients a way to know that a graphic designer is qualified. It would allow designers to distinguish themselves from desktop publishers and other less qualified graphics practitioners. Again, what could be wrong with that?

Well, if there is one thing I've learned in more than fifteen years of running a design business (and a few more years of living), it's that doing something out of fear or greed almost always dooms whatever you are doing. If certification of graphic designers is to have any chance of working, it must he done with worthy motives and clarity of purpose. When a major article in favor of certification (Shapiro's July 1993 *CA* article) begins by showing us a design pretender and revealing that (*gasp!*) his date has a lousy accent ("What d'ya do?" "J'learn that in school?"), we may not be basing the desire for certification on rationality and good will.

Interior designer certification is often held up as comparable to graphic designer certification. However, certified interior designers I have talked to complain that their certification test doesn't reflect abilities, hasn't improved business, and is necessary only because of the threat that licensing is just around the corner. (Certified interior designers would be grandfathered into the licensing system.) Certified business communicators, public-relations professionals whom Shapiro holds up as another product of a successful certification program, say they are paid no more for being certified than uncertified. We hear reports about what a success certification has been for similar fields, but those reports seem to come from the people administering the test, not the people who have taken it.

But graphic design isn't necessarily very much like interior design or business public relations. Let's look at graphic design. Certification, we are assured, would be based largely on an objective test. What is it about graphic design that can be tested objectively? Shapiro gives us a "whole list of technical material"—postal regulations and production information. Are these the things that distinguish "Us" from mere desktop publishers? The assumption is that "real" designers will do better on an objective test than someone who buys a Mac and religiously reads *Publish* magazine. My suspicion is that the opposite is true.

Shapiro lists specifying type as an important objective skill; she fails to mention examining color progressives or sorting to a California case. Her technical anachronism doesn't just point out the problem of keeping a standardized test current. It points out a problem with standardization. In a field moving as rapidly as ours, standardization favors calcification. Certification might benefit some designers in the short run. It is unhealthy for *all* designers in the long run if our business becomes even less relevant to a world in technological and sociological flux.

Standardizing graphic design is like standardizing dance or fishing. It may all go by one name, but it's not the same thing. Please explain to me why Charles Spencer Anderson, Sheila de Bretteville, Josef Müller-Brockmann, Art Chantry, Ed Fella, Tom Geismar, April Greiman, any senior designer for Walter Landor, Scott Mednick, Paul Rand, Deborah Sussman, Rick Valecenti, Rudy VanderLans, and Massimo Vignelli are all in the same business. The strength of graphic design is its diversity. A successful certification program would threaten that diversity.

Proponents of certification tout its benefits for clients, who would be able to discover instantly whether a designer is "qualified." This ignores the fact that our clients and their needs are as diverse as we are. While some clients may look for designers in the vanguard of fashion, others may consider marketing knowledge the key attribute. As technology shifts, professional responsibilities change; proofreading skills may be vital to some clients. Should there be a spelling-errors-not-caught-by-a-spell-checker section of a graphic design certification test?

If our goal is to show that we are competent to do a particular task, particular certification would be much more reasonable. Some designers might want to collect certifications like merit badges, while others would see fit to become just a certified packaging designer, a certified architectural signage designer, a certified financial designer, or what have you.

If design specialties require particular training, knowledge, and skills for a candidate to pass a certification test, at what point would all of this become nothing more than a protection for existing design firms? A few of us are finally waking up to the fact that the real world, unlike the design world, is not all white and middle class. Holding up standards may be appropriate; putting up more barriers is not.

One argument against certification is that it is a collective waste of time. Along with the design business, major design organizations such as the AIGA are going through a period of change and reevaluation. Adjusting to decentralization, broadening our scope, and reaching out to a changing world are formidable tasks for designers, design firms, and design organizations. I don't know about you, but I don't need another thing to do. We risk sinking our design organizations under the weight of a certification bureaucracy, petrifying ourselves and our image with attempts at objective standardization, and generally doing damage to design to prove we are not just desktop publishers. Do we think the desktop publishers are going to say, "Oh, sorry. I didn't realize this was holy ground. I'll pack up and leave"?

In the meantime, certification, if successful, would become a standard, a proof that we are "real" designers. (That is why we're doing it, after all.) Although we might claim it's only for design business owners, every senior designer who wants to keep moving ahead will need to be certified. It will become the measure of success.

Even if there is a required year or two or three between school and certification, certification rates of schools' graduates will become part of that measure of success. Many schools will succumb to the temptation to teach to the test. Since the test will be objective, and objective testing favors production skills, printing knowledge, and legal facts, curricula will also tilt in that direction. Since technology is rapidly changing production, printing, and the law, schools with certification-adjusted curricula will increasingly offer short-term training rather than lasting education and we will have dealt another blow to our already troubled system of design education.

The side benefits of graphic design certification promised by its supporters—continuing education, dissemination of information, creation of benchmarks, and going beyond style and fashion—are all worthwhile goals. They might or might not be side effects of the certification process, but they would certainly be easier to reach if addressed directly, rather than hoped for as a collateral product of a testing scheme.

Another place where direct action would be more efficient is in proving that "We" are not like "Them." If you can do something demonstrably better for a client than a desktop publisher can, then do it. If you can't, certification isn't going to make you rich or gain you respect.

What is it that you do better than the desktop crowd? If you're like most designers I know, your answer primarily has to do with aesthetic refinement. The secondary answer is some combination of business and printing experience. I'd love to see an objective test for aesthetic refinement. (Especially one where "taste and style . . . have nothing to do with it.") Clearly, that's what some certification supporters expect of the process. Massimo Vignelli says that "real" designers are protecting the culture. When challenged whether an objective test could judge cultural protection, he claimed it was easy. "We'd agree 90 percent of the time. . . . There's good typography and there's *Emigre* stuff."

Vignelli is not alone. I think many designers have a fantasy that certification might rid us of whatever we hate in design and would prove that we and those we most admire are objectively better, more qualified, or more *real*. I suspect that, confronted with an actual test and actual standards, most of us would see the folly in such an attitude. So before we expend any more time on this, proponents should produce a portion of a test. An outline and some typical questions would suffice—just enough so that the "real" designers can see whether it could accomplish any of our fantasies. It's time to get real.

Originally published in Print, *January/February 1995.*

IN DEFENSE OF UNPROFESSIONALISM
Michael Rock

A national design conference is something like one of those interminable annuals; but you're right inside it, the work has sprouted arms and legs, and it's all talking a mile a minute. *Ray Gun* is hobnobing with *Emigre,* Aldus is eyeing Adobe across the room, Benetton is whispering in the corner with a Time-Warner annual report. As the critical mass of graphic designers is approached, you cannot help pondering issues of professional association. And so I was not surprised when I found myself cornered into an argument on the subject just as I was planning my escape from the fifth national convention of the American Institute of Graphic Arts and the maudlin lobby of the Downtown Miami Hyatt Regency—replete with waterfall, palm trees, and tropical Muzak punctuated by an endless jack-hammering in the empty lot next door.

The concept of professional standards has plenty of manifestations—educational accreditation, professionalism, AIGA certification—and all the allure that goes along with the image of The Professional: respect, high pay, beautiful lovers. You can't spend an hour at a design conference without someone decrying the lack, the need, the desire for any or all of the above. Journals are peppered with articles entitled "Making Accreditation Work" or "Board Certification: An Idea Whose Time Has Come." It seems like everyone from Paul Rand to Katherine McCoy has taken a shot at the idea. It's a concept that lurks under the move to establish national design councils, motivates debates between designers, and directs the curriculum of art colleges and graduate schools. But what is a design professional and what standards dictate his or her activity? Do we really need a professional organization of graphic design?

The predominant feature that seems to run through any gathering of two or more graphic designers is a certain deep-seated insecurity. Designer anxiety is rooted in a fear that what we do is not respected, worthwhile, important. This feeling is fueled by a business world that, in general, neither respects nor considers design particularly worthwhile or important. As designers seem hell-bent on impressing business, this can be a big problem. Thus the design activity is fraught with a desperate quality. In that desperation, designers turn to professionalism as their savior.

Professionalism works by constructing an artificial wall around an activity by keeping people systematically excluded from calling what they do the same thing as what you do. The logic runs that if we could develop a set of standards, either through the school system or through an exterior organization, we could produce a measure against which we would conclude who is, and who isn't, a graphic designer. (Actually, what it would really conclude is who aligns with the sanctioned definition and who doesn't, telling us more about the values of the tester than the testee.) The medical profession, for example, for better or worse, excludes herbalism, acupuncture, midwifery, and faith healing as outside of convention, therefore exotic, different, dubious. This may make more sense in fields concerning life and death (doctors, cab drivers) or activities involved with things that have to stand up (structural engineers) than it does in a field that has to do with communication, taste, aesthetics, and fashion.

Attendant to the move toward guild-like closure is the development of a specialized jargon and a set of mysterious trade practices. In order to accomplish a separate identity, the graphic design profession has fortified itself against other activities that border on its kingdom. So in a headlong attempt to market themselves to business as a quasiscience, graphic designers have artificially defined the activity by elimination, insisting that they are not artists, not illustrators, not photographers, not industrial designers, not writers, not architects, not printers, not typesetters, and especially not advertising people. Artists— considered suspect, possibly subversive, probably destitute—tend to make the design-buying middle manager, with an eye on the bottom line, twitch. Getting the company to part with its money proves easier for a suited man, preferably graying at the temples, representing an organized profession using an articulate and complex language of technical terms. (One of the great fears attached to the advent of the Macintosh and desktop publishing is that it has initiated others into our secret language; demystified our code of fonts, rags, picas, and leading.) And so like Henry V, to borrow critic Raymond William's allusion, design disavows its disreputable friends, the artists, and the follies of youth once it ascends to the throne of corporate consultancy.

The professional carries a certain prestige within the social hierarchy. A title or an acronym after a name is a class signifier, a sign of position and community approbation. Raymond Loewy was perhaps the first paradigm of the design professional. The expensive suits, elegant cars, elaborate process—like the stories of preparing for days for a big presentation, like a boxer training for a prize fight—all symbolized a suave sophisticate, completely on top of his game and in control of his client. In his analysis of the middle class, C. Wright Mills observed that "United States society esteems the exercise of educated skill and honors those who are professionally trained; it also esteems money as fact and as symbol, and honors those who have a lot of it. Many professional men are thus at the intersection of these two systems of value."

Design professionalism is advanced along these two fronts: the acquisition of high learning that is equated with high culture and the attainment of real-life experience and the big pay-off. Academia posits an image of design as an altruistic service and an intellectual pursuit, safely above the disagreeable association with dirty commerce. Graphic design is promoted as a kind of aesthetic public service through which the world is saved from visual anarchy. The patina of the university and its association with fine printing, bibliophily, and erudite scholarship are exploited, endowing the activity with a certain cultural authority. This model invests heavily in developing a historical canon and may employ complex metalanguages and theory. It is often accompanied by calls for the accreditation of educational programs and aspires to academic goals well beyond those accomplished by the proponents.

The second route is based in nuts-and-bolts pragmatism. It's the bare-knuckles approach to the profession in which one earns his or her stripes by serving time in the trenches. Success is signified by wealth. For this anti-intellectual school of professionalism, the esoteric, pedantic, overly theoretical approach of the academy is dismissed as indulgent and misguided; the real goal of design is to please business and sell product. Out of this position a basic strategy of professional corporate design developed, based primarily in results, rationalism, and a close examination of what exactly it is that business expects.

The strategy has worked, more or less, in the corporate world and a certain normative behavior has arisen in the practices of the big corporate identity studios. But an attempt to adopt the standards of business design as a definition of the wider activity is sure to fail. In addition to narrowing the activity and severing design from other forms of mass communication, the imposition of professional standards shifts the field from a meritocracy, or leadership by the talented, to an artificial system of rules and dictates.

And so professional certification by a group organized to serve those same practitioners would only stultify design, ensuring that a single value system remains predominant and unchallenged. The AGI (Alliance Graphique International) is the example. In addition, certification sends a signal to business that there is a unified and accepted definition of acceptable design that is exterior to performance. The organized profession legitimizes privilege, and promotes success by conformity rather than risk, as well as stresses professional cohesiveness over client or community satisfaction. This gives rise to the condition we have today in which we tend to be more concerned with the intra-professional discourse than our relationship with those who use our products. "Charlatans satisfy clients," notes historian Everett Hughes, "professionals satisfy their colleagues."

Ironically, professionalism is usually advanced as a service to the *clients,* protecting them from unscrupulous practitioners and shoddy workmanship. In fact, professional organizations serve their *members,* limiting competition, excluding alternative practices, and legitimizing and fixing higher fee structures. (In the best cases they do both, like the SEGD's involvement in reworking the ADA guidelines.) Since definitions of what design is and should be are constantly revised and in flux, organizations tend to synthesize an artificially unified image. Often design systems are challenged by the introduction of ideas from outside the profession, from technological development and from development in the arts. Unless standards were constantly revised—which would contradict their very purpose—or made ridiculously broad, guidelines agreed upon one year may be useless the next.

We might be better off if we jettison the idea of a singular definition of what design *should* be, and perhaps that of a single organization for all graphic designers. If we were to do so, much of the divisiveness that plagues and trivializes the activity might disappear. There is no reason why design should have some unified field theory that governs the entire practice. I am always amazed at the sentiment—represented at the AIGA conference by debates between wildly divergent designers like Scott Mednick and Jack Summerford—that there are some overarching principles that should necessarily apply to an alternative magazine, an annual report, a street map, and an album cover.

Rather than model the design activity on architecture or law, perhaps we should view it as a kind of elaborated speech or writing. Writing is a common activity shared by most members of a society and practiced on many levels. Like design, writing is integral to human communication. Yet there is no call to standardize all speech or all writing or even standardize the way in which all writing is taught. Writing and speech are practiced eclectically—from poetry to graffiti, novels, newspapers, tabloids, and love notes. There is academic writing and experimental writing, religious writing and profanity, and "bad" writing that comes, over time, to be considered "good" writing. For every Nabokov there are thousands of Danielle Steeles and millions of hacks pounding out stories and articles at twenty-five cents a word. I can appreciate, in differing amounts, both the back of the cereal box and a poststructural analysis of it. We celebrate the diversity of writing, the diversity of speech, the universe of information, but bemoan the paucity of good design. If we released ourselves from the realm of self-imposed standards, we could see the design profession as a true meritocracy where the cream rises to the top.

A version of this article was originally published in I.D., *January/February 1994.*

NATURE OR NURTURE?
Michael Bierut

When Thomas Watson, Jr. died last year, there was no shortage of ink extolling his extraordinary career. He was, after all, the man who transformed his father's business, a successful manufacturer of adding machines and time clocks, into the world's largest computer company, IBM; who built, in fifteen years, a $7.5 billion-a-year enterprise that came to define American business in the postwar world; who *Fortune* called "the most successful capitalist in history."

No one, though, seemed to mention the real reason why Thomas Watson, Jr. is held to be a heroic figure by designers everywhere; no one spoke of those five little words attributed to him that have been repeated endlessly in articles, in speeches, at design seminars, in slick presentations to hesitant clients, over and over again, like a mantra: "Good design is good business."

The Corporate Design Foundation (CDF) was established in 1985 to "communicate the significance and importance of design to American business." At the 1991 American Institute of Graphic Arts national conference in Chicago, CDF chairman Peter Lawrence helped organize a presentation to discuss the foundation's efforts to introduce design into business-school curricula. Now, designers claim to be desperately interested in matters of business. But conference organizers have learned to their chagrin that given a choice between a thoughtful discussion of ways to communicate the significance of design, on one hand, and a show-and-tell by someone with groovy slides on the other, conferees stampede to the latter.

To remedy this imbalance, conference organizers suggested that Lawrence give the event a hot title: "Creating the Perfect Client."

Thomas Watson, Jr., in the mythology of our profession, was the Perfect Client.

Even his great awakening was the stuff of myth, right out of St. Paul on the road to Damascus: "The inspiration for the design program came to me during a stroll I took down Fifth Avenue in the early 1950s," Watson wrote in his autobiography. "I found myself attracted to a shop that had typewriters on sidewalk stands for passersby to try. The machines were done in different colors and had sleek designs. I went inside and saw modern furniture and bright colors. . . . The name over the door was Olivetti." Later a Dutch friend sent him a bundle of Olivetti graphics, which Watson laid side by side with similar IBM material. "The Olivetti material was filled with color and excitement and fit together like a beautiful picture puzzle. Ours looked like directions on how to make bicarbonate of soda."

What happened next was simple. Watson found Eliot Noyes and appointed him IBM's consultant director of design. Noyes in turn brought in Charles and Ray Eames, Eero Saarinen, and, of course, Paul Rand. The rest is design history.

Funny thing, though. "Business people often have the impression that design is only about styling," Peter Lawrence observes regretfully in the January/February 1994 issue of *I.D.* And certainly few things are as irritating to today's informed and well-intentioned designer as being dismissed as a mere stylist. Yet go back and reread what the real issue was for Watson: beautiful picture puzzle versus bicarbonate of soda. Good design is good business? Maybe. More like, good design just . . . well, *looks* better, for God's sake. In other words, styling.

So what's so bad about styling, anyway? If styling, mere styling, is so dismissively easy, why does everything look so horrible? Not horrible in terms of "Cranbrook: Bold and Experimental or Ugly and Illegible?" or "Modernism: Utopian Functionalism or European Phallicentrism?" but horrible like what you see on the shelves of any convenience store in America. In other words, Tibor and Massimo and *Emigre* can go on about good and right and wrong for years, but you can be sure their arguments are inaudible in the aisles of 7-Elevens across the country. Forget about "communicating the value of design to American business." Can't we just get a few more clients interested in this styling thing?

Historically, it seems as though Perfect Clients have been born, not made. Again and again, for each great corporate design patron, a single person can be identified as the prime enabler: Watson at IBM, Irwin Miller at Cummins, Walter Paepcke at Container Corporation, Frank Stanton at CBS. Designers desperately summon up this pantheon as evidence that good design is good business. It's certainly comforting to assume that these Perfect Clients were driven by something as rational as the profit motive, that it was just good old-fashioned hardheaded business sense that led to all those products by Emilio Ambasz and displays by Rudy de Harak and ads by Herbert Bayer and Alvin Lustig.

But any designer that's been lucky enough to work with their own version of a Perfect Client knows firsthand that something else is at work here, something less rational than the simple good design/good business equation would admit. Meryl Streep was once asked why she devoted so much time to perfecting aspects of her performances that would never be visible to a movie audience. She sheepishly replied, "I guess I'm just the kind of person who likes to clean behind the refrigerator." The disquieting truth is that the factors that motivate good clients may be genetic rather than strategic. Simply and bafflingly, they may just be the kind of persons who like good design, the same way they might be interested in music or wine or motorcycles or porcelain figurines.

Disquieting also has been the occasional selectivity of good taste. It's been observed that while Walter Paepcke was commissioning world-class designers to create those extraordinary "Great Ideas" ads, his Container Corporation was manufacturing vast quantities of truly hideous packaging and point-of-purchase materials untouched by good design by any definition of the word. Even more startling to contemplate is that the exquisite CBS headquarters building by Eero Saarinen was brought to you, at least in part, through advertising revenues generated by "The Beverly Hillbillies." In other words, good design is good business, but good business may not always be good design.

The whole idea of "good design" must have seemed easier to isolate in days when there was more of a consensus about what constituted "good." Taken as a class, the pantheon of Perfect Clients now seems like a pretty insular world, with the same names—Noyes, Saarinen, Eames, Rand, and so on—showing up on everyone's Rolodex. And with the idea of styling held in such low regard these days, the modern Perfect Client seems to be held to a higher standard in nonvisual realms; the many designers who admire the Body Shop's Anita Roddick or Paul Hawken, founder of Smith & Hawken, for instance, obviously do so for more than the way the packaging and catalogues look.

Then as now, the design character of each of these companies seems completely tied up with a specific human being. In an op-ed piece in the *New York Times* last spring, Paul Rand noted how many vaunted design programs collapsed with the departure of their idiosyncratic champions, adding reassuringly, "That so many programs for large corporations have had a short life span is no evidence that design is impotent." Perhaps design isn't impotent, but what about designers?

For it seems that so much time and effort is devoted to solving one basic problem: can truly brilliant design—whatever way you want to define it these days—happen without a Perfect Client, some person who, for mysterious reasons, cares desperately about "mere styling," and everything else, and is willing to devote time and intelligence and money to getting it right? We designers have tried lots of different things as substitutes: thick corporate-identity standards manuals, desktop publishing templates, strategic design-planning documents with lots of charts, and now design-flavored case histories to sneak under the noses of MBAs-in-training—all intended to counter the sense of impotence that comes with sitting and waiting for a Perfect Client to magically appear.

Of course, there is another approach, one borrowed from the world of counter-intelligence. Why not canvass America's schools, find an artistically inclined ten-year-old who might otherwise choose a design career, divert them with CDF and AIGA money to the finest business education available, establish them on the corporate fast track, and wait for this "mole" to become CEO of a major corporation? An anonymous gift subscription to *I.D.* would be all it would take to "activate" the nascent design interests of this influential agent-in-place.

We would then sit back, our lips soundlessly repeating five little words, waiting for the commissions to roll in.

Originally published in I.D., March/April 1994.

GRAPHIC DESIGN: AN UNPROTECTED
FRONTIER OF INTELLECTUAL PROPERTY

DK Holland

In 1979, the Graphic Artists Guild made a presentation to the United States Copyright Office regarding the protection of graphic design by the copyright law. Copyright is the protection of intellectual property. Usually, we think of movies, paintings, books, illustration, software, and music scores as being copyrightable properties. Graphic design is more like a movie or a book than an illustration or painting since it is typically a compendium of many different creators' individual efforts. But while it is trade custom for graphic designers to license their work (i.e., mechanicals) to their clients, they do not generally copyright their efforts. So the question at the 1979 meeting was: how and when is graphic design deserving of copyright?

Before we can make a clear statement of the principles of law that support copyright protection for graphic design, it is essential to understand the subtle issues of definition and judgment. A painting of colored squares by Josef Albers was shown to the Registrar of Copyrights to be much like an abstract poster using typography designed by Milton Glaser. Albers clearly owned the copyright to his painting in the eyes of the copyright office. Yet they struggled with Glaser's rights. Did he design the typography? No. But Albers did not invent the square either. And in the years since 1979, there has been no resolution to this dilemma.

A work is deserving of copyright when it has enough creative expression to be considered protectable. Something as simple and unsophisticated as a child's finger painting is considered unique. The Graphic Artists Guild (GAG) submitted a form to register the copyright for the cover of their *Pricing and Ethical Guidelines* recently and received back a notice that the application presented a claim in "design." "It is the position of the Copyright Office that format and book design fall within the realm of ideas or concepts, which, by law, are not protected by copyright. . . . Please file a new application omitting reference to 'design.' A claim in 'cover art' alone might be appropriate," said Alden Almquist, Copyright Examiner.

This seems to suggest that there is a bureaucratic blind spot in the watchful eye of the Copyright Office, whose mandate is to encourage creative expression by protecting it. Tad Crawford, who handled the guild's presentation to the Copyright Office and recently cowrote *Business and Legal Forms for Graphic Designers,* observes, "The copyright examiner lacks the aesthetic insight of the designer. Calling a work 'art' instead of 'design' may sometimes encourage the examiner to process an application. However, minimal creativity may ultimately be rewarded by copyright protection, while far more subtle and sophisticated designs may have no protection at all." The copyright law is intended to benefit the public by not protecting that which is too simple or generic. At the same time, a lack of clarity in the rights area, in general, has created a gnarly ethical mess within the graphic design industry.

The dilemmas were especially evident at the American Institute of Graphic Arts (AIGA) exhibition called "Influence and Plagiarism." Graphic designers were asked to compare pairs of design projects designed by different people. In each pair, one claimed to be an original designer, the other an imitation. In examining the results, it was easy to see that designers do not understand what infringement means. Many stood falsely accused of imitation. Also, there were many examples shown where the design was not what was imitated; what was actually copied was the illustration within the design, if anything. At any rate, only a small handful of examples could be seen as legitimate infringements.

THE ACADEMIC SCENE

Students are especially easy targets of exploitation, since they are often given assignments that result in the development of valuable intellectual property. Sometimes this property is given away by the schools or students to corporations (frequently in corporate-sponsored contests held in schools), or used by the teachers themselves in their own professional projects. Schools usually are unaware of the rights issue and the ethical implication of such practices. Or they are aware of it but nonplussed as to how to resolve it.

Schools like Art Center College of Design and The Fashion Institute of Technology (FIT) have established thoughtful programs for handling outside interest in students' intellectual property. Art Center, in Pasadena, California, which is internationally known for consistently graduating some of the top graphic design talent, has a corporate sponsored project program. Art Center will set up students in a think-tank situation to tackle a problem; to rethink a process; to think outside the box. The client participates in the process. The cost to the corporation (i.e., the client) is $10,000–$50,000. One half is allocated to materials, one half goes to support scholarships. "The end result, however, cannot be to create an actual product. The experience must be of the highest educational value to the student. The goals of the client must be philanthropic," says Tim Butte, Director of Corporate Sponsored Projects at Art Center. "We screen prospective sponsors very carefully. You can often tell in the first interview what their true intention is. We turn away two to three project inquiries a day which would be better handled on a professional basis.

"We see this as a far-sighted proactive way for companies to identify future designers, while at the same time providing students with 'real world' experience. Students aren't jaded or discouraged. They have an easier time 'blue skying' an approach to problem solving," says Butte (who proudly states that his mother graduated in the class of 1949). "With majors in illustration, fine art, advertising design, we've had as many as six corporate sponsored projects going on at any one time, including Nike (which recently hired seventeen Art Center graduates), Steelcase, Nestlé, NCR, and Honda."

Does the school deserve to benefit from its students' efforts? "Art Center College of Design does not exist in a vacuum—it *is* the students! We are not here to make a profit, and everything we do is calculated to further the process of taking what we believe are today's finest students and preparing them to be tomorrow's premiere designers and artists, well grounded in the realities of the business world," continues Butte. It is hard to believe that corporations, in this day and age, have the time and money to put into purely altruistic, charitable acts. But the truth is they want to expose the best and brightest design students to their corporation with hopes of recruiting them. Publicity coverage is also a good possibility. The tangible results of the projects become the property of Art Center, with rights awarded to the students for use in their portfolios.

The Fashion Institute of Technology has a different approach. "At FIT, particularly in the new toy design department, students are expected to design 'marketable' products and carry them from concept to prototype. All of our students are carefully selected, and have exceptional artistic abilities in combination with a playful and adventurous spirit," says Judy Ellis, chairperson of toy design. "In our department, students are under rigorous guidance of a highly skilled faculty and are in regular contact with the leaders of the toy industry. Students are encouraged to be socially responsible and create products that will inspire, inform, entertain, and sell. We fully expect that, while in the program, students will develop highly marketable toys."

In order to protect the student's concepts and product designs, and to ensure financial compensation for both the student and institution, FIT's toy design department has developed specific guidelines and legal agreements. "These agreements are carefully explained to every student during the initial interview, and all students are required to sign these agreements upon acceptance into the program," according to Ellis.

"The first agreement deals with the matter of royalties. It is a legal document that guarantees that the student will receive 75 percent of all royalties and the toy design department will receive 25 percent, which is earmarked for scholarships. This agreement also states that all other work the student creates while in the program is the joint property of the student and FIT, and that it will remain so until six months after the student graduates. After six months, another legal agreement is signed by the school that returns all rights to the student. Royalties for concepts and products sold to the industry while the student is in the program remain the joint property of the student and the school."

In addition to the royalty agreement, FIT uses other legal documents to protect designers' rights. In one, known as the Faculty Confidentiality Agreement, Ellis notes, "all members of the toy design faculty acknowledge that toy designs and ideas that are developed as part of the program belong to both the student and the school, and agree that all ideas to which they are privy will be kept confidential.

"The educational foundation is another mechanism FIT utilizes to help students interface with industry. The foundation accepts research projects that are sponsored by individual companies, trade organizations, or government agencies. When the educational foundation accepts a design research project, they decide on the format for the project and then select a faculty member to be the project director. The project director, in turn, chooses a group of students to work on the project." In these endeavors, students can, depending on the particular arrangement, receive stipends, awards, and/or royalties.

Overall, Ellis comments, "We emphasize the importance of integrity and honesty. As part of the required course of study, students learn how to operate in the business environment. For example, in the business practices course, which is a requirement, students learn about corporate structure, the rights and obligations of the designer in the toy industry, copyright law, and contracts."

INTEGRITY AND OWNERSHIP OF IDEAS

Similar clarity is also needed outside the academic arena. Clients sometimes rationalize that when they are brainstorming with the designer on a project, they too are designing the work and deserve to own the rights to the work. "After all, what am I buying?" is a common—and naïve—question. The answer, of course, is that they are buying thinking, an intangible product—a response that does not always satisfy clients. In fact, clients sometimes also assume they will own *all* the ideas that are proposed by the design firm, even ones not used or fully developed. Projects that are killed midstream but have gone to the comprehensive stage (i.e., mock-up) are in the most jeopardy. Clients often think they own the comprehensives. Again, the "What-am-I-buying?" mentality is prevalent, and the question is begged: "What are you going to do with the comprehensive? Hang it on your wall?" No one else should be allowed to develop another designer's work without his or her consent. And the trade custom of selling unfinished work is not supported by most creative professions.

Following the client's logic, graphic designers would have rights of co-authorship with illustrators and photographers, whom they direct and with whom they brainstorm. Paul Basista, executive director of the Graphic Artists Guild National, explained how the judicial system is being used to clarify this, "Ever since the landmark decision by the U.S. Supreme Court in *CCNV v. Reid,* which dramatically limited a hiring party's ability to impose work-for-hire on commissioned work in the absence of a written agreement, we anticipated that clients would attempt to retain complete control over works by claiming joint authorship. That's why Senator Thad Cochran's "Artist's Bill of Rights" introduced in the last Congress specifically addressed the joint authorship issue.

"Joint authorship allows either author to exploit economically the work in many ways without the permission of the other. However, the joint author can demand an accounting and 50 percent of any profits derived from that exploitation. There are several problems with this. First, if the client claiming joint authorship is on the scale of a Time Warner, and an individual creator demands an accounting and percentage of the profits, and a Time Warner refuses, who's prepared to take on Time Warner's legal department? Yet, if a Time Warner demanded an accounting and percentage of the profits, how could any individual refuse? Second, what if the exploited work is a promotional brochure or T-shirt that is distributed for free? Third, without controls on this, any client (art director or design firm included) can claim joint authorship merely because they conceived of the project, even if there were no contribution of anything tangible.

"The guild feels that joint authorship should occur only when each author's contribution is tangible and copyrightable in its own right and if both parties agree in writing, prior to the commencement of work that the work is a joint authorship. Clients don't understand that buying art is really entering a licensing agreement. It is the responsibility of the creative community to educate them."

Clearly, graphic design is not yet strong enough in its trade customs. These generally mature with a profession, and in evolutionary terms, graphic design is in "those awkward teenage years." When a design firm hires freelance designers, the common practice is to expect that they have no rights and should be treated as employees—work-for-hire employees. The truth of the matter is that if the work created is deserving of copyright protection, the creator owns the copyright until it is sold, unless the creator is on staff.

Another extremely unethical practice occurs when clients bring already designed formats from a design firm that has been let go, asking the new firm to modify or implement the designs without the previous design firm's knowledge.

Exploitation exists. But if graphic design is to thrive as a profession, these kinds of activities must be brought into check. The integrity of design must be controlled by the creator, the graphic designer, which means controlling the end product, the fate of the mechanicals, the floppy disks or the film produced to create the mechanicals, and, in fact, the concept used to create the design. Clients need to understand this since they have as big a stake in the survival of the profession as designers do. As Roger Whitehouse, principal of the design firm of Whitehouse & Company and chief architect of the AIGA standard contract, put it: "Design is, or should be, the very core and foundation of any project, an essential part of its basic structure and strategy. Clients should demand that the designer protect and monitor the integrity of his or her projects."

The contract states, under Rights and Ownership:

> All final designs provided by the Designer under this Agreement shall be for the exclusive use of the Client other than for the promotional use of the Designer. Upon payment of all fees and expenses, the following reproduction rights for all approved final designs created by the Designer of this project shall be granted.
>
> All drawings, artwork, specifications, and other visual presentation materials remain the property of the designer. The Client shall be entitled to temporary possession of such materials only for the purpose of reproduction after which all materials shall be returned, unaltered, to the designer.
>
> All preliminary concepts and visual presentations produced by the Designer remain the property of the Designer and may not be used by the Client without the written permission of the Designer. . . .

These clauses are significant, supportable pronouncements of the trade customs of the industry.

In addition, if the graphic designer creates a design of value that a client can leverage to greater worth later on, the graphic designer deserves credit and financial compensation for having been instrumental in the success. Illustrators and photographers see their work that way. In fact, due largely to the efforts of organizations like the American Society of Magazine Photographers and the Graphic Artists Guild, clients understand and accept the copyright law as a part of doing business.

Only a few graphic designers exercise these rights, on the other hand, so that professionals are not adequately supported by trade custom in this area. Copyright is complicated, and graphic designers have not been as well educated as they should be regarding the intent of the law and how it relates to their rights. One recommendation is to limit the rights transferred to "those uses described in the proposal or contract." This protects the creator if the design ends up having a greater use than originally intended. A buyout fee can be included in the contract or, later on, based on the rule used by illustrators or photographers, which is "two to three times greater than the original fee."

"I have recently developed a unique new sign system at the request of the Knoll Group," said Whitehouse, who specializes in environmental design. "In this instance, my contract provides for a percentage royalty of all product sold and specifically states that I retain 'full design control over all aspects of the project.' This is an ideal arrangement. It represents, in reality, a partnership between the graphic designer and client in which both stand to gain equally, and in which, more importantly, a sense of mutual trust and respect is reflected. Such an enlightened view has also brought clients like Knoll considerable success with their many products that fully acknowledge the value of design."

THE JOINT ETHICS COMMITTEE—A JURY OF YOUR PEERS

We are entering exciting times for graphic designers. As with all professionals, our ethics are constantly being tested. Besides the rights and ownership issues, environmental safety and truth-in-advertising are among the hot topics with which designers must be concerned. Fortunately, many of these can be addressed in forums provided by the AIGA, the Graphic Artists Guild, and the Joint Ethics Committee (JEC).

In particular, since 1948, the JEC has been the judicial system of the print industry. In New York state, it is recognized as a legitimate alternative to litigation, and JEC decisions—like court decisions—can strengthen trade custom and artists' rights. Yet this forum is underutilized in general and specifically by graphic designers. Although well respected within the judicial system, the JEC has developed little visibility within the advertising, publishing, and corporate worlds that it serves.

The AIGA response has been to take a leadership role in revitalizing the JEC. Within this context, the AIGA/NY has organized a campaign to stimulate its use and have it become a much-watched arena for discussing many of the issues outlined in this commentary. The JEC's seven other member groups can also help in this process—the Art Directors Club, Graphic Artists Guild, Art Buyers Club, the Society of Photographers and Artists Representatives, Society of Illustrators, Advertising Photographers of America, and American Society of Magazine Photographers. Of the supporting organizations, however, the AIGA and Graphic Artists Guild are the largest organizations, together representing more than eight thousand graphic designers nationwide.

Taking the long view, the JEC is another vehicle for establishing stronger ethical standards for our profession, since the results of arbitrations or mediations can be summarized and reported in professional design journals. As New York AIGA/JEC representative Clare Ultimo stated, "The national importance of the JEC is obvious: the wider our scope of influence, the more seriously standards of professional practice will be taken—by clients, other artists, and even the next generation still in design school. Since our world is not made up of 'local' standards, a national scope is imperative."

A DWARF STANDING ON A GIANT'S SHOULDERS SEES THE FARTHEST OF THE TWO

Graphic designers—and their clients—are learning how to be influenced by the work of others, yet to respect that personal expression that belongs to the individual creator. Every new design style or attitude is like a door. Creative individuals open these doors to explore what is inside, to create intellectual property. Allowing others to enter, respectfully, will enhance the evolution of the profession. This is what copyright protection is all about.

Originally published in Design Management Journal, *Fall 1991.*

DESIGN AND BUSINESS: THE WAR IS OVER
Milton Glaser

When I first came to Aspen, the mantra "Good design is good business" was the guiding assumption of our professional lives. Although it sounded beneficial to business, like all true mantras it had a secret metaphysical objective: to transform the listener spiritually. We were convinced that once business experienced "beauty" (good design), a transformation would occur. Business would be enlightened and pay us to produce well-made objects for a waiting public. That public would, in turn, be educated into a new awareness. Society would be transformed and the world would be a better place. This belief can only be looked on now as an extraordinary combination of innocence and wishful thinking.

After forty years, business now believes that good design is good business. In fact, it believes in it so strongly that design has been removed from the hands of designers and put into the hands of the marketing department. In addition, the meaning of "good" has suffered an extraordinary redefinition. Among an ever-increasing number of clients, it now only means "what yields profits."

While we might agree that all of life is an attempt to mediate between spiritual and material needs, at this moment in our work the material seems to have swept the spiritual aside. Hardball is now the name of the game, and the rules have changed. This, of course, is nothing new. The struggle between these issues is as old as humankind. Through the years, as the power of official religion declined, the source and receptacle of truth and morality became "the arts"—and all those who were involved in them formed a new kind of priesthood. Designers very often perceived themselves as being part of this alliance against the Philistines, whose lack of religiosity had to be opposed in order to produce a better world. Now this conflict seems to have resurfaced with a vengeance. One might say that what we are experiencing is merely a question of atmosphere, but the atmosphere is the air we breathe, and it has turned decidedly poisonous. Let me use a recent contract I received from a record company to illustrate this change in spirit. The contract reads, in part:

> You acknowledge that we shall own all right, title, and interest in and to the Package and all components thereof, including, but not limited to, the worldwide copyrights in the Package. You acknowledge that the Package constitutes a work specifically ordered by us for use as a contribution to a collective work. You further acknowledge that we shall have the right to use the Package and/or any of the components thereof and reproductions thereof for any and all purposes throughout the universe, in perpetuity, including, but not limited to, album artwork,

advertising, promotion, publicity, and merchandising, and that no further money shall be payable to you in connection with any such use. Finally, you acknowledge that we shall have the right to retain possession of the original artwork comprising the Package."

The first thing one notices is the punishing tone. This is not an agreement between colleagues, but the voice of a victor in a recently concluded war. It reinstates the principle of "work-for-hire," a concept that presumes that the client initiates and conceptualizes the work in question, and that the designer merely acts as a supplier to execute it. It destroys the relationship between payment and usage so that, although the work has been created for a specific purpose (and paid for accordingly), the client is free to use it anywhere, and forever, without further payments. This violates the most fundamental assumption about compensation of professionals; i.e., that what something is being used for and how frequently it is used is the basis for determining how much should be paid for it. It also claims ownership of the original art, marking the reintroduction of a mean-spirited and unfair doctrine that we all assumed had been legally eliminated. The overall posture, of course, reflects what is seen in the larger culture—a kind of class warfare that occurs when societies lose their sense of common purpose. The collegial sense of being in the same boat, pulling toward a common shore, has been eroded and replaced by the sense that the rowers are below decks and the orders are coming from above.

The Aspen Conference itself was founded in 1951 by Walter Paepcke and Egbert Jacobsen, his art director, to promote design as a function of management. It became, for a time, the preeminent symbol of the modern alliance of commerce and culture. They were joined, at least spiritually, by such remarkable figures as Josef Albers, Herbert Bayer, and László Moholy-Nagy, the last of whom was active in Chicago's New Bauhaus, a school committed to the principles of modernism and the reconciliation of art and consumer capitalism. It is not an overstatement to say that design education in America began here. It is important to remember that the Bauhaus was not simply a trade school but represented nothing less than the "transformation of the whole life and world of inner man" and "the building of a new concept of the world by the 'architects of a new civilization.'" (Walter Gropius in *The New Architect and the Bauhaus*). Cultural reform was at the center of Bauhaus thought, as it has been in many art movements.

In the United States, the social impulses that characterized Bauhaus thought began to be transformed by our pragmatic objectives, such as the use of design as a marketing tool and the elevation of style and taste as the moral center of design. The primacy of individual opportunity and capitalistic efficiency replaced many of the mildly socialist impulses of the modern movement. The metaphysical objectives and the ideal of civic responsibility went underground or were swept partially away. The pressures of professional practice and breadwinning left little room for theoretical inquiry into social issues. Nevertheless, the feeling that the arts in general, and design in particular, could improve the human condition persisted and informed the practice.

In the struggle between commerce and culture, commerce has triumphed and the war is over. It occurred so swiftly that none of us were quite prepared for it, though we have sensed that all was not well in our world. Anxiety, frustration, humiliation, and despair are the feelings that are revealed when designers now talk among themselves about their work. These are the feelings of losers, or at least of loss. The two most frequent complaints concern the decline of respect for creative accomplishment and the increasing encroachment of repetitious production activity on available professional time. These are linked complaints that are the inevitable consequence of the change in mythology and status that the field has gone through. The relationship of graphic design to art and social reform has become largely irrelevant. In short, designers have been transformed from privileged members of an artistic class or priesthood into industrial workers. This analogy partially explains why the first question now asked about designers by clients is more often not how creative or competent they might be, but how much they charge per hour. If screws are being tightened on a production line, it scarcely matters that a worker might be a brilliant poet. He or she still earns only fifteen dollars an hour. The same assumption makes it understandable how a person with six weeks of computer training can become a designer with significant responsibility in a corporation without having any knowledge of color, form, art history, or aesthetics in general. We once thought these things essential to a designer's education.

But why now? What brought us to this unhappy circumstance when there is more interest in design, more graphic designers, and more schools teaching the subject than at any time in history? Overpopulation, in fact, may be one of the problems, particularly when combined with the downsizing that the sense of a contracting economy and the computer have caused. Economic forces and technology have always driven aesthetics, though sometimes the relationship is not obvious.

In the past, the design process seemed esoteric, highly specialized, full of internal rituals, and hard to understand from the outside. These characteristics are all typical of spiritual or artistic activity and serve as a means of protection. The computer, with its unprecedented power to change meaning, has made the process transparent and therefore controllable; and as we know, control is the name of the game. The argument within the field about computers has been mostly concerned about whether they are an aid or a hindrance to creativity. These concerns resemble the semiconscious babblings of someone who has just been run over by a truck. The phrase "it's only a tool" scarcely considers the fact that this tool has totally redefined the practice and recast its values, all within a decade.

Clients can now micromanage every step of the design process, and production has become the central and most time-consuming part of every design office's activity. The overriding values are efficiency and cost control.

The use of the computer encourages a subtle shift of emphasis from the invented to the assembled form. Imagery is now obtained increasingly from existing sources and files more cheaply than it can be produced by new work. Electronic clipbooks have become the raw material for a kind of illustration we might call "computer surrealism."

The computer appears to be an empowering and democratic tool. The operator can achieve results that previously were obtainable only through the long process of study and skill development. This partially explains its addictive effect on the user. For myself, someone deeply shaped by old value systems, all expressive forms that are easily achieved are suspect. There are many more bad examples of clay modeling than stone carving: the very resistance of the stone makes one approach the act of carving thoughtfully and with sustained energy. This may also be a small and passing issue. History has shown us that technologies develop their own standards.

There is something else to consider that may help us understand where we are: the relationship between the victory of entrepreneurial capitalism, the fall of world communism, and the almost universal collapse of liberal ideology. Here, we can see the connection between reduced ecological and social programs, the attack on "soft-headed or subversive do-gooders" (like the NEA and public broadcasting), and our own sense of loss. Flush with success and in the midst of its validating triumph around the world, business is in no mood for accommodation. Recent history has proven to business that unyielding toughness pays, and self-inquiry is a form of weakness. Unfortunately, with the elimination of an external threat, those same convictions have been turned inward. Once again, the wisest phrase in the language comes to mind—Pogo's immortal words, "We have met the enemy and he is us." The tendency of unconstrained business to produce a sense of unfairness and class warfare has emerged dramatically, and most of us have been affected by it.

We may be facing the most significant design problem of our lives—how to restore the "good" in good design. Or, put another way, how to create a new narrative for our work that restores its moral center, creates a new sense of community, and re-establishes the continuity of generous humanism that is our heritage.

The war is over. It is time to begin again.

Originally presented at the Forty-Fifth International Design Conference in Aspen and published in the AIGA Journal of Graphic Design, *Vol. 13, No. 2, 1995.*

THINKING ABOUT COMMUNICATION
John Bielenberg

Just like an addict creates a lust for drugs or alcohol, the designer develops a craving for the new, the visually compelling, and the beautiful. The image becomes an end in itself. The graphic language sometimes takes a dominant role over the message being communicated. Small capitalized type letterspaced and reversed out of a dense black background looks cool because of the dynamic tension of scale and mass even if you can't read the type. Sometimes the graphic language is the message. Not every document needs to be read for its meaning or essence of the communication to be understood. However, the fact remains that the reversed type would be visually interesting regardless of whether it is communicating the proper message.

Why are we interested in viewing small two-dimensional reproductions of layouts in design annuals without much, if any, sense of the context, message, goals, or audience for these pieces? Because graphic designers have developed a hyperliterate visual sense and a highly refined appreciation for the craft of graphic design. I call it the intoxication of craft. Within any field the quest for and celebration of high craft is admirable, but the responsible creation of graphic design involves more than the skillful manipulation of elements on a page or surface.

I concluded that the intoxicating power of the design solutions we see in design shows, and around us daily, interfere with our ability to understand clearly the role of the designer in the communication of a message. Designers overweigh the craft component of visual solutions much like people overweigh the possibility of a shark attack.

DESIGNER AS ENGINEER

The profession of graphic design is principally about engineering a connection between a message and an audience. I use the word *engineering* to define a rational and thoughtful problem solving approach that also accommodates a creative and intuitive phase. In graphic design, the message and the intended audience is usually generated or dictated by the needs of a client rather than those of the designer. Addressing this issue, *I.D.* magazine quotes Tibor Kalman as saying, "Graphic design is a language, not a message." The responsibility of the graphic designer involves crafting the most appropriate and effective visual language given the defined objectives of the assignment.

This relationship between engineering and graphic design should be obvious to anyone practicing in this field. However, discussion about design often addresses the tools and craft rather than the appropriateness of the solution for the specific audience. During the 1993 AIGA conference in Miami, I was perplexed by the debate between Roger Black and David Carson. Although played for laughs and quite entertaining, the discussion revolved around their vastly different typographic approaches to editorial design. The truth, of course, is that each approach can be effective depending upon the criteria of the design objectives. The formal structure and elegance of Roger Black's *Esquire* layout is as successful and appropriate to its audience as the unstructured and informal chaos of David Carson's *Ray Gun* design. "I like it" or "I don't like it" should not be a part of a serious debate about the profession of graphic design.

THE CORE OF MAXIMUM COMMON INTEREST

I developed a diagram that tries to depict the relationship between the design of a graphic language, a message, and an audience. I call it *The Core of Maximum Common Interest*. It shows that you can define a core of common attributes within any given audience. The wider or more mass the audience, the more general the attributes must be. For example, if you are trying to reach a mass audience like *Time* magazine, Carson's design for *Ray Gun* would probably hit outside the densest part of the core on the outer perimeter of the disk. Also note that within a given core the graphic design solution can be created with either high or low craft. The annual reports that Kit Hinrichs of Pentagram has created over the years for Potlatch Paper are firmly entrenched within the appropriate core but at a very high craft level. Unfortunately, a design can also be effective at a low craft level. Almost all direct mail would fall into this area of the core.

It's not coincidental that most cutting-edge design today is created for niche audiences. The youth market is especially ripe for experimental solutions as they are more accepting of change and less prone to the shock of the new. However, if a new design style is powerful and timely it can pull or expand the mass core over so that that style is assimilated into the popular vocabulary. A recent example of this phenomena is the work of P. Scott Makela. He originally developed his unique densely layered approach within the experimental laboratory of the graduate program at Cranbrook. I expect that this style evolved out of both the emerging computer technologies and his ability to explore freely a language to express his own messages. Although originally reaching a narrow audience, I suspect that we will witness a gradual widening of the core to embrace this new visual language.

THE CONFLICT

Conflict often exists when you combine the intoxication of craft, exposure to and interest in cutting-edge design with the engineering of a client-driven message to a client-defined audience. Graphic designers are generally drawn to the profession for reasons that have little to do with the engineering process and lots to do with creativity and self-expression. Whenever I ask my design students at California College of Arts and Crafts why they want to be graphic designers, nobody ever mentions client objectives in their answer. I believe that this conflict between the needs of a creative professional and the needs of a commissioning client has always existed to some degree in the field of graphic design and other creative professions. An understanding of the process does not necessarily equal harmony.

There is a principle in physics that states that *systems tend to attain a state of minimum energy and maximum disorder.*

The energy and motivation of the designer to explore new solutions is required to propel the process of an evolving visual vocabulary forward. It is this very conflict that forces the core to widen and move. Without conflicting agendas, it is possible that the tendency of a system to maintain a state of minimum energy would result in a stagnation or cessation of visual exploration in the field of graphic design.

Originally published in Communication Arts, *March/April 1995.*

MIRROR, MIRROR
Peter Laundy

A constant theme of business bestsellers is that incremental improvement is not enough. Tom Peters, Peter Senge, Peter Drucker, and many other experts, who aren't lucky enough to have Peter somewhere in their names, are telling businesses that they'd better transform themselves fast or die.

A frequent complaint heard from consultants trying to help companies make big changes is that their clients' actions don't follow their words. Phrases like "don't just talk the talk, *walk* the talk" and "your actions are so loud I can't hear what you are saying" have therefore entered the lecture circuit lexicon. James Champy, one of the two consultants who brought us "re-engineering," has just written a sequel in which he expresses the frustration up front. He declares that "Re-engineering is in trouble" and laments that "some managers, misled by wishful thinking, believe that merely repeating the key words in *Re-engineering the Corporation* is enough to bring about a transformation, like the newsboy in the comic strip who yelled 'Shazaam!' and became powerful Captain Marvel. Managers have been saying 'Fundamental!' 'Dramatic!' 'Radical!' 'Processes!'—and, lo, that which they proclaim to be so *is* so . . . they hope."[1]

So on one hand we've got fast transformation seen as a survival issue. And on the other, we've got company after company that can, at best, s-l-o-w-l-y evolve. May I suggest another arrow in the quiver of those helping companies transform themselves?

If your client reads your bullet presentations, listens to your examples of how other companies have transformed themselves, enthusiastically embraces your suggestions, and then blithely goes off and continues to act in ways contrary to them, do not think that your client is insincere, lily-livered, or dumb. Realize that it is hard to see a sea change: to see what is inconsistent in current behavior or see what it would be like to behave in a way that supports fresh thinking. *Also, realize that you can help them to see by showing them prototypes of a wide range of the things they would make if they were to incorporate their new intentions into everyday actions.*

My first experience with the power of prototyping to help companies understand the implications of transformative ideas came in the late 1980s. A consultant gave his client, whose margins had suddenly come under pressure as competitors caught up, a recommendation: shift from being "the low-cost supplier" to being "the supplier that helps its customers buy smart." The company had pioneered warehousing and distribution techniques that had previously provided it cost and speed advantages, but had not paid attention to such things as developing better items, bundling them in ways that added value, or surrounding those items with more useful information. By adding proprietary intelligence to products, services, and communications, rather than just offering the same products as everybody else at a low price, the consultant suggested the company could reverse the margin erosion. We were asked to review some projects in progress, make prototypes of products and marketing communications that would illustrate the consultant's suggestion.

We put together a notebook of very rough prototypes of "afters" to contrast with the company's existing "befores." One was a sketch of a catalog spread showing a redesigned presentation of surgical marks. It helped the customer buy smart by offering only the alternatives that provided performance differences, and made them understandable through written descriptions and a chart of features mapped against each mask type. Previously, the catalog contained a redundant laundry list of options with little explanation. A second prototype incorporated ergonomic thinking into the design of thermal plastic dinnerware as an example of providing a better product rather than just better prices in their current line of undifferentiated products. Other prototypes of packaging and a computer-generated report suggested software that could be developed to help the sales force—who had little confidence in aesthetic decision making—generate pleasing hospital room fabric and finish combinations to present to hospital administrators. Another showed catalogs reconfigured to target vertical markets within and outside the hospital, so that each could access information appropriate to it.

Together these prototypes (and many others) illustrated a pattern of behavior consistent with "helping the customer buy smart," so that the company could see itself as it might become. Before seeing the prototypes, the "help the customer buy smart" idea had sounded interesting, but the client simply couldn't see what it would mean in practice.

Based on our learning on this project, and subsequent ones, I've come to understand that:

- The talk-walking problem is not just a problem of wishful thinking, or just of resistance to change. People often really want to see; they take pride in being among those that "get it." But it's hard to connect the details of behavior to transforming ideas because so much of a company's current behavior has become invisible as part of the everyday routine. And few (if any) employees had ever experienced the behavior that flows from new ideas.

- Old ways are not only embedded in organizational structure and processes, but also in the tangible stuff made by an organization. These things—products, facilities, and communications—are so much a part of habit that their underlying assumptions have become invisible. What Winston Churchill noted about buildings extends to all the things we make—we first shape them, then they shape us.[2] They are manifestations of past ideas, and they help the past ideas quietly endure. Office interior layout schemes and whole furniture systems result from, then prolong the life of, old ideas about hierarchy. Company identification badges that note seniority (purple for up to five years experience, orange for five to ten years, etc.) support the idea that seniority is important and makes the length of one's tenure visible, abetting the tendency of insiders to dismiss the opinion of "fresh blood" (this in a company that for some time has seen a more adaptive culture as essential). Architectural photographic conventions—make it look beautiful and shoot it *before* occupants can mess it up—hinder architects from employing photography to study the use of their buildings over time, which could simultaneously help them understand how people really use their buildings, and show prospects that their aspirations include livability.[3]

  Our ancestors, who, for example, provided us with a document called the Bill of Rights, but no countervailing thing called a Bill of Responsibilities,[4] shaped a set of documents that continue to shape our country. They also shaped names that contain old ideas from whose hold we haven't yet escaped. For example, they gave us the name "Criminal Justice System" for our country's system to reduce crime, with its built-in bias toward actions that involve the processing of criminals. An alternate name, like "Crime Reduction System," would help us take a broader more systemic view, incorporating preventive as well as punitive and corrective approaches.

- As a general rule, examples from home seem to hit home better, and examples of how "they" in other businesses have acted often don't transfer. As cognitive scientists have found, it is surprisingly hard to transfer ideas from one context to another. For example, many college students who have mastered ideas new to them in school—like Newton's laws of physics—will revert to intuitive explanations that violate Newton's laws when asked to apply them to everyday occurrences in their lives.[5] Ideas that go against invisible assumptions (which are precisely those ideas with the power to transform) are especially impervious to transfer.

  While benchmarking (the process of comparing your company's practices to competitors and recognized leaders within a pertinent domain) may seem to be evidence that new ideas do transfer, we suspect that benchmarking works best with ideas that offer incremental improvement rather than a transforming change in pattern. And benchmarking does have a downside: it can lead a company to see things more like its competitors, leading to diminished differentiation.

- Prototyping the things "we" make—a company's products, facilities, communications, and names—puts the "Churchill" effect in the service of transforming ideas. Once made, sketches of things as they could become can turn around and shape us, releasing our imaginations from invisible old patterns of thinking. People can more quickly and deeply see how current behavior is inconsistent with transforming ideas, and what they need to do to transform themselves and their organizations.

- Prototyping works best early in a process—*before* big decisions are made—helping executives get beyond abstractions and understanding the tangible implications of the changes they are contemplating.

PROTOTYPING TRANSFORMING IDEAS: SOME FURTHER EXAMPLES

• A company selling products to biotech researchers in universities over the years grew more distant from them, no longer seeing researchers as colleagues but rather as mere customers. The shift was gradual, helped by traditional ideas about sales and marketing and by decreasing numbers of senior personnel with roots in the scientific research community.

Within this company's marketing department, a desire recently emerged to change course and get closer to its research customers. In looking at their communications, we could see that their *modus operandi* contained a number of behaviors at odds with the emerging intentions. For example:

Ads aimed at their research customers were intended to manipulate perceptions rather than build relationships. To illustrate ad behavior consistent with emerging intentions, we prototyped "advernouncements" that focused on providing useful information about their more differentiated products.

Art budgets went to creating scientific-looking decorations with little information value. We suggested they shift emphasis to creating easier-to-read, more informative diagrams of use to their audience, and prototyped an example that better explained the advantages of one of their new products.

Information technology was being overlooked as a tool to create a better customer relationship, simultaneously serving customers better and learning more about them. We prototyped a system that would simultaneously cut down the time it would take our client's sales force to restock their customers' supply shelves, help their customers allocate their own costs for supplies among their departments, and help our client get beyond their customers' purchasing agents and gather information about end users.

Together these and other prototypes helped the company see what it could become. This vision was embraced in their research products division by key marketing people in the United States, in large part because they could see the implications of the prototypes.

• A contract furnishings leader saw its industry being marginalized by the greater productivity-enhancing potential of the computer industry as well as by flattened organizational hierarchies that resulted in diminished expressions of status through office size and furnishings opulence.

A consultant suggested that the company could build a much more persuasive case for the ability of furnishings to have impact on white collar productivity. To show the client the transforming potential of a focus on performance enhancement, a team prototyped a variety of examples. At the time, the company followed standard industry practice of appealing to designer specifiers by showcasing trendy cutting-edge furniture, showroom, and communication design.

Our team prototyped a furniture system designed to support team practices and to perform well through the full product cycle from furniture specification through refurbishment, at the same time building in cost and performance advantages unavailable on the market. We prototyped an executive furnishing system that focused on providing performance features rather than just expensive materials. We prototyped showrooms designed not as trendy design statements to appeal to interior designers, but rather as stages to make visible performance features. We designed brochures targeted to vertical markets, like law and insurance, containing furnishing tips to help readers in the targeted industry achieve a competitive advantage, and, of course, to see that furnishings could give them their edge and that our contract furnishings client understood this better than its competitors. We even prototyped a separate parent company that focused on research about work performance.

Together, the sketches helped the company see how it could improve its research efforts to understand performance issues, how it would think about products and communications that supported the performance focus, and how much of its current behavior was in the service of status display and aesthetic refinement simply to appeal to designers' tastes.

• A life insurance sales force was encouraged by its company to provide solutions rather than to sell products. However, the latter approach was deeply embedded in the marketing materials and process. Products with snazzy names and glossy brochures continued to be provided to the field and encouraged salespeople to show customers insurance products even as they "talked" solutions. The salespeople who understood solution selling had no use for the materials provided to them and were making do with what they could make for themselves. Less forward-thinking salespeople, however, had simply purged the word "product" from their vocabulary and replaced it with "solution."

To help the company see how to provide solutions, we sketched an array of materials that supported a different process: they included software that allowed salespeople using notebook computers to build a customer insurance need profile, take it back to the office, and build a proposal with the help of an automated computer system; and then print a document tailored to the precise needs of the client and title it something like, "An insurance plan for John and Mary Swift." As a result, the sales force, and those at the central office that provided them with sales aids had a better understanding of what it took to really make the transformation to providing solutions.

In every example, the company had trouble connecting new ideas to the tangible results of those ideas, and therefore had trouble either evaluating the power of the ideas or in implementing them convincingly. The prototypes helped them see the ideas and see what they had to do to pull them off.

THE PROTOTYPING PROCESS AND TEAM

Projects, if at all possible, should occur outside immediate deadline pressures and constraints so that the prototypes can demonstrate a more complete adoption of the new ideas. The process should be designed to involve key development people, build understanding and enthusiasm, neutralize opposition, and make the product as good as it can be. Participants within the client company are generally engaged in the prototyping process in one of four ways:

1. *Project Leaders.* This person or people are the outside consultant's eyes and ears, making sure the right people are involved and political obstacles avoided. The consultant is greatly hindered without a trusting relationship with a good person inside the client company who is respected, is a believer in the new ideas, and who wants the company to achieve the transformation.

2. *Core Advisers.* This larger group of people is kept informed on progress through reviewing drafts of a presentation to get feedback. These reviews have a number of objectives: to build enthusiasm or diffuse opposition among reviewers for the presentations; to build interest at the highest possible levels if the project doesn't begin at the top; to debug the presentation; and to prospect for new sketch candidates that would provide value. Bend over backwards to include as many of these ideas as possible in the final version so reviewers can see their recommendations incorporated, and involve the most influential people possible within the company.

3. *Secondary Advisers.* There is usually a larger group of people than the project team who feel they should be part of the process. Such people should be interviewed at project initiation for their input and then shown a late draft. Every effort should be made to demonstrate the late draft has not been cast in stone. To aid understanding, the ideas that inform the prototypes should be presented in words and diagrams, and the prototypes should be captioned to note their performance features.

4. *Implementors.* Those people that are not part of the approval process, but rather will be part of the implementation process, are shown the presentation as part of receiving their marching orders. However, the presentation should still be presented as in progress and feedback sought.

PILOT PROJECTS

Small companies may not have the budgets to undertake projects without immediate payoffs, and large companies will want to begin the process of embedding new ideas into their deliverables quickly. Projects that pilot transforming ideas should advance the company's ability to deliver consistent with the ideas and help key internal and external audiences understand them. They should be selected to provide opportunities for small, quick wins, and leaders should provide a zone within the company in which old-view rules can be broken. Vigilance is required because the "white blood cells" of the organization built around the old ideas will come out and try to destroy—threatening new ideas.

Beware of defining pilot projects too tightly up front. A key aspect of a pilot project is that it is prototype-driven rather than spec-driven. Specifications bring past learning to bear on current projects, and therefore obstruct change because they define both problems and solutions in accordance with old ideas. Instead, progress in project definition and solution comes as generations of prototypes are revised. The project team uses quick sketches to learn simultaneously what it thinks and to record its progress.

DESIGNERS AND PROTOTYPING TRANSFORMING IDEAS

Designers, who have the ability to prototype things that flow from other people's points of view, are natural candidates for being members of teams to help companies see transforming ideas. Designers from outside a company culture are particularly useful because they can see what is invisible to those inside, and are therefore able to break old patterns more easily. However, to be effective, we designers must adopt some transforming ideas ourselves. We must:

- tolerate initial ambiguity and expect to aid project definition as well as project solution.
- learn to think of artifacts as an anthropologist would—as manifestations of the maker's behavior and culture, rather than just as we normally do—as a combination of delivered functionality and aesthetic composition.
- see ourselves as group facilitators rather than design deliverers.
- encourage client participation and try to help them put new ideas into practice with their traditional resources. If they can begin to do it themselves the transformation is taking root.
- be satisfied without a tangible delivered artifact, because prototypes in this context are means to a changed understanding, rather than an end product.
- learn the difference between "good enough to show the idea" and "a really good design," and not waste time going after the latter in situations that require only the former.
- learn patience, because, from a designer's perspective, an organization's understanding changes slowly.
- realize that seeing is only part of the answer. Once clients start to understand they will be asking you how they should go about changing their organization.

The relationship between the project team and the company, come to think of it, is more like one between a psychiatrist and patient than between designer and client. The subject is the emerging self-understanding of the client and the objective is a transformed company, not a specific new product or communication. The process takes time, requires a lot of careful listening, trust, and candor. It allows the designer to earn a good wage because the effort at transformation is critical. But projects are always in danger of rejection by forces fighting for the status quo.

If you succeed in helping the company transform itself, you, like a psychiatrist, will be dimly, if fondly, remembered, as your client confidently marches into the future proud of their ability to succeed on their own.

Originally published in Communication Arts, *August 1995.*

Notes

1. James Champy, *Re-engineering Management: The Mandate for New Leadership* (New York: HarperBusiness, 1995), 35.

2. Stewart Brand, *How Buildings Learn* (New York: Viking, 1994), 3.

3. Brand, *How Buildings Learn,* 55.

4. Scott Russell Sanders, *Utne Reader* (March–April 1995): 69.

5. Lewis J. Perleman, *School's Out* (Avon Books), 131.

PUBLIC
WORKS

THERE IS SUCH A THING AS SOCIETY
Andrew Howard

In 1964, British designer Ken Garland and a group of twenty-one colleagues issued a manifesto entitled "First Things First." Aimed at fellow graphic designers, it was a succinct and gutsy appeal to reject the "high pitched scream of consumer selling" and omnipotent lure of the advertising industry in favor of what was defined as socially useful graphic design work. The manifesto was reproduced in the publication *Modern Publicity,* together with an interview in which Garland attempted to defend it to Douglas Haines (described as a creative executive with British agency and marketing specialists Mather and Crowther), who was hostile to the idea that there is anything wrong with the marketplace or that the advertising industry does anything other than a good and necessary job.

What makes the manifesto interesting today is the realization that its premises appear as radical now as they did thirty years ago. And more significantly, the issue it addresses is as unresolved now as it was then. But the manifesto also touches on a dimension that seems to be missing from current debate: a concern with the social function and purpose of graphic design. Discussion in the profession in the mid 1990s appears to have crystallized into a debate between two schools of thought. On the one hand there is the "new wave" of Macintosh-devoted design, some of which has been produced under the theoretical auspices of poststructuralist analysis and is guided by an exploration of the formal problems of representation and meaning, as in the work of the Cranbrook Academy of Art. Some of its exponents claim that their output represents a new aesthetic; their critics dismiss it as a form of visual pyrotechnics, a lavish aesthetic feast but low on nutritional content. Such critics believe that despite its stated intentions (where there have been intentions to state), this work is aimless and impenetrable.

On the other hand, a trend has emerged more recently that claims to seek a new clarity—of intention as well as aesthetic. Rick Poynor (*Eye,* Vol. 3, No. 9) suggests that there is a growing reaction by "design students, teachers, and young professionals" against what are seen as the "excesses" of formal experimentation and in favor of a less ambiguous, more message-related program. In the Netherlands, designers Dingeman Kuilman and Neils Meulman are calling for an approach that is not sophisticated, not technological, and not intellectual, just "basic" (*Emigre,* No. 25).

For some designers, and I would include myself and many of those I class as colleagues here, a search for formal solutions has only ever been a part of, not an alternative to, a longer-term socially and politically influenced project. For us (only an "us" in as much as we have histories and influences in common), to interpret much of what is characterized as "new wave" as playfully self-indulgent is not a refusal to "join in the party," nor does it signify lack of interest in new technologies and experimentation. Rather, it springs from a continuing interest that goes beyond a search for parts of the design jigsaw, of which formal visual vocabulary is a piece, to an understanding of how the jigsaw fits together.

It is perhaps understandable that recent debate has centered on conflicting ideas about what contemporary design should look like and what methods it should employ in order to create understanding: how it should function formally. The impact of computer technology has transformed the nature of the design activity, allowing designers to assume control (competently or not) of many stages in the production process that were traditionally shared among a number of people with different skills and expertise. It has also had a profound effect on aesthetics. The computer makes it possible to construct multifaceted compositions with relative ease and at vastly increased speeds. Its capacity for sampling, duplication, and the integrated assembly of all manner of visual elements has given designers the opportunity to view countless variations and to realize more visually complex ideas. Visual, formal possibilities have taken center stage.

Discussion of content, apart from as formal exploration, has tended to concentrate on the internal subject matter of individual works. But there is another sort of content in graphic design: its social content as a form of social production. The significance of this lies in the ways in which function influences form and purpose informs content. It suggests that the character of our work is determined by more than our intentions alone, since production processes and the social context within which the work is received have a profound impact in directing, respectively, its aesthetic and the kinds of understanding it is capable of generating. These issues touch on the very definition of graphic design.

To see graphic design as a form of social production rather than as individual acts of creativity means recognizing that it is subject to the same economic and ideological forces that shape other forms of human social activity. It means that in order to understand the nature of our activity and to think about its possibilities, we must be able to locate it within a historical context that relates it to economic and political forces. This is (strangely) problematic, as Anne Burdick rightly states (*Eye*, Vol. 3, No. 9), because "it is considered outside our role to analyze the content of our work in relation to politics, theory, economics, morals, and so on." But if the present debate is about creating a body of work that is meaningful to people in general, that plays a part in the development of a stimulating visual culture, then it must involve understanding how our culture functions, how it is shaped, and how it shapes our perceptions of ourselves. It means addressing people's need for a culture in which they can participate actively, for which they can help shape the agenda. It will inevitably involve an analysis of what prevents us from building such a culture.

The economic organization of our society depends on the promise of ever-expanding production and the building of markets to absorb that production. We have the means to make goods in sufficient quantity and range to satisfy all our basic needs. But, "goods are no longer sold on the basis that they satisfy a known and voiced human need, but instead demands are developed through 'research' and through marketing in order that commodities may be produced to meet them," explains Owen Kelly (*Community, Art, and the State: Storming the Citadels,* 1984). Goods are only a means to an end: the production of surplus value. Consequently, "there can be no such thing as sufficient production of any commodity, since there is no such thing as sufficient surplus value."

Whether one sees advanced capitalism and the consumer society as good or bad, one cannot ignore the ways they have encroached on previously private areas of consciousness. The building of markets is not a purely economic exercise: it is we, the "citizens" who are the intended markets, and their creation is very much an ideological task. This involves a process, explains Kelly, in which our needs are broken down into smaller and smaller units, "so that they match (and can be met by) the outputs of a profitable production process." "Thus, for example," says Kelly, "the desire to avoid giving off offensive odors is redefined as a positive, and normal, desire to achieve 'personal hygiene,' and is pictured as a continuous, and inevitable, struggle in which only the deliberately antisocial would refuse to participate." Convinced of the need to obtain this "personal hygiene," we are offered our bodies divided into separate marketing zones—underarm, mouth, vagina, feet—within each of which, writes Kelly, "the consumer can be educated to make choices (roll-on or stick, fragrant or natural), and within each of which separate innovations are possible."

This fragmentation of our needs and desires does not operate only in relation to areas of industrialized production. It is paralleled in the operations of the state, from health and medicine to education and leisure, where we are taught to consume professionalized services. In this sense there are no areas of our personal lives that are not subject to the social pressures of the marketplace, wherein decisions that might have been made by consenting citizens are reduced to purchasing choices made by passive consumers. Since the 1950s and 1960s, writers have referred to these encroachments as inducing a state of crisis in personal and cultural life.

In addition, the political avenues through which we might expect to control the decisions that govern our lives are severely restricted. Stuart Hall has talked about "a growing gap between where people are politically and the institutions and organizations which express that in a formal political way." Recent trends reveal a growth in intense pseudo-religious movements, in nationalist and neofascist ideas, in young people embracing directly oppositional lifestyles. Few would deny that at the center of this is a search for something meaningful to believe in, a vision of ourselves as empowered human beings able to act upon our needs and desires as we define them.

It is crucial that we recognize that there is a direct correspondence between the condition of our culture and the ways we organize the production of materials. The form of economic organization we refer to as capitalism ceased long ago to be simply that, and has become a means of organizing the consciousness necessary for that economic system to flourish. As designers whose work is concerned with the expression and exchange of ideas and information and the construction of the visual vocabulary of day-to-day culture, we must establish a perspective on where we fit into this scheme. We must ask in what ways our function helps to organize consciousness. We must also discover to what extent and in what ways the solutions, vocabularies, and dialogues that we are able to conceive and construct are determined for us. The "First Things First" manifesto was an attempt at least to address these issues.

Its conclusions, however, fall short of what seems necessary. Written at a time when the high-intensity market was establishing itself at the heart of the design profession in Britain, it was perhaps a last-ditch attempt to hold back the flood of "gimmick merchants, status salesmen, and hidden persuaders." It starts off in a forcible and radical manner. But at the beginning of the fourth paragraph it extinguishes its own flames when it says, "We don't advocate the abolition of high pressure consumer advertising: this is not feasible"— without making clear whether or not this is perceived as desirable. After its declaration of a rebellion against the techniques and apparatus of high-pressure consumer advertising, there is a trace of retreat here, despite the fact that it would probably be defended as "realism."

Garland echoes this concession in the interview, and the power of his argument is all the less compelling for it. Early on he concurs with Haines that "we are not against advertising as a whole. The techniques of publicity and selling are vital to Western society." But isn't that the problem? This allows Haines's contention that high-pressure advertising and the ideology of the marketplace are healthy and natural to go unchallenged, and leaves an impression that what Garland is arguing for is the same cake, sliced differently. But the logic of the manifesto implies that social and cultural needs are constantly circumvented, if not distorted, by the power of an industry whose primary purpose is to create demand for consumption, regardless of usefulness. Furthermore, that the effect—on young designers in particular—of the absence of an alternative sense of what meaningful work might be is leading to a gradual erosion of enthusiasm and creativity. What is needed is a different cake altogether, but to argue for such a thing is to take a leap into the unknown. The modern advertising industry is the creation of the high-intensity market, and graphic design has always been at the center of its strategy. Its history forms a large part of the history of design. To question that industry and the ideology of consumerism it promotes is to question our whole economic organization. It is easier to argue for more of the cake.

The manifesto's concern with purpose and social function should not be confused with a moralizing preoccupation with "politically correct" subject matter. It should not be interpreted as a determinist concern with "the message," though it does not exclude a commitment to direct (or indirect) political expression. Devotees of the new wave may well demonstrate little interest in the "message as content" approach, perhaps justifiably, when one considers the unbelievably inane work of "cultural ground-breakers" such as Oliviero Toscani and his sponsors, Benetton.

"I want to make people think," says Toscani in an interview in the *Independent* (December 16, 1992). "I want them to remember a name." Thus social criticism is appropriated in the struggle for brand identification. "It [the advertising industry] persuades people that they are respected for what they consume, that they are only worth what they possess," says Toscani, angrily upbraiding the industry for corrupting society. Most advertising, he tells us, is based on the emotions and has nothing to do with the product. One can only wonder what graveyard crosses during the Gulf War, a ship overflowing with refugees, an electric chair, children in Third World slums, and a nun and priest kissing have to do with expensive, multicolored knitwear? But even these are surpassed by Toscani's idea for a "fun" campaign about wife-beating for Guinness. What makes Toscani's ever-so-radical ideas ever so depressing is that his accurate critique of the advertising industry's effect on our aspirations and self-image appears to be of no help to him in establishing the link between the industry and the economic ideology that spawned it.

Whatever his intentions, Toscani's posters are merely a state-of-the-art marketing device masquerading as social conscience. It is extreme arrogance to throw images at people in the belief that they need to be told what issues are of social importance. Radical work is never a question of presenting correct political opinions, but is concerned instead with the nature of the dialogue that is made possible between the author and the audience.

It is not at all clear, on the other hand, in what sense the approach advocated by Dutch designers Kuilman and Meulman is basic, or what is the meaning and significance of what they have to say. Is this perhaps a private argument between them and the technological, intellectual sophisticates about the most effective formal approach to sell spicy sausage or decorative floor tiles? Or is the liberation from confusion they wish to achieve to be reserved for greater purposes? Appending political messages to work as if forms were empty vessels is simple-minded, and advocacy of "basicness" is meaningless if it is concerned only with the internal logic of design. But does this mean that formal exploration, as content, is the way forward?

Writers such as Roland Barthes are said to have been of seminal influence in the development of the work and ideas of at least one agency of the new wave—the Cranbrook Academy of Art. Jeffery Keedy, a former Cranbrook student, says, "It was the poetic aspect of Roland Barthes which attracted me, not the Marxist analysis. After all, we're designers working in a consumer society, and while social criticism is an interesting idea, I wouldn't want to put it into practice" (Eye, Vol. 1, No. 3). Barthes's work is indeed poetic, which gives it a resonance lacking in much Marxist theory, but to disconnect the critique from the form seems a perverse example of literary raiding. The work of other French writers of the same period, such as the situationist Raoul Vaneigem, is also poetic and also concerned with the decay of personal and cultural life under modern capitalism. His book, *The Revolution of Everyday Life* deals with the subjugation of our potential to be active, independent-minded, and creative. It is a complex description of our condition, which focuses on the corruption of our desires, dreams, values, and aspirations, and a ferocious social critique. If it is not on the Cranbrook reading list, perhaps it should be.

The major artistic movements of this century—the futurists, constructivists, dadaists, surrealists—all had a theory of society that guided their explorations. The exploration of the formal structure of language—its signs, symbols, and how these construct and carry meaning—should be the staple diet of designers. Language is a means through which we express our consciousness of ourselves and our relationship to the world; it is our attempts to describe our situation and to think about the future that lead us to search for appropriate vocabularies. Language changes when it is no longer able to express what its users require of it, so unless it is to be of academic interest only, an exploration of language must also take into account the changing consciousness of human beings. It is difficult to comprehend the point of exploring form if it is not related to contemporary problems of vocabulary and the search for meaning. The study of visual form and language is limited if it does not consider the forces of cultural production, which involve a set of social relations between producer and audience.

Whether our activity and its products are open and empowering, whether they contribute to the building of a democratic culture, is not dependent only on the content of our work, but also on the productive social relations that affect the nature of the dialogues we are able to construct. A large advertising poster for multicolored knitwear, for instance, is not a dialogue on equal terms, if it is a dialogue at all. It is designed to make an intervention into our consciousness in ways we cannot ignore; it shouts at us so that we may remember a name that will influence our acts of purchasing. It is a form developed for a social context that the audience cannot control. This is what makes it oppressive. No amount of fiddling with the visual forms it employs or the message it carries will transform it into an open-ended product.

But the ideology of consumerism is not limited to the world of commerce. Our consciousness is fragmented so that we are better able to consume everything: films, music, fashion, diets, healthcare, education, information, even our own history. This problem cannot be avoided simply by choosing between "good" or "bad" products, or between commercial and noncommercial work, since the nature of the problem is not just consumption but the ordering of our consciousness to become consumers in the first place.

Graphic design has a part to play in creating a visual culture that empowers and enlightens, that makes ideas and information accessible and memorable. Many designers may argue that their job is not politics, and they would be right. But this does not prevent us from developing ideas about cultural democracy. We cannot separate our work from the social context in which it is received and from the purpose it serves. If we care about the integrity of our design decisions, we should be concerned that the relations implicit in our communications extend active participation in our culture. If what we are looking for is meaning and significance, then the first step is to ask who controls the work and whose ends does it serve.

The computer revolution that brought us new aesthetic possibilities has given us other opportunities too. The technological condensing of the production process has the potential to alter our notion of authorship, and with it our aspirations. The technical self-sufficiency the computer has allowed may give us the conceptual space to develop a more complete consideration of our work in relation to the way it is received and the purpose it serves. It may encourage us to initiate more often, and in the process to establish partnerships and collaborations in which design is not simply a means to sell and persuade, but also a means of organizing ideas and finding forms of expression that suit the interests of a more specific audience.

The work that flows from such a practice cannot be prescribed. It may or may not be sophisticated, technological, and so on. It will in no way preclude an exploration of the formal representation of language. Its content may be concerned with what it is we are able to think about (subjects), or the ways in which we are able to think (forms). It will recognize that how something is produced and distributed socially carries with it specific relations that affect the dialogue that is possible between author and audience and limit the sort of meanings that can be constructed. Above all, it will acknowledge the link between our choices as designers and the sort of culture we wish to contribute to.

Originally published in Eye, *No.13, 1994.*

HITLER'S CHILDREN: NAZI ICONOGRAPHY IN CONTEMPORARY GRAPHIC DESIGN

Steven Heller

Washington, April 16: A problem that has long plagued downtown Washington, the defacement of newspaper boxes and trash bins by spray painted swastikas and SS logos, appears to be spreading into residential communities . . . (*New York Times*, April 12, 1996)

A cultural literacy exam given to selected New York City high school students, within months after the release of Steven Spielberg's movie *Schindler's List*, revealed that more than 30 percent of those tested could not place the Holocaust—the genocidal murder of six million Jews and millions of others—in a proper historical context. As this cataclysmic event further fades in time, there is a very real threat that kids will become ignorant of Nazi crimes.

The evidence of such ignorance takes many insidious forms, including the increasingly popular and flagrant abuse and reapplication of Nazi-inspired iconography as logos for products like skateboards and music CDs. Infusing very dangerous symbols with romance not only steals historical relevance from heinous imagery, but reduces its cautionary power. The young, who are not as well versed in this vocabulary, are hence desensitized to the political red flags around them.

In Germany, a constitutional law prohibits the public display of the swastika and other Nazi symbols of any kind, punishable by harsh penalties. In America, no such law exists. Nor should there be, given the doctrine of free speech. This license, however, does not mean that these venal icons can be used for commercial whim. Their meaning is as unambiguous as the Final Solution. Not just the swastika, but other Nazi graphic emblems represent the ideology of a barbarous regime. Even today, fifty years after the Third Reich was defeated, Nazi-inspired images have become benign clip art to be decoupaged on skateboards, fashion labels, and CD covers. In an age where sampling and biting corporate brand logos is an expression of political frustration, some graphic artist/designers contend that stealing Nazi images is also a polemical act. Reclaiming or co-opting the swastika neutralizes, satirizes, or demystifies these images, they claim. And these are the smart ones. The less astute find Nazi imagery, well, just kinda cool. Sometimes its difficult to know which group is the most ignorant; the ones who strive for the intellectual high ground or the ones who are clueless. And while most view the symbols mindlessly, all you have to do is surf the Internet to find those marks emblazoned on a score of home pages for white supremacists, skin heads, and hate mongers.

Granted, popular art has been eroding the historical memory of the symbol since the 1950s, when men's magazines reduced black-shirted Nazis to villainous Simon Legrees. "In the popular culture of the West, Nazism was often no more than a source of lighthearted amusement of distraction, perverse fascination, and even sado-masochistic pornography," writes Robert S. Wistrich, in *Weekend in Munich: Art Propaganda and Terror in The Third Reich* (Trafalgar Square, 1996). "Clearly, any moral and political lessons to be drawn from Nazi terror and genocide are bound to be dulled by such mischievous and irresponsible approaches to the past." The reduction of Nazism to nothing more than the object of fun is an example, says Wistrich, of the "politics of forgetting."

More recent memory loss can be traced back to 1973 when the rock group Kiss began playing heavy metal music and wearing fright makeup. Their logo, inspired by comic book lettering in a gothic style, became the standard for heavy metal graphic design. It also marked the first time since the end of the Third Reich that Nazi iconography was re-aestheticized for mainstream consumption. The last two letters of the band's name, "SS," are virtually identical to the insignia of the Schutzstaffel, or SS, Hitler's elite branch of the Nazi military/police that administered the Final Solution. Few critics questioned the reference, but there was no mistaking it for the Nazified lightening bolts, known as SS runes, which was also a letter that type founders were required to include in the official German alphabet during the Third Reich.

A fan denied the association in a letter to the *AIGA Journal of Graphic Design* (Vol. 14, No. 2). He said, "The stylized S's in the logo were never intended, nor do they have anything whatsoever to do with, the Schutzstaffel. The logo was created by the original guitarist, Paul 'Ace' Frehley, who has said time and again that the Nazi reference was never intended."

In any case, intent is not the issue; history is. Unless the SS insignia is forever consigned to the cabinet of inviolable icons, the mark should remain a symbol of evil. Its history is robbed, its symbolism sanitized, when flagrantly displayed as an accouterment of rock performance. Whether they knew it or not (and since three of the original Kiss members are Jewish, it is probable that ignorance probably prevails over malicious intent), Kiss's adaptation of this image, which was printed on twelve albums, a score of T-shirts and other souvenirs, and spawned countless imitators, is an insult to the victims and survivors of Nazi terror.

The graphics of the Nazi party have been referred to as the most effective identity system in history. The swastika, which Hitler claimed to have personally designed but was actually an ancient icon for good fortune, by 1933 was strictly controlled by the "Law for the Protection of National Symbols." Although it was prohibited from being commercially applied (i.e., no Swastika brand soft drinks), it was integrated into hundreds of official logos, emblems, and insignia. In addition, it inspired unofficial versions, which were also popular political and commercial graphic devices. Today, collector's catalogues of Nazi-era imagery, including equally charged ancillary icons, are widely available and used by contemporary designers as a resource.

Of the growing litany of depoliticized Nazi forms, the Boy London™ logo is a vivid example of historical amnesia and flagrant misappropriation. The motto for this fashion manufacturer and retailer is The Strength of the Country Lies in Its Youth. Its trademark is nothing less than the seal of Großdeutschland, or greater Germany, the official emblem of the Third Reich. The original version is an eagle with outstretched wings, its talons firmly embedded in a circle containing the swastika. Boy London's adaptation has the eagle sitting atop the "O" in the word boy.

Although the swastika is eliminated, the appropriation of such a historically charged image begs inquiry into the designer's motives. It is doubtful that this particular retailer, which markets to a gay clientele, wants to be associated with the Nazis. Yet when posed with the problem of designing a logo, the designer must have felt the seal of Groß-deutschland made tremendous formal sense. It is imposing, memorable, and, for godsakes, an eagle. On Boy London's expensive metal-covered diary and address book, it looks like the official papers the Nazis where so fond of issuing.

Another example of reused Nazi imagery was found in supermarket butcher departments throughout the American South and West in 1988. As reported in *Time* and *Newsweek*, the Fleming Food Companies, an Oklahoma City-based food wholesaler, distributed promotional posters that resembled a forgotten Nazi-era image originally designed by Ludwig Hohlwein to promote the Hitler Youth. The Fleming version, designed by the ad agency Sully & Wood, is a painting of a heroic-looking cowboy wearing chaps and tightly holding an American flag above which a headline reads "America's Meat Roundup." Its Nazi roots went unnoticed until a college student was reminded of an illustration in his history textbook titled *Der Deutsche Student,* a recruitment poster. A company spokesperson insisted at the time that the Fleming artist had worked from a live model, the resemblance to Hohlwein's Aryan superboy was indisputable.

Although Ludwig Hohlwein is a renowned poster artist, some of his best work was done for the Nazi party. Does the fact that he was a master of poster art mitigate the heinous acts for which his posters now stand? Can the lessons of that era be so distant from reality that form can be separated from content? Nazi propaganda was extremely efficient, should contemporary designers desecrate the memory of the twentieth century's most bloodthirsty period by separating good design from bad Germans? Design responsibility does not end with refusing to design for bad clients, but in refusing to design with bad images that have indelible connotations.

> I've never used the swastika directly in my work, but I have twisted it around and distorted it while keeping the strong graphic look . . . While I don't want [my] band to be perceived as skinhead or right wing, the logo is just so damned strong, and what's more, the war's been over for fifty years. (A designer who preferred to remain anonymous talking about the logo of his New York band, quoted in the *AIGA Journal of Graphic Design,* Vol. 14, No. 1.)

Perhaps this is also the rationale for designers who use Nazified forms as logos for skateboard and hip sportswear clients. In an age when even the crucifix has been reduced to a stylish fashion accessory, images reminiscent of Nazi totalitarianism and neo-Nazi racism are exposed to an ever-younger market. In the October 1995 issue of *Thrasher,* a skateboard monthly that dabbles in alternative politics, advertisements for skateboards exhibit overt and covert Germanic/Nazi influences. Among them, the Iron Cross, the traditional German army medal for valor (indeed the only medal that Hitler ever wore on his tunic), appears as a component of an Old English Logotype for Beer City Skateboards; a Kiss/SS-inspired lightening bolt is the centerpiece in the Germanic spiky Fraktur type for the Real Skateboard logo (Fraktur, incidentally, was one of the two official typefaces of the Third

Reich); a variant of a Flemish SS divisional badge is part of the logo for Vision Streetwear; and the logo for Focus skateboards draws its striking form from a combination SS and other neo-fascist emblems. The above can be explained, though not excused, as mindless nostalgic sampling, but other applications reveal a more sinister influence.

A tear-and-peal promotional sticker for a Los Angeles rock band, Follow For Now, derives its logo directly from the mark for the Aryan Nations, a neo-Nazi hate group linked to a variety of political assassinations. The sampling of this logo does not trivialize the movement of hate. Those designers who believe that they are doing the world a service by reducing the symbols of brutality to the equivalent of happy faces are deluding themselves.

> We see the competition for market supremacy as a big game: Battle of the Logo-
> Dinosaurs or Clash of the Icon Titans or something. On this level, it sounds fun
> and we just want to join in. (Ian Anderson, member of Designer's Republic, in
> an interview in *Emigre,* No. 30)

In the spirit of logo demystification, Designer's Republic (DR), the innovative English graphic design firm that specializes in music packaging, has commandeered and reconfigured various multinational brands in the service of their hip clients. Most are benign-enough samplings of mainstream corporate trademarks. But in a letter to the editor in *Emigre,* No. 31, Jeffery Keedy restates and critiques DR's position on the sampling of logos: "I guess I worry that since 'there is no hierarchy in the Age of Plunder' and 'whatever captures the imagination in a split second is what's important,' DR will appropriate the swastika because it is a cool-looking symbol and if anyone can make it look even cooler DR can."

Indeed one of their pieces, a promotional T-shirt for Supersonic, is a bitmapped derivation of the Nazi-era logo for the Deutsche Arbietsfront (German Workers Front), the 25-million man cadre of German workers that served as the bulwark of the Nazi regime. Granting that the Designers Republic's image distorts the original symbol of an eagle with talons holding a machine gear and eliminates the swastika originally found in that gear, it nevertheless remains a flagrant abuse of the past and, perhaps unbeknownst to DR, a variant of an emblem currently used by an outlawed neo-Nazi group in Germany.

The Nazis arguably began the popular chic for wearing logos and emblems. Nazi icons were strong enough to seduce a nation and still contain a graphic power that can be unleashed today. This is not simply the allure of a well-designed form, like the Coca Cola logo, nor is it the stuff of nostalgic fads, like hoola hoops and flower power buttons. It is the embodiment of a rare and dangerous hypnotic quality that expresses the passions, emotions, and aspirations of the masses. Playing with it is playing with fire. Which is why the most dangerous pyromaniac in the past couple of years is a rock band called The Residents and their album graphics for *Third Reich and Roll.*

Embedded in a visually dense package are pictures of Hitlerian characters and Nazi images (the CD disk is a pattern of swastikas and the band's logo is a six-pointed star medallion of German eagles and a swastika in the center). The package was considered contraband in Germany where it was called *Censored and Roll.* But in the United States, it was just another example of shock rock. And appearances to the contrary, *Third Reich and Roll* is no neo-Nazi hate rock group album, but a "scathingly satirical look at sixties bubble-gum rock somehow twisted into a shocking seventies bubble-gum avant guard [sic]. With a swift kick in the balls . . . ," say the liner notes, that truly tests the limits of satire—and fails. This is more like R. Crumb's lamely parodic pair of comic strips published in *Weirdo* in 1994 that "satirically" told of how the "dirty niggers" and "Jews" would take over America. The strips were reprinted last year (without permission) as if they were real hate propaganda in *Race & Reality,* an international neo-Nazi magazine. *Third Reich and Roll* attempts to toe the fine line between reality and humor and falls prey to stupidity.

History reveals many brilliant examples of how Hitler and his henchmen were humorously ridiculed for propagandistic purposes during and after the rise of the Nazis in Germany. Charlie Chaplin's film, *The Great Dictator,* makes the person of Hitler into a megalomaniacal clown, and the swastika into the Double Cross. And as anti-Nazi attacks go, John Heartfield reclaimed the fascists' own symbols as the basis for caustic and acerbic caricatures in *AIZ,* the communist worker's magazine. When he made the swastika from four blood-dripping executioner's axes, Heartfield was not poking fun but revealing the truth about the regime. The imagery always hit its target. Whereas a misfire like *Third Reich and Roll* is easily misconstrued and ultimately supports the forces of evil.

As Nazi atrocities are challenged by revisionist historians who brazenly question the conclusive evidence of mass genocide (or in today's argot, ethnic cleansing), the trivialization of iconic forms contributes to the real threat that these acts will someday be reduced to a historical footnote. Designers who ignorantly play with the swastika and other Nazi emblems are not only perpetrating a crime against history, they are mutilating a universal language. The various symbols devised by the Nazi imagemakers are a vivid reminder of systematic torture and murder. These pictures, signs, and emblems are not merely clip art for designers, but evidence of crimes against humanity and should remain so.

Originally published in Speak, *October 1996.*

CRITICAL WAY FINDING
Ellen Lupton and J. Abbott Miller

The pyramids of Egypt are mythic monuments to the origin of Western culture, from its architecture to its alphabet. These oversized tombstones have always fascinated the West; they are testaments that a human society could actually design something that could last for five millennia. At the edge of another millennium, a glass pyramid marks the entrance of a more modern form of tomb: an art museum in contemporary Paris. The grand concourse of the Louvre looks, sounds, smells, and feels like an airport or a hotel lobby or a department store. What reminds one that it's an art museum is the Mona Lisa—or rather backlit transparencies of the Mona Lisa—visible from across the broad hall in which visitors congregate.

What links the Louvre to other public spaces—aside from its stadium-capacity entryway—is its use of pictorial symbols addressed to an international public. Such icons participate in a broader phenomenon in the cultural landscape: the emergence of a hieroglyphics of communication, which overlays the contemporary experience of cities, buildings, products, and media with a code of repeatable, reduced icons, compacted chunks of information that collapse a verbal message into a visual mark. The expanding domain of this hieroglyphic speech poses subtle problems for designers in the next millennium: how can we create cross-cultural communication without flattening difference beneath the homogenizing force of a single dialect?

Perhaps these dubious achievements are what makes graphic design the black sheep of the design family. Graphic design lacks the spatial drama or *presence* of architecture and product design. Architectural criticism often contrasts the plentitude of architectural form with the one-dimensionality of "sign," "communication," "illustration," "anecdote," and "information"—the very modes of expression that graphic design traffics in.[1]

Like an overeager, pimply-faced younger sibling, graphic design is what architecture never wants to be: namely, packaging, ornament, frame, and sign. Architecture says "Experience, Space, Tactility, Drama, Eternity," while graphic design says, "Can I help you? Do I look okay? Buy me. Read me. Eat me. Drink me!"

Yet graphic design is a frame that makes spaces, places, and objects legible. Graphic design continually mediates contact with the environment. Signs, arrows, instructions, "you are here" maps, advertisements, and other kinds of information set up the conditions in which experience takes place. And this process of wayfinding—the term used by environmental graphic designers—is increasingly more visual than verbal. The semantic and visual reduction of international symbols—their concise generality—gives them their paradoxical status. They are simultaneously open and closed, vague and specific, ostensibly neutral and yet loaded with connotations and stylistic mannerisms.

Environmental signage is simultaneously there and not there—not really a "part of" the architecture, yet indispensable to its functions, its lived use. The signs that lead visitors to the Mona Lisa are like the frame around the painting: they direct attention to the object and yet are considered extrinsic to it. Graphic design—signage in particular—is largely a framing activity. Graphic design occupies the space *between* a product, building, or text and its user. Graphic design is the margins of a book, the buttons of a boom box, the friendliness of a computer interface, or the label wrapping a tin can.

In common usage, the term *graphic* describes a high-contrast image: black against white, white against black. The silhouette is the dominant strategy behind the language of international pictures, suggesting an objective shadow of material reality, a schematic index of fact. The ideal of an international picture language has been part of modernist design since the 1920s, and reached the intensity of an obsession during the 1960s and 1970s. Sign systems, such as the U.S. Department of Transportation's 1974 symbol set, designed under the guidance of the American Institute of Graphic Arts, aspire to the semiotic consistency of a typeface.[2] The quest for uniform symbols for public information parallels the rise of coherent corporate identity programs and the emergence of an international consumer hieroglyphics.[3]

Such civic and commercial marks signal the challenges of cross-cultural communication in the next millennium. For as the globe is rendered increasingly accessible by communication technologies and forces of economic consolidation, it is at the same time segmented by diverse national, racial, and ethnic identities. Differences must be maintained to counter the domination of what Herbert Marcuse has called "one-dimensional man," whose culture has been robbed of ambivalence and negativity in favor of a mass media capable of assimilating, and thus neutralizing, any form of cultural difference or dissent.[4]

International communication carries the dangers of homogeneity and hegemony alongside the hopeful promise of an integrated global village lined with universally legible street signs and uniformly available products. Designers working at the edge of the millennium are faced with the conflicting imperatives to both expand and contract these formal languages: to reach a diverse public without succumbing to the dangers of assimilation. The one-world, one-language ideal of heroic modernism is an untenable solution for design in the next century.

The simultaneous expansion and contraction of markets for products and media has encouraged the compression of messages into more compacted units. Visual, verbal, and aural—texts transmitted through print, television, film, radio, computers, products, and exhibitions—are increasingly reduced to a code of repeatable icons, or what we call a hieroglyphics of communication. These hieroglyphics punctuate daily life with a pattern of generalized, repeatable signs or marks that signal ownership or information.

Historically, hieroglyphs occupy the space *between* pictures and writing; it is the passage connecting the concrete depiction of objects with the abstract, mechanical coding of the alphabet. The hieroglyph marks the clash between the soft, continuous, flowing substance of visual experience and the hard, polarized, digitized articulations of writing. The power of the phonetic alphabet, in contrast with the older forms of the ideogram, lay in its ability to ignore the "ideas" or "meaning" of a language and to represent only its material side—its sounds—disconnected from the objects and ideas that a language refers to. The alphabet, unlike the hieroglyph, is blind; it is a neutral grid, an automated device capable of converting any word into a graphic mark, regardless of its referent.[5]

The alphabet claims to represent only the *outside* of a given language—its exterior envelope—rather than its interior content.[6] The hieroglyphic script is the checkpoint *between* the mechanical abstraction of the alphabet and the vivid particularity of the image. In hieroglyphics, the specificity of pictures embeds itself in the schematic abstraction of the typographic sign. Through repetition and conventionalization, the picture enters the realm of writing. The soft becomes hard, the fluid becomes fixed, the concrete becomes abstract. In between these two extremes stands the hieroglyph, a rebus that is both silent and spoken, a full-bodied depiction of an idea and a standardized abstraction.

Modern communication has returned to the transitional medium of hieroglyphic writing. The logotype, the corporate symbol, and the international pictogram combine the generality of the typographic mark with the specificity of pictures. In corporate identity the image becomes the "personality" behind a mass-produced product, a sign of uniqueness stamped into an intrinsically multiple object. The fictional character Betty Crocker, for example, is regularly updated by her image managers, who have enabled her features to slowly evolve over the decades while keeping her identity—her status as a proprietary symbol—intact. She is at once naturalistic and schematic, changing and fixed, a rendered portrait and a conventionalized mark.

How does the return of the hieroglyph affect everyday life? Writers from diverse ideological positions have described ways in which the media that supposedly "record" events have come to play a central role in shaping those events—sometimes initiating the event in the first place. From Daniel Boorstin's "pseudoevent" to Jean Baudrillard's "simulacrum" to Stuart Ewen's "all consuming images," critics of culture have noted that representation has come to *inhabit* reality, not content to document it after the fact.[7] This by-now familiar critique has attacked network television, mass-market publishing, advertising, and Hollywood film for substituting an endless stream of superficial images for the lost fullness of experience.

This diaphanous veil of commercial imagery is punctuated with a pattern of hieroglyphics, signs that are neither strictly image nor text but occupy a middle ground between them. Such signs, whether generated in the name of private commerce or public information, are attempts to anchor or regulate the ongoing barrage of pictures and products. Like digital rocks in an analog stream, hieroglyphics guide the flow of communication by directing the interpretation of events, the consumption of goods, or the navigation of public spaces.

Baudrillard has criticized the function of signs in contemporary media, arguing that they have organized reality into a reductive pattern of oppositions. Baudrillard describes how the symbolic plenitude of a concept is emptied when it becomes *instrumental,* when it is strictly coordinated against its semantic opposite. Baudrillard's example is the sun, which for nonindustrialized cultures is a concept approached with considerable ambivalence: it is a source of destruction as well as growth. To this he contrasts the vacation sun of the tourist economy, which is "a completely positive sun . . . source of happiness and euphoria, and as such . . . is significantly opposed to nonsun (rain, cold, bad weather)." The vacation sun results front a semiological reduction: the ambivalence of the sun is lost when opposed to the idea of nonsun. This yes–no, on–off operation of the sign is what Baudrillard describes as "semiological organization"—the process through which signs are given a cultural value.[8]

A comparable pattern of semiological difference governs the cultural boundaries of sexual identity, a phenomenon inadvertently expressed in the official U.S. Department of Transportation travel symbols. The difference between male and female bathrooms is signified by the addition of a cultural mark to the generic human form: the finlike extrusions representing the woman's dress. Rather than express the difference between male and female lavatories with an anatomical representation, as in the more sexually explicit signs proposed by *National Lampoon* in the mid 1970s, the DOT design committee stayed with the already conventional device of the finlike party dress.

The semiotic pattern male–female disappears in other signs in the DOT system, however, in which the male figure represents humanity in general, just as the word "man" becomes a generic title in many verbal contexts. The supposedly neutral pattern of linguistic oppositions breaks down in this particular sign, which happens to depict a service relationship between an employee and a consumer. The DOT sign system thus unwittingly brings home the fact that sexual relationships are determined not solely by biological fact but also by culture, customs, images, and structures of power.

The symbols used in commerce, information graphics, and environmental signage draw upon and reinforce dominant cultural ideas. With the rise of television journalism in the 1960s, pictograms became an important element of news graphics as symbolic logotypes for issues or events. In the television industry, such symbols are called "over-the-shoulders," referring to their ubiquitous location in the void behind a talking head. Over-the-shoulders draw upon a stock vocabulary of flags, maps, hearts, doves, and olive branches. Over-the-shoulders became visually more complex with the introduction of the Paint Box system in the 1980s; conceptually, however, they are virtually unchanged.

The idea of pictorial logos for news stories crossed over into print media in the late 1970s, when Nigel Holmes and Walter Bernard revamped *Time* to make it more competitive with television. Such logos continue to provide news events with a corporate identity. The 1970s also witnessed the renaissance of pictorial information graphics, or what Edward Tufte has called "chartoons," in which numbers are projected into entertainingly figurative scenarios.[9] A pictographic chart from *Time* showing an Arab "over a barrel" belies the supposed objectivity of journalistic statistics by resorting to caricature. The ethnic stereotype is itself a kind of hieroglyphic form, consisting of a set of conventionalized, exaggerated features.

The hieroglyph has also found its way into the verbal features of broadcast news. The ascendancy of the "sound byte" as the basic unit of news speech reflects the media's increasing reliance on condensed chunks of information in favor of extended linear discourse. The term "sound byte" couples the immateriality of speech with the materiality of a product—a bite-sized portion, a compacted blip of information.

The replacement of linear discourse with visual and verbal hieroglyphs in the news media is exemplified by the newspaper *USA Today,* which favors illustrations over text and serves up its articles in TV-sized portions. *USA Today*'s "snapshot series" presents pictorial statistics on mass habits, supporting the publication's desire to be everybody's hometown paper by celebrating the uniformity of taste and canonizing the myth of a national consensus on such issues as how eggs should be prepared.[10] *USA Today* came of age in the 1980s, a decade that was also fascinated with bringing comic books to life. In films such as *Who Framed Roger Rabbitt?* live-action cinema was merged with the flat, caricatured aesthetic of the cartoon, laying an opaque hieroglyphics over the depth of the filmic image.

The modernist ideal of the sharp, crisp graphic symbol is giving way to a logic that favors the folding of signs *into* experience. This softening of the edges between signs and reality reflects the ongoing conquest of the real by the abstract, the will to impose a legible pattern or symbol over the amorphous mass of experience. The grafting of hieroglyphic signs onto the fullness of experience—to bring the sign *to* life and *into* life—is seen in numerous advertising campaigns. Absolut vodka projects its product silhouette into various settings with its endlessly transformed bottle, while other ads merge the corporate hieroglyph with naturalistic settings and live-action drama. Either we see living objects becoming signs, or we see corporate symbols acting as life-size elements in the landscape.

Architecture also increasingly participates in the phenomenon of the hieroglyph. Numerous office towers have come to function like graphic logos for a corporation, their silhouettes serving as massive commercial signs across the script of urban skylines, such as San Francisco's Transamerica pyramid or New York's Citicorp building.

The expansion of global advertising strategies has been another agent in the internationalization of the public landscape. Initiated in the mid 1980s by British firms such as Saatchi and Saatchi, global advertising relies on images and messages that function across diverse markets. An early example is a series of Coca-Cola ads called the Mean Joe Greene series, which features American, Brazilian, Argentinean, and Thai sports stars, each giving a youngster a football jersey in gratitude for a Coke. Such "universal" narratives of heroism and identification are considered general and durable enough to cross cultural contexts. Global strategies increasingly preoccupy advertisers, who wish to control their worldwide identity centrally rather than entrust their marketing to local firms.

The success of this centralization depends upon the pairing of sufficiently general messages with equally generic imagery. The production of a single ad to run across different national markets has created a demand for a new "everyperson"—or "everyconsumer"—a full-bodied, full-color corollary to the international man of airport signage. It has created a need for what a marketing director at Coca-Cola described as a "global teenager."

> There is global media now, like MTV. And there is a global teenager. The same kid you see at the Ginza in Tokyo is in Piccadilly Square in London, in Pushkin Square, at Notre Dame.[11]

Of course, Coca-Cola and MTV have a vested interest in the concept of a universal teenager, though Tokyo, London, and Moscow hardly fulfill the definition of "globalness." Yet the projection of a globally consistent consumer—through advertising, marketing, and packaging—increasingly will inform the public representation of cultural identity.

For example, the international marketing of Frosted Flakes uses a young man whose racial, ethnic, and national identity are uncertain. His generic good looks allow him to function as a logotypical consumer in American, Latin American, and European contexts. Tony the Tiger presents another approach within global advertising: the cartoon–mascot/spokesperson who escapes questions of cultural identity entirely. The cartoon–mascot is a speaking, acting logo—a proprietary beast of burden who is trademark and spokesperson rolled into one.

The economic and bureaucratic advantage of global campaigns is that advertisers can approach divergent audiences as a unified market, as in the United Colors of Benetton campaign. In contrast to Frosted Flakes, Benetton has constructed a global market not by blurring cultural difference but by *incorporating* cultural difference as its theme or trademark. While Frosted Flakes attempts to override racial and cultural specificity, the Benetton campaign makes a fashion statement about cultural difference.

The possibility of a "world culture" in the next millennium brings with it the same anxieties that attended the postwar uniformity of American culture. The loss of individuality and the sense of placelessness in American suburbia can be extrapolated to a worldwide context. Mass media, internationalized markets, and tourism suggest a future "world culture" of stunning sameness.

Internationalization, especially as expressed in the U.S. Department of Transportation symbols, has been viewed as a democratizing force that facilitates intercultural communication and contributes to an *ecology* of information through an economy of signs. What many instances of internationalization show, however, is a hegemonic relationship between the officially sanctioned "language of internationalism" and the specific cultural contexts they inhabit. The sign for "women's toilet" in a Saudi Arabian university has been modified by the addition of the silhouette of a veil, since the long dress depicted could just as easily signify the traditional robes worn by Muslim men. The use of pictorial symbols is, in itself, problematic for Muslim religious codes, which discourage representations of the body.

Consider also the poorly conceived sign that has been used on San Diego freeways to alert drivers to Mexican immigrants who run across the freeway trying to avoid the customs checkpoints. The image of the family in that sign was interpreted by Spanish-speaking people as a directive to "cross here." Thus the very audience most in danger was misled by a sign directed at drivers rather than pedestrians.

Modern hieroglyphs crystallize through simplification and repetition: by offering schematic icons for film genres, news events, or corporate messages, the hieroglyph visually categorizes experience into tidy packages, often reducing it to a flattened cliché. One of the chief functions of graphic design is to generate such tidy icons. But are designers only in the business of purveying dominant ideologies and pandering to the reduced attention spans of contemporary audiences? Could the code of repetitive symbols and schemes that provides the bulk of our visual diet be used for something more than passive instruction or the caricature of complex ideas into univocal statements? If graphic design provides an interface between people and products, could it not also provide an interface between people and culture? We call this utopian project for design in the next millennium "critical wayfinding," or the construction of interfaces that serve not to package corporate messages but rather to provide alternate routes of access to media and information.

For example, one of the chief inventors of international pictograms was Otto Neurath, a Viennese philosopher and social scientist who pioneered the use of pictorial symbols in the 1920s and 1930s as a means of public, cross-cultural education. Although his pictograms are remembered now as the ubiquitous signage found in train stations, airports, and art museums, in his own lifetime he used them to display social statistics in a visually accessible way.

Designers working in the critical spirit of Otto Neurath today include Dennis Livingston, a Baltimore-based activist designer who uses pictorial symbols to track distribution of wealth across the categories of race, sex, profession, and family organization. His chart of "Social Stratification" allows readers to see vertical paths running upward through the economic heap, expressing the fact that for many people social identity is formed more by profession (e.g., office work vs. factory work) than by income.

A billboard-sized poster created by Michael Lebron, a New York-based artist and designer, uses the language of advertising and information design to compare the amount of money spent preventing terrorist attacks on international airplane travel to the amount of money spent preventing the death of poor children across the globe. A 1988 billboard designed by Sheila de Bretteville and the Brooklyn 7 entitled "Can-U-Read-Me?" uses a combination of pictures, letters, and symbols to encourage people to learn to read. By showing nonreaders how much they already know just by living in a literate culture, this hieroglyphic billboard helps to demystify literacy and thus make it more accessible.

In a more comic vein, the designers of *Spy* magazine in the 1980s created a mode of information graphics that derails the intellectual paternalism of mainstream news media and explores instead the messy subconscious of the information age. The tongue-in-cheek yet meticulously archival style of *Spy*'s news graphics invented by Stephen Doyle and Alex Isley in the mid 1980s, is an example of design that works within yet against the dominant codes of the media.

These examples taken from both the context of activist design and the commercial media, indicate some paths that designers could pursue at the edge of the millennium.

Graphic design, as the interface between people and products, information, and environments, has the potential to interpret, revise, and critique the world as well as to simplify and condense it. The notion that design should be transparent, and that we are simply legibility and problem solvers, offers a recessive and reactive role for desire that is ultimately disempowering.

Originally published in The Edge of the Millennium: An International Critique of Architecture, Urban Planning, Product and Communication Design, *ed. Susan Yelavich, Cooper-Hewitt National Design Museum and Whitney Library of Design, 1994.*

Notes

1. Kenneth Frampton questions the legitimacy of "communication" as an architectural value in his essay "Critical Regionalism: Six Points for an Architecture of Resistance," in *Anti-Aesthetic: Essays on Post-Modern Culture,* ed. Hal Foster (Port Townsend, WA: Bay Press, 1983), 16–30.

2. On the history and theory of international pictograms, see Ellen Lupton, "Reading Isotype," in *Design Discourse: History, Theory, Criticism,* ed. Victor Margolin (Chicago: University of Chicago Press, 1989).

3. On corporate identity, see Maud Lavin, "Design in the Service of Commerce," in *Graphic Design in America: A Visual Language History,* ed. Mildred Friedman (Minneapolis and New York: Walker Art Center and Harry N. Abrams, 1989), 126–143.

4. Herbert Marcuse, *One-Dimensional Man* (Boston: Beacon Press, 1964).

5. I. J. Gelb, *A Study of Writing* (Chicago: University of Chicago Press, 1952).

6. Jacques Derrida, *Of Grammatology* (Baltimore: Johns Hopkins University Press, 1974), 30–44.

7. Daniel J. Boorstin, *The Image: A Guide to Pseudo-Events in America* (New York: Atheneum, 1971); Jean Baudrillard, *Simulations* (New York: Semiotext(e), 1983); Stuart Ewen, *All Consuming Images: The Politics of Style in Contemporary Culture* (New York: Basic Books, 1988).

8. Jean Baudrillard, "Fetishism and Ideology: The Semiological Reduction," in *For a Critique of the Political Economy of the Sign* (St. Louis: Telos Press, 1981), 88–101.

9. Edward Tufte, *Envisioning Information* (Cheshire, CT: Graphics Press, 1990).

10. J. Abbott Miller, "*USA Today*: Learning from Las Vegas," *Print* 44:6 (December 1991): 90–97.

11. Peter S. Seeley, Senior Vice President and Director of Global Marketing for Coca-Cola, quoted in the *New York Times* (November 18, 1991).

COUNTERING THE TRADITION OF THE APOLITICAL DESIGNER

Katherine McCoy

This decade finds us in a crisis of values in the United States. Our increasingly multicultural society is experiencing a breakdown in shared values—national values, tribal values, personal values, even family values—consensual motivating values that create a common sense of purpose in a community.

The question is how can a heterogeneous society develop shared values and yet encourage cultural diversity and personal freedom? Designers and design education are part of the problem, and can be part of the answer. We cannot afford to be passive anymore. Designers must be good citizens and participate in the shaping of our government. As designers we could use our particular talents and skills to encourage others to wake up and participate as well.

Before the United States congratulates itself too much on the demise of communism, we must remember that our American capitalist democracy is not what it used to be either. Much of our stagnation comes from this breakdown of values. Entrepreneurial energy and enthusiastic energy and enthusiastic work ethic have deteriorated into individual self-interest, complacency, corporate greed, and resentment between ethnic groups and economic classes. Our common American purpose is fading—that sense of building something new where individuals could progress through participating in a system that provided opportunity. Consumerism and materialism now seem to be the only ties that bind. The one group that seems to be bound by more than this is the Far Right; but their bond is regressive, a desire to force fundamentalist prescriptive values on the rest of us.

We have recently experienced the Reagan era during which we were told it was all okay, that we could spend and consume with no price tag attached. During this period, graphic designers enjoyed the spoils of artificial prosperity with the same passive hedonism as the rest of the country. Now we are beginning to realize it was not all okay. The earth is being poisoned, its resources depleted, and the United States has gone from a creditor to a debtor nation. Our self-absorption and lack of activism has left a void filled by minority single-issue groups aggressively pushing their concerns. There are serious threats to our civil liberties in the United States from both fundamentalist censorship on the Right and political correctness on the Left. We have seen the dismemberment of artistic freedom at the National Endowment for the Arts in the past three years and aggressive attempts to censor public schools' teaching from Darwin to Hemingway to safe sex. As graphic designers specializing in visual communications, the content of our communications may be seriously curtailed if we do not defend our freedom of expression.

AN ACT OF SELF-CENSORSHIP

But even more troubling is our field's own self-censorship. How many graphic designers today would feel a loss if their freedom of expression were handcuffed? Most of our colleagues never exercise their right to communicate on public issues or potentially controversial content. Remove our freedom of speech and graphic designers might never notice. We have trained a profession that feels political or social concerns are either extraneous to our work, or inappropriate.

Thinking back to 1968, the atmosphere at Unimark International during my first year of work typified this problem. Unimark (an idealistic international design office with Massimo Vignelli and Jay Doblin as vice presidents, and Herbert Bayer on the board of directors) was dedicated to the ideal of the rationally objective professional. The graphic designer was to be the neutral transmitter of the client's messages. Clarity and objectivity were the goal.

During that year, the designers I worked with, save one notable exception, were all remarkably disinterested in the social and political upheavals taking place around us. Vietnam was escalating with body counts touted on every evening newscast; the New Left rioted before the Democratic National Convention in Chicago; Martin Luther King and Robert Kennedy were assassinated; and Detroit was still smoking from its riots just down the street from our office. Yet hardly a word was spoken on these subjects. We were encouraged to wear white lab coats, perhaps so the messy external environment would not contaminate our surgically clean detachment.

These white lab coats make an excellent metaphor for the apolitical designer, cherishing the myth of universal value-free design. They suggest that design is a clinical process akin to chemistry, scientifically pure and neutral, conducted in a sterile laboratory environment with precisely predictable results. Yet Lawrence and Oppenheimer and a thousand other examples teach us that even chemists and physicists must have a contextual view of their work in the social/political world around them.

During that time, I became increasingly interested in the social idealism of the times:

the civil rights movement, the anti-Vietnam peace movement, the antimaterialism and social experimentation of the New Left, and radical feminism. Yet it was very difficult to relate these new ideas to the design that I was practicing and the communication process that I loved so much. Or perhaps the difficulty was not the values of design so much as the values of the design community. About all I could connect with was designing and sending (to appalled family members) an anti-Vietnam feminist Christmas card and silkscreening T-shirts with a geometricized "Swiss" version of the feminist symbol. Meanwhile, we continued to serve the corporate and advertising worlds with highly "professional" design solutions.

The implication of the word *professional* is indicative of the problem here. How often do we hear, "Act like a professional," or "I'm a professional, I can handle it." Being a professional means putting aside one's personal reactions regardless of the situation and carrying on. Prostitutes, practitioners of the so-called oldest profession, must maintain an extreme of cool objectivity about the most intimate of human activities, disciplining their personal responses to deliver an impartial and consistent product to their clients.

This ideal of the dispassionate professional distances us from ethical and political values. Think of the words used to describe the disciplined objective professional, whether it be scientist, doctor, or lawyer: *impartial, dispassionate, disinterested*. These become pejorative terms in a difficult world crying out for compassion, interest, concern, commitment, and involvement.

Disinterest is appropriate for a neutral arbitrator but not for an advocate. In fact, most often design education trains students to think of themselves as passive arbitrators of the message between the client/sender and audience/receiver, rather than as advocates for the message content or the audience's needs. Here is the challenge—how to achieve the objectivity and consistency of professionalism without stripping oneself of personal convictions.

Our concept of graphic design professionalism has been largely shaped—and generally for the better—by the legacy of twentieth-century modernism as it has come to us through the Bauhaus and Swiss lineages. However, there are several dominant aspects of this modernist ethic that have done much to distance designers from their cultural milieu. The ideals, forms, methods, and mythology of modernism are a large part of this problem of detachment, including the paradigms of universal form, abstraction, self-referentialism, value-free design, rationality, and objectivity.

A MUCH-NEEDED ANTIDOTE

Objective rationalism, particularly that of the Bauhaus, provided a much-needed antidote to the sentimentality and gratuitous eclecticism found in nineteenth-century mass production, visual communications, and architecture. Linked to functionalism, objective analysis formed the basis of problem-solving methods to generate functional design solutions to improve the quality of daily life. Expanded more recently to include systems design, this attitude has done much to elevate the quality of design thinking.

Linked to the ideal of the objective clear-sighted designer is the ideal of value-free universal forms. Perhaps a reaction to the frequent political upheavals between European nations, especially World War I, early modernist designers hoped to find internationalist design forms and attitudes that would cross those national, ethnic, and class barriers that had caused such strife. In addition, a universal design—one design for all—would be appropriate for the classless mass society of industrial workers envisioned by early twentieth-century social reformers.

But passing years and different national contexts have brought different results from the application of these modernist design paradigms. The myth of objectivity unfortunately does much to disengage the designer from compassionate concerns. Strongly held personal convictions would seem to be inappropriate for the cool-headed objective professional. Functionalism is narrowly defined in measurable utilitarian terms. Too often this means serving the client's definition of function—generally profits—over other concerns, including safety, the environment, and social/cultural/political/environmental impacts.

Universalism has brought us a homogenized corporate style that is based mainly on Helvetica and the grid, and ignores the power and potential of regional, idiosyncratic, personal, or culturally specific stylistic vocabularies. And the ideal of value-free design is a dangerous myth. In fact all design solutions carry a bias, either explicit or implicit. The more honest designs acknowledge their biases openly rather than manipulate their audiences with assurances of universal "truth" and purity.

Abstraction, modernism's revolutionary contribution to the visual language of art and design, further distances both designer and audience from involvement. Stripped of imagery, self-referential abstraction is largely devoid of symbols and disconnected from experience in the surrounding world. It is cool and low on emotion. Abstraction is predictable in application, polite, inoffensive, and not too meaningful—thereby providing a safe vocabulary for corporate materials. Imagery, on the other hand, is richly loaded with symbolic encoded meaning, often ambiguous and capable of arousing the entire range of human emotions. Imagery is difficult to control, even dangerous or controversial, often leading to unintended personal interpretations on the part of the audience—but also poetic, powerful, and potentially eloquent.

TENDENCY TO AVOID POLITICAL DIALECTICS

The modernist agenda has conspired to promote an apolitical attitude among American designers, design educators, and students, building on the pragmatic American tendency to avoid political dialectics. American designers consistently take European theories and strip them of their political content. Of the various strains of modernism, many of which were socially concerned or politically revolutionary, American design either chose those most devoid of political content or stripped the theories of their original political idealism.

More recently we have seen a strong interest in French literary theory. But its original element of French contemporary Marxism has been largely ignored in the United States, perhaps rightly so. The American political environment is far different from the European; European political dialectics may not be appropriate to us. Yet we cannot assume that no political theory is needed to ground our work—all designers need an appropriate framework to evaluate and assess the impact of their work within its social/ethical/political milieu. Perhaps an appropriate evaluative framework would be different for each individual, reflecting our strong tradition of American individualism.

Designers must break out of the obedient, neutral, servant-to-industry mentality, an orientation that was particularly strong in the Reagan/Thatcher 1980s, and continues to dominate design management and strategic design. Yes, we are problem-solvers responding to the needs of clients. But we must be careful of the problems we take on. Should one help sell tobacco and alcohol, or design a Ronald Reagan Presidential memorial library for a man who reads only pulp cowboy novels? Design is not a neutral, value-free process. A design has no more integrity than its purpose or subject matter. Garbage in, garbage out. The most rarefied design solution can never surpass the quality of its content.

A dangerous assumption is that corporate work of innocuous content is devoid of political bias. The vast majority of student design projects deal with corporate needs, placing a heavy priority on the corporate economic sector of our society. Commerce is where we are investing time, budgets, skills, and creativity. This is a decisive vote for economics over other potential concerns, including social, educational, cultural, spiritual, and political needs. This is a political statement in itself, both in education and practice.

ART IGNORES THE ISSUES TOO

Postwar American art has greatly ignored the issues as well. The self-reference of abstract expressionism and minimalism has been largely divorced from external conditions. Pop art embraced materialism more than it critiqued it. The more recent postmodernist ironic parodies have been full of duplicity and offer no program as antidote to the appalling paradigms they deconstruct. Nevertheless recent years have brought a new involvement by artists in the social/political environment around them. A recent book, *The Re-enchantment of Art,* advocates a second postmodernism, a reconstruction that moves beyond the detachment of modernism and deconstruction. Suzi Gablik, the author, wants an end to the alienation of artists and aesthetics from social values in a new interrelational audience-oriented art.

There are signs that this is happening. Issue-oriented art has been spreading like wildfire among graduate students in the fine arts. At Cranbrook Academy of Art and at a number of other design schools, fine arts students are attending our graphic design crits, eager to learn design methods for reaching their audiences. Fashion advertising is beginning occasionally to embrace issues—perhaps humanistic content is good for sales. Witness Esprit, Benetton, Moschino. That these clients are prepared to make social advocacy part of their message signals both a need and a new receptiveness in their audiences. Graphic design is a powerful tool, capable of informing, publicizing, and propagandizing social, environmental, and political messages as well as commercial ones. But are many graphic designers prepared to deal with this type of content?

Undertaking the occasional piece of compassionate graphic design as a relief from business as usual is not the answer here. The choice of clients or content is crucial. The most fortunate can find a worthy cause in need of a designer with the funds to pay for professional design services. Unfortunately, good causes often seem to have the least resources in our present economic system. Is it possible to shape a practice around nonbusiness clients or introduce social content into commercial work? The compassionate designer must plan an ethical practice strategically—and be an informed, involved citizen in a Jeffersonian participatory democracy, agile and flexible, prepared to turn the tools of visual communications to a broad spectrum of needs.

AN END TO DETACHMENT?

How does one educate graphic design students with an understanding of design as a social and political force? Can a political consciousness be trained? Can an educator teach values? The answer is probably no in the simplistic sense. However, the field of education has a well-developed area referred to as values clarification that offers many possibilities for graphic design educators. Too often we take individuals with eighteen years of experience and strip them of their values, rather than cultivate those values for effective application in design practice.

In teaching, these issues must be raised from the beginning for the design student. This is not something to spring on the advanced student after their attitudes have been fixed on neutrality. At the core of this issue is the content of the projects we assign from the very first introductory exercise. Most introductory graphic design courses are based on abstract formal exercises inherited from the Bauhaus and the classic Basel school projects.

The detachment problem begins here. These projects either deal with completely abstract form—point, line, and plane, for instance—or they remove imagery from context. The Basel graphic translation projects, so effective in training a keen formal sense, unfortunately use a process of abstractional analysis, thereby stripping imagery of its encoding symbolism. (I have to admit to being guilty of this in my assignments in past years.) Divorcing design form from content or context is a lesson in passivity, implying that graphic form is something separate and unrelated to subjective values or even ideas. The first principle is that all graphic projects must have content.

The type of content in each assignment is crucial. It is disheartening to see the vast number of undergraduate projects dedicated to selling goods and services in the marketplace devoid of any mission beyond business success. Undoubtedly all students need experience in this type of message and purpose. But cannot projects cover a broader mix of content, including issues beyond business? Cultural, social, and political subjects make excellent communications challenges for student designers.

Project assignments can require content developed by the student that deals with public and personal social, political, and economic issues and current events. The responsibility for developing content is a crucial one; it counteracts the passive design role in which one unquestioningly accepts client-dictated copy. On a practical level, we know how frequently all designers modify and improve client copywriting; many graphic designers become quite good writers and editors, so closely is our function allied to writing. In a larger sense, however, self-developed content and copy promotes two important attitudes in a design student.

One is the ability to develop personal content and subject matter, and an interest in personal design work, executed independently of client assignments. This method of working is much like that of fine artists who find their reward in a self-expression of personal issues. Second is the challenge to develop subject matter stimulates the design student to determine what matters on a personal level. A process of values clarification must go on in the student before a subject or attitude to that subject can be chosen. And the breadth of concerns chosen as subjects by fellow students exposes each student to a wider range of possibilities.

CLARIFICATION THROUGH CRITIQUE

The critique process for issue-oriented work can be a very effective forum for values clarification. This is particularly true of group critiques in which all students are encouraged to participate, rather than the authoritarian traditionalist crit in which the faculty do all the talking. In evaluating the success or failure of a piece of graphic communications, each critic must address the subject matter and understand the design student's stated intentions before weighing a piece's success. This expands the critique discussion beyond the usual and necessary topics of graphic method, form, and technique. Tolerance as well as objectivity are required of each critique participant in that they must accept and understand the student's intended message before evaluating the piece.

For instance, two fundamentalist Christian students recently brought their religiously oriented work to our Cranbrook graphic design crits for two semesters. It was a challenge—and a lesson in tolerance—for the other students to put aside their personal religious (or nonreligious) convictions in order to give these students and their work a fair critique from a level playing field. It was quite remarkable—and refreshing—to find us all discussing spirituality as legitimate subject matter. This has held true for many other subjects from the universe of issues facing our culture today. These have included local and global environmental issues, animal rights, homelessness, feminism, and reproductive choice.

The point here is content. As design educators, we cast projects almost as a scientist designs a laboratory experiment. The formula and the variables conspire to slant the results in one direction or another. The project assignment and the project critique are powerful tools that teach far more than explicit goals, and carry strong implicit messages about design and the role of designers.

Design history also offers a rich resource for understanding the relationship of form and content to sociopolitical contexts. We all know how often works from art and design history are venerated (and imitated) in an atmosphere that is divorced from their original context. By exploring the accompanying cultural/social/political histories, students can see the contextual interpendencies and make analogies to their own time.

Am I advocating the education of a generation of designers preoccupied with political activism, a kind of reborn sixties mentality? I think rather what I have in mind is nurturing a crop of active citizens, informed, concerned participants in society who happen to be graphic designers. We must stop inadvertently training our students to ignore their convictions and be passive economic servants. Instead we must help them to clarify their personal values and to give them the tools to recognize when it is appropriate to act on them. I do think this is possible. We still need objectivity, but this includes the objectivity to know when to invoke personal biases and when to set them aside.

Too often our graduates and their work emerge as charming manikins, voiceless mouthpieces for the messages of ventriloquist clients. Let us instead give designers their voices so they may participate and contribute more fully in the world around them.

Originally published in Design Renaissance: Selected Papers from the International Design Congress, *Glasgow, Scotland, 1993; Jeremy Myerson, editor.*

WOMEN WHO TURN THE GAZE AROUND
Pamela A. Ivinski

WAC is watching me. Don't think I'm I'm paranoid—they're watching you, too. Especially if you're in the business of constructing images of women. The advertisements, book covers, movie posters, and magazine spreads that you laid out yesterday are being scrutinized today by the Women's Action Coalition, a feminist group with a gift for visual analysis. If WAC finds your design to be sexist, racist, or homophobic, they'll let you know.

WAC doesn't have anything against graphic designers. Neither do SisterSerpents of Chicago, nor the Guerrilla Girls and WHAM! (Women's Health Action Mobilization) in New York. In fact, designers and artists are key members of these activist organizations and the graphics they produce are considered powerful weapons. But these groups want you to know that they've got an eye on the media, the medical profession, government, schools, the art world; in short, any person or institution perceived to be attempting to limit the rights of women. They're going to make sure their voices of protest are seen as well as heard.

Activist graphics, in the form of posters, placards, and banners, are, of course, traditional tools of dissent. What sets the most recent wave of feminist protest design apart is an understanding of the ways in which images have been used to maintain power structures that oppress women. Film and literary critics in particular have demonstrated how women are rarely portrayed in art and the media as participating in the full range of activity allowed to men. Despite advances achieved by women in the real world, buxom blondes (however cliché) still sell. Professional women rarely find themselves able to identify with media-generated female images, and lesbians might as well not exist.

Guerrilla Girls, SisterSerpents, WHAM!, and WAC draw strength from the kind of visual theory about the social construction of gender roles that is more at home in academic journals than on protest posters. Fluency in the visual arts, however, allows them to deploy this theory with a dry sense of humor that makes their design all the more effective. Aware of having been observed and objectified, these women have turned the gaze around. They fight graphics with graphics, exposing offensive images in some cases, creating images with the intention to offend in others.

Steven Heller has written that "design in the service of social activism is not always pretty," due to the low-budget, high-urgency nature of most protest projects. For feminist groups, resisting the "pretty"—the burden of beauty placed upon women—is more than a side effect of production. It is an aesthetic and philosophical stance.

Guerrilla Girls, an anonymous group of women who proclaimed themselves to be the "conscience of the art world" in the mid 1980s, challenge the preference for feminine attractiveness over achievement. Their original goal was to make visible the invisibility of women artists in New York galleries and museums. Recent efforts and collaborations have seen them expand into current social and political issues such as sexual harassment and homelessness.

The initial Guerrilla Girls posters, "sniped" on Soho walls in 1985, made women their subject while eschewing their images. Unadorned columns of Futura listed the plain facts of the art world: "WHAT DO THESE ARTISTS HAVE IN COMMON? THEY ALLOW THEIR WORK TO BE SHOWN IN GALLERIES THAT SHOW NO MORE THAN 10% WOMEN ARTISTS OR NONE AT ALL." The first four years of posters repeated this basic formula, naming names in bold text and avoiding images of the body.

Transferring graphic style to public practice, Guerrilla Girls likewise have refused the female image in their instructional appearances. Members give lectures and serve on panels, with a twist: their identities are hidden under hideous gorilla masks, sometimes worn coyly with miniskirts and heels. Taking as their *noms de guerre* the names of dead women artists, Guerrilla Girls at once honor their predecessors (still absent from many histories of art) and deflect attention from their own individual traits.

Secrecy still holds with Guerrilla Girls. When asked if graphic designers are counted among their members, "Rosalba Carriera" responded, "We don't give out that kind of information." She was more forthcoming about the design process, describing design-by-committee. "Someone comes up with an idea—'Let's do something about . . .'—and others have to agree before we proceed. Everything is done by consensus."

According to "Rosalba Carriera," there was no conscious decision among Guerrilla Girls to avoid the female image. "We wanted something clean and effective—statistics. We found a typeface we liked early on, and we continue to use it. We like our identifiable style." However, their bare-bones graphic aesthetic suggests a reaction against women's art of the 1970s, especially two-dimensional work that emphasized decoration and performance art that used the naked female body.

By the mid 1980s, under the sign of feminist theory and out of the Age of Aquarius, the female image was considered taboo by many women artists. The female body (clothed and naked) had for too long been the primary vehicle of masculine avant-garde art and mass-media advertising. Its celebration, even by women, came to seem more limiting than liberating.

Guerrilla Girls' concentration on text at the expense of imagery mimics the art of Jenny Holzer, who pasted her "Truisms" posters on New York buildings in the late 1970s. Although she has characterized her lists as "mock clichés," a number of individual statements with special resonance for women were popularized by hats and T-shirts reading "MEN DON'T PROTECT YOU ANYMORE" and "ABUSE OF POWER COMES AS NO SURPRISE."

Guerrilla Girls have been criticized for their obvious desire to be allowed member-ship in a contemporary art world that still has the feel of a boys' club. Yet it seems more judicious to view their project in a continuum with that of conceptual artists like Holzer and Barbara Kruger, who represent an eighties trend in art and scholarship by women that preferred to interrogate existing systems of power rather than to propose alternatives.

In their unadorned graphics, Guerrilla Girls respected an unspoken feminist proscription against the female image. But through their public performances, they pay homage to women's performance art, which had its roots in activism. They underscore the fact that women, like children, are still encouraged to be "seen and not heard."

In an unusual example of an early poster employing the female image, Guerrilla Girls expose how the ubiquity of idealized female images in the visual arts has hidden the invisibility of real women. Ingres's *Grand Odalisque*, perhaps the most languorous nude in the history of painting, is made an honorary Guerrilla Girl by being hidden under her own gorilla mask. At her side is the query: "DO WOMEN HAVE TO BE NAKED TO GET INTO THE MET. MUSEUM? LESS THAN 5% OF THE ARTISTS IN THE MODERN ART SECTIONS ARE WOMEN, BUT 85% OF THE NUDES ARE FEMALE."

Guerrilla Girls originally targeted the specific injustices of the mid-eighties art world and can take partial credit for the improved status of women artists. Those of a conceptual bent, like Kruger and Holzer, Cindy Sherman and Sherrie Levine, as well as artists like Susan Rothenberg and Jennifer Bartlett, who work in more traditional media, achieved distinction. Ironically, the greater presence of women in the art world was counteracted by the constriction of civil rights of women in the broader sphere of American culture, so well illustrated in Susan Faludi's recent bestseller, *Backlash* (Crown, 1991).

In 1989, it became clear that there was more at stake than an increased number of one-woman art exhibitions. Women's control over their own bodies was at issue, and naming names *à la* Guerrilla Girls, while to some degree effective, wasn't enough. Spurred to action by the recent attack on abortion rights (where the Supreme Court threatened to overturn *Roe v. Wade* in a ruling on Missouri's abortion law), and inspired by the success of the AIDS activist group ACT UP, a new feminism began to emerge.

ACT UP (AIDS Coalition to Unleash Power) has provided a valuable model for women's activism, dealing as it does with related issues of sexuality, invisibility, and health. Founded in New York in 1987 and devoted to political action, ACT UP has brought attention to the AIDS crisis through savvy manipulation of the media.

Like Guerrilla Girls, ACT UP has been fueled by visual arts participants. Wresting the pink triangle from Nazi infamy, the Silence = Death Project produced a rallying point for AIDS activism that was embraced outside the homosexual community. Another graphics collective, Gran Fury, is responsible for some of the most sophisticated images in recent activist history. At the same time, Gran Fury realizes, "WITH 42,000 DEAD/ART IS NOT ENOUGH/TAKE COLLECTIVE DIRECT ACTION TO END THE AIDS CRISIS."

Activist graphics are, in a sense, advertisements for change. Barbara Kruger, the graphic designer and artist whose signature style influenced ACT UP, knows how to sell a point, having shaped her terse style within the very media machine that she would later disassemble. Soon after completing her fine arts study at Parsons School of Design, Kruger was named chief designer of *Mademoiselle.* Her graphic skills, honed in the construction of the feminine ideal, became, as she noted in Kate Linker's *Love for Sale* (Abrams, 1990), "with a few adjustments, my work as an artist."

Perhaps as an antidote to her role in promulgating the "can't be too rich or too thin" aesthetic of Condé Nast, Kruger freelanced in radical politics. Her book cover designs from the period include titles like *Peasant Uprisings in Seventeenth-Century France, Russia, and China* and Kropotkin's *The Anarchist Prince.*

Condé Nast meets Kropotkin in Kruger's art. "WE WON'T PLAY NATURE TO OUR CULTURE." "YOU THRIVE ON MISTAKEN IDENTITY." "YOUR MANIAS BECOME SCIENCE." Her visual style is glossy, but her tone is accusatory "BUY ME I'LL CHANGE YOUR LIFE."

The forceful critique embedded in Kruger's high-art practice lends itself well to activist causes, and throughout the 1980s she created her own protest posters. In "YOUR BODY IS A BATTLEGROUND," a call-to-arms for the 1989 prochoice march on Washington, Kruger's art became, with a few adjustments, her work as an activist. The lipsticked and mascaraed positive image juxtaposed against the radiograph-like negative encapsulated the terms of the debate over women's bodies: where is the boundary between inside and outside, private and public, and who will control it?

A number of women, many of them too young to have participated in earlier manifestations of the women's movement, and frustrated by the bureaucracies of established prochoice groups like NOW and NARAL, chose to form their own, defiantly militant, organizations. The masculine rhetoric of war employed by feminist activists like Sister-Serpents and WHAM! might be distasteful to some women, and the point is well taken. But with real violence against women on the rise (even among groups like Operation Rescue, who claim to protect women), a peaceful exchange of words is not enough.

SisterSerpents snipes posters that make men cringe. The group's manifesto boasts, "SisterSerpents is fierce and uncompromising, refusing to plead, or gently persuade. We recognize and confront the misogyny that exists deep within society. We will sever our connection with men who do not care to recognize our oppression because we realize that this is a survival mechanism. . . . Concerns about judgment or keeping up appearances are totally irrelevant."

While comprising women who work in the visual arts, who presumably were schooled in the "pretty," SisterSerpents cultivates a brutal aesthetic. Where an earlier generation of feminists called for women to "take back the night," SisterSerpents seeks to take back the fetus from the religious Right. "FOR ALL YOU FOLKS WHO CONSIDER A FETUS MORE VALUABLE THAN A WOMAN," they suggest on one poster, "HAVE A FETUS COOK FOR YOU," "HAVE A FETUS CLEAN YOUR HOUSE." "CRY ON A FETAL SHOULDER," among other things, and at center, "FUCK A FETUS."

Collage is a favored design technique of SisterSerpents, especially when used for disjunctive effect. Where Kruger uses cool irony to nudge mass-media images toward self-destruction, SisterSerpents stages violent collisions between the real and the advertised. The naked profile of an anorexic woman is pasted next to the elegant, long-legged model in a Superslims cigarette ad. The surgeon general's warning is altered to admonish: "QUITTING DIETING NOW GREATLY REDUCES SERIOUS RISKS TO YOUR HEALTH."

SisterSerpents pokes gruesome fun at the penchant for female body parts in graphic design by creating corresponding images of disembodied male genitalia. In one juicy example, Julia Child emerges from behind an outsized banquet of foodstuffs (including a prominent lobster claw). With a smile, she brandishes a very large knife, a set of male genitals stuck on its point. "Julia's simple method for stopping a rapist/GO FOR THE GROIN, GALS!"

While SisterSerpents targets media-generated misogyny in its posters, WHAM! aims to uncover the sexist bias of organized medicine. Prompted by the fact that medical studies, such as those conducted by the Centers for Disease Control, have until recently excluded women, WHAM! has produced stickers such as "SUPPORT VAGINAL PRIDE BECAUSE WOMEN'S HEALTH CARE IS POLITICAL."

WHAM! is best known for intervening in the reproductive rights conflict by providing escorts to abortion clinics and squaring off against Operation Rescue. WHAM! also publicizes the tragedy of breast cancer much in the way that ACT UP focuses on the

AIDS epidemic. Stickers citing breast cancer statistics can be found decorating women's bathrooms around New York City. A recent poster, sniped around Soho, features a woman wearing a plaster breast plate—with one breast removed.

Despite an increased feminist presence at the start of the 1990s, many women perceived the continuing erosion of women's rights. The concurrent unfolding of a number of sensational rape cases, as well as the heightened awareness of sexual harrassment in the wake of the Clarence Thomas hearings, impelled a group of women from the New York art and design worlds to form another feminist organization dedicated to direct action, WAC.

It was no longer enough to be part of the silent and (reasonably liberal) masses, especially with the Moral Majority making very vocal claims to preeminence. The time had come for women to openly identify themselves with the feminist cause. As a Planned Parenthood placard featured at a 1992 reproductive rights march announced, "I AM THE FACE OF PRO-CHOICE AMERICA." The examples of ACT UP and WHAM! and their willingness to put their own bodies on the line in order to protect the bodies of all, were crucial to WAC's formation.

WAC's original membership was composed mainly of artists and designers, well-versed in both graphic techniques and feminist theory, and willing to lend their names to the cause. The group's graphic identity was a priority from its inception. Their mission statement proclaims, "We will exercise our full creative power to launch a visible and remarkable resistance."

The WAC blue dot symbol was the brainchild of performance artist Laurie Anderson. The blue dot was based on the television blip used to obscure faces in televised trials, such as that of William Kennedy Smith. Marlene McCarty, designer and artist, elaborated on the idea, creating the "WAC Is Watching" logo, with its unblinking, all-seeing eye.

WAC uses graphics to establish solidarity among women. The WAC logo is omnipresent at Soho gatherings as well as protests, on buttons, T-shirts, baseball caps, even on bodies in the form of a temporary tattoo. Graphic designer and WAC member Bethany Johns recognizes the motivational force of design. "Women showed up at the [April 1992 Washington] march in part because the graphics were good," says Johns. "They were all so excited to hold Marlene's posters up."

Johns and McCarty, who collaborated on many of the powerful graphics utilitzed during early WAC actions, emphasize that their design training and experience prepared them well for activism and "guerrilla problem solving." In order to confront issues at the height of media attention, McCarty reports, "Things had to happen overnight. We had to develop an idea, get it approved, and get it done for about twenty dollars."

WAC originally coalesced around a shared desire to make a feminist presence felt at the 1992 rape trial of a group of students from St. John's University in Queens, New York. An ad decrying rape was taken out in the school newspaper and a demonstration was planned. Some group members proposed bringing materials to the courthouse and making posters on the spot, but the designers knew that working outdoors in below-freezing weather might not lend itself to the generation of catchy slogans and effective graphics. "Our work for WAC is content-driven. But the graphics have to be legitimate," says Johns.

The idea of carrying placards in the shape of a blue dot was then conceived, and Johns and McCarty put their skills to work, not only to create designs, but also to find suitable low-cost materials and to set up an assembly-line and demonstrate production.

Cardboard "cheesecake rounds" served as dots, with tongue depressors for handles, as other types of sticks were banned as a security precaution.

Despite the "do-it-yourself" aspect of the production process, WAC graphics reflect technological advances in image reproduction. Desktop publishing has done more than change the worlds of print and design: it has revolutionized the business of revolution. As Roberta Bernstein notes, "Our graphics must be sophisticated in order to engage the public's attention. We want people to think 'it looks like a Gap ad.'"

Photography has entered feminist graphics with a vengeance. In addition to naming names, WAC pictures its oppressors and labels them with the dis-honorific "PUBLIC ENEMY #_____" And while feminist activists have been criticized for privileging negative over positive images, WAC has heroes as well as enemies, identified clearly as such. Popular singer K. D. Lang, poet and performance artist Saphire, and Rabbi Sharon Kleinbaum are among those women cited as role models for their vocal support of feminist, as well as gay and lesbian, causes and concerns.

WAC has also availed itself of desktop publishing in the production of its first book, *WAC Stats: The Facts About Women*. Stylistically, *WAC Stats* harks back to early Guerrilla Girls posters, marching fact after fact in sans-serif type unrelieved by images. Arranged alphabetically by subject ("Abortion, AIDS, Art, Breast Cancer, Cosmetics and Cosmetic Surgery . . ."), the individual statistics are often horrifying ("Over 2,000 women die from hysterectomies annually"; "At least 70 percent of men who batter their wives sexually or physically abuse their children"). Yet, the accumulated effect is strangely empowering: someone has finally taken the time to worry about women.

Guerrilla Girls, in turn, have begun to examine a broader range of women's issues outside the art world and have collaborated with the Artist and Homeless Collective on a new series of posters. WAC joined forces with Guerrilla Girls in the summer of 1992 to protest racism and sexism in the inaugural exhibition at the Guggenheim Museum branch in Soho.

Guerrilla Girls are unusual in that they now represent nearly a decade of sustained activism. WAC's media visibility has led to a swollen membership that hampers its ability to move at a moment's notice, as was possible in its earlier phase. Splinter groups like Lesbian Avengers already have been formed.

Yet, in terms of sheer numbers, the response to WAC by concerned and creative women is encouraging. Roberta Bernstein points out, "It's not just a New York leftist liberal phenomenon: there are thirteen other very active WACs around the country." Even if these groups disband, their members have learned how to deploy their visual skills in the service of women's issues, issues inextricably linked to the world of appearance.

For now, WAC is still watching. Even better, as WAC reminds us, "Women are watching, we will take action." Consider yourself warned.

Originally published in Print, *September/October 1993.*

NORM AND FORM: THE ROLE OF GRAPHIC DESIGN IN THE PUBLIC DOMAIN
Hugues C. Boekraad

In "Strukturwandlung der Oeffentlichkeit," the German philosopher Habermas sketches the historical development of the public domain in a number of European countries. He outlines an ideal model of this domain in which decisions regarding public matters are taken on the basis of arguments rather than of status, power, or tradition. This is clearly a prerequisite for the functioning of a democracy. The public domain is the medium in which the arguments are formulated that ultimately underlie political action. The quality of the arguments and the number of participants in the debate are crucial in determining the democratic level of the decision making. A specific form of communication turns out be *sine qua non* for a democratic system.

In his historical sketch, Habermas indicates who formed the basis for this early public domain: the city burghers. They were wealthy and educated and shared the values of a certain lifestyle—bourgeois culture. So only a limited segment of the population was involved; women, the poor, and children played no role in the debate. The burghers controlled the material and other conditions for taking part in this debate. At once owners of capital, participants in a common culture, and keepers of the relevant information, they turned the public debate into the exclusive preserve of a particular social group.

The question is whether the actual public domain achieved between the seventeenth and nineteenth centuries can continue to serve as a model in the twentieth century. Not only has the number of participants increased dramatically, but also the nature of public debate has changed. It is no longer carried on or mainly carried on between equal citizens but between the representatives of organizations who make use of increasingly complicated information and media networks. Ownership of the economic machinery has been divorced from its management—the so-called managerial revolution. The internationalization and increased scale of the economy alone ensure that the classic model of public domain cannot be retained. But it is not only economic powers of decision that have gained independence from the bourgeoisie: the same is true of the production of knowledge and information. Bourgeois culture has long ceased to be identical with capitalism; the bourgeois lifestyle is no longer rooted in positions of economic power. Bourgeois values such as thrift, lack of ostentation, etc. have become antique in a culture of conspicuous consumption. In his novel *Buddenbrooks,* Thomas Mann shows how the early bourgeois culture yielded to the new capitalism that took over in the second half of the last century in sociology, it was Max Weber who described the end of Enlightenment ideals: the society of rationally thinking, speaking, and acting citizens ended up as a bureaucratized state/society that subjected its own citizens to its administrative procedures. In "Diälektik der Aufklärung," Horkheimer and Adorno outlined the working methods of a culture industry that constantly and professionally manipulates the behavior of the masses. In their somber view, in the twentieth century the masses who had become politically aware were robbed of this awareness by being permanently embedded in a mass culture in which entertainment and fun took the place of pleasure, culture, and knowledge.

Graphic design is a young discipline. As an independent field, it is related to the rise of modern mass culture and opposed to it. Graphic design came into being as a by-product of the development of modern mass communications—as an autonomous professional function between the creation of text/image and its printing and circulation. Its object is the form in which all kinds of information are presented. As a independent discipline, graphic design is tied to the decline of the bourgeois public domain as described by Habermas.

The profession originated at the end of the nineteenth and beginning of the twentieth centuries. It emerged from low, rather than high, culture. As a producer of images, the poster designer gave a banal treatment to themes and techniques from painting to meet the needs of business and the entertainment industry. As the arranger of information, the graphic designer applied architectonic design methods to two-dimensional work. At the same time as this new field of commissioned work was developing, book design became the domain of those graphic designers who had made the traditional forms, typefaces, and page forms of the Renaissance book the standard.

It is remarkable that both traditional book design and the new typography were at odds with the reality of the print media that dominated the field of communications at the beginning of the century. Dutch traditionalists wanted to see a revival of the bourgeois culture, which had achieved its finest form in the seventeenth century. In the Dutch version of Art Nouveau (known as *Nieuwe Kunst*), a new feeling was given expression in a curious amalgam of traditional forms and a new idiom. Obvious examples include the furniture that Van de Velde designed for his own use or for high-minded clients such as Osthaus, and the design of the volumes of poetry published by Kloos and Corter. The specialized book designers retained the classic outward form of the book while trying to extend its range to include the masses (from the *Arbeiterbildung* of social democracy to postwar ideas about bringing culture to the people). They tried to reaffirm the central value of the book and the library as the seat of the collective memory at a time when the real foundations of the survival of society were to be found in the anonymous, inconspicuous archives of bureaucratic institutions. They refined the outward appearance of the book at the point when it lost its dominant position as the repository knowledge and medium for argument. They were concerned to defend not only the book's form, which was threatened by mass production, but also its function in society. They were upholding the rights of a humanist tradition. One of the central figures in this movement, the scholar and typographer Stanley Morison, displayed a sharp awareness of the political significance of design (see his "Politics and Script"). In *First Principles of Typography* (1929), he describes the role of the graphic designer as servant of society. The designer makes himself invisible and obeys the rules that centuries of experience have found to be valid. Surrounded by the new media, Morison was a proponent of "the European tradition of the written and printed word." The forms of this tradition may be adapted only to the extent that this is necessary for modern technology. By definition, the designer has nothing at stake; he has no artistic interest of his own in the forms he creates and is simply the intermediary between text and reader. An ethic of self-effacement, dedication, and service lies behind Morison's celebrated book, which became the standard work for the traditionalists among graphic designers. He is appalled by the idea of autonomous or artistic design. Respect for the text and the reader is at the heart of his concept of professional integrity. Design is a service to society. The strategic objective of his definition of design is the realization, on an extended scale, of the model of public domain as shaped by bourgeois culture. He rejects the reality of the mass culture of the early twentieth century in the name of a tradition to be restored or updated.

The modernists were no less averse to the communication practices current in their day. However, they tried to create new forms for the new contents of contemporary culture. New content and a new audience—the urban masses—required new forms that would adequately reflect the spirit of the age. From the beginning, they took account of the new production methods; the machine and technology were the natural parameters of their formal vocabulary. But they also had a different society in mind. Their experiments with form were meant to anticipate a new material and nonmaterial culture. Their prototypes were intended to exemplify new social relations. Their products were to be suitable—in due course—for mass use. They also rejected the idea of personal motives for designing. At stake were the collective interests of the masses excluded by bourgeois culture. The high expectations of a new society lay behind their ethic giving first place to collective interests. Thus, an ethic of service was common to the modernists and the traditionalists, as was the tendency to put their ideals into practice in utopian communities or small groups. This is not the place to go into the complicated process by which the proposals of the avant-garde in art and design had their subversive element removed. These proposals were implemented in circumstances that were entirely different from those the avant-garde had anticipated. Their innovative forms were integrated into a capitalist culture that continually renewed itself. The avant-gardes were normalized, assimilated, seduced by money and prestige. Salvador Dali was renamed "Avida Dollars" by André Breton. The moral integrity of individual participants in the avant-garde could not prevent its disintegration under Stalinism and capitalism. Caught in the web of the new fields of town planning and mass communications, most members of the avant-garde lost their individuality.

When postmodernism became dominant in Dutch graphic design around 1980, designers could let their hair down. The strict rules of both traditionalists and modernists were overturned—anything went. The designer's personal pleasure was central to the philosophy of Studio Dumbar, a leader in this new movement. Respect for client and public gave way to an attitude that gave priority to the aims of the designer. A certain disdain for the external conditions of the design was accompanied by a concentration on the formal possibilities available to the designer. What disappeared was the relation of the design to the public domain, however defined. The designer as a specialist serving public interests had gone. The designer's frame of reference had narrowed down to the world of design itself: what was his/her relation to the established names in that world? Fame and fortune became acknowledged aims of design activity. The norm of design became the positioning of the designer. If we look at the attitudes to design held by architects and graphic designers or students in these disciplines, several categories can be distinguished.[1]

The theoreticians. They are text oriented. They are more interested in philosophies and theories about design than in design itself. If they practice design, they prefer to work on the basis of theoretical ideas or concepts. Among architecture students, Libeskind and

Eisenman are the popular figures at the moment, and Heidegger and Derrida are widely read. Theoretically inclined graphic designers are interested in texts on the role of design with a social or cultural slant.

The handymen. They are manually oriented. They focus on the material and the form is created in the encounter with the properties of the material. They want to let the materials speak for themselves and to bring the form back to the essence. Naturalness in form and material are high priorities. They attend workshops and have a real interest in the craft aspects. Cut and paste is back in favor with this group of graphic designers. What matters to them is the pleasure of form, but without frills.

The designers. They are visually oriented. They search for the image of the age. They find it in cinemas, magazines, on the streets and in museums, at video festivals and fashionable events. Their working method is usually collage—combining existing images to create a new one. They are sensitive to trends and reduce the design process to image invention.

The artists. They use the methods and tools of design but for strictly subjective purposes. They are concerned with their own preferences in form and image; they aim to create an image of their own. They express themselves without regard to communication or pragmatic concerns.

The technophiles. They are fascinated by the technical aspects of their discipline: the materials, the construction, the new design tools. The graphic designers in this category are Apple freaks.

In all these cases, design is made independent from commissioning and the use of the designs realized, if realization is desired. In his inaugural address *Beeldende kunst: boegbeeld of zinsbegoocheling voor de architectuur?* of November 1992, Jean Leering pointed out the general tendency towards autonomy among young architects—an abbreviation of the overall responsibility they bear towards society. His observation is confirmed by the typology I have outlined. None of the five categories relates to the practical world in which designs are initiated, realized, and used. The social context of design is placed, mathematically speaking, outside the brackets, the communicative meaning of a design eliminated. This means that for graphic designers, the profession's right to exist is in jeopardy.

In reality these attitudes are forms of resistance to or attempts to escape from the way the commissioning relationship has developed. Increasingly, design commissions are given by professionals mandated by the commissioning body. Nor do the users come into the picture these days. The result is that the commissioning body's definition of the public is adopted. The designer's subjective nonconformism leads finally to indifference to and maintenance of the *status quo,* which is accepted as the natural framework of professional activity. The possibility of transforming social reality (or parts of it) through long-term, well-thought-out design strategies is outdated.

It is exactly when students or young designers adopt a "critical" approach that this conformism becomes all too apparent. The critical content is taken from official ideologies, such as antiracism, feminism, or environmental awareness. These are all—at least in our part of the world—state ideologies accompanied by penalties for breaking the laws derived from them. Personal experience as a source for design is generally lacking in the treatment of these subjects, which is heavily dependent on images put out by the media. The result is often a collage of different genres; in content, the "critical" designs are full of good intentions and permeated by officially encouraged patterns of thought.

What is the nature of a graphic design ethic now that it can no longer, as it could until recently, rely on the vision of a social alternative? Now that it can no longer rely on one of the big stories that are dead and buried according to Bell and Lyotard? Many replace the big narratives with micronarratives or, as we saw, with the "critical" ideologies adopted by the great majority, which retain at least the prospect of a better world. How is the self-centered ethic of the designer yearning for the status of an artist to be avoided?

Two concepts seem to me important as the foundations for a proper design ethic. The first is respect for the other. By that I mean something quite different from taking account of the preferences of a target group as determined by marketing techniques based on consumer panels, etc. In this respect, what I have in mind is not the other insofar as s/he can be equated with still others who are part of the same target group of a marketing strategy that basically reduces everyone to a consumer. What I envisage is the other insofar as his or her values and images differ from mine. Few designs show this openness towards the other—or question the implicitly assumed hegemony of their own culture. The second concept is the desire of the designer him- or herself for which a design ethic should leave ample scope. S/he could be present in the design of the subject of desire, not as the manipulation of the demands, needs, and wishes of others. So does this mark a return to the romantic image of the designer as autonomous subject in order to escape from the false romanticizing and sentimentality of commercial communication? No. Desire is a source of poetic production. It aims for the utopian element, the dream character of reality in the strongest sense of the word. Desire transcends the world of available objects and does not cover up the fundamental shortcoming of the human condition with the endless repetition of satisfying needs.

Desire accepts the shortcoming as an insoluble characteristic of human existence and is diametrically opposed to promises that (consumer) needs will be met. Desire for the not-present object keeps the line to the future open. It can only be put into words by a rich voice.

We can now see that a desire formed the basis of both the traditionalist and the modernist ethic, though this was not recognized as such by the spokesmen for each movement. It is the desire for a rational society in which strength of argument will triumph over power and violence, the desire for a society in which justice will be done to everyone, not just to an elite.

Can design be more than it now is: streamlining of communication controlled by the system of power and money? The affirmative answer to this question is based on two observations.

First, this system is not monolithic; fractures and contradictions can be seen. It is not uncommon for these to be intensified by the still operative ideals and sense of responsibility of policy makers. Designers can cooperate productively with them, though often only on a temporary basis.

Second, the system constantly sets its own limits. At the edge of its territory, an extraterritoriality arises in which the interests and wishes of marginalized groups and individuals ask to be articulated. Since the 1960s, a rival public domain has existed that has bombarded the system from the flanks with unwelcome counterinformation and counterimages.

Strategies aimed at the general good and social/cultural/political priorities form the points of action to a kind of design that positions itself beyond the status quo and wants to be more than the *basso continuo* of power and the market.

Design like this breathes fresh air into the polluted and blocked lungs of the body of society. It is inspired as much by the rejection of injustice as by the desire for the sublime. Its field is a public domain that must itself be constantly redesigned.

Based on a lecture given at the Jan van Eyck Academie, Maastricht, Holland, this article was originally published in Engagement in Graphic Design *(Kogeschool voor de Kunsten, Arnhem, 1992) and has appeared in* Kunst & Museumjournal, *Vol.4, No. 5, 1993, and* Emigre, *No. 32, 1995.*

Note
1. I owe this typology to discussion with Ben Loerakker, architect and professor of architectural design at the Technological University of Eindhoven, on differences and similarities between students and practitioners of the design disciplines architecture and graphic design.

PHOTOGRAPHY, MORALITY, AND BENETTON
Tibor Kalman

I currently edit *Colors,* an international magazine sponsored by Benetton. It is a multilingual magazine pairing English variously with French, German, Italian, Spanish, and Korean. *Colors* takes outside advertising and its format changes from issue to issue. One of its fundamental aims is to challenge assumptions about what a magazine can be. Benetton funds *Colors* without exercising control over its contents.

Benetton, of course, is the company that has generated worldwide controversy by using emotionally charged imagery in its own advertising. Charges of intrusion, cynicism, inappropriateness, and bad taste abound. Central to the controversy is the issue of the nature of photography. The moral questions often arise out of people's belief that Benetton is using "real" photographs for "unreal" advertising purposes.

Whatever Benetton's motives, I believe that this whole question of some photography being "true" and some "untrue" is a nonquestion. Photography is not objective; it never has been objective. It has never told the truth any more than any other form of artistic communication can. In the first days of cinema, people ran from the movie theaters thinking the train on the screen was going to come crashing out into the audience; more recently some people were scared of the monsters in *Jurassic Park.*

Early in the history of photography models were used to enact situations for a camera to record. Later, we learned how to retouch images, first by hand, later by rearranging the tiny dots that make up the images. Meanwhile, there has always been the cheapest and easiest way of making photographs lie—simply changing the caption to change the meaning of the image.

Some people accept this but still argue that the photograph remains in some way uniquely "honest." They say that for it to exist, some kind of real-life situation also had to exist. They claim that the fact that a camera can be set up by remote control to record whatever passes in front of it somehow confers objectivity. They cling to the idea that the photograph is an inherently "real" or honest image and as such is always on a different plane from an obviously subjective form of visual communication, such as painting.

However, I believe that photography is just like painting and that it can lie just as effectively. I do not accept that there is necessarily a "true" moment that the camera captures, because that moment can be manipulated as much as anything else.

A QUESTION OF CONTEXT

That argument is really a diversion from the real issue, which I believe to be one of context—the way we react to images presented in different contexts, such as editorial or advertising. Literal-minded people say "we must legislate" and that there is a need for some code that newspapers and television should obey to prevent them from manipulating readers and viewers with images willfully used out of context. This is impossible. You simply cannot pass a law that says magazine editors or reporters cannot lie. Instead you have to learn (and then to teach others) to mistrust everything.

The development of new and sophisticated retouching techniques has intensified the debate about how "real" photography is. This is a good thing because it highlights the fact that photography can never be objective. Photography should always be questioned the way all kinds of authority should be questioned.

THE BENETTON CAMPAIGN

So how do we educate everyone into questioning the images they are constantly bombarded with by billboards, books, newspapers, TV, movies, and magazines? One way to approach the Benetton campaign is to allow that it may have an educational contribution to make. Instead of accusing Benetton of trying to sell sweaters with images of human suffering, think of their advertising as an exercise in challenging assumptions and raising issues: a media experiment sponsored by a clothing company.

Consider the famous Benetton example of the newborn baby that appeared on billboards and the cover of the first issue of *Colors*. If we had been photographing this baby for a pretty moms' magazine, we would have cleaned the baby with retouching. Instead we chose not to. This is an example of contextualization. In the first place, Benetton paid for a photograph from a news organization. They then recontextualized it into an advertisement. Then—for the cover of *Colors*—we recontextualized it back to editorial again.

An even more controversial Benetton image was that of the dying AIDS victim. Here I believe what Benetton thinks it is doing is sponsoring education by raising social issues. However, one incontrovertible result of that poster is that there has been widespread discussion about it. In the press, that discussion has been negative and concerned with the assumed objective of selling sweaters in a dubious way. However, among the public the real subject of discussion has been the picture itself and the unsettling implications of using that sort of image in an unfamiliar context.

A HEALTHY SKEPTICISM

We should value anything that encourages us not to believe in both pictures and the media. After all, the media are subject to manipulation by the government, police, and business. I'd be lying if I did not say that media is subject to manipulation by Benetton, too. So to be responsible, those of us who work in the media have to tell people not to believe us. In the final analysis, it is the only honest course open to us.

Originally published in Design Renaissance: Selected Papers from the International Design Congress, Glasgow, Scotland, *1993; Jeremy Meyerson, editor.*

Editor's note: This article is taken from comments made in 1993 by Tibor Kalman at the International Design Conference in Glasgow, Scotland, when he was editor-in-chief at Colors. *He resigned that position in 1995.*

CRITICAL
PROFILES

PAUL RAND
Janet Abrams

T
alking to Paul Rand over two days in May, shortly after the publication of his third book, *Design, Form, and Chaos, I* could appreciate why one of his clients, Steve Jobs of NeXT Computer, would describe him (in a forthcoming film profile) as having "the exterior of a curmudgeon but a heart of gold." And how he could inspire such contradictory feelings among those who have encountered him during an exceptionally long career as a designer and educator: on the one hand, undying devotion from many former students and colleagues; on the other, a kind of weary resignation, invariably "not for quotation," on the part of those who regard him as an unreconstructed modernist, rigid in his views and dismissive of new approaches to graphic design.

Now professor emeritus at Yale University, Rand continues to work solo, as he has done for some thirty years, from a studio at his home in Weston, Connecticut. Here, under a bright red Le Corbusier–inspired skylight illuminating a long wooden desk, the dialogue begins.

If I had been looking forward to a friendly chat about some of the ideas in Rand's new book, I was in for a surprise. After only a few minutes it becomes clear that his conversational style and writing style are two entirely different things. Face-to-face conversation is like a boxing match, with swift jabs back and forth. Rand doesn't suffer fools gladly, and those who try to engage him in debate had better be prepared for tough combat. Slight deafness tends to exacerbate a characteristic gruffness, and his tone becomes thoroughly stentorian when you cross him, with firm thumps to the table supplied for emphasis. Rand bluntly repeats the terms of enquiry when he prefers not to answer, frequently asserts that "it's obvious" until pressed to offer elucidation of a given point and, when push comes to shove, throws back, "So, what's the question?" by way of response.

On certain topics, however, his voice abruptly softens, his right hand settles on his right cheek, and you can tell that the curmudgeonly exterior is just defensive armor plating to a vulnerable, even endearing, core. Often, he'll finish sentences with a sort of schoolboy chuckle, a mischievous wheeze of amusement—sometimes denoting self-deprecation, sometimes egging on the questioner to take up a particularly egregious challenge. Ten minutes into the interview, he decides to call it off; an hour and a half later he's suggesting we meet again the following day to carry on the conversation, which we duly do, this time on the beach a few miles from his home.

Readers must use their imagination to identify his *bêtes noires,* since Rand follows up his more unbuttoned flourishes with instructions that the foregoing remarks are not for publication. Suffice it to say that Armin Hofmann, London-based designers Abram

Games, Derek Birdsall, and the late Hans Schleger figure highly in his pantheon of admired associates; former students Lorraine Wild (now teaching at CalArts) and Sheila Levrant de Bretteville (current head of graphics at Yale) do not. Although he was on the Yale faculty from 1961 to 1992, Rand resigned shortly after de Bretteville took up her appointment, and professes disdain for academia and its denizens. (He still teaches the first week at Brissago, Yale's summer school in Switzerland.)

But he reserves his greatest scorn for design critics and theorists because they take things "literally" and lack hands-on experience of the process of design; on the scale of things, they are scarcely higher than the marketing executives who come in for a drubbing in his essay "Good Design is Goodwill," the first in his new book. "People who write about art and are not artists are very suspect in my library," he remarks.

In contrast to his pugnacious spoken persona, Rand's own essays are lucid and eloquent, larded with references from Vasari to Bacardi by way of the brothers James and Alfred North Whitehead. On closer examination, they are also studded with arbitrary value judgments passing for objective analysis, and statements that might be considered merely sententious if they did not happen to issue from one of the *Grands Seigneurs* of graphic design.

Nevertheless, the carefully hewn prose is obviously the fruit of long cogitation. On the dashboard of Rand's gray BMW a small notepad is fixed at the ready for any passing *pensée*: its front sheet currently declares "Depends on the context" in slightly jerky, on-the-move pencil script, an insight he mentions is destined for his next book.

In consistently reflecting on his own work, starting with *Thoughts on Design* of 1946, Rand is one of the few practitioners who has seriously attempted to codify a theoretical position, and his writings have served to consolidate his reputation. Yet he is not necessarily willing to discuss his ideas, once committed to print, still less to acknowledge differences of opinion. "This is very serious stuff," he tells me later. "I don't write for your benefit. I'm writing for myself, to understand. The by-product is a book for other people."

Over the years, Rand has worked on magazines and in advertising, as well as on corporate identity programs, producing benchmark logos for IBM, Westinghouse, ABC television, and United Parcel Service. At the precocious age of twenty-three, he was art director of *Esquire* magazine, which he left in 1940 to join Elkan Kauffman and Bill Weintraub in a new advertising agency launched with funds from Weintraub's sale of his 50 percent interest in *Esquire*. Rand clearly relished the variety and hectic pace at the agency, where jobs often had to be executed in a matter of hours for the following day's publication. "It's good experience to work fast and efficiently. That's the thing about design—or art: you have to have your hand in it or you lose the immediacy of good work, which is what makes the job pleasant."

During the next fourteen years, Rand produced some of his most memorable advertising designs, for El Producto cigars, Dubonnet, Ancient Age, and Disney (the other Disney) hatmakers. He also turned out a prolific assortment of book jackets and magazine covers, perhaps the most celebrated being those for *Direction,* from 1938 to 1945. Identities for Cummins, The Limited, IDEO, and NeXT are all documented in Rand's new book, and he continues to design posters for various institutions.

The "later," pared-down Rand typically deploys figurative and geometric forms in a bright paintbox palette on a simple white plane, or plays photographic and typographic elements against each other to produce a visual pun. To an eye acclimated to the work of younger designers, whose experiments he finds so dismaying, Rand's recent work is tempered, but in its restrained formal clarity, sometimes leaves one wishing for more.

On the Sunday just prior to our meeting, the *New York Times* had carried not only design historian Victor Margolin's review of *Design, Form, and Chaos,* but also an op-ed piece on why, as Rand so delicately puts it to me, "corporate design stinks." In it, he basically bemoans the absence of great corporate design programs in contemporary America—the kind in which he had been involved at IBM and Westinghouse—and argues that this is due to a lack of great business leaders as well as of good designers. The brief duration of many such programs "is no evidence that design is impotent. What is evident is that somebody is not minding the store, and that management does not really appreciate the contribution that design (art) can make, socially, aesthetically and economically."

Rand's article inadvertently invites us to consider the role played by the all-powerful paternalistic company chairman—an oft-celebrated, if rare, species—whose obsessive passion for order and identity tends to have been a prerequisite for noteworthy corporate design. But which comes first: the design program that makes a company look organized, coherent, and impressive (when it may be a managerial shambles), or the corporate culture that merits such representation? Lamenting the lack of good design programs seems a bit like looking through the wrong end of the telescope. I put it to Rand that surely what's actually at stake has less to do with design per se than with the transformation of American culture in the years since companies like IBM rose to become unassailable benchmarks of white-collar capitalism. Rand is quiet for a few moments. Then, having sized me up, he begins an oration. "The questions you are asking me are unanswerable. It's like asking 'what is art?'"

That was going to be my next question.

"Oh, I know what it is. Art is an idea that has found its perfect visual expression. And design is the vehicle by which this expression is made possible. Art is a noun, and design is a noun and also a verb. Art is a product and design is a process. Design is the foundation of all the arts."

A splenetic outburst about Victor Margolin follows. "The review of my book was written by an academe character, not a practicing artist. He makes absolutely irresponsible statements about me at the end of the essay: that I'm not interested in social things and that it's too bad I'm not interested in the latest stuff. He's dead wrong. I could flunk this guy in two minutes on a design history test."

What would you ask him?

"I would ask him things that he doesn't know. Listen, I've lectured to Germans in Berlin about German design. Things they knew nothing about."

Fortunately, the tirade is interrupted by a phone call.

Rand returns, and resumes. "See, my life is what I do. When people start picking on me I get very angry. And to be accused publicly of not being interested in social issues is an outrage."

I discern that I have, unwittingly, aroused his wrath.

"The very fact that this guy gave me a good review and then starts criticizing me means that he doesn't know what he's talking about. It's completely untrue what he's saying, because he doesn't read things properly."

I read out loud the offending section of the review in which, in fact, Margolin has taken exemplary care to present Rand's position accurately. Far from misrepresenting him, Margolin has merely stepped on his Achilles heel. "Part of the problem, he believes," writes

Margolin, "is that design classrooms have been turned into forums for social and political issues."

"Absolutely," Rand confirms. "And it's the reason I left Yale. I resigned."

Turning to what I hope will be a less inflammatory topic, I ask Rand what he thought of Thomas Watson Jr., whom he credits in his op-ed piece with having "almost single-handedly put the IBM design program to work." The tactic proves effective. Rand immediately softens. "This guy was the reverse of Jefferson's definition that 'All men are created equal,'" he chuckles. "This guy was not created equal: Thomas Watson was handsome, rich, tall, and bright. Still is. He's my age, maybe a couple of months older."

Presumably he worked quite closely with Watson?

"No . . . I don't know much about him. I would see him, you know, in the hallway. I had dinner once at his house on the occasion of his giving Eliot Noyes and Charles Eames and me a trophy."

Convinced of the importance of access to the company chairman, Rand has actually forfeited work rather than deal with underlings—or rather Marion Swannie, who runs his business, has done so. (Rand's second wife, known affectionately as Swan, was manager of design at IBM for thirty years, relinquishing the post when they got married. "Her department would pay us but the work came from the different divisions. She never used her influence for me. In fact I got ten times as much work after she left the company.")

During the late 1980s, in one of the country's most fascinating outbreaks of mass superstition, rumors began to circulate that Procter & Gamble's century-old logo, comprising a Man-in-the-Moon and thirteen stars, was a coded sign for the devil. "Two people from Procter & Gamble came to me because they were having problems with their logo. My wife wrote these guys and said 'we don't deal with anybody unless he's the CEO.' She just gave up the job. We know that in order to get anything done, you have to deal with the top guy."

Rand has a simple template for what makes a good client: they don't interfere, don't tell you what to do, and appreciate whatever the designer proposes without questioning it. So much for the ideal situation, with a hot line to the top. "Most clients are nice clients. It's the people in between who give you the problems: the account executives, the marketing people. They destroy people's work: 'this should be bigger, this should be up here, there should be a sun here with a price.' What else have they got to show for their accomplishments? If they don't change your work all they can say is you've done a good job. It's much more convincing to show something graphic!"

Another noteworthy aspect of Rand's relationship with his clients is his fee structure. His compensation has entered graphic-design mythology; he is said to have commanded more than $100,000 for doing the NeXT logo. While he insists that he has no interest in the financial side of life ("My wife is the money girl in this family; if I need money I have to ask her"), Rand is nevertheless attuned to his own market value. "When somebody pays me a lot of money, he's not doing so because he likes to. He pays me because this is what I deserve."

How much would he have charged for doing a new logo for P&G, I wondered.

"One or two hundred thousand."

And what do you actually buy with that?

"You buy a logo. I write a brochure, go through the steps, like in the book. That's the market value: what studios get, though some get $300,000."

What's the fee measured on?

"It's measured on nothing. If it takes me an hour, I do it in an hour. If it takes me a year, it takes me a year. I don't work on time. You give me the problem, I let the idea come. Most of the time it's immediate. I don't start making sketches—that throws you."

No second thoughts?

"Very rarely."

On occasion, however, Rand has looked back and seen fit to revise a design, as with the logo for UPS, originally created in just one week in 1961. "I offered to make some modest changes," he explains, "to make it right. I changed the bow and the drawing of the P. It wasn't right before. If there's something wrong with the drawing, then you change it." But UPS stood firm, and declined. "They didn't give any reasons. They just said no."

It would be quite far-reaching and costly to implement such a change, given the extensive applications—surely something of an indulgence unless the company had undergone managerial changes that it wished to express visually.

"It's not far-reaching to change the shape of a bow. Nobody would notice it."

Then why bother doing it?

"Because it bothers me. Just as much as it bothered my mother not to clean above a molding that you didn't see. It's just not right."

One of the more intriguing aspects of Rand's life is how this son of a Viennese immigrant fabric cutter, brought up in a very poor, strictly orthodox Jewish household, turned out to be the graven-image maker to *echt*-WASP America in its most institutional form: the great corporations of the fifties and sixties. Born and bred in Brownsville, Brooklyn, Rand had an older sister and a twin brother who became a professional jazz musician, playing sax and clarinet. "Guy Lombardo!" Rand chuckles, recalling the kind of music he played. Then, in an undertone, "He's gone . . . killed in an accident. She died years ago. My family's gone. Everybody's . . . dead." A few more sentences pass between us, and the mood has grown suddenly so poignant I can hardly hold back tears. "It's sad," he concedes, and at such moments one cannot but forgive this man his usual hectoring manner.

Although he is at pains to keep his observances a private matter, he is clearly a devoutly religious man. On each of our two days of conversation he thrusts his left arm toward me, proud to show the impression of his tefillin, the ritual thongs bound around a man's arm for daily morning prayers. It is hard to resist making a connection between his deeply held religious tenets and the strength of his commitment to orthodox modernism: both rigorous systems of belief, each in their way striving toward a kind of mortal perfection. When I asked him how he chose to become a designer, his answer was unequivocal: "I didn't choose. God chose." There is no trace of guile when he explains that he performs these rituals "because I want to. Because I think God is more important than I am. It's important to be modest in the world. To think there's somebody who is better than we are, and more significant. Right?"

A major portion of our first meeting is taken up with discussing the importance of doing pro bono work, and donating to charity. He relates at some length, and in his customarily pugnacious storytelling mode, the occasion when he was moved to give his copier-machine repair man several thousand dollars, to help bring the latter's family out of the Soviet Union. "And I didn't even know this guy." I remark that his gesture seems very generous. But he's off again.

"This is a social issue, right? Or is it not? It has nothing whatsoever to do with design. Design issues are form and content and proportion. And color. And texture. And scale. You can't say any of these things about social issues. Design can help elucidate or explain social issues. Social issues are not design issues, though the visual arts have done a hell of a lot for social issues. They're two separate things, as different as milk and corned beef." (And as we know from the scriptures, "thou shalt not souse a kid in its mother's milk.")

It's not that Rand isn't interested in social issues. Rather, he has made his own decisions about which ones matter to him and attends to them in his own, sometimes narrowly focused, idiosyncratic way. And he vehemently rejects what he sees as the corruption of design education, that is as he conceives it and practiced it at Yale. "They don't teach design because they don't understand what design is. They'll give you a poster to do, let's say, for some social issue and they consider that teaching design."

OK. So if we accept that design issues are only form and content . . .

"That's all they are. They're never anything else."

. . . then, what if the *content* of the poster is a social issue?

"Then . . . then . . . Then the designer deals with it. He uses the power of design to express the social issue."

Hoping to steer back to safer ground, I ask which pieces of work he's most pleased with, meaning, of course, his own work. The answer, needless to say, is indirect.

"I don't know. If I'd done this"—he points toward a lively abstract print by Henryk Tomaszewski on the wall behind me—"I'd probably be most pleased. I'm going to use it in my next book as an example. I think it's terrific."

Why?

"Here, I have this little note and I was going to print it." He rummages on the desk for a scrap of paper, then reads aloud: "Better to be silent and have folks think you are a fool than to speak and remove all doubt."

He looks up. "If I start talking about it, then maybe I'd better not. I think it's obvious."

But what's obvious? *Why* is it terrific?

"The colors. They happen to be the colors I always use, red and green. The way it's done. The idea, which is very expressive of circus activities . . . calisthenics, twirling and twisting. This childlike quality that it has. Not child*ish*. The distinction is tremendous. It has all the good qualities that children have: honesty, spontaneity. Most people who try to imitate that kind of stuff do lousy drawings, rather than understanding the spirit of childlike drawings, I mean, as in Klee, Picasso, Miró. Picasso said about Miró that he ought to stop playing with his hoop. In other words, grow up. But I think Miró was a genius, as was Picasso."

For Rand, as for his heroes, childhood creativity is still vivid. "I always drew. Since I was a little kid—three or four years old. During the first World War. I used to use a chair as a drawing table. I'd sit on a little tiny stool or on my knees, and draw soldiers and trenches and photographs. My education was mostly from books, and magazines, not from teachers. I used to be so admiring of people, I would stand in the rain, I would just stand there *looking,* for hours, in the drugstore, for example, or the gasoline station." Rand studied with George Grosz for a while when the German artist first came here, at the Art Students League. "He didn't even speak English. He would say a few simple words. But design I just picked up. From libraries, bookshops. From magazines. German magazines."

In "A Mentor" (on the typographer Jan Tschichold), Rand mentions the initial "indifference or outright hostility" that greeted painters, architects, and designers of the modern period, before their work became recognized and subsequently acclaimed. Yet, in "Cassandre to Chaos," the most indignant and bare-knuckled of the essays in his new book, he fulminates against (unspecified) designers who are experimenting with formal vocabularies and production technology. This "bevy of depressing images . . . collage of chaos and confusion . . . art deco rip-offs . . . sleazy textures . . . indecipherable, zany typography" is mostly "confined to pro bono work, small boutiques, fledgling studios, trendy publishers, misguided educational institutions, anxious graphic arts associations, and a few innocent paper manufacturers . . . comforted by the illusion that this must be progress." But such rhetoric puts him at risk of proving himself as blind to innovation as were the critics of his early twentieth-century heroes. Isn't he being a bit harsh toward today's young innovators?

"I don't consider these 'young innovators' innovators. I consider them a pack of undisciplined gibberish. I'm not going to mention any names . . . mostly posters for the AIGA and crap like that. The difference is a difference of talent. These people are untalented people."

How does he measure talent?

"By looking."

That, I find, is a rather haughty position.

"Well, I'm haughty."

It's potentially a very unpleasant attitude.

"I know it is, but that's the way it is. I've been doing it sixty, seventy years. I am the judge of a good designer. I don't consider myself an old fuddy-duddy. I haven't changed my mind about things and I don't consider it a weakness. I'll debate with people that I respect and do good work, and if I think their work is lousy I want nothing to do with it because we don't talk the same language. I have my track record. If you like it, fine. If you don't like it, that's too bad. I expect a certain kind of respect from people. Not only because I'm a great designer—which is not my opinion, this is the *world's* opinion. But because I'm older than you are. You question me in a way which elicits a doubt. What did you major in—psychology?"

I smile. We sit across from each other in silence, enjoying a temporary cease-fire. Despite his vexatious and, by his own declaration, "impatient" mien, I have to admit I'm warming to this guy. I can imagine why his students—especially the one who, according to Yale lore, once punched Rand on the nose after a particularly fractious crit—would never forget him. From time to time it's crossed my mind that perhaps Paul Rand has no sense of humor. But actually he does; it just takes patience. Just then, he pipes up.

"See, I know what your problem is. You lack humor. That's your problem. You take things too seriously. Le Corbusier—you know who he was?—he said that to me. He said 'young man, you're much too serious.' So I can say it to you."

We're made for each other . . .

Returning to Manhattan after our second meeting, I catch a serendipitous image through the train window: a huge parking lot in which dozens of UPS delivery vans stand in serried ranks, like mechanical cows in a paddock, presumably a distribution hub. There is Rand's logo, multiplied dozens of times, receding into the distance—a cattle brand on each van's haunch. I'm forced to think afresh about the design, to *notice* rather than merely perceive it out of the corner of my eye, a reliable motif for an ubiquitous service. The dark brown livery, the spindly lowercase letter forms, the grace note of the bow: altogether the identity looks dated, a vestige of another era, that age of men in hats and men in charge. Yet strangely timeless, by now a piece of the visual landscape, a bearing mark against which America goes about its business. To have been the creator of that symbol must be a very satisfying feeling, a bit like naming a species.

I think about Rand's wish to perfect what has already served quite well for a long while. If it were suddenly changed, even only slightly, the entire edifice of trust that inheres in that arrangement of lines on a surface might suffer a seismic jolt.

Rand would surely enjoy the scene, having extolled (in *A Designer's Art*) the "exciting spectacle of marching soldiers . . . neatly arranged flower beds . . . crowds at football games . . . rows of methodically placed packages on the grocer's shelf." I think about his appreciation of repetition, with respect both to the arrangement of items in space (that is, as a formal device), and in terms of regular activity—as much in the ritual of daily prayer as in creative practice.

As the train rushes past, I realize what's missing from the UPS logo, and yet scarcely needs adding: that looping signature, like the vapor trail from an aerial acrobatics display, whose freehand strokes—child*like* but not child*ish*—appear on much of his earlier work. An unmistakable trademark: the artist's guarantee of authenticity.

Originally published in I.D., *September/October 1993.*

RUB OUT THE WORD
Rick Poynor

It must be just a little unsettling to be crowned "the first graphic design superstar," to achieve a degree of recognition by the age of thirty that most designers will not be granted in a lifetime, to be the subject of a book, a crowd-pulling retrospective in one of the world's great museums, and an avalanche of admiring publicity, only to find—when you quite naturally assume you have well and truly arrived—that you have been written off as a "stylist," that fellow designers are publicly questioning whether you merit such treatment, and, worst of all perhaps, that most of your clients have vanished so that within only a few months of your triumph you are on the brink of bankruptcy with no choice but to start all over again.

Such has been the remarkable career of Neville Brody. In the period immediately after he published *The Graphic Language of Neville Brody* in 1988 he entered a kind of limbo from which he is only now, six years later, beginning to emerge. Once a continuous, monthly presence in the pages of *The Face* and *Arena,* Brody is these days effectively invisible to many of his British colleagues. "I couldn't actually tell you what he's been doing with his life for the last five years," says a Pentagram London partner. It is not that he has not been busy. As his new book, *The Graphic Language of Neville Brody 2,* shows—it is sixteen pages longer than the first—he has been busier than most.

Brody leads a curious, binary life. He is the rebel with boardroom access, a potentially mainstream talent who prefers creative life in the margins, an aloof and glamorous figure who doesn't return calls with the soft-spoken, easy-going, genuinely likeable manner of the boy next door. "On one level he's the international star who travels everywhere club class," says collaborator Jon Wozencroft. "On the other he's a north London lad who wants to go home and watch a video with his girlfriend." Brody gets short shrift from British colleagues. "He's an interesting sideline," one corporate identity specialist told me. "A fashion designer who works in graphics," says another. "He never figured for me personally," says a third. Yet he is judged by more historically minded and perhaps less partisan observers to be one of the most notable designers of the last ten years. When Philip Meggs published his revised history of graphic design in 1992, Brody was the only recent non-American addition. Richard Hollis's new *Graphic Design: A Concise History* singles out Brody over many of his detractors—only to damn him with faint praise. Brody, writes Hollis, "tamed punk into the consumer graphic idiom of the 1980s."

Was it really no more than this? While Brody would be the first to suggest otherwise, he knows there is a problem. He is remembered (and in some quarters blamed) as much for the paper mountain of advertising and retail graphics inspired by his work for *The Face* as for the pages of the magazine itself. "Essentially, I think I failed," he told me in 1990. "My ideas were weakened into styles. The very thing I used in order to get the ideas across—a strong personal style—was the thing that defeated reception of the ideas." His switch to stylistically neutral Helvetica for *Arena* headlines was an act of both atonement and self-denial ("I hate Helvetica"), but it did no good. They copied that, too: for the last eight years in Britain a spotlessly white, drip-dry neomodernism has been the dominant graphic style. When, as a juror at last year's ACD "100 Show," Brody came across a Pentagram Prize poster that looked like one of his *Arena* spreads circa 1987, he selected it only to give it a public dressing down: "This is, to me, a perfect example of getting it totally wrong," he fumed. "This sort of thing shouldn't happen."

As if this were not enough, Brody has sustained damage in more sensitive areas. He believes he has something important to tell us, wants to be taken seriously, and in numberless interviews, culminating in the text of his first book, urges us to consider the substance of his ideas. But his critics, like his imitators, have a tendency to linger on the seductive surfaces where, they argue, the true meaning lies; and this meaning is never quite what Brody intended. In a superb essay on *The Face,* Dick Hebdige, now dean of critical studies at CalArts, argues that the magazine's use of advertising rhetoric, its urge to compress and condense—most pronounced in Brody's "sometimes barely legible typefaces"—creates "an absolute homology of form and meaning which cannot be assimilated but can only be copied." The exact opposite, in fact, of what Brody set out to do.

In December 1988, following the success of *Graphic Language,* a British newspaper gave Brody and Wozencroft an unprecedented opportunity to state their case against "the set up" of contemporary design and explain their desire to call a halt. Casting aside *The Guardian*'s usual grid and typeface, they filled the page with tall columns of tiny Helvetica, huge, arbitrary arrows, and meandering pontification rendered in fathomless prose. Unfortunately, as readers pointed out, these strategies embodied precisely the qualities of "designerism" that the authors claimed to deplore. "The biggest contradiction is between the 'designed' form it takes, and its criticism of the role of design," ran one tightly argued riposte. "Significance has been sacrificed on the altar of style."

For Brody the manifesto was a turning point. He had mounted the pulpit, delivered his most withering sermon on what he saw as the iniquities of design, and the audience had merely shrugged and turned its back. "At some point after the article there was a commonly held agreement not to talk about me any more," he told me a year later. "My name and my work were almost unmentionable." Even his status as a professional communicator was now being challenged. "Is Brody a designer?" concluded one skeptical letter to *The Guardian*. "I don't think so."

Brody quietly regrouped. In 1988, he moved to a new top-floor studio under the exposed rafters of an old furniture warehouse in east London. He became a partner in FontWorks, the British arm of FontShop, the international font distributor started by Erik Spiekermann. "I don't want to have to rely on the whim of the client," he says. In the 1990s, Brody went digital with a vengeance. Through the Macintosh he has found his way back to the painterliness that is the basis of his talent. The halting angularity of his earliest experiments has been superseded by a sensuous organicism. In 1991, he launched the quarterly experimental type magazine *Fuse,* with Wozencroft as editor.

No longer fashionable in Britain, Brody found new clients in Europe and Japan. He redesigned and art directed the men's magazine *Per Lui* and redesigned the fashion title *Lei* for Italian Condé Nast. Then, in 1991, he put in a hectic year as airborne art director for *Actuel,* the Parisian news magazine—some of his most un-Brody-like and, it has to be said, ordinary work to date. Assisted by the Neville Brody Studio, a collection of freelancers who work for him as projects arise, he has undertaken cultural commissions in Germany (where his stock remains high), an on-screen identity for ORF (the Austrian state broadcasting company), and a signing project in Tokyo. He is currently setting up an office in Miami with Spanish fashion and industrial designer Chu Oroz.

This is the fourth time I have interviewed Brody, and, hoping for some environmental clues to his character, I ask if we can meet at his home. I am politely but firmly rebuffed. One phone call too many at three in the morning from devoted fans who have somehow obtained his phone number has left Brody with a horror of invasion and a determination to keep his home life off limits. There is no computer, he says (and in his case this *is* saying something—he's an obsessive game-player), and the phone number is only known to four or five people.

So we meet at Brody's new north London office, a small, purpose-built block in muted high-tech that looks, unlike his previous offices, as though it is inhabited by designers. For the first time he has a reception area with regulation-issue black leather sofa, a secretary with a telephone manner and something resembling a meeting area occupied (let's not get too corporate) by a dart board, a pool table, and an electric racetrack that the studio bought itself for Christmas. This is where we sit down to talk.

Brody looked boyish well into his thirties. These days, at thirty-seven, he sports a beatnik beard and goes easier on the hair gel. He talks fluently, with conviction, but there is nothing messianic or overbearing about him. He makes the improbable sound reasonable, inevitable. Brody has got it all worked out—up to a point, and that point is where the contradictions start. Some of his analysis makes sense. But he cannot resist the provocative sound bite—"If [graphic design] was a truly honest means of communicating ideas," he once said on TV, "then there would only ever be a need for one typeface in the world"—and such loopy pronouncements do little for the *gravitas* of someone who made his name "painting" with type and now distributes fonts (nine thousand at last count). "He's a wind-up artist, Neville," says Wozencroft. "He courts the media in an Andy Warhol-like fashion. Sometimes it's very witty and sometimes it's just . . . gulp!"

Language. It's a word that recurs throughout our conversation. "Language is a kind of hypnosis," Brody begins. "When language stops evolving and changing, it's because people have stopped thinking and evolving." At first, I assume he is talking about verbal or written language; there may be other kinds of language, but its primary meaning, clearly, is the formation of words. I find myself wondering why Brody should presume to step in where an army of writers, poets, lexicographers, and linguists already treads. "Language," it soon emerges, is his own shorthand—so thoroughly internalized that he forgets it might need to be explained—for "visual language." It's an inversion that, once again, gives precedence to appearance over content.

"We've now got the opportunity in language to do what William Burroughs did in text," Brody continues. "What Burroughs did was extremely important, necessary, and intellectual." He suddenly turns inquisitor. "Would you question that statement?"

"Well, no," I reply. "Within a well-defined area of literary research he was important. But his innovations have yet to be applied to the airport best-seller."

"They never will be," says Brody. "*Fuse* will never be applied to the *Daily Mirror.* But we've never had the opportunity to experiment with visual language in the same way that Burroughs experimented with written language, and I think that process of experimentation is necessary in itself because our world and the way we communicate are changing. Language is formed by social needs and philosophies. I'm talking about visual language almost strictly in the sense of the letterform and what happens after we've written something. I'm divorcing the look of the word from what the word says."

Since the late eighties, Brody has been talking about making "a typography devoid of words," an organized set of abstract digital marks that carry no linguistic meaning and bear only a passing resemblance to the alphabets we know. *Fuse* is his decidedly non-commercial attempt to force the pace. Brody's own typeface, State, introduced in *Fuse* 1, though still just about readable, was a step in this direction. Other *Fuse* contributors have clung stubbornly to the notion of typography as a vessel of language, however clouded or chipped the goblet. Barry Deck resisted pressure to push Caustic Biomorph any further toward illegibility. Jeffery Keedy also declined to go the full distance with his goth-metal typeface Lushus. "I had a long series of discourses with Jeff Keedy when I met him in Chicago," says Brody. "He didn't get it." Not many people do, so Brody and Wozencroft are upping the ante. Issue ten, entitled "Freeform," makes the commitment to abstraction explicit.

"But language implies a common understanding," I suggest. "These private visual languages you're exploring can't have a wider application because the rest of us don't speak the language." This is the closest Brody comes to losing his patience. "What you're saying is an exact echo of what journalists would have said when the first Dada exhibition was put on, or when they saw the first Paul Klee painting, or Cézanne. They would have said, 'This makes no sense, we've got a set of modular objects with very little relationship to realistic representation, I don't understand it, it's not important.' Would you have said the same thing to Cézanne?" Another appeal to a higher authority. Then he realizes what he has said. "I'm not comparing myself with Cézanne," he adds hastily. "I'm not saying that. What would you have said to Jackson Pollock?"

"It's not the same, though. As painters, Cézanne and Pollock worked with wordless visual form. As a designer, whose medium is words, you are talking about draining off linguistic content so that only design remains."

"No, we're talking about representation. It's moving from representational to expressive typography. I think the parallel with what happened in painting is absolutely precise. Until the arrival of photography, painting was understood as a way of representing either fantasy or the real world. It had a very specific role just as typography has a specific role in Western society as a carrier of words."

"But why would you want to take representation out of language? It's a contra-diction in terms. What, ultimately, is the point?" Brody replies at some length, but circles the question.

Developing the analogy with photography and painting, he argues that putting desktop technology in the hands of the nondesigner liberates the designer from the necessity of representation in the same way that the camera liberated the artist. The project of design, he seems to believe, is almost complete. The sign systems and identities are now largely in place. In-house staff equipped with digital templates can take care of implementation, freeing designers such as Brody to pursue other, more painterly ends. The digital future, he suggests, will be "more to do with art than with design communication as we knew it." He doesn't explain the point of such private "languages"—why do we need them? how will we use them?—or why we should want, *Ray Gun*–style, to "treat printed media as painting." Why bother with text at all? Why not simply set up as a digital artist with a palette of pixels?

Returning to art history, Brody concludes with a question of his own. "The main point about Dadaism was a question mark. Why art? Why painting? And I think we are at the same junction in design and graphics. Why design? Why graphic designers?" What is his own answer? I ask. "Well, I've got no idea," he says, "and to be honest, graphic design is dead."

A couple of weeks later, still wondering what the point is, I call Jon Wozencroft. As cofounder of the audio-visual publishing company Touch, Wozencroft has been exploring the edges of print and performance since the early 1980s. A designer by training, he attempts feats of synthesis (drawing on art, design, literature, philosophy, sociology) in his heavily footnoted writings that would make even subject specialists think twice. They don't always come off. He has produced the text for two Brody books, collaborated on the manifesto and assorted commercial projects, talks like Brody's conscience ("I try to un–sound byte him"; "I'm always trying to improve his politeness"), but stresses his "distance" from the studio. He is in most days, though, according to Brody, and it is clearly a relationship that benefits them both. Through Brody, Wozencroft gains immediate access to client areas it would take him "ages of attrition" to reach. Brody, in turn, enjoys the services of his own resident theorist and gets taken seriously by the hip subculturalists who converge on Touch.

Wozencroft, with little prompting, spells out things that Brody only hints at or implies. "They need to take more drugs!" Brody had joked at one point, as I described the difficulties even experimental typographers have with his ideas. Later he says: "I'm excited by the computer as a tool for exploring a mental reality. It's the biggest LSD drug ever invented." But these are off-the-cuff remarks, not statements of a coherent program. Wozencroft comes right out and tells me that *Fuse* is an attempt to apply "psychotropic, narcotic elements in a purposeful way to the visual realm.

"We're trying to reinvest a kind of magic and indeterminate meaning in what we are doing and at the same time to make it clearer," continues Wozencroft of the *Fuse* collaboration. The two aims don't seem particularly compatible. The problem for Wozencroft, as for Brody, seems to lie in the nature of language itself, the difficulty in stepping back from its mediations, and there is the same ambiguity about what kind of "language" he means. "I strongly disagree with the title [of the new book]," he says. "This one is not about graphic language. Both of us in the best of all possible worlds would like to call it *Language* period." Like the historical sources he cites in support of *Fuse*—Kandinsky's spiritual abstraction, the automatic writing of the surrealists, Burroughs and Brion Gysin's cut-ups— he wants to break free from "the trap of words." As so often with theories of this kind, it takes an awful lot of words to pry open the trap.

A great deal rests on *The Graphic Language of Neville Brody 2,* though it isn't, as it happens, the book we were promised. Brody was already talking about his projected follow up, to be called *The Death of Typography,* even as the first book began to fly from the shops. Why, I ask him some way into the interview, does he feel the need to produce another book so soon after the first?

His reply is uncharacteristically short. "Because I felt I had to. It's very simple."

I press him. "Because the first book was such a . . ." He can't quite say it. "Because people still assumed the work coming out of the studio was . . . All they'd seen was the first book, and, as you know, very little since then. The purpose of the second book is to kill the preconceptions that the first book created."

There, he's said it. And he is right. The first book, like all such books, was a kind of ending. At the age of just thirty-one, a mere ten years into his working life, it froze him, labeled him, in the public mind. It was one of the best-selling design books of the 1980s. Every studio has a copy. The only way to erase its memory, or at least to counteract it, and reassert his centrality to graphic design in the 1990s, is with another equally commanding book. Brody said at the time he wanted *Graphic Language* to open a dialogue (he said the same thing about *The Face*), and he says it again about *Graphic Language 2.* He seems genuinely unaware that it might appear presumptuous to glorify yourself in this way every six years.

"Do you see yourself as a leader?"

"No, no, no." He seems really taken aback. "It's not a case of leading. The group of people who work here have come together because we're all interested in, as I said, research and exploration and pushing and challenging things. This book focuses much more on the work. I'm almost loath to do portraits or interviews for this at all, but the publisher expects it. People should be able to look at the book and get what they need because it's about the work, it's not about me."

There will be another book, says Brody, in a couple of years. But, perhaps because his mood is less apocalyptic than it was immediately after *The Face,* the death of typography has been indefinitely postponed. "In fact," he says, "I think we've missed the point." The new title is in any case much cleverer: it both affirms and negates. Brody plans to call it *Beyond Typography.*

"Are you a Net user?" I ask Brody at one point, convinced his answer will be yes.

"I'm not. I'm not."

"Why not, given your interest in computers?"

"I don't know. That's something that I've never been fascinated with."

Then, just as the tape is about to run out, he says something completely unexpected, making me wonder if I have misheard him—just lets it slip and moves on to something else, an admission that seems, the more I think about it, to crystallize everything, the last thing he probably should say and the most revealing thing he could. Brody says, *"I enjoy creating modes of communication, but I don't enjoy communicating,"* and I begin to see why he finds the thought of a typeface with which you can say nothing quite as exciting as he does.

Originally published in I.D., *September/October 1994.*

PAGANINI UNPLUGGED
Rick Poynor

With the publication of his book this fall, David Carson will attain a level of personal celebrity and influence that many designers dream about, but only the rarest will achieve. Constantly on the move between lectures and workshops all over the world, rarely out of the design magazines, and increasingly the subject of wide media interest in glossy magazines and on television, Carson is now, unquestionably, the most famous graphic designer to have emerged in the 1990s.

In his laid-back, genial way, David Carson has shown a talent for putting himself about that verges on genius. Everyone you talk to about him singles out his knack for publicity in tones close to awe. "He can promote himself like nobody else I've ever met," says *Emigre* magazine editor Rudy VanderLans, no slouch himself in the promotions department. Acutely sensitive to criticism and hungry—even by design business standards—for awards and acclaim, Carson is the most advanced model to date of a comparatively recent invention: the graphic designer as pop star. In his work, attitude, and wanderlust, he is, in the words of his New York collaborator Mike Jurkovac, a "rock and roll typographer."

Carson's résumé unfolds in a series of exemplary subcultural moves. In the late 1970s, he was a pro surfer, achieving a top ranking of eighth in the world. After four years as a part-time designer at the "glorified fanzine" *Transworld Skateboarding* (by day he taught high school sociology) and a brief interlude at *Musician,* he caught the wave in 1989 as art director of the thinking sand-jock's surfing magazine, *Beach Culture.* Six little-seen issues and some 150 relentlessly press-released design awards later, Carson was firmly established among colleagues as the nineties art director most likely to succeed. *Ray Gun,* Marvin Scott Jarrett's "alternative" music magazine launched in November 1992, became Carson's most visible platform to date, winning him a following among disaffected young designers the world over.

Along the way Carson has made some important friends. For David Byrne, who wrote the foreword to his book, *The End of Print,* Carson's work "communicates on a level that bypasses the logical, rational centers of the brain and goes straight to the part that understands without thinking." Albert Watson, who agreed to Carson's type-only front cover for his photography book, *Cyclops,* is equally certain of his status as a fellow artist. They have already collaborated on a number of advertising projects, including a Superbowl spot for Budweiser, and more are planned through two newly launched companies—David Carson Design (partners Carson and Jurkovac) and Cyclops Productions (partners Jurkovac and Watson)—that share the same building and floor in New York's Flatiron district. Jurkovac says roughly half of Carson's time will be spent in the city.

Carson resists any suggestion that he consciously sets out to appeal to Generation X-ers, but whatever the intention, his way with youth codes is manna for American advertisers. "David has tapped into an area of communication that a lot of people have been trying to figure out," explains Jurkovac, formerly of the ad agency Foote, Cone & Belding. "Younger America, people who are looking at multiple options and choices, or different ways of interpreting things from past generations: the MTV-quick-cut-barraged-by-information-all-at-the-same-time society." With projects in his portfolio for such high-profile companies as Nike, Pepsi, Levi's, Vans, Citibank, and American Express, Carson is already a significant ad world player. His growing ambition to do work for television and his New York support system mean he is poised to get even bigger.

For anyone who has followed the development of experimental design over the last ten years or more, David Carson is a fascinating—and pivotal—figure. He has produced some of the most striking and era-defining designs of the decade. I once flew from London to Philadelphia to debate the "new typography" with him at an AIGA evening event and had looked forward to talking to him again with a view to writing about his work in depth. I had many questions—questions that have still, even with the publication of his book, not been fully addressed. But Carson declined on three separate occasions to be interviewed for this article. He doesn't like the few things I have written about him previously, and he didn't think this would be an "objective" piece. "I think you are going to put your own spin on the thing regardless of my input," he told me. It seemed a slightly curious objection coming from a designer who has often stressed the personal and emotional nature of his design method and has urged other designers to do the same.

One of the most striking aspects of *The End of Print* is its unabashed attempt to uproot Carson from the surrounding terrain, and, in the process, rewrite recent history. Carson, the British edition's jacket blurb claims, has "single-handedly changed the course of graphic design." Given that the book has been produced with Carson's full cooperation—

his design for it uses a battery of *Ray Gun*–esque type treatments—this presumably represents the designer's current view of himself. The text by Lewis Blackwell, editor of the British magazine *Creative Review,* lionizes him as a transcendent originator whose work somehow eludes the theoretical frameworks and categorical definitions that, according to Blackwell, bedevil and constrain other less popular forms of experimental design. It is misleading, Blackwell writes, to associate Carson with the "deconstruction" graphics of Cranbrook. At one point, in an interview, he raises the question of Cranbrook and CalArts. "The focus of my work has become quite dissimilar in theory and practice to those schools," replies Carson. "Perhaps in some of the small regular sections of *Ray Gun,* which are often done by an intern, the content is not explored as much and there is more of a style at work."

When I spoke to some of Carson's colleagues about the issue of influences, I received reactions ranging from wry amusement to fierce resentment. The more positive are glad to see their ideas vindicated by Carson's commercial success. Educators such as Lorraine Wild of CalArts have staked their reputations on the belief that the controversial experiments of the academy might some day find a home in the mainstream. "I think it needs to be stated," says Wild, "that it was accomplishment enough for him to figure out that [experimental] work was quite valuable and of interest." Barry Deck, who supplied Carson with prerelease versions of his typefaces for use in *Surfer* magazine and *Ray Gun,* is more critical: "I think he's taken almost everything he does from the CalArts/Cranbrook community and sort of ripped out the heart—that is, de-ideologized it completely and delivered it to the masses."

While this is clearly a matter of personal interpretation, what can be said with certainty is that from *Beach Culture* on, Carson's path has intersected with the experimental design community at many points. Christopher Vice, a graduate of North Carolina State University, designed a fragmented contents page for issue two of *Beach Culture* that inspired Carson (according to an article he wrote for *How* magazine) to go even further in his own dismantling of a next-issue announcement page. Many of the typefaces that were vital to *Ray Gun*'s abrasive texture and reader appeal were designed by students and alumni, such as Deck and Susan LaPorte of CalArts, and Lisa Vorhees, Brian Schorn, David Shields, and P. Scott Makela of Cranbrook. The names are listed in the front, but exactly who did what is not made clear, to the annoyance of some. "He got so famous for work that included some of my own," says Deck, "that when people look at my work they sometimes think of him."

Many of *Ray Gun*'s single pages and later, as the magazine developed, whole spreads were the work of interns such as Cranbrook graduate Martin Venezky. A detail from a poster by CalArts professor Ed Fella was used as *Ray Gun*'s masthead. Carson seemed happy enough two or three years ago to acknowledge these connections. "Overall, the most interesting work, writing, and attitude I've seen from a grad school in the past year has come from Cranbrook," he told Rudy VanderLans in a notoriously prickly *Emigre* interview. "And CalArts has such an amazing pool of talent." He went on to say that he had spent three days at Cranbrook, giving a lecture and sitting in on critiques, and had considered going there himself.

For Ed Fella, who hand-lettered a page for *The End of Print,* Carson is best understood as "the Paganini of typographers." "Maybe Carson is the most virtuoso player of this kind of stuff," he explains. "The truth is, of course, he doesn't invent it all. He's not the Beethoven or the Mozart. He's the performer of these ideas that come from other sources."

Some of the ideas that Carson presents *aperçus* go back decades. Quite apart from the century-old artistic tradition of the found object or image, his use of the street for design inspiration has a recent Anglo-American lineage that stretches from Robert Brownjohn's early 1960s photographs of street typography to the well-documented vernacular reworkings of the 1980s. Similarly, the anti-design that he has built a career on was explicit in 1970s punk graphics, aggressively applied by Dutch provocateurs Hard Werken in the early 1980s, theorized a few years later at Cranbrook, and brilliantly explored by Fella before *Beach Culture* was so much as a distant wave in its publisher's eye. This is not to invalidate such ideas in Carson's output, or to deny that he "performs" them with panache; it is simply to reintroduce a sense of context missing from much of the press about him and *The End of Print.*

Everyone I spoke to about David Carson felt that his real gift was for synthesis. "He's a great art director," says Rudy VanderLans. "He knows where to get the good talent. He has an incredible eye for what is hip, for what is cool, for what is current." As a designer, though—particularly of text—Carson has a more limited toolbox. While his opening spreads for *Ray Gun* can be stunningly unexpected and painterly patchworks of illustration, photography, splotches of broken type, and scintillating rushes of white space, his treatment of the story that follows the initial flourish has rarely—even on its own idiosyncratic terms—been as convincingly resolved. "For the most part his designs are based on shock value," agrees VanderLans. "David is constantly thumbing his nose at typographic convention. For someone who's considered such a design wunderkind, it's disappointing that there's been so little progress toward something a bit more challenging."

Even to the most casual reader of *Ray Gun* it will be obvious that Carson has enjoyed exceptional freedom. I learned exactly how much freedom when I caught up with the magazine's founder and publisher, Marvin Scott Jarrett, on a recent visit to London, where he lectured to the Typographic Circle. Jarrett clearly has enormous regard for Carson's talents; at the talk he calls him a "genius." But there is an undercurrent to what Jarrett tells me at his hotel that only makes sense some weeks later when he confirms that following a disagreement over the cover of the October issue he has let Carson go.

Carson and Jarrett have always worked at a distance—Carson in San Diego, Jarrett in Los Angeles—with few meetings, "not even once an issue," according to Jarrett. He and *Ray Gun*'s executive editor, Randy Bookasta, supplied Carson with edited copy on disk and most of the photography; Carson commissioned some of the photography and all of the illustration. From then on he was completely on his own. The editorial office did not insist on page proofs. Often Jarrett would not even see the magazine, except for the cover, until it was printed.

Magazines are by their nature team creations. Their best moments are often forged in the close collaboration between editors and designers. The unusual circumstances of *Ray Gun*'s production, with Carson's "interpretations" arriving as a *fait accompli,* meant these interactions could not occur. There could be no discussion, response, refinement, or rethinking. It was already clear, during our London conversation, that Jarrett missed this involvement; his other magazines, *Bikini* and *huH,* are produced in-house.

Does he now believe, following Carson's departure, that the previous arrangements represented—as some design world observers committed to graphic authorship might have hoped—a viable model for magazine publishing? It was certainly an interesting test, Jarrett says. "It worked for me for a while, but then it just started to get old." What he now wants to achieve with *Ray Gun* is a "creative energy" between editors and designers. Portland design team Johnson & Wolverton have designed issue thirty-one, with Bookasta working alongside them in their studio. "I am still giving my art directors more creative freedom than any other publisher on the planet," claims Jarrett, "and I'm a tremendous fan of great graphic design. But there comes a time when you've just got to say, 'Hey, wait a minute. This is a case of the tail wagging the dog.'"

Whatever its long-term viability, *Ray Gun's* first incarnation has been a notable success. The magazine has a readership of 150,000 and rising, and you only have to scan its letter pages—"*Ray Gun* is me!"—to see how it thrills its young audience. Yet beyond offering a sophisticated outlet for ordinary teenage rebellion, what does *Ray Gun's* much-vaunted visual "radicalism" actually stand for? "We still believe that music and the people who make it can change the world," spiels a sixties-sounding paean to rock and roll in issue one. Written by former *Beach Culture* editor Neil Feineman, who lasted four issues as *Ray Gun's* editorial director, this is clearly not Carson's view. "Graphic design will save the world right after rock and roll does," he observes ironically in *The End of Print*. It doesn't appear to be Jarrett's view either.

Jarrett told his Typographic Circle audience that he and Carson were non-conformists and anti-authority. But when I ask him later what exactly he is rebelling against, he answers—as Carson tends to answer such questions—in purely inward-looking professional terms: "I'm rebelling against traditional publishing, constantly being challenged by my magazine distributors and consultants telling me I'm doing the wrong thing."

Feineman says that his own conception of the magazine "was all about giving disenfranchised people in the arts a voice." Still loyal to Carson, he seems wholly disenchanted with *Ray Gun's* routine music-biz content as it has developed. "What is amazing is that David has taken such standard fodder and put a new graphic spin on it," he says. "I can't think that without David, or at least somebody of David's ilk, that magazine would have lasted as long as it has, because it's certainly not worth reading." Earlier this year, Carson himself expressed a similar point of view a little more diplomatically in an interview on British television: "I firmly believe if you had done *Ray Gun* traditionally it wouldn't have survived. It's not that unique in the writing and it's a pretty narrow scope—a lot of band bios and things."

From the time of his earliest interviews, Carson has always insisted that his design approach is "conceptual." In other words, beneath the agitated surface lies a problem-solving response to the content of an article based on his close reading of the text: there is an explainable reason for what you see on the page. His famous "surfing blind" spread in *Beach Culture*—two pages of solid black, with only the headline for text—is a quintessential "big idea." What is genuinely remarkable, and a credit to Feineman's vision, too, is that Carson was able to realize such an idea, and others just as memorable, without compromise in the pages of a magazine; many editors would have balked.

Ray Gun, though, is less clear cut. If Carson's later method really was a "conceptual" response to the editorial content, it would have been enlightening to learn from his book about the concepts behind familiar spreads. But when it comes to the inside story, *The End of Print* doesn't get much hotter than such lukewarm revelations as, "the attitude of this design involves a quiet laugh at optimum line length." Perhaps David Byrne comes closer to the essence of Carson's *Ray Gun* work when he talks about a form of "understanding without thinking" and likens the design's communicative effects to music.

Carson says in the book that as well as being a graphic designer, he considers himself an artist; the ultimate source of a designer's work, he once suggested, must come from within. "I set out to do things in an emotional way. When I turn to a page in a book, to a magazine, to any graphic design, I want an emotional reaction. That's probably the basis for how I judge it." Artists, of course, are under no obligation to explain what they do.

Seen in this way, Carson's huge appeal to advertisers makes perfect sense. For a designer without ideological baggage, pursuing a path of design for design's sake, it is the obvious next step. Advertising targets the emotions. It bypasses the logical centers of the brain. It has no critical relationship to its own content (though as a strategy it sometimes pretends to). Mike Jurkovac worked with Carson on the launch of L2 worker jeans for Levi Strauss: "David came back to us with a phenomenal packaging program that really helped reposition the brand. It was to appeal to the same target that David's *Ray Gun* magazine appeals to; the work he did was like a Rorschach collage. When we did the testing on it, the kids were saying, 'this is exactly how I feel in terms of life.'"

Does Carson's work (and other work like it) herald some fundamental shift in the way not just youth subcultures, but all of us will soon be communicating? Jurkovac is sure that it does.

He points to the usual technological factors, the Internet and 500-channel TV. "If you are going to try to do marketing or communication, you have to take that into account." Carson himself has often explained his typographic operations in terms of a changing audience: "You can't give an eighteen-year-old a page of solid gray type and expect him or her to read it." Yet any magazine worth its salt, for any age group, proceeds from the starting point that unrelieved gray type looks dull, that pages should be lively and varied, and that the uncommitted browser will need to be seduced into reading. It's a gigantic conceptual and cultural leap from here to tangled columns, mutilated type, and Carson's empirically untested claim in the *New York Times* that making readers work to decipher text may mean they remember more of what they read. It is certainly clear from *Ray Gun*'s letters that many of its readers do find it heavy going, or even impossible to read on occasion. That is what they say they like about it. One of *Ray Gun*'s writers observed in a recent issue, "Just by opening this very magazine, you've gained admittance to an exclusive club."

New York–based designer Bill Drenttel—well known for his commitment to publishing and literature, and a *Ray Gun* admirer—speaks for many Carson watchers when he suggests that the "eighteen-year-old reader" argument is cynical. "I'm not sure I buy that," he says. "I don't think reading is a lost cause. Employing alternative strategies of engaging people is great, but that doesn't necessarily lead to the conclusion that those are the only strategies. Or that people won't read if you don't engage in strategies that are only about new typography, as defined by people like David."

Excitingly iconoclastic as it seemed for a time, car-crash typography is now everywhere. Jarrett is bored with it. Some of *Ray Gun*'s letter writers are bored with it. Carson may well be bored with it, too. Before his exit cut short any plans he might have had, he had been talking about redesigning *Ray Gun* for more than a year. During his London lecture, Jarrett referred to something he called "the new simplicity." Issue twenty-eight contained a story on Neil Young consisting—perhaps it was a joke—of tall columns of solid gray type. With issue twenty-nine, Carson trashed the retinue of grunge font suppliers for just three contributing typeface designers and some low-key, largely sans serif fonts arranged in orderly rows.

The End of Print, on the other hand, is very much in his established, convention-busting style—a style that, despite the surprise value of seeing it within the traditionally more reserved pages of a book, is beginning to look distinctly tired. Is Carson, as Rudy VanderLans suggests, a "one-trick pony," whose lack of formal education in typography will limit what he can accomplish? Or does he have the natural ability—the "genius" as some see it—to reinvent himself and retain his vanguard position? The new simplicity? The new something else? Or more of the same? All eyes are on him and it's his move.

Originally published in I.D., *November 1995.*

NOTES ON EDWARD FELLA:
"DESIGN IN A BORDERTOWN"
Lorraine Wild

1. (FROM A DESCRIPTION OF GIULIO CAMILLO OF VENICE, WHO, IN THE 1530s, WAS ATTEMPTING TO BUILD A "MEMORY THEATRE" THAT WOULD HOLD SIGNS OF ALL EXISTING KNOWLEDGE IN THE WORLD)

> The work is of wood, marked with many images, and full of little boxes: there are various orders and grades in it. He gives a place to each individual figure and ornament . . . he stammers badly and speaks Latin with difficulty, excusing himself with the pretext that through continually using his pen he has nearly lost the use of speech. He is said however to be good in the vernacular . . .[1]

Has that much ever really been said about the incredible scavenging that shadows commercial art practice? The miles of "clip files," the piles of reference books, the endless gobbling up of magazines, the flea-marketing, the insatiable collection of ephemera? This mania surfaces every once in a while, for instance, during the recent public revelation that an illustrator of a *TV Guide* cover had collaged Oprah Winfrey's head on Anne Margaret's body . . . because Ann Margaret's body had on *just* the right outfit. To anyone acquainted with common illustration methods this episode implied that the exposed illustrator had probably collected a universe of dressy torsos in some file folder, *just in case* the right assignment came along—and sure enough, it did.

To understand Edward Fella's work one has to recognize the age-old project undertaken by so many artists, writers, and thinkers: collecting, reordering, and restating everything about the surrounding culture that can be observed and remembered, thereby laying claim to (one's own interpretation of) the universe.

There's a didactic, crackpot edge to the classifying impulse to "get it right" or "set the record straight" but in the process of creating a new canon or catalogue, the talented ones end up defining themselves and creating that new culture, by and by. For Edward Fella the starting point of his catalogue was the towering pile of any illustrator's reference material: the books, the photos, the lettering guides, the type books, old postcards, clip files, and a mental encyclopedia of visual style, all of it *just in case.* True, he did mix some peculiar things into the investigation: way too much interest in higher forms of art, literature, and cultural history than can be explained by his high-school trade education, or by the environment of the commercial art studios in Detroit that he worked in so diligently and successfully for the first fifteen years of his design life.

2. (A QUOTE FELLA REPEATS IN THREE DIFFERENT SKETCHBOOKS)

This "I" which approaches the text is already itself a plurality of other texts, (EF notes: it's what you already know [too much!]) of codes which are infinite or, more precisely, lost (whose origin is lost).

The path of Edward Fella's work spirals out from inside the conventions of commercial art/design, to its borderlines—and then stops just at the edges, or straddles the fence between whatever separates design from something else (and many think his work is just beyond the pale). Far from being a "hand" (an illustrator who can mimic any number of styles), Edward Fella's illustration originally consisted mainly of pen-and-ink line drawings that were referred to as "cartoons": not in the comic book and animation sense, but in the older definition of the cartoon as a sort of caricature, a visual skewering. Inflexibility of style and media was more than compensated for by wit and humor. Fella's mordant drawings poked fun at all categories of human type and endeavor, and (when the assignment was decorative borders or headlines) at typography, too. Although he received a fair share of awards and recognition for the commercial work, it was always considered by his peers to be somewhat eccentric: he claimed that the strangeness in his work stemmed from desperate attempts to circumvent the limits of his "hand." He developed a fast, funny, and perfectly executed commercial product. It was not for nothing that his fellow illustrators jokingly referred to him as "the king of zing."

The decorative illustration had real impact on what was to follow. Fella's preferred lettering style was a parody of art deco faces that he called "shiny shoe" or "cleaners' modern," in reference to the style of many Depression-era laundries built in and around Detroit. This ornate stuff was constructed by hand with circle guides and triangles, and was in no way an accurate reproduction of anything seen during the 1920s, but like the rest of his caricature, it got at the essential nature of the original lettering that was laughable but dead on. He did the same with hand-scrawled versions of Victorian flourishes and parodies of other vernaculars as well. Years later, while pursuing a graduate school education (quite removed from the commercial art business), he began to confront the typography of high design culture—and his approach was completely consistent. Fella's deep structure is embedded in those illustrator's reference files, and the files are horizontal, not hierarchical—so high design was just more stylistic grist for his mill, to personalize by "getting it wrong." Many graphic designers look at Edward Fella's work and, unable to see anything but error, cannot believe that it is there by design. But that only indicates the severity of the split between "high" art, "mid" design culture, and "low" commercial art culture. One of the many ironies about the current fascination with the synthesis of high and pop cultures that allegedly marks our age is the fact that work that truly challenges the classifications

is still met with great difficulty, particularly if it emanates from the mid range of design—
and this is the story of Edward Fella's project.

3. (FROM A CLIPPING IN ONE OF ED'S SKETCHBOOKS)

> Dear Ann Landers: I am seventeen years old and want more than anything in the
> world to be an artist. The few people who have been shown my work discouraged
> me by saying I'm not "with it." Any advice? —Downbeat in Torrance
> Dear T: Take heart in the words of Orson Welles. He said, I passionately hate the
> idea of being "with it." A true artist is always out of step with his time. He has
> to be. (Ed adds comment: "Another great popular cult of art myth.")

By the early 1970s art was made out of a lot of things, including neon tubes, and very big
holes bulldozed out of the earth (and of course fifty years earlier it had been made out
of porcelain urinals and snow-shovels); it wasn't until ten years later that it would be made
out of type and large half-toned photostats. Pop-art made commercial art into a subject
for painting that was obliquely flattering to commercial artists but which absolutely did
not include them. (Author's note: the wall between graphic design and commercial art is
dwarfed by the wall separating all of it from art. For instance, at least some graphic designers
keep up with *Art in America, Artforum,* etc. How many "real" artists do you think will see
this issue of *Emigre?*) Fella's Bauhaus-influenced education taught him to idealize a
combination of art and design practice: but still, art was painting and that was something
he only got to do on weekends. As art dematerialized in the 1970s it remained difficult
to integrate as a motif into promotions for car dealerships and florists and banks and other
typical clients. Fella turned to marginal art practices, especially photography, to augment
his work. It helped that photography was pictorial, but it was not the pictures that became
his subject matter. It was the detail of seeing, the little conceptual moves that turned the
act of photographing from a banal procedure to a vehicle for meaning and a work of art
that became so interesting. Ed Ruscha, Andy Warhol, Robert Frank, Lee Friedlander, "artist's
books," folk art, "mall" art, and flea-market antiques—all were added to Fella's frame of
reference, and it was at this point that the edges began to blur.

 Staff illustrators in design studios have lots of downtime between assignments, and
Edward Fella used his the way most illustrators do, to make "samples" that are comps of
imaginary projects meant to demonstrate one's capabilities in a way that printed samples
did not, which a salesman would take to show to potential clients, which might bring about
a real job where the experiment could be put to use. When not cartooning, Fella used
samples to tread into art territory. In 1974, he used his studio's first direct-positive photostat
system to produce a book of collages instantly composed of found imagery and type. He
had always made collages, but now because of the stats, they were easy to translate into
graphic media. The pages are based on the genre of magazine design (where most of the
imagery come from) but the sparse juxtaposition of images and tiny bits of type is like a
caricature of the minimalism of late Swiss corporate design. However, the content, which
is mostly cryptic, contradicts the clarity of the style. It is all wrong, which leads you to
inspect individual elements more carefully. Suddenly everything is "strange." ("Nothing
is more fantastic ultimately than precision."[2]) What Fella had ingested from art and
photography—an obsession with process, art defined not by an identifiable visual style but

by a series of intellectual moves in space and time—was conflated with the puns and pop images of commercialism in his new sample book—and it did not yield him any commissions. But it set him permanently on the course that led to his current work. It also had a large impact on the design program that the McCoys were setting up at Cranbrook, just a few miles away. Fella would show his experimental work to the students (a more appreciative audience than his art business peers) and his scavenging of art and design became a model for much work produced there. From the McCoys and Cranbrook, he developed a more refined appreciation for the rational methodology of design: you see him synthesize it with his old caricaturing mode in a series of rigorous but intuitively "friendly" symbols designed for several departments of Detroit's Henry Ford Hospital. The program is straight out of any corporate manual but the visual style is a funny version of stenciled images, completely unlike the typical institutional identity system.

4. (FROM A 1984 SKETCHBOOK)

I force myself into self-contradiction to avoid following my own taste.
—Marcel Duchamp

Between the time that Edward Fella began to produce his hybrid art/design work (which could be interpreted as art about design, in materials not usually encountered in anything recognized as art, at least fifteen years ago) and the next ten years or so, when he gradually pulled out of commercial practice to concentrate on his own education, he began to work with a variety of alternative arts organizations in Detroit: the Detroit Focus Gallery, the Poetry Resource Center, the Detroit Artists Market. He began to produce printed material for openings, announcements, temporary signs, small catalogues—all of it extremely low-budget, but free of constraint. Through his work in the "samples," then a set of photocopied collages and little books, and finally a set of sketchbooks, he had wandered even farther into the *terra incognita* of the professional graphic designer—but the work was still "design," it was made up of type and photographs arranged clearly. Fella's work was always "legible" but not in the completely linear way most design is. For a designer like Fella, who had been used to working with professional suppliers paid by big production budgets, stepping down to the erratic quality of cheap typesetting and "quickie" offset printing was a radical move, but one that he had to make (since it was all the organizations could afford) in order to see the experiments of his collages and sketchbooks realized. He slowly built an audience out of the Detroit arts community—and eventually they took him as seriously as he took them.

Fella claims that he could never figure out how to modulate his experimental work into the routine commercial design and illustration projects that he produced, that he was only able to flourish when he had complete creative control over the projects for the arts organizations. But in that work he did develop hierarchies of experimentation that imitate the range possible in "real" work. For instance, the *Detroit Focus Quarterly* is typographically conservative, true to the genre, but there are visual puns and buried themes in photo choices (for instance, everyone will be posed similarly, etc.) that are not blatant but can be appreciated upon closer inspection. In a series of posters for photography exhibitions, an angle of vision or composition will be echoed in the ostensibly minimal typography; in the case of the Rauhauser poster, typographic detail from the image of the Leica is integrated into what appears to be quite normal, tasteful "art" typography. It is usually considered to be very bad form for graphic design to provide anything but the most reverential, neutral frame when the subject is art. But Fella insists on intervening with the subject. In 1987, he produced two remarkable catalogues: one on the work of Morris Brose (published by the Detroit Artists Market) and the other for an exhibition of the work of Phillip Fike and Bill Rauhauser at the Detroit Focus Gallery. In the Brose catalogue, big chunks of type move muscularly across the pages, mimicking the weight and gravity of Brose's work. Photographs are cropped in extreme shapes that induce a visual anxiety by emulating the formal strategy of Brose's sculpture in the "wrong" media.

In the Fike-Rauhauser catalogue, photographs of the artists are embellished with shapes that Fella has added, which seem disconnected from their work. The presence of the designer is noted more aggressively than custom ever allows, and design as one of the many invisible support systems in the art world is highlighted with a vengeance.

5. (E.F. SKETCHBOOK, NOVEMBER 1985)

Tell the truth but tell it slant/Success in Circuit lies —Emily Dickenson

Now Edward Fella is a faculty member in the graphic design program at CalArts, where he works with fourth-year and graduate students. He keeps designing Detroit Focus announcements (by express mail) and he diligently produces sketchbook after sketchbook of drawings and collages; these two projects are the main "lab" where Fella keeps performing his new experiments. (Fella is an unusual teacher; he possesses decades of experience but he rejects it as a source of authority since he is almost entirely involved with speculation).

There are not many precedents for Fella's position in graphic design now. He produces work that, because of its media, scale, and audience, is usually called graphic design, but that flaunts the professional conventions of it. Rotten work is nothing new, since it is more often done, knowingly or unknowingly, by printers, artists, or anyone with access to "desktop publishing"—but Fella toys with the border between what is acceptable and what is not from deep within the establishment, thirty-some years of design practice, and a graduate education from Cranbrook. He cannot be accused of any sort of naïvete.

The first position Fella takes, which can only make many designers wince, is to declare that his formal experimentation is purely in the service of his own aesthetic gratification and nothing else. (This, of course, is not quite true, or we would not be looking at his work right now—but that is his cross to bear). Fella proceeds from the point that all standards (particularly typographic ones that imply a kind of mastery or expertise) are not necessarily wrong, but in his particular case, irrelevant. He refuses to find the solution in the problem (a great design cliché if ever there was one); in fact, conveying a message is never a problem in his work—messages are usually as clear as bells. But he does concoct enormous problems by upsetting every rule associated with functional typography (while remaining completely cognizant that design is defined in part by its "obedience" to a highly mutable set of standards of public tastes).

For instance, how easy is it to compose a page using only typefaces whose names rhyme? What new aesthetic emanates from that small but strange decision? He is not trying to perfect an old style or invent a new one; all situations are unique and deserving of a whole new approach. It is this quality that is so relevant to the kinds of design now possible on the computer. Even though his work is painstakingly created by hand, it is a model of complexity that is really only viable on the computer. Fella talks about looking for crude archetypes for lettering, and while many designers have appreciated the vitality of amateur lettering, few have had the nerve to actually incorporate its characteristics into their work. While a graduate student at Cranbrook, he began by taking photostats of existing faces and "adjusting" them by slicing serifs or strokes with his x-acto knife. He has continued to do this, guided by a set of formal precepts that celebrate discordant or unbalanced elements; irregularities of shape, letter, and wordspacing; ambivalent baselines; and almost imperceptible degrees of contrast rendered by types of slightly different weight. Fella's own standard of "similar differences" or "inconsistent irregularities" are in direct opposition to the simplified notions of contrast inherited from modernist typography (as articulated by Moholy-Nagy and Tschichold) but again are much more reflective of the plasticity made possible in contemporary computerized typesetting. So, although he has avoided the computer so far, his work does address the complete and total technological change sweeping over typography today. It has been noted that the grand technological change that we are now witnessing has to have some impact on the aesthetic principles of design: perhaps Edward Fella's work is demonstrating what those shifts might be.

But to look at his work only for that is to distort what it really is, which cannot possibly be described in its entirety because, like Camillo's Memory Theatre, it contains so many bits and pieces, quotations and signs, organized in such a personal manner, that it can't really all be rationalized. In the flyers for exhibitions at the Detroit Focus gallery, all sorts of elements and techniques are catalogued, sometimes in reference to the subject, sometimes so obliquely that the joke just lies there waiting for the most astute observer. He reserves the prerogative to interact with the artists or to stage a sideshow. A very subtle example of this is his design for the *10th Anniversary* catalogue for Detroit Focus. Its style is typical of the sort of conventionally subdued form that design takes when the subject is an art institution. But the entire eighty-page book is pasted up by hand without tools, columns of type and blocks of photographs simply "eyeballed" as if there is a grid; but of course it wobbles, *ever so slightly*. From the design, you could infer that the presence of this alternative institution has positively destabilized the more closed cultural milieu that existed before its history; or you could infer that the institution itself is flexible, or perhaps even on shaky ground. Or, if you are not prone to close reading, you could miss the whole thing!

6. (E.F. 1986)

Finger on exactly identifying that meddlesome art touch in the design pie . . .

In many of the real professions whose status is envied by the quasiprofession of design, there is a very clear distinction made between levels and genres of practice. The neighborhood no-fault divorce lawyer is different from the academic specialist, and they in turn are different than the highly paid corporate counsel or the idealistic public defender. But genres of graphic design practice are rarely distinguished from each other and therefore the common assumption is that all design has to rest upon a set of shared "values," which are mostly based on style and production quality. Look at *Print's* Regional Annual—there is no perceptive difference between the work that is chosen from different parts of the country, because the representatives of the profession that curate the work would tend not to recognize anything that falls outside of this very generalized set of specifications as graphic design at all. This delusion stems from the time not so long ago when self-conscious graphic design was produced by a small group of modernist initiates. Some nostalgic designers (mostly over fifty) are somewhat bitter about it passing, dismayed by the hordes of young designers and the (inadvertent) loss of production control brought on by the new technology. Edward Fella, fifty-three, continues to play in his self-defined "bordertown" of design practice (declared in the bordertown of Detroit, unconcerned with the mainstream of either one of the coasts), surrounded by the piles of clip files, books, type samples, art magazines, novels, polaroids that he has been trying to make sense out of for thirty years. It is in Fella's style to discount the work, to insist that it is all for fun and without consequence, and maybe he has to maintain that line in order to be able to continue to produce it when it is not recognized by many as being art or design. But there are many who appreciate his work for the tough questions implied by its very existence. Can graphic designers ever really be accepted as anything other than obedient mediums lubricating the messages of their clients? Is there any room in the transmission of messages for the designer's static? Is friction a vital element in "problem solving"? Are designers really smart and creative enough to be able to see the opportunity to take a more aggressive role in their work? Can work that is produced for practically nothing be taken seriously in our slick profession, or is a budget (and a map) now attached to the definition of design? Can design that embraces the culture of design as subject matter be understood by other designers without them becoming defensive ("Oh that's just design about design!") and fearful, or must designers wander about in a state of perpetual ingenuousness? Must design always be put to work? Edward Fella doesn't presume to have the answers, but he just keeps rephrasing the question in a million permutations, *just in case.*

Originally published in Emigre, *No. 17, February 1991.*

Notes

1. Francis Yates, *The Art of Memory* (Chicago: University of Chicago Press, 1966), 131.
2. Alain Robbe-Grillet, quoted in John Hejduk, *Mask of Medusa* (New York: Rizzoli International Publications, 1985), 39.

IN MEMORIAM

PROJECTS OF OPTIMISM
Dan Friedman

In the relatively short history of modern design, certain periods (such as the 1930s and 1950s) sustain special fascination for me. They were moments when designers envisioned a future that occasionally allowed fantasy to supersede functionalism. Objects designed with this futurism may have been inspired by an organic nature, an aerodynamic technology, an artful sculpture, or an irrational glamour, but, most important, they embodied a culture of *optimism*.

At the end of this century, it has become a much greater challenge for design to inspire. There are fewer assurances that our future will be better than our past. How will it be possible to express a sense of balance, vision, and optimism in a world moving toward complacency, cultural conformity, or anarchy? How can we sustain the need for play, fantasy, and dream in the midst of our exhaustion from harsh realities? Is there still authenticity and originality in the fast world of appropriation and simulation? Does the preoccupation with the way things look (style) preclude design from ever again becoming radically progressive and meaningful? Will our multitude of personal visions prevent us from reconceiving an enlightened sense of community and social purpose?

At a time when the values of the individual, family, corporation, and community are being debated in society, not enough corresponding dialogue exists among designers. This book has tried to demonstrate that the issues of culture are products of design and vice versa. It has tried to reposition design so that it is viewed as a part of culture and not only as a service to industry. It has tried to suggest that when art and design are a more broadly accepted part of culture, they become a more passionate universe of discourse and theory. The radically modern agenda which follows might just suggest a basis for optimism.

- Live and work with passion and responsibility; have a sense of humor and fantasy.
- Try to express personal, spiritual, and domestic values even if our culture continues to be dominated by corporate, marketing, and institutional values.
- Choose to remain progressive; don't be regressive. Find comfort in the past only if it expands insight into the future and not just for the sake of nostalgia.
- Embrace the richness of all cultures; be inclusive instead of exclusive.
- Think of your work as a significant element in the context of a more important, transcendental purpose.
- Use your work to become advocates of projects for the public good.
- Attempt to become a cultural provocateur; be a leader rather than a follower.
- Engage in self-restraint; accept the challenge of working with reduced expectations and diminished resources.

- Avoid getting stuck in corners, such as being a servant to increasing overhead, careerism, or narrow points of view.
- Bridge the boundaries that separate us from other creative professions and unexpected possibilities.
- Use the new technologies, but don't be seduced into thinking that they provide answers to fundamental questions.
- Be radical.

Originally published in Radical Modernism *by Dan Friedman, Yale University Press, 1994.*

CONTRIBUTORS

JANET ABRAMS is a critic and creative director of Leading Questions, a New York–based communications consultancy. She is writer-at-large at *I.D.* magazine, a contributor to many other journals, co-founder of the Digital Algonquin, and curator of the "DIALogue" series at Cooper Union in New York.

TIMOTHY BARRETT is an associate research scientist and director of paper facilities at the University of Iowa Center for the Book.

JOHN BIELENBERG is principal of Bielenberg Design, which has offices in San Francisco, California, and Boulder, Colorado. He teaches graphic design at the California College of Arts and Crafts.

MICHAEL BIERUT is a partner in the New York office of the international design consultancy Pentagram.

ANDREW BLAUVELT is director of graduate studies in graphic design at North Carolina State University's School of Design. He is also a designer and a writer about graphic design from a cultural perspective.

HUGUES C. BOEKRAAD, philosopher and design critic, is a lecturer at St. Joost Academy, Breda, The Netherlands.

ROSEMARY J. COOMBE is an associate professor of law at the University of Toronto and the author of *Cultural Appropriations: Authorship, Alterity and the Law.*

MEREDITH DAVIS is a designer and a writer who teaches graduate studies in graphic design at North Carolina State University's School of Design in Raleigh.

ROB DEWEY is a design manager, editor, and writer living in Minneapolis. His work has appeared in *Eye, AIGA Journal of Graphic Design,* and *Communication Arts.*

WILLIAM DRENTTEL is a partner of Drenttel Doyle Partners in New York and a publisher of poetry, fiction, and writing on design.

KEVIN FENTON is a writer for the Minneapolis communications agency Kilter Incorporated. He also edits the quarterly *Two Cities*.

TOBIAS FRERE-JONES is a senior designer at Font Bureau in Boston. He has lectured at Yale School of Design, Pratt Institute, Royal College of Art, and at the Rhode Island School of Design.

DAN FRIEDMAN was an artist whose subject was design and culture, and the author of *Dan Friedman: Radical Modernism*. He passed away in 1995.

MILTON GLASER is president of Milton Glaser, Inc., and has taught design at the School of Visual Arts for more than thirty years.

JESSICA HELFAND runs Jessica Helfand Studio, is a contributing editor to *I.D.* and *Print*, the author of *Six Essays on Design and New Media*, and a visiting lecturer at Yale University and The Cooper Union.

STEVEN HELLER is editor of the *AIGA Journal of Graphic Design*, a senior art director at the *New York Times*, and author of more than fifty books on graphic design.

DK HOLLAND is a partner in the Pushpin Group, design issues editor of *Communication Arts*, and business editor of the *AIGA Journal of Graphic Design*.

ANDREW HOWARD studied fine art before becoming involved in design and print in London. He has specialized in work for social and cultural organizations and now lives and works in Portugal.

NATALIA ILYIN teaches cultural and design theory at The Cooper Union in New York and at Yale University. An art director and a writer, she is working on a book about mythic images of American culture.

PAMELA A. IVINSKI is a PhD candidate in art history at the graduate center of the City University of New York. She writes on graphic design for *Print* magazine.

KARRIE JACOBS is known for her essays on the politics of design and the culture of technology. She is a contributing editor to *New York* magazine, where she writes the "Cityscape" column on architecture and urbanism, and is also a contributing editor to *I.D.*

TIBOR KALMAN is the founder of M&Co., New York, and was editor-in-chief of *Colors* magazine.

JEFFERY KEEDY is on the faculty of the program in graphic design at California Institute of the Arts. He received an MFA from Cranbrook Academy of Art, and he is known internationally as an educator, writer, and type designer.

ROBIN KINROSS is a typographer, writer, and publisher in London. He is author of *Modern Typography* (1992).

PETER LAUNDY is a designer with the Doblin Group in Chicago.

ZUZANA LICKO is the co-founder of Emigre, a digital type foundry based in Northern California.

ELLEN LUPTON is the curator of contemporary design at the Cooper-Hewitt National Design Museum. Her exhibits include *Mixing Messages* and *The Avant-Garde Letterhead*.

LAURIE HAYCOCK MAKELA is the former design director at the Walker Art Center in Minneapolis.

KATHERINE McCOY was co-chair of the design department at Cranbrook Academy of Art for twenty-three years. Currently she is a senior lecturer at Illinois Institute of Technology's Institute of Design in Chicago, a visiting professor of the Royal College of Art in London, president of the American Center for Design, and a frequent writer on design criticism and history.

PHILIP B. MEGGS teaches graphic design history at Virginia Commonwealth University and is the author of *A History of Graphic Design*.

J. ABBOTT MILLER is the principal of Design Writing Research in New York.

RICK POYNOR is the founding editor of *Eye* magazine, a contributing editor of *I.D.* and *Blueprint,* and a contributor to the *AIGA Journal of Graphic Design*. His books include *Typography Now: The Next Wave, The Graphic Edge,* and *Typography Now Two: Implosion*.

PHILIP C. REPP teaches environmental design and computer imaging in the department of art at Ball State University, Muncie, Indiana. He is editor of *Snowy Egret* and writes about nature, design, and technology.

MICHAEL ROCK is an associate professor at the Yale School of Art and a partner in the graphic design firm, 2 × 4.

FATH DAVIS RUFFINS is a historian and head of the collection of advertising history at the National Museum of American History, Smithsonian Institution. She is currently at work on a book and exhibition on ethnic imagery in twentieth-century American advertising.

PAUL SAFFO is a director at the Institute for the Future in Menlo Park, California.

SUSAN SELLERS is a graduate student in the American studies department at Yale University and a partner in the graphic design firm, 2 × 4.

ELLEN SHAPIRO, a graphic designer and writer, is president of Shapiro Design Associates Inc. in New York.

PAUL STIFF is reader in typography and graphic communication at the University of Reading, England. He edits *Information Design Journal* and *Typography Papers*.

GUNNAR SWANSON is a graphic designer in Duluth, Minnesota, and the head of the graphic design program at the University of Minnesota Duluth.

VÉRONIQUE VIENNE writes about design, photography, and cultural trends. Her articles have been published in *Metropolis, Graphis, Print, Emigre, Eye, Communication Arts, AIGA Journal of Graphic Design,* and many general-interest magazines.

LORRAINE WILD is a designer and educator. She has been teaching at the California Institute of Arts for ten years and also serves as a project tutor at the Jan van Eyck Akademie in Maastricht, The Netherlands. She has her own design practice, focused on collaborations with architects, curators, and publishers in the United States and abroad.

JON WOZENCROFT is managing editor of the audiovisual publisher *Touch* and assistant course director in MA Interactive Media at the Royal College of Art in London. He is the author of *The Graphic Language of Neville Brody 1 & 2*. In 1990, he and Brody set up *FUSE,* a showcase of experimental typography.

INDEX

BOOKS FROM ALLWORTH PRESS

Looking Closer 3: Classic Writings on Graphic Design
edited by Michael Bierut, Jessica Helfand, Steven Heller, and Rick Poynor
(softcover, 6½ × 10, 304 pages, $18.95)

Looking Closer: Critical Writings on Graphic Design
edited by Michael Bierut, William Drenttel, Steven Heller, and DK Holland
(softcover, 6½ × 10, 256 pages, $18.95)

Graphic Design Time Line: A Century of Design Milestones
by Steven Heller and Elinor Pettit (softcover, 6½ × 9⅞, 272 pages, $19.95)

Graphic Design and Reading: Explorations of an Uneasy Relationship
edited by Gunnar Swanson (softcover, 6½ × 9⅞, 240 pages, $19.95)

Design Connoisseur: An Eclectic Collection of Imagery and Type
by Steven Heller (softcover, 7½ × 9⅜, 208 pages, $19.95)

Design Literacy (continued): Understanding Graphic Design
by Steven Heller (softcover, 6½ × 10, 296 pages, $19.95)

Design Literacy: Understanding Graphic Design
by Steven Heller and Karen Pomeroy (softcover, 6½ × 10, 288 pages, $19.95)

**Design Culture: An Anthology of Writing from the AIGA Journal of Graphic
Design** *edited by Steven Heller and Marie Finamore* (softcover, 6½ × 10, 320 pages, $19.95)

Design Dialogues
by Steven Heller and Elinor Pettit (softcover, 6½ × 10, 272 pages, $18.95)

The Swastika: Symbol Beyond Redemption?
by Steven Heller (hardcover, 6½ × 9½, 176 pages, $21.95)

Sex Appeal: The Art of Allure in Graphic and Advertising Design
by Steven Heller (softcover, 6½ × 10, 288 pages, $18.95)

AIGA Professional Practices in Graphic Design
The American Institute of Graphic Arts, edited by Tad Crawford (softcover, 6½ × 10, 320 pages, $24.95)

Business and Legal Forms for Graphic Designers
by Tad Crawford and Eva Doman Bruck (softcover, 8½ × 11, 240 pages, includes CD-ROM, $24.95)

Please write to request our free catalog. To order by credit card, call 1-800-491-2808 or send a
check or money order to Allworth Press, 10 East 23rd Street, Suite 510, New York, NY 10010.
Include $5 for shipping and handling for the first book ordered and $1 for each additional book.
Ten dollars plus $1 for each additional book if ordering from Canada. New York State residents
must add sales tax.

To see our complete catalog on the World Wide Web, or to order online, you can find us at
www.allworth.com.